Richard Overy's award-winning writing on the history of World War II and the Third Reich has been praised as, 'highly effective in the ruthless dispelling of myths' (A.J.P. Taylor), 'original and important' (*New York Review of Books*) and 'at the cutting edge' (*Times Literary Supplement*). Professor of Modern History for ten years at Kings College, London, Overy is also a Fellow of the Royal Historical Society, Fellow of the British Academy, Fellow of King's College and currently Professor of History at Exeter University. In 2001 he was awarded the Samuel Eliot Morison Prize of the Society for Military History for his contribution to the history of warfare and in 2004 The Wolfson History Prize for his book, *The Dictators*.

'The richest book on the whole subject that I have read for a long time.'
Norman Stone, *Sunday Times*

'A closely argued and detailed analysis providing a new and proper insight into an evil and inefficient war machine.'
The Economist

'This is a major contribution to our knowledge of the history of the German Reich... absorbing reading will remain a standard authority on the subject for a long time.'
Michael Dockrill, *Journal of Strategic Studies*

RICHARD OVERY

GOERING

HITLER'S IRON KNIGHT

I.B. TAURIS

LONDON · NEW YORK

New paperback edition published in 2012 by I.B.Tauris and Co Ltd
6 Salem Road, London W2 4BU
175 Fifth Avenue, New York NY 10010
www.ibtauris.com

Distributed in the United States and Canada Exclusively by Palgrave Macmillan
175 Fifth Avenue, New York NY 10010

First published in 1984 by Routledge, Kegan Paul

ISBN: 978 1 84885 932 6

A full CIP record for this book is available from the British Library
A full CIP record is available from the Library of Congress

Library of Congress Catalog Card Number: available

Printed and bound in Sweden by ScandBook AB

CONTENTS

	List of Illustrations	vii
	Preface to the 2012 Edition	ix
1	The 'Iron Man'	1
2	Building the Goering Empire	22
3	Goering and the German Economy	48
4	Goering and Hitler's War	76
5	Building the Nazi Empire	109
6	The Era of Egotism and Incompetence	138
7	The Failure of the Luftwaffe	164
8	The Decline of the Goering Empire	205
9	Goering and the Politics of the Third Reich	231
	Notes	242
	Bibliography and Sources	293
	Index	306

ILLUSTRATIONS

PLATES

1 Goering wearing his decoration 'pour le mérite' (*BBC Hulton Picture Library*)
2 Goering relaxing with Hitler (*Imperial War Museum*)
3 Hitler, Goering and other party faithful (*Imperial War Museum*)
4 Goering shortly before the seizure of power in 1932 (*BBC Hulton Picture Library*)
5 Goering the politician (*BBC Hulton Picture Library*)
6 Goering the soldier (*Imperial War Museum*)
7 Hitler's 'first paladin' greets his leader (*Imperial War Museum*)
8 Commander-in-chief of the air force (*Imperial War Museum*)
9 The civilian leader and economics overlord (*Imperial War Museum*)
10 Goering the fanatic (*Imperial War Museum*)
11 Ernst Roehm (*Imperial War Museum*)
12 Hjalmar Schacht (*Imperial War Museum*)
13 Werner von Blomberg (*Imperial War Museum*)
14 Joachim von Ribbentrop (*Imperial War Museum*)
15 Ernst Udet (*Imperial War Museum*)
16 Fritz Todt (*Imperial War Museum*)
17 Erhard Milch (*Imperial War Museum*)
18 Albert Speer (*Imperial War Museum*)
19 Goering in captivity (*Imperial War Museum*)
20 Goering at the Nuremberg Trials (*BBC Hulton Picture Library*)

TABLES

1 German military expenditure 1934/5–1937/8   38
2 Selected German economic statistics 1935–8   55
3 Selected statistics on German investment 1936–42   60
4 German sources of iron ore 1929–35   63

5 German wage statistics 1928–38   83
6 German explosives production plans, 1938   86
7 Military expenditure, state expenditure and national income 95
   in Germany 1938–44
8 Distribution of the workforce by nationality, Reichswerke AG 129
   Salzgitter/Watenstedt
9 Distribution of labour in Germany 1939–44   148
10 German air force combat strength 1939–43   175

CHARTS

Chart I   The organisation of the Four Year Plan   58
Chart II   The Reichswerke and main subsidiaries,   67
            September 1939
Chart III   Czech and Austrian holdings of the Reichswerke 115
            'Hermann Goering'
Chart IV   The Reichswerke organisation, 1942   134–5

PREFACE

In a series of interrogations carried out by the American officer Ernest Evans shortly after Goering's capture in May 1945, the prisoner explained the drama of the last days of the Third Reich, during which he came to realise that Hitler, surrounded by the Red Army in his bunker in Berlin, was no longer in a position to carry out his leadership duties. Goering was Hitler's designated successor. 'In a flash,' wrote Evans, 'the idea came to him: "I am the Führer, only I don't know it."'[1] Goering sent a telegram from Berchtesgaden to Hitler explaining that he was going to function as leader in his place. The dream was rudely punctured when a telegram arrived from Hitler condemning Goering and his entire family to death for treason. Goering was Germany's 'Leader' for no more than a few hours on 23 April 1945. He was arrested by an SS troop, but later rescued by loyal air force soldiers. When Hitler committed suicide on 30 April, he left a document appointing Joseph Goebbels his successor as chancellor and Grand Admiral Karl Dönitz, commander-in-chief of the navy, as president. Goering's 23-year political career had come to an inglorious conclusion.

Any biography of Goering must acknowledge that he might have been Hitler's successor. If one of the many assassination attempts had succeeded during the war, Goering was supposed to take over. Would this have happened? Probably not. There were other powerful National Socialists in the wings who might have pushed him aside, not least the head of the SS and the German police, Heinrich Himmler. The army high command might have declared martial law and finally taken over the state after planning and plotting a coup for years. Goering told Evans in another interrogation that by 1942, 'My star was sinking'.[2] Around him there was a growing chorus of criticism and complaint about the failure of the German Air Force to stem either the bombing or the advance of the Red Army, but most sharply from Hitler. Most accounts of Goering's career illustrate the growing gap between his political aspirations and his military and administrative competence.

One of the things this biography tried to do when it was first published more than 25 years ago was to take Goering more seriously as a politician, commander and organiser. Subsequent biographies have also shown his significant contribution to the diplomacy of the 1930s, which plays a smaller part here.[3] For all the popular image of Goering as the butt of popular jokes and rumour, too idle to do a job properly and too fond of the good life to abandon his position without a struggle, there was much more to his personality than that. It is perhaps significant that among the cohort of unhappy characters arraigned before the International Tribunal at Nuremberg, Goering stood out from the crowd. The effort in 1945–6 to identify National Socialist leaders as both evil and psychologically disturbed had greater difficulty with Goering, who did not seem as suitable a case for treatment as the others. The interrogations conducted in the six months before the trial show a man who was not as ill-informed or unintelligent about his responsibilities as many of his subordinates and colleagues suggested. On the detailed issues of aircraft production and distribution in 1944 and 1945, Goering's responses to questions have been broadly verified by the available documents.[4] When he was asked for the principal explanation for the defeat of the German Air Force he opted, rightly, for the introduction of the Allied long-range fighter: 'Without this escort, the air offensive would never have succeeded'.[5]

Goering's problems were only partly a result of his ambitions and foibles, as this biography has tried to show. The key issue that Goering had to contend with was the virtual impossibility of fulfilling what Hitler wanted, either as head of the Four-Year Plan for armaments and substitute materials, or as commander-in-chief of the German Air Force. In spring 1941 his air force units were battering British cities, at the cost of a steady attrition of German bombers, while plans were laid to transfer almost all the aircraft to the east for the assault on the Soviet Union in June. Goering was among those who favoured finishing Britain off first, either by bombing, or through seizing Gibraltar and the Suez Canal and closing Britain off from the Mediterranean and links with the empire. Goering told Evans in 1945 that he found Hitler's strategy flawed: 'Hitler's decision for war against Russia put me in doubt. I knew well that we could bash the Russians, but how could we ever come to a peace settlement with the Bolsheviks? In the end we could not march all the way to Vladivostok.'[6] Goering no doubt deserved some of the blame for exaggerating what the air force was capable of doing, and he used air force success regularly as a way of inflating his own political prestige. But the sheer range of activities required of the air force, in circumstances where the aircraft industry failed to respond to the demands for new models and inflated output, doomed Goering's military ambitions. The explanations for the failure of Goering's military enterprise lie in economics and technology as much as strategy.[7] In these fields, it is argued here, Goering's limitations as a leader were most fully exposed.

One aspect of Goering's activities did not get the coverage it deserved when the book was written. Goering played a part in the policies of discrimination, spoliation and murder of German and European Jews, and that part was not sufficiently emphasised or explored in what follows. Awareness of the extent to which the racial policies of the regime intruded into every area of German life during the Third Reich was not as widely appreciated in the 1980s as it is now.[8] It is not altogether clear in Goering's case, as in the case of other perpetrators, how much of his anti-Semitism was opportunistic, and how much of it reflected the same visceral hatred shown by a Himmler or a Streicher. In conversations with the psychiatrist Leon Goldensohn during the Nuremberg trial he claimed that he joined the Party because of its political programme, not its anti-Semitism.[9] Yet Goering's role as virtual economic 'dictator' in Germany in the late 1930s made him responsible for the policy of 'Aryanisation' and the spoliation of Jewish businesses and wealth, and he did nothing to avoid this responsibility. There is now a much richer literature on the economics of German race policy in the Third Reich than there was 20 years ago.[10] Goering was the political force behind imposing a fine of one billion marks on Germany's Jewish community following the Night of Broken Glass on 8 November 1938, and in introducing on 3 December 1938 a decree on 'The Deployment of Jewish Wealth'. The new legal claims allowed the state to close down Jewish businesses or compel their sale at disadvantageous rates or, in some cases, to seize them outright. A further decree in January forced all Jews to bring their jewellery, precious metals and securities to central collecting centres (many of them municipal pawn shops) where they were given a nominal sum in exchange. The metals were melted down to fund German arms spending, and the jewels sold to Swiss dealers in exchange for much needed industrial diamonds.[11] This was one way of solving the problems that Goering's Four-Year Plan had in funding overseas purchases of essential materials and equipment.

On Goering's direct involvement in the switch to the 'Final Solution' in the summer and autumn of 1941 the evidence is still less certain. The document often cited – it is in this biography on p. 128 – was issued by Goering on 31 July 1941, ordering Reinhard Heydrich, head of the Reich Security Main Office, to find a final solution to the Jewish question. Recent research has shown that the document originated in the Jewish Affairs Office of the Gestapo, run by Adolf Eichmann. It was drawn up by Gestapo officials who then ran it past Heydrich before putting it on Goering's desk for final signature. It is not known how closely Goering read the document. His signature was secured partly perhaps as insurance for Eichmann and Heydrich that they would be seen to be just obeying orders (which Eichmann eventually used at his trial in Jerusalem twenty years later), partly so that Heydrich could exploit Goering's authority for his own purposes.[12] Goering seems to have played little direct part thereafter in the genocide, which passed entirely into the hands of the Gestapo and the SS. When one of Eichmann's deputies asked to be shown evidence that genocide had been ordered, Eichmann chose to show him a document signed by Himmler on Hitler's behalf, rather than the 'final solution' document signed by Goering in July 1941.[13]

Goering was sentenced to be hanged at Nuremberg nonetheless for his role in German aggression, crimes against humanity and crimes against peace. He was treated as one of the principal conspirators in the charge of conspiracy brought forward by American lawyers to make sure that 'obeying orders' could be no-one's excuse. Although his influence on Hitler waned during the war, and the economy, armed forces and the apparatus of genocide were gradually shifted from his areas of supervision, he could have had no complaints about the judgement. When it suited him he was ruthless with people in his way. He told Evans that when an officer returned from a visit to the Soviet Union shortly before the German invasion with news that a single Soviet aero-engine factory was as large as half-a-dozen German ones, Goering threatened him with a concentration camp for his defeatism.[14] Goering was a deceptive personality, charming and larger-than-life in the right environment, but a callous bully in others. It is striking that those closest to him in the air force committed suicide or contemplated it – Ernst Udet, head of Air Force procurement, killed himself in November 1941; Hans Jeschonnek, chief-of-staff, in August 1943; Erhard Milch, deputy air minister, threatened to follow suit. This was an unusually high proportion, and it says something about the frustrations of working with a leader who took out his own failings regularly on those below him. In the end Goering himself committed suicide on the night before his execution, one of thousands of Germans who opted to choose the manner of their death after the collapse of the Third Reich.[15]

Over the 25 years since this biography was first written there has been a great deal of new writing on almost every aspect of the history of the Third Reich. Many of those areas touch on things that concerned Goering, but in general the picture presented here of Goering's political activities, military command and economic responsibilities has not greatly altered. He was a key player in the history of the Reich, with fingers in a great many pies, regarded for a long time by Hitler as his fixer when there were problems to confront. The political history of the period cannot be understood just as the history of Hitler's dictatorship. The inner circle around Hitler were delegates for the leader, delivering what was wanted, and doing so with a good deal of their own discretion and activity. They were each a fragment of dictatorship. Goering was one of the largest, 'Almost the Führer', but not quite.

NOTES

1 Ernest Evans, 'Göring – beinahe Führer', *Interavia*, 1 (August, 1946) p. 16.

2 Ibid., p. 14; see also his comments to Leon Goldensohn in 1946 during the trial in Robert Gellately (ed.), *The Nuremberg Interviews Conducted by Leon Goldensohn* (London, 2006), pp. 102–3.

3 Stephan Martens, *Hermann Göring, Erster Paladin des Führers und Zweiter Mann im Reich* (Paderborn, 1985); Alfred Kube, *Pour le mérite und Hakenkreuz: Hermann Göring im Dritten Reich* (Munich, 1986).

4 See, for example, National Archives, College Park, MD (NARS), RG332 Box 115, Interview with Reichsmarshal [sic] Hermann Goering, 'Organization and planning of aircraft production', pp. 1–5.

5 Ibid., p. 7.

6 Evans, 'Göring' Teil II, *Interavia* (September, 1946) p. 17.

7 On all these issues see the excellent analysis by Lutz Budrass, *Flugzeugindustrie und Luftrüstung in Deutschland 1918–1945* (Düsseldorf, 1998).

8 See, for example, Christopher Hutton, *Race and the Third Reich: Linguistics, Racial Anthropology and Genetics in the Dialectic of the Volk* (Cambridge, 2005); Gerald Feldman, Wolfgang Seibel (eds), *Networks of Persecution: Bureaucracy, Business and the Organization of the Holocaust* (Oxford, 2005).

9 *The Nuremberg Interviews*, p. 116. Although Goering had an interest in distancing himself from the mainstream anti-Semitism of the Hitler movement, his remarks to Goldensohn show that he picked up anti-Semitic rhetoric opportunistically: 'extermination of the Jews,' he was reported as saying, 'was unjustifiable.'

10 These new perspectives are discussed in Richard Overy, 'Making a Killing: The Economics of the Holocaust', Fifth Glasgow University Holocaust Memorial Lecture 2005. See particularly A. Beker (ed.), *The Plunder of Jewish Property during the Holocaust* (London, 2001); Martin Dean, *Robbing the Jews: The Confiscation of Jewish Property in the Holocaust 1933–1945* (New York, 2008); Gerard Aalders, *Nazi Looting: The Plunder of Dutch Jewry during the Second World War* (Oxford, 2004).

11 H. McQueen, 'The Conversion of Looted Jewish Assets to Run the German War Machine', *Holocaust and Genocide Studies*, 18 (2004), pp. 29–30.

12 Yaacov Lozowick, *Hitler's Bureaucrats: The Nazi Security Police and the Banality of Evil* (London, 2000), pp. 51–2; David Cesarani, *Eichmann: His Life and Crimes* (London, 2004), pp. 94–5.

13 Richard Overy, *Interrogations: The Nazi Elite in Allied Hands* (London, 2001), pp. 359–60.

14 Evans, 'Göring', Teil II, p. 18.

15 Christian Goeschel, *Suicide in Nazi Germany* (Oxford, 2009).

1

THE 'IRON MAN'

Hermann Goering has emerged from the bleak history of the Third Reich as a corrupt rather than evil figure. He has done so for obvious reasons. His greed, corruptibility and incompetence contrast with the ascetic fanaticism of the other leading Nazi politicians, and make him at once a less threatening and more forgivable character. His apparent lack of scruple and his opportunism diverge from the obsessive idealism of the mainstream of German fascism. Goering symbolises fascism in its most venal and fallible form; recognisably human where Hitler and the little Hitlers are not. Goering appears superficial where Hitler, from whatever perspective, is a deeply complex historical figure. He remains the political gangster; the man described by a British ambassador as a 'typical and brutal buccaneer'.[1]

Yet this image of Goering, the cheerful if vicious booty-hunter, could not be further from the truth. While it is certainly the case that Goering was flamboyant and conceited, and equally true that he profited unscrupulously and ruthlessly from the plundering of Europe's great museums and households, these are not what make him historically important. For most of the period of the Third Reich he was second only to Hitler in the Nazi movement and in the state. He shared Hitler's ambitions and played a crucial role in the attempt to fulfil them. Moreover he was compelled to work closely with the day-to-day reality of German politics and strategy, thus forming an important bridge between Hitler and the wider political world of the Third Reich. Much of the history of this period has been written as the history of Hitler. This is perhaps excusable, given the character of Nazi rule. But this preoccupation with Hitler has obscured the wider political context in which he worked. If Hitler can, in a sense, be abstracted from German political life and enjoy a history of his own, the same cannot be said of his subordinates. Any history of Goering becomes at the same time the history of the institutional and political world in which he operated; the history of the 'Goering empire' as well as Goering himself.

There can be no doubt that Goering justifies such a history. His contemporaries took him seriously enough. His brutality and lack of scruple earned for him the nickname 'der Eiserne', the 'Iron Man'.[2] His reputation abroad led to the publication in 1940 of a book with the title *Goering – Germany's*

most Dangerous Man. Robert Vansittart, no great admirer of Germans generally, judged Goering to be 'pathological ... completely irresponsible, and
much more dangerous than Hitler'.[3] His reputation at home earned him
the loyalty and confidence of Hitler until almost the end of the war. Even
as Allied bombers penetrated deeply and dangerously into the Reich in
1944 Hitler was prepared to tell his staff that 'a better man cannot be
found'.[4] He embodied the restless and violent nature of the Nazi movement
as a whole and played a central and active part in its development.

Goering was a completely committed Nazi and was no mere political
opportunist. He worked from a deep conviction that the course on which
Hitler and Germany had embarked was the right one. Unlike Hess and
Keitel, for example, who were merely Hitler's echoes, Goering brought his
own ideas and his own political style to invigorate the efforts of the party.
He demonstrated a deep and enduring loyalty both for Hitler himself and
for the movement's wider aims in domestic politics and foreign expansion.
Indeed for a great deal of the period after 1933 he had greater responsibilities and greater authority than any other leading Nazi except Hitler, and
used this position to see that these wider aims were fulfilled. From his
regular and direct contact with economic, military and judicial offices he
earned the further responsibility for shaping much of Nazi policy. The long
list of offices that Goering held, and the specific services that he rendered
to the movement, betray the image of a man very much at the centre of
state affairs; if no Thomas Cromwell then at least a Wolsey.

For the historian Goering's most important contribution came from his
role in the economy and the waging of war. Goering was permitted a degree
of autonomy in his leadership of the air force and in his capacity as overlord
of the German economy between 1937 and 1942 enjoyed by few if any of
Hitler's other subordinates. It is on this particular aspect of Goering's
political life that the following chapters will concentrate. During the period
between 1936 and 1942 Goering not only controlled the Luftwaffe but
intervened extensively in strategic and military matters as a whole. In the
economy he gradually extended his power and authority from selected areas
of industry and economic administration to embrace the whole structure of
economic policy-making. He was charged by Hitler with the task of
preparing the German economy for the Nazis' imperial ambitions. In the
words of Rudolf Hess, wrongly attributed to Goering, he did indeed choose
guns before butter.[5] Once war had broken out Goering continued to
consolidate his authority in economic affairs while at the same time accepting
Hitler's commission to organise the creation of the economy of the New
Order in Europe. It was Goering who was responsible for fixing the level
and nature of economic exploitation.

In this respect Goering played a crucial role in establishing the necessary
relationship between the Nazi movement and German capitalism that would
make such imperialism possible. This he did not by integrating private
capitalism in its pre-Nazi form into the programme of war-preparation and

imperialism, but by attempting to transform the whole relationship between state and economy. This was done by extending direct Nazi control over businesses through a system of regulatory offices and by establishing state industry in those areas where it was felt that private capitalism could not, or would not, serve the interests of the community. This effort to establish a more thoroughly Nazi economy, to remodel German industry, and to redefine the purposes of economic life was part of a wider movement, increasingly evident after 1936, to speed up the transformation of German society along fascist lines. The administrative and institutional empire that Goering established contained the political ingredients necessary to effect this transition.

The central role played by Goering during this period in the reorientation of the economy is worth emphasising because Goering has often been characterised as the moderate in the Nazi party, a friend to big business and an opponent of radical change. While it is true that he approached all such questions in a gradualist way, realising that changes in the economy would take time, he was nevertheless committed to making the changes. He saw the relationship between the economic structure and the political system as a critical one in defining the nature of the regime. Goering believed that it was his personal responsibility, together with the party apparatus over which he ruled, to create a fascist economic system. This was not simply an empty threat as it turned out to be in Italy during the 1930s. Goering, unlike Mussolini, did not have to make a series of tactical concessions to industry of the kind that effectively undermined Italian efforts to remodel the economy. Goering exercised direct authority over the private sector, seeing the relationship as a relationship of power, not as a merely formal constitutional one. The power base that he established represented, as it was meant to do, a direct threat to the traditional political position of big business and the military establishment in German society, held since the time of Bismarck. The degree to which Goering's power encroached on that of the traditional elites was the measure of how far the Nazi movement was capable of creating new institutions and a new political class. Under these circumstances Goering emerges every bit as revolutionary a Nazi as those victims of his vengeance in the purge of 30 June 1934.

The historian has to set limits for such a study. Goering's fingers stuck in many pies, some large, some small. It is the large ones that really matter. The years 1936 to 1942 are clearly more important than those beforehand or afterwards. His role in the early stages of the movement was unspectacular. The story of his personal life, while it says something about his political affairs, is less intrinsically interesting than Hitler's and is already well-known.[6] His many and more minor offices pay tribute to how extensive his political interests and ambitions were, but were of slight historical weight. What all his many activities did amount to was the largest political and administrative empire controlled directly by any of Hitler's paladins. Goering's history thus becomes to an important extent the history of his political

empire rather than his personal history. This in turn sheds important light
on fascist political systems in general and on Nazi party politics in particular.

The existence in the Third Reich of what Professor Trevor-Roper has
called 'a confusion of private empires' has long been accepted by historians.[7]
That Goering controlled such an empire is clear. It is perhaps misleading
to call it private, for these empires were primarily made up of public
institutions, of departments of state, and were run ostensibly on behalf of
the people and the movement. Through the political empires the Nazi
community, the *Volksgemeinschaft*, was imposed on Germany. They demonstrate certain important features of Nazi rule. Hitler and the party expected
the new German elite to be recruited by a system of political natural
selection. The fittest to rule were those who rose to the top. Those who
were at the top were, *ipso facto*, the fittest. There was no need for any
conventional demonstration of competence to rule. Second, the creation of
powerful administrative empires illustrated the Nazi emphasis on substance
over form. The important thing was the establishment not of formal constitu-
tions and jurisdiction but of direct and coercive rule; action rather than
words. This was the style of fascist politics, with its irrational and primitive
values and its urgent revolutionism. Goering's empire was one of the clearest
examples of Nazi political life. In its internal power-structure, its dynamic
for expansion, its personnel and its ideological orientation it was a miniature
of the larger Nazi empire that spawned it. Through its confrontation with
the conservative forces in German society it became, like the SS during the
war, a major instrument in revolutionising German and European political
life.

These, then, are the fruitful areas of Goering's personal history: preparation for, and prosecution of, the Second World War; the attempt to transform the German economy; and a dominant position in the fluid, revolutionary, politics of the party. They are linked together by that set of
ambitions and attitudes that made up the Nazi world view, the desire to
create a community run from above by a hierarchy of corporative agencies
in the form of a racial absolutist state; and the desire to use this ordered
German community to expand and extend German world power at the
expense of 'declining' or 'inferior' peoples. Both these main ambitions
Goering shared. His experiences during the First World War and its immediate aftermath he also shared with other leaders of the movement. His
early history, like Hitler's, gives few enough hints of his future place in
German politics but it does tell us something about the sort of people who
were attracted to German fascism and the historical circumstances that
shaped the movement.

Hermann Wilhelm Goering was born at Rosenheim in Bavaria on 12
January 1893. He was descended from a long line of bureaucrats and jurists
who had hovered on the fringes of aristocratic and royal life in Prussia for
two hundred years. His father, Heinrich, was a soldier who fought through
Bismarck's wars and subsequently joined the consular service of the new

Reich. At the time of Goering's birth his father was consul-general in Haiti. His was a typical service family, positioned uncertainly between the real German upper classes and the commercial middle class, with which it had no connection. The family made little money, status and pension being its reward. The lower levels of the bureaucratic and military establishment in Germany formed an important part of the pre-industrial world that was able to survive and even extend its influence in the Bismarckian Reich, supporting colonies and German expansion, as Goering's father did, as a further avenue to jobs and influence. The nationalism and sense of duty that these classes displayed blended with a growing fear and resentment at the threat to their social position posed by the new social forces thrown up by industrialisation. It was from this blend that German fascism was to draw at least some of its support.

Goering followed his father willingly into German military life. A failure at more conventional studies, he was a distinguished cadet at Karlsruhe and at the military training college at Lichterfelde. But in some important ways Goering did not share the conventional Prussian upbringing of his fellow cadets. He remained living in Bavaria, although his father was a Prussian. In a castle at Veldenstein near Nuremberg, provided for the family by the man whose mistress Goering's mother became, he was surrounded by a curious neo-medieval pageantry.[8] It was here, rather than in Prussia, that Goering absorbed and developed a romantic sense of Germanness that finally blossomed under National Socialism. His early life symbolised a curious fusion of southern and northern Germany, producing a romantic, ethnic nationalism invigorated by the rigorous service mentality of the north. Although Goering was clearly anxious to be absorbed into the Prussian military world, his Bavarian background instilled a kind of restlessness and sense of isolation that prevented him from being fully accepted by, or from accepting, the Prussian establishment. Goering inhabited a world of heroes and legends that the declining Bismarckian system was ill able to provide. The irony for Goering, as for other ambitious but conservative young Germans, was that the very system that fuelled their romantic traditionalism, and held out the promise of fulfilment, was itself on the point of dissolution.

The First World War was the high watermark of the world into which Goering was hopefully moving. It gave him ample opportunity for acts of heroism of which there can be no doubt. His medal *pour le mérite* was awarded for repeated and exceptional acts of bravery in the field. But the war also brought about the complete collapse of the system that had provided the Goerings with their livelihood, and provided the soldier and bureaucratic classes with a sense of common identity. In this respect Goering shared with many other Germans the sense of disorientation and frustration brought about by defeat in war. What made such a situation so much worse for soldiers like Goering was that they had very little else to fall back on; neither money nor good connections. He was rudely reminded of this by his fiancée's upper-class family who broke off the engagement when he returned penniless from the front in 1919.[9] It was possible for the wealthy and aristocratic elites to adjust to the world after 1918 for they retained their wealth and considerable social and political influence under the Weimar Republic. For those who had always been on the fringes of upper-class society in the Second Reich it was much harder to salvage anything from the wreckage.

From the point of view of the birth of fascism in Germany it was essential that people like Goering should experience a double sense of betrayal. Not only a deep conviction that the socialists had been responsible for the 'stab-in-the-back', a legend which Goering took over uncritically in 1918, but also a sense of mute betrayal by the conservative classes which he had aspired to enter. Through their failure to win the war and their subsequent withdrawal from defence of the old system, the conservatives left the lower levels of the traditional German community vulnerable to industrial society and democratic politics. This rejection of pre-war conservatism was a central feature of Nazi politics. Goering wrote contemptuously of the German upper classes who, in 1918, 'hauled down their once glorious standards and were not to be found in the ranks of the warriors who were passionately fighting for Germany's rebirth'; of the German generals among whom 'there was not one who was willing to hoist the standard of resistance'; of the 'possessing classes who were at least prepared to represent their own personal interests, but not the interests of the German people as a whole'.[10] Goering was not an exception to the rule among leading Nazis, an aristocratic island in a petty-bourgeois sea, but was very much a part of the mainstream of Nazi politics; an ex-soldier unwilling to restore the old world but fundamentally alienated from the world of Weimar. A product of that social zone between the traditional conservative elites and the new industrial classes, which the old Reich had protected and supported for its own political ends but which was a social anachronism in the 1920s.

Unlike Goering many Germans did adjust, however grudgingly, to Weimar democracy. But Goering's deeply emotional nationalism and sense of bitter rejection by the society for which he had fought prevented him from settling down to extract what he could from the new system. His political response to the Republic was naive and incoherent, reflecting the uncomprehending resentment which conservative Germans felt towards the Versailles settlement and the rule of Social Democrats. He allegedly read political pamphlets and attended Freikorps meetings in the first two years after the end of the war, but remained only on the fringes of political life. For some time he imposed an exile upon himself in Denmark and Sweden before moving back to Bavaria with Carin, his first wife. In Sweden he recaptured the sense of mystery and pageantry that he had experienced in Bavaria in the 'Edelweiss Chapel', a select and mystical Nordic society run by Carin's mother, Baroness Huldine Beamish-Fock.[11] Under pressure from Carin, Goering returned to Germany to instil his nationalist romanticism into local politics. Like Hitler and other leading Nazis, Goering clearly made the commitment at some stage in the two years after the end of the war to become involved actively in politics; not in the conventional political parties, which only imperfectly accommodated the politically active elements of the traditional middle class, but in the creation of new political movements that represented in a direct sense those alienated groups who were unwilling any longer to allow the conservative elites to represent them. What particularly attracted Goering to National Socialism was Hitler's ability to express in words that feeling of alienation and frustration that Goering could not express for himself. It was this sense that Hitler provided an explanation for what had gone wrong that drew Goering towards the movement, as it drew many others.

Hitler and Goering first met in 1922 in Munich. Having heard Hitler speak Goering requested an interview during the course of which Hitler briefly explained his *Weltanschauung*. The interview went well. Hitler offered Goering the leadership of the SA, in deference to his war record. Goering declared an oath of allegiance to Hitler. It would be wrong to read too much into this early relationship. Hitler wanted a soldier with a distinguished war record to lead the SA, the small party police force. This Goering did effectively enough until the Nazi's abortive *Putsch* in November 1923.[12] But the movement as a whole was of relatively minor significance and Goering's role within it not a prominent one. If anything it was Carin who earned Goering a place in Hitler's circle as much as Goering himself. When the *Putsch* failed Goering left Germany and the link between himself and Hitler became attenuated and finally almost non-existent. Goering continued to drift in and out of the underworld of radical conservatism. If nothing else Goering could claim to be one of those who had actively struggled and opposed the Weimar system from below, as Hitler was always able to claim. Goering capitalised on this when he later became active again in the Nazi movement but it was a poor investment in the renewed exile in Italy and Sweden.

During his period in exile – he was a wanted man in Bavaria – Goering lived in poverty and considerable hardship. The serious injury he sustained during the *Putsch* drew him towards morphine addiction from which he slowly recovered in Swedish hospitals. The historian has little material to show what interest Goering maintained in politics or what the formative influences were in shaping his ideas. In 1924 he met Mussolini through the offices of friends he made in the Fascist Party. He continued to read and absorb political literature. It would be fair to conclude that his basic political and social attitudes only hardened during this period, but that they did not change substantially. After recovering from his addiction, and benefiting from an amnesty, Goering returned to Germany in 1927 to find paid employment and to re-establish his contacts with the political right. He visited Hitler in Munich, rejoined the party and established himself in Berlin as a salesman for the Bayerische Motorenwerke.[13] His party activity was confined to making contact with Goebbels's Berlin-based organisation and taking his turn in electioneering and propaganda. The turning-point in Goering's personal fortunes coincided with a turning-point in that of the party as a whole.

Between 1926 and 1928 the Nazi Party tried to win a mass base of support in the German industrial cities. The strategy was an almost complete failure. In the Reichstag elections in May 1928 the Nazi Party could only achieve 800,000 votes, enough to gain twelve seats, but not enough to become a serious political force. At some stage early in 1928, when Hitler paid a visit to Berlin from his Munich headquarters, Goering was successful in persuading Hitler to put him forward as a candidate in the elections. Quite why Hitler made the choice is open to speculation. Indeed Röhm opposed the choice, for it implied a threat to his role in the SA, which Goering had once led. Goering held no office in the movement, had been out of the country for three years and had an insecure job as a sales representative. What he did have was a very considerable personality, great ambition, and the ability to appear to be at the centre of affairs. His one advantage was that unlike so many of the Nazi leaders he had at least been on the fringes of the Wilhelmine upper classes and knew enough about how conservative society worked in Germany to be useful to Hitler. He was chosen for his qualities as a serious candidate rather than his qualities as a dedicated Nazi.[14]

It was in his position as one of the twelve Nazi deputies elected to the Reichstag that Goering at last assumed any significance in the Nazi movement. And it was in this capacity as a public-relations officer for Nazism that Hitler tolerated and finally welcomed Goering. His role within the party itself remained undefined and peripheral. His political power depended on Hitler's success in national politics and he based his personal influence almost exclusively on his role in the Reichstag and his importance as an intermediary between the party and other groups in German political life. It seems to have been a tactical decision on Hitler's part to use Goering as a political ambassador but the decision had important implications for Goering's own career. It meant that he became increasingly indispensable to Hitler without becoming deeply involved in internal Nazi political squabbles. It also meant that Goering was both better informed and more involved in national issues than most other Nazis and could use this expertise to bolster his influence with Hitler and his intimate circle. How little Goering featured in internal Nazi politics can be gathered from the fact that he figured not at all in the memoirs of leading Nazis in the period between 1923 and 1930 nor in Goebbels's diaries of the same period.[15] His importance for the movement at a national level can be gauged from the fact that much of the foreign press talked of Goering and Hitler but of few of the other leading Nazis. Here were the roots of Goering's political empire-building.

Goering's political position also depended on his loyalty to Hitler and the success of his efforts in the Reichstag to have Hitler taken seriously as a political figure. The first factor assumed a special significance since the growing success of the party at the polls coincided with a sharpening of the conflict between the northern-based party group led by the Strasser brothers and the Munich headquarters of the party. The division was as much a tactical one as an ideological one. Hitler wanted complete control over the methods and tactics used by the party. He also wanted undivided loyalty to the party's supreme leader. Goering, who was himself so dependent on Hitler's favour, became identified with Hitler's efforts to exert full control over the party. Hitler too was keen to exploit his loyalty because of changing political circumstances outside the conflicts within the party. To maintain momentum after 1928 it was necessary to acquire more funds for the party and also to establish links with the conservative forces in German politics. Such links were necessary in order to make the party look more respectable and less iconoclastic in its attempts to win the votes of the peasantry and the small-town officials and property-owners upon whose support the party fully depended. Goering played an important part in operating such tactics. He conducted his election campaigns accompanied by conservative recruits to the movement – including the Hohenzollern Prince, August Wilhelm – and established the necessary contacts with businessmen and bankers who were sympathetic to the movement, such as Fritz Thyssen and Hjalmar Schacht.[16] Goering was by no means the only Nazi engaged in the task, though he was one of the most conspicuous, nor did the Nazis succeed during the period in attracting the conservative elites in any real numbers. But it did have the effect of making the Nazi Party appear to be more respectable to the lower levels of the German bourgeois and agrarian world.

The role Goering assumed as Hitler's 'ambassador' – his party nick-name – should not be exaggerated. Not until late in 1932 was any real success achieved in negotiation, and then only because the shifts in the political power balance encouraged the threatened political elite around Hindenburg to adopt a new strategy for survival. Despite Goering's histor-ical reputation as a conservative bridge between the traditional military and agrarian elite and the Nazi Party, it is clear that Goering neither considered himself as part of the ex-Wilhelmine political elite nor was accepted or respected by them. Goering lacked a respectable social position and was compromised, like Hitler, as an ex-putschist and populist orator. Most important of all Goering himself did not lose that implicit rejection of the old aristocratic Germany, the strong desire to establish something identifi-ably new, that replaced or transcended the old Bismarckian Reich but avoided the democratic alternative. This deeper rejection of conservative Germany was symbolised by Hitler's decision to contest the presidential election in 1932 against Hindenburg. Goering was conspicuous in his support for Hitler's decision, even though it offended potential friends among the conservative circles with which he had contact, because he believed that Hindenburg was being manipulated by socialists and Catholics. Conservatives were useful for Goering, as for the whole movement, only inasmuch as they could be mobilised or manipulated for the purpose of achieving power.

It was in the achievement of final power in January 1933 that Goering appeared to Hitler to play such an important part and which cemented what had otherwise been an uncertain and unpromising political relationship between the two men. Goering was helped in his own political career in 1932 by his election as President of the Reichstag, a tribute to his flamboyance and energy as a Nazi deputy. 'I'm glad that he's now well taken care of,' was Hitler's comment.[17] It was from this position that he was able unscrupulously to conduct negotiations with other parties, ostensibly from a disinterested desire to form a stable government that could command a parliamentary majority: in practice to find an avenue whereby Hitler might complete the 'legal revolution' and gain the chancellorship. His position was still very much that of a go-between. His ability to achieve anything from the negotiations depended first of all on continued Nazi success at the polls. Only on the basis of being the largest Reichstag party could the Nazis hope to lay claim to the highest office. It also depended crucially on the attitude of the conservative parties and the military group around the President. In this respect Goering's role, like Hitler's, was essentially negative, depending upon initiatives over which both men had very little control. Indeed Goering, whose reputation with the party rested on his ability to establish and maintain contacts, was conspicuously excluded from the inner discussions between the leading conservative political figures and was consulted only when conservatives chose to consult him. The important political discussions took place with Hitler rather than Goering, with the single exception of the meeting arranged by Hindenburg's son, Oskar, to offer Hitler the chancellorship if he would agree to enter a government composed of Nazis and conservatives.[18]

In the last week before the Nazis came to power Goering became a central figure in discussions. The circumstances of German political life changed substantially when the conservative forces, compelled on the one hand by the very size and vigorousness of the Nazi movement, on the other by their increasing desperation in finding a conservative national solution that worked, finally decided that Hitler should be included, on their terms, in the government. This represented a complete reversal of the President's position and that of his agrarian and military allies who had opposed giving Hitler power throughout the months of crisis after the fall of the Brüning cabinet in May 1932. The reasons for this initial opposition were clear; there was no guarantee that Hitler could be controlled and every indication that the movement was opposed to the main interests of the traditional elite. What changed the conservatives' minds was the recognition that something at least could be salvaged from the constitutional crisis by co-operating with Hitler, whereas a failure to stabilise German political life might well lead to the exclusion of the conservative nationalists from all political influence.

This change on the part of the conservatives brought a flurry of political intrigue at the end of 1932 and in the first few weeks of 1933. Hugenberg, leader of the nationalist DNVP, reached the decision to co-operate with the Nazis in December 1932 and was prepared to share power with Hitler to forestall the complete eclipse of his own power-base.[19] Von Schleicher, during his short-lived chancellorship, attempted unsuccessfully to reach agreement with Gregor Strasser to bring some of the leading Nazis into the government. Goering and Hitler opposed such a scheme because it gave greater prominence to Strasser's 'Prussian' Nazis and did not promise the chancellorship itself for Hitler, or any role for Goering.[20] Finally the conservative elite around Hindenburg, operating under the illusion that Hitler could be tamed once in power, arrived by the middle of January at the decision to include Hitler in a coalition in a final effort to maintain some influence over the traditional Bismarckian alliance of industry, agrarians and the conservative mass. Where such a tactic was workable in the 1860s it failed utterly to cope with the circumstances of a mass radical party whose sympathies with the conservatives were transparently tactical and whose heritage was 1848 rather than 1866.

Goering had the enviable task of bearing the news to Hitler that the conservatives had at last agreed to give Hitler sufficient support to form a majority government, and the final reward of telling Hitler that Hindenburg had consented to his appointment as Chancellor. Hitler, whose grasp of how affairs were moving in January 1933 was at best hazy, was inordinately grateful to Goering, assuming wrongly that Goering had in some sense been instrumental in persuading the conservatives to concede the chancellorship. Goering was rewarded with a post in the prospective new cabinet and the important position of Prussian Minister of the Interior. Yet throughout all this period Goering did little within the party itself in the more mundane tasks of mobilising mass support, for he held no important party office. No doubt his force of personality was important in establishing his claim to a leader's role within the movement. But certainly until 1933 this claim was ambiguous. The strength of Goering's political position within the movement depended as it had done since 1922 on his loyalty to Hitler, and on the supreme demonstration of that loyalty in the days before the seizure of power. Had the efforts to achieve power failed in January 1933 it is unlikely that Goering would have long survived the crisis.

Goering brought to the movement a forceful and ambitious personality moved by a simple and typical fascist outlook. His intellect was shallow; his ideological apparatus was shaped by the circumstances of his personal history and closely resembled Hitler's, whose more articulate expression of the ambitions of the radical conservative mass Goering came to imitate. His ideas took shape on the foundation of a deeply-held and romantic sense of nationalism. This nationalism was the product of both positive and negative intellectual forces. In the positive sense it was a blend of the traditional patriotism of his class and a sentimental view of German history and the German character. His view of history was the same kind of vulgar Hegelianism common in pre-1914 Germany, a belief that Germany was destined through the historical process to emerge as the swordbearer of a superior culture, to secure the triumph of the Germanic ideal. Although Goering's nationalism was strongly influenced by the events of the war and the Versailles settlement, his was not a restoration mentality. 'If one looks back', he later wrote, 'at the time before the war, one is amazed to see how weak the leaders of the nation really were.'[21] Goering's ideas betray a consistent desire to create something essentially new, implying all the historic virtues, but unlike any Germany of the past. This was the root of his subsequent claim that he joined the party 'because it was revolutionary'.[22]

The negative influences that created his sense of nation were like those of other Nazis: a powerful anti-semitism and a deep loathing of international Marxism. His view of the Weimar state as a Jewish Marxist Republic seems to have pre-dated his first contacts with the Nazi movement and suggests that he had already formed an independent view of the historic enemies of 'Germandom'.[23] The exact source of his anti-semitism can only be guessed at though it was a consistent and firmly-held attitude. He was no doubt influenced by the upper-class anti-semitism of his cadet school and his army companions. It may well be that Goering bore a deep resentment against his Jewish godfather who continually humiliated Goering's father in his last years. He lived openly with Goering's mother as his mistress and compelled the father to live on his charity in the gatehouse of his castle. But this can only be speculation. It is more likely that his anti-semitism was picked up uncritically, like most of his ideas, from the literature of radical right-wing politics in post-war Germany. Anti-semitism was part of a general explanation of the German crisis rather than the product of a specific hatred.[24] The source of his anti-Marxism is more obvious. The Marxist parties before 1914 were the enemies of the poorer, status-conscious bureaucrats and soldiers because they threatened the tradition-bound world upon which they depended. The experience of 1918 and the creation of a democratic system only hardened his inherited hatred of Marxism.

Goering's own answer to the problem of asserting Germany's historic role and defeating its enemies was twofold. It depended first of all on defeating democracy and establishing a unifying authoritarian political structure. Goering rejected the parliamentary principle instinctively with its 'anonymous ideas of the Majority'. 'The Laws of Nature demand', he wrote, 'that authority should be exercised from above downwards and responsibility from below upwards.'[25] Second, it depended upon the continuation of German imperialism and expansion. Goering shared with those of his own background a regular exposure to geo-political writings that saw world affairs in terms of nations rising and falling, of living-space and raw materials, an international Darwinism. The difference between Goering's response and that of the traditional conservative lay essentially in the kind of society he wanted to create in Germany, and the kind of people who would run it. The new society was what Nazis called the 'third way', neither bourgeois society with its redundant conservative elites, nor working-class democracy with its threat of national subversion, but a society based upon a unity of all groups working under the authoritarian guidance of a Germanic elite, allegedly 'national' and 'socialist' at the same time. By this route Nazis could claim the right of the party to totalitarian control, to extirpate Marxism, eradicate old class interests and define the nature of 'Germanness'.[26] By this route Goering later justified his central control over the economy and his challenge to what he called 'egoistic capitalism'.[27] In effect he was attempting, like fascism in general, to give a universal validity to a narrow pre-industrial ideal.

This new society had to be led by what fascists called 'the New Man'. This, too, was an essentially social-Darwinian concept. For Goering the concept implied the rediscovery of heroism and the rejection of bourgeois virtue. Goering's view of history was itself heroic, and his heroes were exclusively the great military leaders from Charlemagne to Napoleon. The virtues which he exalted were those of the soldier: honour, obedience, loyalty, daring. In warfare he believed that 'personal heroism must always count for more than technical novelties'.[28] More significantly, perhaps, he accepted uncritically the fascist emphasis on 'action', as opposed to the bourgeois emphasis on 'reason'. After his election to the Reichstag he wrote that ·We had but one task then – to attack everybody and always. Like pikes in the carp pool we stirred up the well-fed parliament-men. . . .'[29] The will to act with a ruthless and brutal determination was for Goering a defining characteristic both of the movement as a whole and of its leaders. In 1933 he announced 'I do not have to exercise justice. I have only to destroy and exterminate'; and on another occasion, 'I am proud of not knowing what justice is.'[30] He prided himself that he was always prepared to take brutal decisions when necessary, and without reconsideration. 'I don't just say I'm going to do something,' he told his staff, 'I actually do it.'[31]

Goering's whole world view was coloured by this pessimistic perception of human nature. He himself became the personification of his own ideas on struggle and action. His personality blended perfectly with his intellectual conviction that man was a 'Raubtier', a 'beast-of-prey'.[32] At Nuremberg he asked 'What do you know of the possibilities of evil? Why do you write books and make philosophy, when you only know about virtue and how to acquire it, whereas the world is fundamentally moved by something quite different.'[33] It was this unspoken or unspeakable force that Goering pretended to have found in National Socialism. For Goering the movement was not simply a political instrument for rescuing the conservative masses from destruction within industrial society, and for preserving and extending Germandom, but was an instrument for releasing human energies glimpsed at during the war but submerged beneath conventional morality and bourgeois culture; here was the Futurism of the front-line soldier. In all these respects Goering showed himself to be typical of the mainstream of German fascism: a frustrated and desperate member of the traditional middle class;

convinced of Germany's national 'mission' and of the Marxist and Jewish enemies that stood in its way; a firm believer that national life in Germany could only be transformed by a revolution of values, through the agency of the party.

These attitudes do not tell us everything about Goering's personality, though what they do say is not prepossessing. That he was ambitious, unscrupulous, vicious, and boastful is not mere legend but is, on any count, substantially true. That he was loyal, naive, sentimental and brave is little redemption, for these were the characteristics of his German service background, prompting Goebbels's patronising description of him as an 'upright soldier with the heart of a child'.[34] He lacked any discriminatory moral sense or humanity. He had much political cunning despite his apparent ingenuousness and had, at least for most of his life, a genuine native authority that stood him in stead for his lack of intellect. As a leader it would be wrong to pretend that he was liked, except perhaps by a circle of old wartime associates. What he was admired for as a leader was what Hitler admired in him: his energy, his coldness, his directness. This political and personal style was closely related to his style as a soldier when he had shown himself to be impulsive and daring. He liked to be thought of as a hard man. When it came to leading men during the period of the Third Reich his personality was still that of the rebarbative young officer.

Goering's barrack-room values made him bullying and boastful. Perhaps such characteristics stemmed from a deep-seated insecurity. He was deeply dependent upon Hitler and could be reduced to bouts of tearful self-mortification if he aroused Hitler's displeasure. But for most of the time Goering sought to impose his own will on others by sheer weight of personality, resorting to vengeful tactics if crossed in purpose or argument. Throughout the period he expected to achieve what he wanted by threats and brow-beating. If some believed that his bark was much worse than his bite, it was only because he got others to do his biting for him. He was also a boaster, filling out the reputation for hardness with his own exaggerated view of himself. This was partly the pattern of the regime as a whole. Its propaganda was designed to build a world of illusions peopled with superlatives. The Third Reich was a political jungle in which failure was penalised and dramatic success rewarded. Goering spent much of his time convincing Hitler and others that he had done all and more of what was required of him. His subordinates quickly discovered how far flattery would get them. But in Goering's case it was not simply the nature of political life that encouraged his boastfulness, but a deep desire to convince himself that he had achieved something: that he was no longer the powerless ex-soldier drifting away from the Wilhelmine world of his frustrated youth. Even if he had been more intellectually capable of self-criticism, his personality and the circumstances of its development were against it. He preferred to live in a bizarrely optimistic world of his own creation, shutting out reality, using his political power for its narcotic effects. Like others of his fascist contemporaries who found the reality of social and political change in Germany too difficult to face up to, he created his own world of illusion to protect himself psychologically as well as politically from the conflict between the world as it ought to be and the world as it was.

In one respect at least Goering was honest with himself. He recognised his intellectual limitations. This would not necessarily have mattered, and Goering himself clearly believed that it did not, had it not been for the fact that for most of his period in office the work with which he was associated was of a highly technical and complex nature. This was the case with both the air force and the economy. Nor would it have mattered had Goering simply delegated the technical decision-making. But in almost all cases he insisted upon his own responsibility for making technical judgments and forming policy. Schacht's view that he had 'a complete lack of understanding for economics' is well known, and is supported by the verbatim accounts of Goering's discussions as economic overlord.[35] Goering himself was openly in agreement with this judgment. In 1937 he complained when his subordinates brought economic problems to him: 'It is no good my trying to talk about them: how can I be expected to understand these complicated problems of economics?'[36] When he was commissioned by Hitler to run the Four Year Plan to create an autarkic, war-orientated economy, he told a distinguished audience that 'My department is not economics. . . . Neither am I an agriculturalist. Except for a few flower-pots on a balcony I have never cultivated anything.'[37] Goering instead made his anti-intellectual attitude and his lack of any technical competence into a virtue. This was a frustrating virtue for those who worked with him because of the incompetence and ignorance that accompanied it. 'A right decision, or critical judgement in technical matters', wrote one of his officers, 'was often a matter of pure luck in his case.'[38] The stenographic reports of his many conferences do indeed betray the image of a man trying to take technical decisions or even deal with questions of a broader strategic nature quite beyond his grasp.

Goering's political and administrative life, which forms the substance of this book, reflected both his personality and his intellectual make-up. He was excessively jealous with his authority, arguing endlessly with other offices over questions of jurisdiction and competency. He was unwilling to concede that important ideas or innovations were not his own, insisting that all decisions and every initiative should lie with him. He assumed the right to interfere in any affair, however trivial, in what was often an arbitrary and unsystematic way. In this his administrative method resembled Hitler's. Like Hitler, Goering had responsibility for a wide range of offices for which he was not inclined to do routine work. Had he been so inclined it would have been apparent from the outset that one man could not hope to master so many departments of state effectively. But instead Goering was able to disguise his lack of administrative endeavour behind his many and varied duties. He always appeared to be occupied by moving rapidly from one

responsibility onto the next without doing justice to any of them. The
records of his day-to-day activities kept by his personal staff show a constant
round of interviews, conferences and discussions.[39] The problem was not
administrative indolence, although there were times when Goering could
not be stirred to do anything at all, but an excess of administration, which
often amounted to the same thing.

Under these circumstances Goering came to depend on others to do
much of his work for him; Milch in the Air Ministry; Koerner and Pleiger
in the Four-Year Plan office and its industries; Gritzbach and Goernnert
on his personal staff. He instinctively disliked doing this, unless he was sure
that he could effectively dominate his deputy in some way. He preferred
Udet, an ex-flyer and stunt-man, to Milch, the officer and businessman,
because the former knew little about his job while the latter knew too much.
Goering was never reconciled to Milch politically because he took initiatives
that should rightly have been taken by Goering. But whether he liked it or
not most of his many offices were run on a permanent basis by his deputies
– state secretaries, special commissioners and civil servants. This dependence was reflected in the lack of initiative that Goering showed in practice
in the making of day-to-day policy. He set the broad conditions and aims
of all the major policies and knew what end-product he wanted from them,
but in their execution he was often ill-informed and inept. Like Hitler,
Goering was easily swayed by the last person to speak to him. In discussion
or argument Goering would attach himself firmly to what he could understand or what caught his interest. There was little weighing of evidence and
rational assessment on his part. He refused to read any policy document
longer than four type-written pages and professed not to understand graphs
or statistics.[40] His staff learned to cope with this and in fairness Goering
himself was willing to concede error. Moreover the effectiveness of the
bureaucratic and military establishment in maintaining routine and inter-
preting general policy directives meant that many of Goering's assignments
were fulfilled to some extent in spite of him. That is why any history of
Goering in the Third Reich is simultaneously a history of the apparatus of
state that he controlled.

Goering's administrative style reflected the unusual complexion of
German political life under Nazism. For most of his period in office Goering
was far more isolated from his political colleagues than was the case in, say,
Britain or the United States. There was none of the long and fruitful
correspondence between them that serves the historian of British politics.
Goering's contact with other Nazis, with the exception of Hitler, was
irregular. On the occasions when they did meet there were seldom discussions of policy or collective decisions. Meetings were contrived and formal,
ritual occasions. Political life was confined within the frontiers of administrative empires organised vertically, with little co-operation between them.
These power-blocs manoeuvred for advantage, drawing their strength from
their link with Hitler and the party, each seeking to profit at the expense

of the others. This situation encouraged the physical separation and isolation of Nazi leaders. Their direct political relationships were with those who worked lower down the hierarchy, not with other Nazi leaders. The characteristic feature of politics was a highly centrifugal institutional structure animated by mutual hostility and rivalry, held together with a rhetoric of solidarity.

This was, of course, how Hitler wanted it. The achievement and retention of power conformed with the jungle values of Nazi politics. Other Nazi leaders were, to Goering, rivals rather than partners. Power had to be competed for and fiercely retained; it did not come simply from the fact of holding office. For much of the time Goering trespassed on the authority and prerogatives of other office-holders, indifferent to their claims. Might was right. Nazi political morality was derived entirely from this central premise. The problem was that this made power a very brittle commodity. Signs of personal weakness were mercilessly exploited. So too was the loss of Hitler's favour. Once the sustaining bond of Hitler's confidence was broken, Nazi leaders were vulnerable to all those who still enjoyed his trust. Any power thus lost was immediately swallowed up by rival Nazi empires. Nazi leaders rose and fell not because of incompetence or electoral defeat, but because they lost out in the personal, and even physical, contest for power and the restless efforts to provide Hitler with what he wanted.

As a result, political life was never still in the Third Reich. There was never any sense of permanence, despite all the propaganda of solidarity and unity. The competitiveness of the movement's leaders led to constant and rapid shifts in political allegiance, the distribution of responsibility and in policy. The unstable and dynamic properties of this system produced remarkable twists and turns in the character of political life, in diplomacy, in economic affairs. The speed with which Goering built up the Luftwaffe and constructed his economic empire did not simply reflect his personal energy but was a product of the system itself. This perhaps explains the underlying fragility of both the air force and the economy when faced with general war. One initiative followed another, with insufficient time for recuperation and consolidation. Moreover Goering's formal ministerial responsibilities suffered from the fact that for much of the time he was fending off rivals outside his empire and potential rivals within it.

Deliberate isolation, power-seeking and rivalry coloured the way in which other people perceived Goering. Few got close to him. Indeed for all his excessive sociability he remained an outsider, keeping people at a distance. Fellow Nazi leaders saw him as ambitious, energetic, vain and unscrupulous; as one of themselves. They were for the main jealous of Goering and critical of his sumptuous life-style. Goering had no illusions about their feelings. He surrounded himself with bodyguards wherever he went. Like Hitler his cars were armour-plated and bullet-proof, built without running-boards to make it harder for would-be assassins to get near him.[41] No doubt he had more to fear from other Nazi leaders than he did from the public, for one source of their jealousy was Goering's popularity. To the party and the public at large Goering's image was that of the colourful ex-soldier and old party fighter, bluff and approachable, energetic and loyal. This was indeed the public face that Goering displayed; blunt, direct, jovial and above all trustworthy. Foreign diplomats and German conservatives alike were among those taken in by his habit of straight-talking, his apparent willingness to listen to reason and to sympathise with what he was being told, Goering appeared at times to be all things to all men. This was partly an uncontrollable reflex. Goering liked to feel important. His accommodating behaviour gave him an immediate significance in any discussion and won over the confidence of his interlocutor. But in fact he seldom told the truth on such occasions; his sociability was a mask; his openness and reasonableness a ploy. This ability to dissimulate was an important and calculated tactic. Within the broad framework of ambitions laid down for the movement by Hitler, Goering explored every possibility of making political capital and extending his personal power. Beneath his public persona was a thoughtful, unscrupulous and vengeful politician who manipulated those with whom he had contact as they believed they might manipulate him.

Because of the contrast between public image and private ambition it is difficult to decide how much other people actually influenced Goering in either his ideas or his political actions. His family, respectable and thoroughly middle-class, seems to have had a negligible influence, and to be largely unaware of the exact nature of Goering's political life. His sister believed, for example, that in 1939 the strong desire for peace expressed by his family acted to turn Goering against war and against Hitler's diplomacy.[42] But in fact Goering's arguments for peace were Hitler's too: that Britain's feeble politicians could be bought off as they had been in 1938 and the Polish crisis be localised. Goering's first wife, Carin, clearly did have considerable influence upon him. Her premature death in 1931 encouraged him to work in politics with an ever greater energy. In 1934 he erected an elaborate mausoleum to her memory.[43] But even her influence took the form of reinforcing ideas and attitudes that were already formed. His second wife, the actress Emmy Sonnemann, was a political innocent, enjoying the high life that Goering's power made possible but distant from his political life and uncritical in her views.[44] From her comes the evidence of how fond Goering was of children and animals. Goering preferred this relationship. 'She could have her way in the household,' he said, 'but as far as my basic code is concerned nothing can sway me . . . when it comes to the basic things in a man's life it is not a woman's affair.'[45] Goering never involved her in his politics and she never interfered.

Two influences on Goering were of great importance: Hitler, and public opinion. That is not to say that he did not hesitate to take unpopular measures when necessary; nor to deny his belief that policy should be handed down from above, not influenced from below. But he was anxious to make a good impression, to be liked by the crowd. That was why he spent much more time cultivating a public personality than other Nazi leaders. Nor was this all vanity. A central theme of Nazi ideology was the belief that the German working class, once rid of its Marxist leadership, would be reunited with the German community. Goering shared this hope, having first made it his responsibility to eliminate working-class political institutions and persecute socialism.[46] Of course this romantic view of the working class should not be exaggerated. Public opinion did not strongly influence Goering's day-to-day actions. It did nothing to blunt his draconian efforts during the war to mobilise labour reserves. It is even doubtful if less public popularity would have reduced his claim to power substantially. The pursuit of public approval was as much an expression of vanity and insecurity as it was a political insight. At Nuremberg he expressed the hope that in 'fifty or sixty years' time there will be statues of Hermann Goering all over Germany. Little statues maybe, but one in every German home.'[47]

The influence of Hitler on the other hand was without question a decisive one. Goering's political acts were derived from Hitler's world view and inspired by his messianic leadership. Hitler was the central reference point. 'God gave the German people a champion in Adolf Hitler,' Goering wrote.[48] The strength of the bond of loyalty transcended everything that Goering did, partly because he wanted to believe that Hitler could determine Germany's destiny, partly because this bond was the single most important key to political survival. His motives were influenced at every turn by this effort to realise Hitler's ambitions.

This is not to minimise Goering's own political significance, for his large empire was a tribute to his vast appetite for political power. His overriding priority was to create a political power-structure, with himself at its core, for the purpose of sharing with Hitler in the transformation of German life. That his conception of the new Germany was class-based and sterile did not matter. Goering's belief was sincere enough that the revival and expansion of Germany depended on the struggle of great individuals with a sense of mission. 'World history', he wrote, 'can show few parallel examples.'[49] He played for a role on a world stage. Intoxicated by this longing for significance, Goering, like Hitler, hoped to transcend his more mundane social and political environment, the pressures of class and interest of which he was, in reality, a violent product.

This tension between romantic longing and the reality of modern politics remained suspended and unresolved. Indeed it could be argued that the final decline of Goering's political power and personal drive was a precise reflection of this tension. Real life was not as Goering perceived it, even in the irrational world of Nazi politics. World-historical significance did not come from simply claiming it. Goering accepted some of the effort necessary to create his new world, particularly in his prolonged attempt to transform the German and European economies. He accepted for much of the period that his political power had to be earned by constant vigilance against the efforts of other Nazis to undermine his influence and claim to leadership.

There was no escape from this kind of continuous, trivial political combat in Hitler's state, except for Hitler himself. But for much of his time in power he was dogged with failure: failure to transform German society from its class base; failure to mobilise the economy effectively enough for war; failure in the air war. For Goering the means eventually defeated the end. His self-constructed image of the Nazi hero was compromised by the constant need to justify and defend it against critics within and enemies without. During the final period of the war Goering appears to have realised that the battle was lost long before Hitler.

During the final months of the war Goering returned to the melancholy life-style of the 1920s, to bizarre efforts to blot out reality and to sustain the illusion. It was widely rumoured that he had become a drug addict. Such rumours were exaggerated. His addiction was not to narcotics but to the habit of taking pills. His physicians provided him with large numbers of harmless coloured pills, each containing a small quantity of paracodeine. The hundred pills consumed each day contained not much more than a number of asprin tablets. The doctors who treated him after his capture at the end of the war found no difficulty in ridding him of the habit. He took pills at meetings and in interviews as other people might smoke.[50]

But he had other vices which he continued to indulge. He retreated more often to Carinhall, his extravagant home in which he lived the life of 'the last Renaissance man', crowding his days with lavish entertainment, art-collecting and looting, hunting and pageantry.[51] His personal papers are littered with the efforts of his staff to requisition the finest wines and foods for Goering's table at the height of the war.[52] His vanity and flamboyance became notorious in the face of the privations of ordinary Germans. Speer judged that 'he had sunk into his lethargy, and for good'. Late in 1944 Goering told General Koller that he was 'sick and tired of the whole business . . . wished he were dead'.[53] He continued to attend meetings and consult with Hitler but on increasingly unfavourable terms. His subordinates had no other recourse but to bypass him in order to get anything done. Goering himself intervened randomly and unpredictably in his many affairs, making through his efforts a substantial contribution to defeat. This was the supreme irony: to have risen to power in Germany to reverse the soldiers' betrayal by the home front in 1918 only to fall from power for military failure in 1945. Eighteen months later, judged a criminal by the Allies at Nuremberg, he committed suicide.

Goering's personal history follows step-by-step the history of German fascism. He was a typical fascist recruit from those classes in German society caught out by the collapse of the old system and unable or unwilling to compromise with the democratic society that replaced it and the industrial and bourgeois values that it encapsulated. Like other fascist activists he fought to create a political mechanism that appropriately expressed the interests of the conservative masses with their desire for authoritarian government, a revisionist foreign policy, and German 'culture'. He was part of a movement from below, not part of an aristocratic stratagem to cling on to power. Once in power, in which he enjoyed a substantial share until almost the end of the war, Goering was active in consolidating Nazi authority and then in hastening the creation of a Nazi empire through military pressure and war. His historical importance derives much more from his role in the economy and in pursuing grand strategy than from any intrinsic personal claim to significance. The 'Iron Man' divorced from his political empire and the apparatus of Nazism was an historical creature of little substance.

2

BUILDING THE
GOERING EMPIRE

On the night of 30 January 1933 Goering broadcast to the German people
news of Hitler's assumption of power: 'We are closing the darkest era of
German history and are beginning a new chapter ... bread and work for
the German people, freedom and honour for the nation.'[1] Despite the fact
that Hitler was sharing power with other right-wing groups that were anxious
to maintain a semblance of continuity, Goering expressed the widespread
feeling in the Nazi Party itself that a real revolution in German political life
was now possible. While the conservative allies of the movement believed
that Hitler could be tamed and manipulated, as popular groups had been
before 1914, the Nazi leaders saw the opportunity to confront their democratic enemies and undermine the institutions of parliamentary government.
This political revolution was indiscriminate, directed against German
communists and socialists as well as the traditional conservative groups that
had helped Hitler to acquire the chancellorship. While the left had no
illusions about Nazi intentions, the nationalist right miscalculated their
ability to contain the Nazi movement and failed to find any tactics that could
cope with Nazi methods of infiltration and usurpation.

The Nazi political revolution began with two basic assumptions. The
first was the necessity for centralising political control under Hitler's sole
authority, at the expense of the provincial political power-holders, the
political parties and the institutions of the state. The second was in some
ways the more important, for the Nazis assumed rightly that the nominal
transfer of political authority would be meaningless if it was not at the same
time accompanied by changes in personnel, in institutional structures, in
the distribution of social power. The Weimar Republic had suffered from
the difficulty of challenging the entrenched social position of the old conservative groups and in democratising German institutions. The Nazi Party
determined from the outset to provide an alternative set of institutions or
to so dominate those that remained that they could not constitute a source
of alternative power in the Nazi state. In this the Nazi revolution in 1933
resembled that of the Bolsheviks sixteen years before, with Lenin's insistence on a fusion of party and state and Bolshevik control of, and penetration
into, the lower levels of administrative and political life.

Hitler shared another political insight with Lenin. During 1933, as in 1917, the Nazi leaders deliberately encouraged the growth of lawlessness, administrative anarchy and a restless dialectic of violence in order to dissolve the old social and political bonds and create the conditions for totalitarian control. The police repression, the emergency decrees, the closing down of the trade unions and the political parties, were only the outward manifestations of the Nazis' concerted efforts to overturn existing social and political relations and to replace them with a network of allegiance and obedience to Hitler and the movement. By the autumn of 1933 this process was largely completed. Reliance on the expertise and experience of older officials, army officers and businessmen was re-established, not because Hitler was forced to compromise and restore the political balance in favour of the conservatives, but because he had achieved the aim of dominating the political system and compelling loyalty. The crisis that led up to the Roehm affair at the end of June 1934 must be seen in this context, not as a concession to the army and big business, but as a necessary consequence of the period of revolutionary violence and confusion created in 1933. These dynamic and violent forces released in the spring and summer of 1933 had to be contained within the new political structure as well. The continuation of violence by Roehm's stormtroopers threatened the establishment of Nazi political power and the Nazis' ability to operate the apparatus of the German state which they had now taken under control. The SA, like the Kronstadt sailors, were a necessary but dispensable part of the revolution.

In the period of 'struggle' between January 1933 and the end of the year, and in the succeeding period of what Hitler called 'Machtbefestigung' (consolidation of power), Goering had a central, if ambiguous, role to play. Lacking any real power-base in the party itself, Goering's claim to influence with Hitler lay entirely in his capacity as a leading parliamentary figure. Since Goering himself expressed the view that the Nazis 'were, are, and will always be foes to the death against the principle of democracy'[2] it was clearly necessary to find some alternative claim to authority. Parliament itself was destined to become irrelevant. His position as speaker of the Reichstag, and as a national political figure, remained important during February and March as Goering manoeuvred between the various political parties in the Nazis' efforts to strengthen their parliamentary position, and in the search during the aftermath of the March election for a majority to agree to an Enabling Law which would give the Nazis unrestrained power. Goering's contacts with the centre and with Hugenberg helped to ensure the necessary two-thirds support while shielding from them the full intentions of the Nazi movement once such an act was in force.[3] But with the passing of the act and the gradual elimination of all rival political parties Goering's position in the Reichstag, like that of all parliamentarians, became supernumerary.

Goering's real power lay with his appointment as Prussian Minister of the Interior. As Reich Minister without Portfolio, a post which he also acquired on 30 January as part of the bargain struck with von Papen, he had a presence in cabinet, but the minutes show that he contributed little to these early discussions.[4] The Prussian post was of much greater significance, even though Goering was nominally subordinate to von Papen as Reich Commissar for Prussia. Hitler had intended on assuming power to make either Goering or himself ruler of Prussia in place of Gregor Strasser who had previously laid claim to it, but in the event von Papen insisted on keeping his commissarial position as part of the price for co-operation.[5] In this von Papen, like Hitler and Goering, recognised the special position of Prussia in German political life. To give Prussia back to the conservatives, who had themselves begun the purging of the social democrats in the Prussian administration in 1932, would be to abandon one of the major institutions of the old state and provide a powerful rallying point for conservative forces. Goering's appointment as Prussian Minister of the Interior gave the Nazis an avenue into Prussian politics, and gave Goering control of the Prussian police force. In this capacity Goering embarked immediately, and with only cursory reference to von Papen, on the task of combating the Nazis' political enemies and rivals. On his first day as Minister he cancelled political demonstrations to be held by the Communist Party and suspended the publication of the social democrat newspaper *Vorwaerts* for three days.[6] This began a pattern of harassment and repression under a cloak of semi-legality.

Goering saw as his primary task the rooting out of socialism and communism within Prussia, though that was not his only one. The elimination of the 'enemies of the state' meant the releasing of posts that could be given to Nazis or Nazi sympathisers. Opponents on the right or centre were not immune either, where they constituted a threat to Goering's authority and the ambitions of the movement. Most important of all Goering assumed the responsibility in Prussia for releasing a widespread movement of political terrorism consistent with Hitler's desire to create a new order out of the confusion and dissolution of the old. Within a week Goering procured a list of police officers and government officials to be purged. For this he depended on contacts established with the Prussian police department in 1932, and on the willing co-operation of conservative officials who wanted to eradicate socialist influence in the civil service. One of these officials, Rudolf Diels, had already approached Goering with a list of candidates for replacement. On 8 February the first purge was carried out. At the same time Goering arranged that elements of the SA and SS should be given official police status so that they could speed up the process of cleansing Prussia. On 11 February auxiliary police were sworn in for the Rhineland area with instructions to assist the ordinary police in their fight against subversive left-wing elements in the Ruhr cities. On 22 February the auxiliary police force was sanctioned for the whole of Prussia. The SA was now given the licence to do legally what they had been willing, but unable, to do during the period of the rise to power.[7]

The burning of the Reichstag building on the night of 27 February was thus not the occasion for the onset of attacks on the Communist Party but merely allowed the scope of such attacks to be extended. The evidence is now well established that Goering was not the fire-raiser.[8] But he used the opportunity created by the fire to speed up and legitimise the actions already being taken against the German left wing. No doubt the fire helped to make police oppression more acceptable to the German public, and was thus good propaganda. However, Goering needed no excuse. 'The record of Communist crimes', he wrote, 'was already so long and their offence so atrocious that I was in any case resolved to use all the powers at my disposal in order ruthlessly to wipe out this plague.'[9] The Communist Party was effectively outlawed. Indeed Goering used the radical literature already confiscated from leading communists and the KPD headquarters during February as evidence of communist complicity in the fire. The repression that followed the Reichstag Fire Emergency Decree merely completed a process well under way.

In the wake of the crisis provoked by the fire Goering was able to move against the Social Democrats as well, on the basis that all left-wing parties shared the same 'corrupt Liberal-Marxist state ideal'.[10] By the time of the general election called in March Goering's apparatus of repression was widespread and indiscriminate. The Prussian police were instructed to shoot anyone who demonstrated against the regime, and although few regular policemen seem to have taken the instruction literally, the SA was given a blank cheque to take what steps they saw fit to intimidate the political opposition and destroy socialism. Goering was fully aware of the forces that he was unleashing, bypassing all protest with the explanation that the nature of the political emergency justified brutal methods. Some conservatives, including the vice-chancellor von Papen, welcomed the Nazis' initiative, for it resembled their own efforts during 1932 to overthrow social democracy in Prussia, and it confirmed their fears of the KPD's revolutionary intentions.[11] However illusory the prospect of a communist-led revolution in Germany in 1933, it was a fear that Goering, for one, took very seriously.

The Nazi victory in the elections of 5 March thus took place against a mounting wave of official oppression. Although the final result did not achieve the outright majority that Hitler wanted, support for the Nazi Party was extensive enough to persuade him to dismantle the alliance set up in January. He was able to bring more Nazis into official positions, and to take the first steps in establishing complete political authority. To achieve this it was necessary to eliminate the independent provinces and centralise all administration in Berlin. Such a step allowed Hitler to remove von Papen from his position in Prussia and leave him in the much more vulnerable role of vice-chancellor. The problem with this course was that it threatened at the same time to remove Goering's authority and to place the Prussian Interior Ministry under the direct control of the Reich Minister of the Interior, Wilhelm Frick. Early in April a compromise was reached. The

Prussian government would remain in being, although most Prussian ministries would be fused with those of the Reich, leaving Goering as a new
Minister-President with diminished responsibilities. Von Papen's commissarial role in Prussia was ended by a law promulgated on 7 April and Goering
assumed control as Hitler's direct deputy.[12] The constitutional position
nevertheless remained confused for Goering feared that the centralisation
would in reality deny him any effective power base of his own. The additional bonus of the Air Ministry, which became his Reich portfolio in
March, was small compensation for it still left military aviation in the hands
of the army and navy.

Perhaps for this reason Goering continued to extend the Nazi terror in
Prussia and to establish institutions independent, as far as possible, of
central control. The SA were encouraged to continue their police role and
began setting up concentration camps and special interrogation centres.
Goering established state-run concentration camps for political prisoners in
Prussia, and set up an independent political police force under his direct
control. This force was constituted from the political police department of
the Prussian police and was placed under Diels, as a reward for previous
service. The new force, known as the Geheime Staatspolizei (Gestapo), had
its headquarters in a building adjacent to Goering's presidential residence.[13]
The new office came directly under Goering's authority. It was responsible
for all political and security police work in Prussia. The ordinary police,
now under SS leader Kurt Daluege, were confined to routine police work.

Throughout the months following Goering's new appointment the
process of 'cleansing' the administration continued. Catholics were sacked
for their Catholicism, national conservatives were replaced with Nazis, Jews
were expelled everywhere. In many offices and firms Goering set up special
commissars, or permitted the SA to do so, who replaced the existing administrative officials, or those who had already fled their office.[14] Much of the
administrative revolution in Prussia was carried through by these commissars. Commissarial rule brought Goering a number of advantages. It gave
him much greater influence over events and allowed him to override conventional channels of appointment and administration at will. At the same time
he established a new Prussian State Council which he intended should have
an advisory role as a college of experts, along the lines laid down in Hitler's
own discussion of political systems in *Mein Kampf*. The disadvantage for
Goering of these developments was that they ran counter to the centralising
process initiated on Hitler's express instructions, while they carried the
additional danger that the SA might be given uncontrolled power at a local
level. As a result Goering found himself in an increasingly ambiguous and
isolated position.[15]

Frick's efforts to centralise political control on Hitler's behalf could only
be resisted by Goering up to a point because he was well aware of how
much he relied on Hitler for his political position. Frick therefore argued
from a position of some strength. Moreover it became apparent to Goering

by the summer of 1933 that the SA that he had unleashed in February was slipping out of his control and that a return to more stable and regularised administration, away from the system of commissars, would also help to keep his own political power intact. There was always the danger that he, too, might fall victim to revolutionary violence. Through the Gestapo he began to close down unofficial concentration camps and the SA interrogation centres. The occupation of business premises by SA commissars was suspended and the businesses returned to competent managers. In June he agreed with Frick that a concerted effort should be made to restrain the SA and to initiate a 'systematic' (*planmässig*) revolution more closely under his supervision.[16] On 17 July Goering issued a decree giving himself responsibility for all Prussian provincial appointments, official and academic. Although the SA continued in places to flout his authority some degree of normality was restored.[17] In the interval between February and July Goering had achieved what was wanted from the confusion and terror. Opponents of all kinds had been eliminated and the administration filled with Nazis, or those who were no longer in a position to oppose. The dissolving of old bonds was complete enough to allow Goering to turn against the violent groups that had been used to achieve it.

The efforts to rein back the SA met with only partial success. It was difficult for Goering to challenge the SA on the grounds of their violent behaviour since he himself had established institutionalised violence and had talked openly of the need for vicious methods. Yet the more difficult it became for him to discipline the SA, the more difficult it was to resist the pressure from Frick and the centralisers, without whose help the restoration of full state authority in Prussia could not be achieved. For some months he manoeuvred between the two contradictory forces. He agreed to allow the SS to replace the SA in the concentration camps, but resisted the efforts of the Commission of Reorganisation set up by the Reich to investigate the activities of the Gestapo. In November he issued a decree making the Gestapo independent of the Interior Ministry and responsible only to him.[18] In the end, however, Goering abandoned his ambiguous role. The Prussian police force was taken under Reich control in January 1934, and the Prussian Ministry of the Interior followed, merged with Frick's national ministry. Despite a renewed statement in a decree of 14 March on the autonomy of the Gestapo, that, too, was finally abandoned in April.[19] Although Goering remained nominal head of the Gestapo until 1936, in practice the installation of Himmler as his deputy and Heydrich as its director marked the end of an independent Prussian force. The ordinary police and political police forces of the Reich now came under the joint control of Frick and Himmler.

The loss of Prussian and police powers constituted a double blow to Goering's prestige which he accepted with ill grace. In both cases Hitler's decision was final. In the confused party politics of the period the one consistent feature was the political success of those who demonstrated a powerful loyalty to Hitler. Goering could not afford to sacrifice Hitler's goodwill. As it was, Goering was identified both at home and abroad as one of the leading Nazi radicals, a proponent of violent overthrow and terror. This Jacobin image suited Hitler during the first months of 1933 but less so thereafter. With the decision to proceed more cautiously through the formal apparatus of a centralised state machinery, evidence of lawlessness became more politically embarrassing. Goering's henchman Diels was dismissed as head of the Gestapo in September 1933 on Hindenburg's insistence. Hitler preferred different methods once the early stages of the political revolution were completed. Although Goering concurred with this tactical change in the summer of 1933 it was difficult for him to be rid of the image of one who had promoted the rowdy and politically dangerous terrorism of the SA. Himmler was able to make capital out of the fact that his police methods were systematic, secretive and considerably more efficient than those in Prussia. Frick supported him in this and was able to persuade Hitler to grant secret police powers in the Reich as a whole to Himmler. The débâcle of the Reichstag fire trial, in which Goering was publicly exposed as an unrestrained and unintelligent bully, lent weight to these arguments. The price Goering was forced to pay for dissociating himself from the SA radicals was the abandonment of his newly-won Prussian power.

Goering's reluctant acceptance of the solution proposed by Frick and Himmler must be seen against a changing political balance within the party itself. The power enjoyed by the SA in Prussia under Goering had fuelled the ambitions of its leaders to become the new rulers of Germany. The SA leader, Ernst Roehm, who also enjoyed cabinet rank, was in direct competition with the party leadership. Unlike his colleagues he did not regard Hitler as an indispensable part of the political system built up by the Nazi Party since January 1933.[20] Opposition to Roehm was thus not merely an expression of personal ambition, but an expression of loyalty to Hitler. Goering could not oppose the centralisers in the party without implicitly supporting Roehm. By accepting the loss of his Prussian and police powers Goering re-affirmed that loyalty to Hitler and avoided association with the radical elements in the SA demanding a 'second revolution'. Gradually during the course of 1934 Goering aligned himself with Goebbels, Ley and Himmler against Roehm and the SA.[21] He had reasons of his own, too, for isolating Roehm. During 1934 rumours circulated that Roehm had ambitions not only to take over the army but the air force as well. This revived tensions that had existed between the two men since 1928, when Goering failed to regain the leadership of the SA that he had forfeited when he fled from Germany in 1923.[22]

It would be a mistake to see the conflict between the SA and the other figures of the party as a concession to the conservative forces still politically active in Germany. It was largely a conflict over personalities and over political tactics. Hitler's desire to restore a degree of stability and system to the political structure was by no means a declaration against the radical ideology of the movement. It was a recognition of political realities. In order to get the state and its institutions to work on behalf of the movement it had been necessary to carry out the centralisation and political 'cleansing' completed by 1934. Now it was necessary to use the organs of state and the economy to extend Nazi power and promote a business revival. Further revolutionary action of the kind argued for by Roehm contained the danger that what had already been gained might be thrown away through an excess of revolutionary zeal. The correct tactic was not a 'Second Revolution' but a permanent revolution, a continuous elimination of 'un-German' values and institutions in favour of those that were racially acceptable. To Hitler this was an organic process, no longer a revolutionary one.

To some extent conservatives inside Germany miscalculated both their own strength and the nature of the internal party struggle. Those that had survived the purges of 1933 saw in the attacks on the SA an indication that Hitler was willing to pursue a more moderate nationalist line with which they could identify. There was even hope that the monarchy might be restored although Goering himself, whom they regarded wrongly as a monarchist, announced in public five days before the Roehm crisis in June that the restoration was out of the question.[23] The fact that the army had been approached by leading Nazis in order to get the promise of support against the SA fuelled the conservative belief that in the summer of 1934 they might once again hold more influence over Reich affairs.

In fact this belief was an illusion. The Nazi Party leaders who opposed Roehm were every bit as radical as the SA in their long-term plans to revolutionise German society and extend the movement's power. Moreover, conservative political fortunes had been considerably reduced during 1933, largely because of the conservatives' preoccupation with questions of foreign policy at the expense of any real political initiative within Germany. Hugenberg was eliminated as a political figure through his obsession with the restoration of Germany's colonies, while his efforts to revive conservative-nationalist fortunes through the Deutsche National-Front (the revamped DNVP) in the summer of 1933 broke down in competition with the populist Nazis. Von Papen and von Neurath had diverted the energies of the surviving conservatives to questions to do with disarmament and the League of Nations, again at the expense of domestic politics.[24] Von Papen's loss of Prussia in April 1933, changes in the army high command and the purging of the upper levels of the Reich and provincial administrations contributed further to the rapid erosion of a conservative political power-base. Symbolically, Bismarck's great-nephew, Herbert, was among those harried from office.[25]

During 1934 it was no longer the conservatives who were 'taming' the Nazis, but the reverse: Nazi manipulation of the old conservatives. Hitler needed, and used, the expertise and experience of army officers, officials and businessmen but he did so from a position of political strength. For example, when Goering approached von Fritsch, the army chief, in February 1934 to insure army support in the event of action taken against the SA it was done with the veiled threat that without it both the SA and the SS would become uncontrolled forces, dismantling and overthrowing even the old armed forces.[26] The threat of violent and radical revolution used to calm conservative fears about Nazi excesses in 1933 was raised once again in 1934 in order to make the armed forces accept Nazi rule. The army, moreover, could be bought off with the promise of more rearmament. This tactic was used successfully to weaken links between conservatives in industry and the army, for in the summer of 1934 the Economics Ministry under Schmitt, and a number of leading industrialists opposed excessive rearmament and the growth of state intervention in the economy.[27] The appointment of Schacht to the Economics Ministry, and the retirement of Schmitt and von Papen in the wake of the Roehm crisis, brought economy and armed forces closer together but brought them both into a position of greater dependence on the Nazis. It was on this foundation of increasing dependence that the surviving influence of the old army officer corps, the economic elite and the traditional foreign office was finally supplanted in 1938, when Hitler felt strong enough to complete through stealth what Roehm promised through force in 1934.

This is not to minimise the importance of the Roehm crisis when it was finally resolved at the end of June. But it must be seen as a function of intra-party politics not as part of a conservative renaissance. In the atmosphere of revolutionary tension in the summer of 1934 it is plausible that Roehm's enemies, including Goering, genuinely believed in the possibility of an SA putsch. Indeed the potential constellation of forces that had threatened to overturn Hitler in December 1932 was still in existence in 1934. The criticism of Hitler among SA leaders and growing tensions within the party revived memories of the earlier crisis. Gregor Strasser, von Schleicher and Roehm stood at the centre of the political crisis in 1932. All three were still free in 1934, though the first two were politically inactive. Von Papen's speech at Marburg directed against the excesses of the regime in June 1934 was interpreted by Goebbels and Goering, in the light of their experiences of 1932, as the beginning of another period of political realignment and uncertainty.[28] On this basis they spent the second half of June persuading Hitler of the necessity for eliminating Roehm, disciplining the SA, and imposing his political authority more firmly. In practice Hitler's authority was firm enough, and there was no direct putschist threat either from the SA or the army. Indeed when an SA leader in the Rhineland received information at the end of June about an impending crisis, he assumed that it was Goering who was preparing a putsch against Roehm, and not the other way around.[29]

In some sense this was precisely what Goering was doing. Although the evidence is circumstantial, it is clear that Goering, Himmler and Goebbels collaborated to produce a list of SA leaders and other political figures to be eliminated on Hitler's orders as a pre-emptive move. The date chosen coincided with an SA gathering in Bavaria and a period of SA leave that would make opposition harder. Goering deliberately distorted the degree of danger in order to persuade Hitler to act. Once Hitler gave the express order Goering carried out the purges in Prussia, Himmler in Bavaria. The most important victims were the intriguers from 1932, Strasser, von Schleicher and Roehm. Von Papen escaped on Goering's orders but was broken politically.[30] The remaining victims were drawn either from the SA or from among the remaining anti-Nazis in the political or administrative establishment who had not been silenced during 1933. Goering and Hitler justified their actions by emergency decrees, stressing the danger to the state that the SA had constituted. The army and the foreign office were given details of Roehm's alleged plans, including the SA candidates for foreign minister and commander-in-chief of the armed forces. Hindenburg sent Goering a congratulatory telegram.[31] Other conservatives, obsessed with the fear of popular risings, saw Hitler as the guarantor of stability and the protector of old institutions. Ironically, a large part of those executed in the purge were aristocrats.[32]

Although Goering secured his political survival in 1934 by playing off one set of radical Nazis against another, his political position in the Reich still rested on a fragile foundation. He enjoyed less direct ministerial authority than he had had in the spring of 1933. In cabinet minutes his name appeared ninth (and occasionally even lower) in order of seniority.[33] His work in Prussia and his police activity left him more isolated from the mainstream of Reich and Nazi Party politics. He had contributed to, but not directed, the undermining of the conservatives and the elimination of the unions and political parties. He failed to benefit from the redistribution of economic posts following Hugenberg's eclipse in 1933 and the sacking of Schmitt in 1934. Other leading Nazis combined both high party office and important administrative and governmental posts. Goering held no major party post while his position as Minister-President of Prussia was purely nominal, since all major decisions on provincial policy were taken at the centre. The Prussian ministry and the Prussian State Council were retained as dignified parts of the constitution. His control over the Gestapo was also purely nominal. The secret intelligence that it provided was gradually sealed off from both Goering and Frick by its SS controllers.[34] During 1935 Himmler argued for unified and complete control over all police matters to be placed in his hands.[35] This move was finally confirmed by Hitler in 1936. Although Goering retained an interest in juridical and police matters, it was not a source of power.

Nor did Goering succeed in his efforts to assume greater responsibility in foreign affairs or military planning. Hitler certainly discussed questions to do with foreign policy and rearmament with Goering, but his formal responsibility extended only to the air force. He was given no official position in foreign-policy making and was subordinate to von Blomberg, the War

Minister, when it came to military questions. His main role in his unofficial capacity as Hitler's confidant was to establish informal contacts as special emissary in Italy, Austria, Poland and the Balkans. It was partly due to Goering's efforts that Mussolini accepted Hitler's assurances concerning the independence of Austria.[36] It was Goering, too, who assumed some of the responsibility for winning support for Germany in the Balkans and who, as Minister-President of Prussia, handled the negotiations over the economic problems of Danzig with the Poles between 1934 and 1936.[37] He also argued on ideological grounds for closer links with Japan, although the general trend of policy in the foreign office and the army favoured closer ties with China; and even though Goering himself was involved in selling old First World War weapons to the Chinese for his own profit.[38]

As a result of these activities he earned the hostility of the Foreign Minister, von Neurath, and the distrust of the German diplomatic corps. Under pressure Hitler respected the views of the diplomatists and used Goering sparingly.[39] For his part, Goering handled individual episodes so ineptly that his exclusion from foreign policy was as much a product of necessity as deliberate choice. While Hitler still needed to conduct his foreign policy with circumspection, Goering was a liability as an ambassador. In late 1934 Goering clumsily tried to detach the Little Entente in eastern Europe from its connection with France by suggesting that Germany was not interested in treaty revision. Apart from the statement's general implausibility in the context of German foreign policy, it had the effect of alienating both Italy and Hungary and left the foreign ministry with the awkward position of having to explain Goering's conduct.[40] Von Hassell in Rome was moved to assure Mussolini that Goering, 'a high-spirited military man', 'was not in charge of foreign policy'.[41] Mussolini had already formed this impression on his own. He disliked Goering, declaring him to be the 'ex-inmate of a lunatic asylum: not conspicuous for reason or logic'.[42] Goering's contacts in Italy with Renzetti, who was head of the Fascist Party office for foreign affairs, and Balbo, head of the Italian air force, reinforced Mussolini's misgivings, for he was suspicious of their political ambitions. In 1933 and again in 1934 he insisted that German-Italian relations be conducted through normal diplomatic channels and not through Goering as a special emissary. Hitler accepted the request.[43]

Goering's interest in foreign policy stemmed from Hitler's general concern with treaty revision and territorial expansion. So too did his interest in rearmament and military planning. Yet here he was faced with further difficulties. His control of military aviation took time to secure against strong army resistance. His hopes of enjoying a wider influence on military policy foundered on the opposition of the War Minister and the other armed services. Although Goering had Hitler's promise of the air ministry in his favour, the army had forceful arguments for keeping military aviation in their hands.[44] Until 1933 the Air Office set up in the defence ministry had co-ordinated all air affairs and undertaken secret air rearmament. Both the army and the navy were reluctant to abandon their control over any future air force. Under Blomberg the armed forces were committed to undivided control by the supreme commander, and were hostile to the idea of bringing any service under the direct control of a political party. Goering's acquisition of control over military aviation threatened both these principles. Only strong pressure from Hitler brought the Air Office under Goering in May 1933. The army and navy succeeded for some months after that in keeping aircraft and air weapons development in their hands in the army ordnance office. Only in 1934 were they compelled to relinquish these activities to Goering as well, who then established an independent structure of procurement for the air force.[45] For the next two years the two sides argued about the nature and extent of Goering's military authority. In April 1936 von Blomberg made one final effort to undermine the autonomy of the air force in a decree on the unity of the armed forces. However, by then Goering's position was much more secure politically. The failure of von Blomberg's initiative brought to an end the uncertainty that surrounded Goering's responsibility for air affairs.[46]

Goering's determination to establish an independent air force stemmed largely from political considerations. As a major party figure he was able to use his position as air minister to undermine the monopoly in military affairs enjoyed by the traditional armed forces. The air force served the purpose of identifying the Nazi movement, and Goering in particular, with the most spectacular and modern of the three services. The glamour of aviation served a specific propaganda purpose. Moreover Goering believed that a future war might be won through air power alone, thus making the older services redundant. Certainly both Hitler and Goering hoped that a powerful air force, and the threat of its use, would bring diplomatic dividends in the short term without having to wage war at all.[47] For this reason Goering overturned the more cautious aircraft production plans of the defence ministry in favour of a rapid expansion. For this reason, too, priority was given from the start to the production of a bomber fleet to be equipped in the long run with heavy bombers capable of conducting independent strategic operations. Despite von Blomberg's protests over the enormous expenditure of resources required by the air force both before and after the declaration of remilitarisation in 1935, Goering successfully defended the expenditure on the grounds that future conflicts would depend much more on the exercise of air power.[48] Strategic air warfare was a cheaper, faster and ultimately more 'national-socialist' way of solving Germany's military problems.

Goering's politicisation of the air force extended to its leadership as well. In the early stages of rearmament he was compelled to take a large number of ex-army officers who had the organisational experience or technical ability necessary to set up an air force in a short space of time.[49] This was balanced by his appointment of friends and contacts who were Nazis or shared Nazi ambitions. As his state secretary he appointed Erhard Milch, the head of

Lufthansa, and an enthusiastic Nazi. The two groups worked uneasily together. The ex-army officers distrusted the civilians and resented the fact that both Goering and Milch were given high military rank even though they were military outsiders. Goering at first hesitated to appoint a Luftwaffe staff for fear that they would ally more closely with the army staff and be a centre of independent power in the air force.[50] Only in 1936 did he create a full air staff under a proven Nazi supporter, Albert Kesselring, owing direct allegiance to him. At the same time influential ex-army airmen were replaced by outsiders. The head of the Technical Office, Wimmer, was replaced by Ernst Udet, Germany's most colourful airman and stunt-flyer, partly on Hitler's insistence, partly on Goering's. In this way the political influence of the army on the new air force was reduced and its links with the party strengthened.[51]

Goering's political role in the two years between the Roehm purge and his assumption of control in October 1936 over the second Four Year Plan depended less on formal ministerial power than on the special relationship that he enjoyed with Hitler. It was this informal relationship that provided Goering with political sustenance and indeed led contemporaries to regard him as Hitler's 'erste Paladin', his 'first paladin'. Goering's appeal for Hitler lay partly in the fact that he was a large political personality, enjoying a degree of popular support and prestige. He was fanatically loyal, and sufficiently ruthless to ensure that others less loyal would be unable to undermine Hitler's power. Hitler came to regard Goering as a special deputy, not detailed to one particular aspect of policy, but available for discussion on a wide range of affairs and for activities which suited Goering's political style more closely. Goering assumed the role of special representative both at state occasions and on foreign tours. Once the furore over Roehm's corruption died down, Goering re-established the regular party feasts for diplomats and officials.[52] Moreover Goering, like Goebbels, enjoyed establishing a new 'high society' to rival that of the German upper classes. Much of the ritual of the Reich was bound up with Goering's own affairs, from the bizarre interment of the remains of his first wife ten days before the Roehm purge, to his wedding to the actress Emmy Sonnemann in April 1935 which was popularly nicknamed the 'Crown-Princely wedding'.[53] This lavish spectacle led the British Ambassador, Sir Eric Phipps, to remark caustically that 'General Goering would seem to have reached the apogee of his vainglorious career: I see for him and his megalomania no higher goal . . . unless indeed it be the scaffold.'[54]

It was on this precarious foundation that Goering established the first steps in building his political empire. Goering's other great asset was his network of contacts and acquaintances, built up over years of political sociability, which served as a means for securing loyal subordinates and of filling offices with placemen. During 1933 and early 1934 many official positions, in the bureaucracy, the universities, the research institutes and the judiciary, had fallen to Goering's patronage. This made him at once a source of political power for a large number of Nazis and non-Nazis who saw contact with Goering as an avenue to political advantage.[55] Some were friends from the First World War: Paul Koerner, who was his Prussian state secretary, Erhard Milch, Bruno Loerzer, Karl Bodenschatz.[56] Others were acquaintances made during the period in Berlin after 1928. With a Napoleonic generosity he sought to bring his own family into politics and society. His cousin, Herbert Goering, was a small trader and businessman who acted as an intermediary between Hermann and foreign trading interests. He was a member of Himmler's 'Freundeskreis', the circle of businessmen sympathetic to the Nazi Party.[57] His Austrian brother-in-law was an intermediary between Goering and Starhemberg in discussions over the future of Austria in 1936.[58] His sister Olga and cousin Ilse became leading socialites, entertaining diplomats, politicians and soldiers, repeating Goering's views and passing back those of their guests.[59] Despite his lack of formal political power after the takeover of Prussia by the Reich, Goering was able to extend informal influence through those whose jobs he had found or whose fortunes he could direct. This was of considerable value when he began the establishment of a more formal administrative empire after 1936.

This network of contacts and supporters was underpinned by Goering's personal intelligence and research agency, the *Forschungsamt*, which he established immediately on his assumption of power in Prussia, housed in an office in the original air ministry building. The *Forschungsamt* was proposed to Goering in February 1933 by an employee of the *Reichswehr* cypher centre who had been a Nazi early in the 1920s. Goering made the office subordinate directly to himself, not to a particular ministry. Its main concern was intercepting information from other agencies, including foreign embassies, through telephone-tapping (which Goering took over from the Reichswehr Ministry) and the monitoring of radio and telegraph communications. Goering accepted requests from other agencies for information, particularly where some trade could be arranged, or marshalled the important information to pass on to Hitler or his ministerial colleagues. By the outbreak of war the *Forschungsamt* had listening stations all over Germany, intercepting a very large amount of international communications, as well as providing Goering with detailed information on what his political rivals and friends were doing. This gave him a considerable advantage in domestic politics. It also helped to constrain his rivals, whose knowledge of Goering's telephone-tapping prompted discretion.[60]

Goering's responsibility for intelligence-gathering taken together with his network of informal contacts and supporters provided a framework of a sort for his political empire. But it was an unhappy substitute for a firm set of administrative responsibilities and duties. Goering was too ambitious to be satisfied for long with honours instead of power. Hitler, however, while pleased enough with Goering's loyalty and his role in the seizure of power, was aware of his deficiencies and at first denied him high office.[61] During

1934 and 1935 Goering was forced to watch other Nazi leaders establish a secure base for themselves within the party or in the government. Ley, Goebbels and Himmler in particular enjoyed power both nationally and through the party. The Labour Front and the SS contained considerable potential for further political growth, and were led by ambitious and jealous Nazi empire-builders. Nor could Goering dislodge the remaining conservatives as long as Hitler accepted the necessity for a more gradualist approach while the early stages of rearmament and economic recovery were carried through. The economy remained the only area in which there was no prominent Nazi in a position of real authority. It was therefore no coincidence that Goering began to lay the foundation for greater involvement in economic affairs in the eighteen months after the Roehm purge. This was not altogether a conscious decision on Goering's part, but was dictated to him by the political circumstances that confronted him. By taking an active interest in economic affairs he would not be displacing any well-entrenched rival, and would be able to contribute more directly to the achievement of Hitler's long-term aims. For Goering, as for Hitler, a healthy economy was the precondition for greater rearmament and an active foreign policy.

Goering's contacts with economic affairs went back to the days in Berlin when he had first become a Reichstag deputy and had sought funds and support from conservative businessmen. Bankers and industrialists figured in his circle of influential contacts, for some believed Goering to be more tractable and less socialistic than other Berlin Nazis.[62] In this they were deceived by appearances. Goering's economic ideas were naive and derivative but they lay nevertheless in the mainstream of more radical thinking on the economy. In 1932 he confessed to being strongly under the influence of the ideas of Otto Wagener, one of the party's leading economic spokesmen.[63] Wagener, like Gottfried Feder, who had drafted the party programme, favoured a mixture of artisan socialism and state intervention based around new economic institutions.[64] During 1932 Goering fought his election campaigns around some of these ideas, promoting state intervention work-creation and labour controls. He was also influenced by the ideas of economic self-sufficiency, autarky, which he grasped with great enthusiasm not only because it was a simple economic concept, but because it fitted in with nationalist politics.[65] Autarky promised independence from the hated economic system of Versailles, while it enlarged people's sense of Germanness. When he later entertained diplomats at Carinhall, his large country house, he insisted on serving only German food, while on guided tours of the house and grounds he boasted that every material used in their construction was German.[66]

Once in power he kept up an interest in economic questions, supporting work-creation programmes and road-building. During 1933 he took responsibility for some of Prussia's state economic policy, including a scheme for re-employment in Berlin known as the 'Goering-Programme', under whose terms unmarried male workers were sent into rural areas to work and their jobs given to unemployed married men.[67] But lacking any formal economic training he held little influence in the party itself on economic questions. As it turned out, this was greatly to his advantage. The most prominent Nazi economists suffered during the internal party struggles from the summer of 1933 onwards. Feder and Wagener in particular were closely identified with the more extreme elements in the SA. Wagener, appointed by Hitler as commissar for the economy in February 1933, was sacked at Goering's instigation in July for encouraging the SA occupation of factories. His office fell into abeyance. Goering opposed Wagener not because he disagreed with his ideas but because he was anxious to protect his authority in Prussia against Wagener's SA commissars.[68] As the influence of the radical economists declined Goering associated himself more closely with Wilhelm Keppler, an engineer who acted as Hitler's economic adjutant and was in close touch with Himmler. He emerged after the 1934 crisis as the most senior of the remaining Nazi economic theorists, and was appointed by Hitler as his Economic Commissioner. Goering supported him for the post of Economics Minister to replace Schmitt in the late summer of 1934 because of his close contacts with Hitler. Although Keppler refused the post on the grounds of ill-health, Goering had made an important, if temporary, ally.[69]

It was the air force and the wider question of rearmament that gave Goering his most direct avenue into economic affairs. From the start he argued for large-scale rearmament and for a policy of autarky to free the economy from dependence on foreign raw materials in the event of war. In 1934 he introduced a bill before the cabinet for full state control of armaments factories in order to supervise the pattern of rearmament more closely. He also urged the setting up of state-owned raw material plants to guarantee the supply of strategic resources, an idea to which he was to return during the Four Year Plan.[70] Von Blomberg rejected both ideas, driving Goering further still into the arms of the Keppler circle who were also searching at the time into ways of increasing domestic raw material production.

Goering's commitment to a high level of rearmament pre-dated the seizure of power.[71] Through his control of the air force he was able to influence the level of rearmament substantially. The army was compelled to accept large increases in air expenditure between 1933 and 1936. Milch's 'Rhineland Programme' increased the planned number of air force squadrons from 37 to 51 and speeded up their introduction into service.[72] This meant higher expenditure on barracks, airfields and equipment, and an increase in investment in the aircraft industry. During 1934 and 1935 Goering was one of the main influences on Hitler in his rejection of any serious attempt at disarmament, particularly in the air. Not only did Goering reject plans for a reduction of air forces or the international renunciation of bombing, but he pressed Hitler in the summer of 1935 for a further doubling of air strength.[73] This involved Goering in arguments with Schacht, von Blomberg and the Finance Ministry over the allocation of

resources for the arms industry and the size and nature of government
expenditure. Goering was a conspicuous consumer, taking up a large share
of government military expenditure (see Table 1). The air force was particularly expensive because it required large installations such as airfields and
training centres, and a complex and high-cost technology. Its weapons
required a more prodigal use of raw materials. The economic crisis that
threatened at the end of 1935 and during 1936 was in no small part due
to this enormous expansion of German air power.

Table 1   *German military expenditure 1934/5–1937/8 (billion RM)*

Year	Total	Army/Navy	Air force	Air force as % of total
1934/5	1.953	1.311	0.642	32.9
1935/6	2.772	1.736	1.036	37.4
1936/7	5.821	3.596	2.225	38.2
1937/8	8.273	5.015	3.258	39.4

Source: R. J. Overy, 'The German *Motorisierung* and Rearmament: a Reply', *Economic History Review*, 2nd
Ser., vol. 32, 1979, p. 113.

Goering expected at first that Schacht would be able, and willing, to
supply almost unlimited funds for rearmament.[74] Indeed the assumption
was that Schmitt's dismissal over the very question of rearmament expenditure would make it easier to compel Schacht's compliance with escalating
military demands. Instead Schacht insisted during 1934 and 1935 on a
more orthodox and conservative approach. While Goering had demonstrated
some sympathy in the past with financial orthodoxy, his approach in 1935
was that nothing should be allowed to get in the way of rearmament.
Schacht's financial conservatism was demonstrated personally to Goering
in the crisis over the municipal finances of Danzig and relations with
Poland.[75] Because of his contacts with the Polish authorities and his position
as Prussian Minister-President, Goering assumed the responsibility from
Hitler for carrying out negotiations over the Danzig economy. While unwilling to aggravate the Polish government, Goering's position was sympathetic
to the Danzig Germans, particularly as Nazi political success in the city
clearly depended on the ability of its Nazi council to make the Danzig
economy work. Schacht and von Krosigk at the Finance Ministry had a
different view. If Danzig could not balance its budget it must deflate. It
must also accept more co-operation with the Poles, and the introduction of
Polish currency. Goering could not accept this. On several occasions in
1935 and again in 1936 he promised financial help for Danzig, and obtained
Hitler's support in the face of Schacht's considerable hostility.[76]
     More important was the food crisis at the end of 1935. Schacht saw in
this not simply an example of how poorly Nazis managed economic affairs

on their own, but the force of his arguments that the pace of rearmament should be slowed down in the face of trade difficulties abroad and a high level of deficit-financing at home. In reality the food shortages were a product of poor harvests and larger, and more expensive, imports.[77] But Schacht blamed Darré, the Agriculture Minister, for poor planning. In this he took particular satisfaction for the Nazis had removed responsibility for agricultural policy from the Economics Ministry in the Hugenberg crisis of 1933.[78] Schacht wanted it restored to his control. As the Minister responsible for foreign exchange and trade any miscalculation over food requirements meant that all his calculations suffered as well. In December 1935 he wrote to Blomberg over his dissatisfaction with Darfe, arguing that rearmament levels would have to be cut to cope with the problem of foreign exchange and to preserve the currency.[79] Schacht took the same complaint to Hitler, refusing to accept Darré's demands for more foreign exchange to pay for food imports with the argument that the Reichsbank's holdings of gold and foreign exchange were already dangerously low.[80] Hitler responded by asking Goering to intercede as arbitrator between the two ministries. To the surprise of businessmen and ministers Goering crossed Schacht, insisting on more food and the foreign exchange necessary to finance it.[81]

Although they appeared unaware of the fact, Goering was gradually manoeuvring himself into a position between Hitler and the conservative political groups around Schacht and the army leaders. The conservatives in fact believed that their fortunes were improving as a result of the slowing down of the Nazis' revolutionary zeal in 1934. Though they had made substantial concessions that undermined any real claim to power, they still harboured the illusion that the party was tameable. Some conservatives even believed that Goering was more sympathetic to their cause than other Nazis, and saw him as a possible replacement for Hitler.[82] They hoped that in the milder political climate after the Roehm crisis it might be possible to restore something of the 'Sammlungspolitik' of pre-war Germany. They wanted to link together conservative institutions, particularly the army, with big business and the moderate elements of the Nazi Party, in order to control the radical enthusiasm of the Nazi rank and file and the restiveness of the working classes.

The conservatives' main fear during 1935 and 1936 was the recurrence of popular political unrest. This fear was aggravated by the Nazis' food policy. Schacht told the British Ambassador that if food supplies failed 'Communism in Germany would be the outcome'.[83] Sharing this deep class fear, the conservatives failed to understand that the Nazi leadership, while not unmindful of the need for domestic stability, were committed entirely to war preparation at the expense of every other consideration. This clash between conservative pragmatism and Nazi idealism became more open in 1936 and 1937 and finally led Hitler, egged on by Goering, to eliminate the leading conservatives. Like the SA before them, the conservatives became dispensable when they threatened to compromise Nazi plans.

This conservative miscalculation led Schacht and the army to an ingenious solution. Faced with growing difficulties in foreign exchange, which Schacht blamed on the fact that Nazi leaders were ignoring currency regulations, he and von Blomberg recommended that Hitler should give Goering a special commission to investigate the currency and raw material sectors of the economy.[84] By inviting Goering into the economic establishment the conservatives hoped to be able to improve their own political position. On the one hand, Goering could be used as an ally in restraining the more radical Nazis and reducing the party's extravagant expenditure because of his reputation as a friend to business and a conservative in economic questions. On the other hand, if Goering turned out to be just as unreliable in his economic attitudes, then any subsequent disaster could be blamed on the party, not on the Economics Ministry or the army. No doubt Schacht hoped that it would not in fact go as far as this. Once Goering discovered how difficult economic questions were it was to be expected that the Nazis would come hurrying back to Schacht, admitting that he had been right all along. Goering would then retain nominal authority, which would keep the party in place, while real economic power would continue to be exercised by the moderates.[85]

This was an important, if understandable, misjudgment. Goering may well have been technically unskilled in economic matters, but he had a clear grasp of the central political questions involved. As an autarkist and a champion of large-scale rearmament, he approached economic problems with quite different priorities from Schacht. Nor was he likely to discipline the party financially since he too was involved in business adventures of dubious legality. Moreover his appointment by Hitler to head a new Raw Material and Foreign Exchange Office at the beginning of April 1936 was not simply the result of conservative cunning, as Schacht later suggested, but was part of Hitler's growing preoccupation with bringing the economy more closely under party supervision. Hitler intended, one way or another, to structure the German economy so that it could serve the needs of war and imperial expansion. Hitler was determined not to be caught, as Germany had been in 1914, with an economy unprepared for major war. Schacht's practical objections to pursuing this course did nothing to dissuade Hitler, but in the long run encouraged him to bring the economy into the orbit of the party. Goering's appointment thus marked the beginning of the end for conservative hopes of manipulating economic and military policy for their own advantage.[86]

Hitler's active interest in raw material questions went back to the summer of 1933 when plans for synthetic fuel production were first laid.[87] At the annual party conference at Nuremberg in September 1935 he publicly announced his intentions of achieving self-sufficiency in food and raw materials.[88] Synthetic production was well under way by the time Goering was appointed, but it was not expanding rapidly enough for Hitler in the light of Germany's escalating raw material requirements abroad and the insecure position of the balance of payments. Hitler's intentions were frustrated further by Schacht's efforts to curb the synthetics programme and his general hostility to autarkist thinking. Early in 1936 a fresh crisis arose with Schacht over Keppler's efforts to speed up the development of domestic iron ore resources. Schacht argued against such projects on the grounds that they would increase domestic steel prices and make Germany's exports even less competitive.[89] These discussions were conducted side-by-side with a sharp deterioration in the level of fuel imports early in 1936, which strengthened the autarkists' case. Threats from Roumania to cut off oil exports to Germany, and hostile Soviet trade policy, promised a significant reduction of oil imports during 1936. The War Ministry believed that on mobilisation only 50 per cent of oil requirements could be met and that that figure would continue to deteriorate unless special action were taken.[90] In the middle of 1935 the War Ministry began to explore the possibility of setting up a special commissioner for oil because of its vital strategic importance. Keppler was anxious to get the job, while Schacht and the army had their own business candidates. Goering's interest in aviation fuel made him a contender as well. In March 1936 he told Kesselring that he was to be named 'fuel dictator' by Hitler in the near future.[91]

In March the economic crisis reached a new pitch. Darré demanded more foreign exchange to buy food, in addition to what he had obtained the previous December. The armed forces painted the blackest possible picture of Germany's strategic position. Schacht angrily rejected efforts to encroach on his jurisdiction during the crisis, both from Keppler, whom Schacht ordered to be physically debarred from his ministry, and from Goering, who had re-opened negotiations with the Poles on the Danzig question and the more vexed subject of German capital holdings in Poland, against Schacht's express wishes.[92] Goering was at or near the centre of all these squabbles. He met Hitler frequently during the period and both were in possession of a wide range of information on the political discussion going on, through Goering's telephone-tapping. Since Hitler had already brought Goering on to the centre of the economic stage as arbitrator between Darfe and Schacht, and in the absence of any clear alternative candidate, Goering was an obvious choice when Hitler decided to resolve the various disputes through a party appointment. In all likelihood Hitler had decided on this course before Schacht suggested Goering's name, for the scope of the new commission was much greater than Schacht had envisaged and the decree confirming the appointment was produced with surprising haste. No doubt Hitler was awaiting the outcome of the re-militarisation of the Rhineland in March 1936 before taking up fresh political initiatives at home.[93] The fact that von Blomberg and Schacht also supported Goering was an additional and unexpected bonus, making it much easier to extend party influence over the economy than Hitler could have expected.

The appointment was of critical importance. It gave Goering an immediate avenue into the machinery of economic control denied to any Nazi until then. Indeed Schacht's efforts until 1936 had been directed to excluding as far as possible any senior party leader from economic office. Goering's appointment opened up a breach which had unpredictable consequences. 'Control', Schacht later complained, 'was now in amateur hands.'[94] Why did Hitler make such a choice? In the first place he was determined that the economy should now be brought more closely into line with his longer-term ambitions for war. A leading party figure would be more likely to do this than the conservatives. But the choices open to him from the party were severely limited. Keppler, his economic adjutant, expected the job and later expressed surprise at the appointment of Goering. He attributed it to the fact that Hitler was looking for a man of energy and authority for the delicate task of interceding with Schacht, and that he himself lacked these qualities. This was certainly the case. Keppler was an ineffectual politician. He suffered from a chronic heart condition which severely circumscribed his activities. His relations with Schacht were poor and he had proved unable to combat the Economics Ministry on any major aspect of economic policy.[95] As his economic influence waned Hitler looked for someone who was more independent and more ambitious.

Goering fulfilled this requirement on both counts. Himmler, Ley and Darfe were too involved in their established offices to play a wider economic role. The party's remaining economic expert, Walther Funk, was a weak and unambitious subordinate; like Keppler, an unlikely choice for such an important commission.[96] Whatever doubts Hitler had expressed about Goering's technical qualifications and administrative capabilities were set aside. What he wanted were Goering's qualities as a forceful political schemer. For extending party power ruthlessly against the prevaricating conservative elite Goering was, in Hitler's view, 'the best man that I possess, a man of the greatest will-power, a man of decision who knows what is wanted and will get it done'.[97] Goering needed no second bidding. Far from remaining a mere figurehead for keeping the party radicals at bay, as Schacht had intended, he began at once with great energy to establish the commissarial role denied to him in 1933. At the first meeting called to explain the function of his new office he explained that he was not heading 'some kind of investigation committee, but that he would take over responsibility for the necessary regulation'.[98] Schacht was horrified, complaining to von Blomberg that they had miscalculated Goering's role. He appealed to the Nazi government to behave with moderation, to pursue 'a steady, prosperous economy ... and renounce the execution of other irrational ideas and aims of the party'.[99] Goering repudiated this appeal. On 15 May he announced that 'the primary political necessity is to maintain the same tempo of rearmament'.[100] Far from being a force for moderation, Goering now showed himself to the conservatives as a force for change.

Goering's official position in charge of the Raw Materials Office broadened out immediately into a general concern with the central issue in 1936 of maintaining or reducing the level of armaments expenditure. Upon this question turned the nature of economic policy and diplomacy in Germany. This is not to say that Goering's influence on either of these things was as yet decisive. The shift in power implied by his new office was a slow and uncertain one. Schacht and the army still had wide influence in the summer of 1936, and used this in their attempts to manipulate Goering and the party. Both were wary of Goering. Both, for their different reasons, wanted greater control over economic affairs for themselves. They deliberately exaggerated the difficulties facing the German economy, in food, in exports and strategic raw materials, in order to persuade Hitler to give them greater responsibility for economic planning and war preparation; to reverse the trend to greater party influence.

But here the attitude of the civilian and military conservatives diverged. Schacht was disappointed that he had misjudged Goering's ambition. He emphasised the dangers of inflation and internal unrest if Goering insisted on maintaining a high level of rearmament. He wanted greater priority for exports and a re-integration of the Food and Economics Ministries, to remove agriculture from Nazi hands.[101] He argued that Germany wanted more trade and the return of the German colonies lost under the terms of the Versailles Treaty, the reverse of the autarkists' priorities.[102] His concern with colonies became more pronounced the further Goering moved away from his position on the economy. It showed once again the conservatives' traditional tactics of using foreign policy to stabilise an awkward domestic situation, reflecting a growing pessimism in conservative circles over the course of Nazi policy. The colonial policy was a particularly transparent example. Schacht urged the British Ambassador to persuade the British government to return Togoland and Cameroon to Germany as a first step in re-integrating her into the world's imperial trading structure. He remained obstinately impervious to the objection that the return of these territories would hardly bring the expansion of exports and raw materials he was looking for.[103] Of course Schacht knew this. In October he confessed with more candour that the colonies were really useful as a place to send Nazi party extremists, leaving domestic policy in the hands of conservatives.[104] While the renewed campaign on colonies did produce popular anti-British feeling in the Nazi Party, it left Goering largely unmoved. His chief concern was not African expansion, but European.[105]

While the War Ministry and the army were clearly unhappy with the failure to control Goering, their priorities were different from those of Schacht. Von Blomberg accepted the arguments for agrarian reform, greater exports and colonies, but only because he saw these as essential means for ensuring the security of the military economy and avoiding the dangers of blockade.[106] The main priority of the armed forces was to maintain or increase the level of rearmament, and to establish unified military authority over economic preparations for war. At the meeting of the Reich Defence Council in May Keitel announced the army's agreement with Goering on rearmament at the expense of civilian consumption.[107] In August the army published a plan for a large increase in army armaments at precisely the time that Schacht and his civilian allies were arguing that rearmament should be cut back.[108] The attitude of the War Ministry to this disagreement was that while the army was willing to work with Schacht if he accepted the rearmament programmes, it was also prepared to abandon him if he would not. In such a case the army was prepared to take over areas of the economy crucial for defence into military hands alone, opposed alike to civilian critics and party rivals.[109]

This division between the two conservative groups played into Goering's hands. The failure to produce a united front during the summer of 1936, the frantic arguments over economic choices, only served to strengthen Goering's position. By chance the outbreak of the Spanish Civil War in July gave Goering a further opportunity to bypass both the Foreign Office and the Economics Ministry. With Hitler's approval a special raw materials and trade commission, the so-called *Hisma-Rowak*, was set up in Seville under Goering's supervision, responsible for directing economic relations with Nationalist Spain, and in particular for safeguarding the flow of Spanish iron ore. These new responsibilities strengthened his argument that his new office was indispensable in finding a solution to the economic difficulties and that its powers should be increased.[110] His own ideas on the economy began to crystallise during the summer months. He accepted the arguments of the Keppler circle for greater domestic production of food, raw materials and synthetics.[111] He was a leading advocate of higher levels of rearmament, and of higher levels of deficit spending to finance it. He now became fully identified in Hitler's eyes as the leading champion of autarky and increased military spending, which was the way in which Hitler's own mind was moving. Moreover Goering was able to prove that the 'amateurs' were after all capable of taking over areas of economic responsibility. Up until 1936 Schacht and his circle had insisted that only they had the technical expertise and competence to conduct economic affairs. Although Goering clearly did lack such qualifications, he rejected the argument all the same. By recruiting a wide range of technical experts and economists, many of whom were party members or supporters, he could get round the problem posed by his own ignorance. This was an important discovery for the Nazis who had always been more politically timid in areas where they felt out of their depth. By 1936 there was a sufficient number of officials and engineers in the economy who were Nazi Party members to provide the technical expertise necessary to run the day-to-day administration of the economy.

Indeed through a new series of decrees on foreign exchange and vigorous state encouragement and subsidising of exports, the 'crisis' that Schacht predicted throughout 1936 did not materialise. He had, after all, deliberately exaggerated its seriousness. After a period of consultation and investigation during the summer, Goering authorised the takeover of all sources of foreign exchange abroad held by German nationals. The threatened foreign exchange deficit of 630 million marks turned into a surplus of 550 million for 1936.[112] Goering succeeded, too, in making a start with his raw material plans. Keppler's assistants, Paul Pleiger and Hans Kehrl, were bullied into accepting Goering's authority. The technical research they had already undertaken was used to initiate plans to save some 600 million marks of foreign exchange by developing domestic synthetic oil, rubber and textiles, and by extracting larger quantities of domestic iron ore.[113] Goering drew on his wide circle of contacts and friends from the air ministry, the Prussian ministry, his personal staff and the Nazi Party in filling new posts and in providing himself with competent technical advice. In this way an alternative apparatus was quickly constructed to challenge Schacht's monopoly of economic control.

As a result of these early successes, which contrasted with the failure to resolve the conflicts between party, army and economy, Hitler determined to bring economic planning more closely under party supervision. There were important reasons for this decision. Hitler was faced with a new set of international circumstances in 1936. Mussolini's invasion of Abyssinia, and the economic sanctions that it provoked against Italy, revived German fears of economic blockade. This made autarky a more attractive proposition. So too did deteriorating relations with the Soviet Union over the Spanish Civil War crisis, which brought with it the fear of encirclement again by the old enemies of the First World War. Against such a background it was even more necessary to secure a firm economic base at home and reduce dependence on distant sources of raw materials. For Hitler this was an essential precondition for the active foreign policy programme he now wanted to pursue. By strengthening the hands of the party autarkists Hitler hoped to resolve some of these problems. A policy of autarky also meant a rejection of the moderates' demand in 1936 for a reduction in rearmament and an increase in trade and domestic consumption.

Of all the factors that influenced Hitler's decisions in 1936 this was perhaps the most important. He later complained that there was 'a mass of people working against me behind my back' to restrict and control the military budget. By July and August the campaign against any increase in armaments and related expenditure came to a head. Schacht, who had openly argued against more armaments from late 1935 onwards, spoke publicly on 20 August at a conference of senior civil servants of the folly of greater rearmament and the foolishness of Nazi economic policy.[114] Shortly before, one of Schacht's industrial allies, Albert Voegler of the Vereinigte Stahlwerke, had also publicly criticised autarky and excessive rearmament, arguing instead for closer trading ties with the Soviet Union.[115] Carl Goerdeler, who had been Price Commissioner until 1935 under

Schacht, submitted a memorandum to Goering in late August in which he stressed the need to hold up rearmament and synthetic production and concentrate on trade and home demand.[116] Even the War Ministry, which had contributed to the general climate of panic over foreign exchange and trade, became critical of party projects and of Goering's handling of economic questions.[117]

Both Goering and Hitler had access to all this information. It clearly contradicted the principle that Goering had emphasised across the summer months that rearmament was the first priority in any consideration of economic policy.[118] Together the two leaders arrived at a decision late in July or in early August to cut through the political crisis over the economy by giving Goering a wide-ranging commission to prepare the economy for war. Exactly when the decision was made is not known. Goering announced at a meeting on 6 July that he would discuss the whole raw material question with Hitler 'in order to prepare for the future situation'.[119] During this critical period he met with Hitler almost every day.[120] During August, at his retreat in the Obersalzburg, Hitler drafted a memorandum which formed the basis of the second Four-Year Plan announced in October. By the end of August four copies of the memorandum were prepared. One was given to Goering, another to von Blomberg, a third to Fritz Todt, who was building the *Autobahnen*. Goering later recalled that he had been summoned to Berchtesgaden by Hitler who then read the whole memorandum through; 'subsequently we went for a long walk, during which my appointment was put into effect.'[121] By 1 September when Goering told Keppler of the plans, it was already widely rumoured that Hitler would shortly announce a number of important changes in the economy which would bring to an end the long period of uncertainty and administrative confusion over the summer months.[122]

Hitler deliberately chose the Party Rally in Nuremberg as the forum in which to announce the new policy. The leading conservatives were invited to attend but most refused. Schacht, who by now had nothing but regret for the tactical blunder that allowed Goering to penetrate the sanctuary of conservative economics, wrote urgently to von Blomberg asking him to warn Hitler of the folly of pursuing a policy of autarky and unrestricted rearmament. He tried to alert sympathisers abroad to the dangers of the growing influence of 'crazy' or 'wild' Nazis.[123] While von Blomberg understood Schacht's arguments he refused to do anything that directly contradicted Hitler.[124] This flurry of activity can only have confirmed Hitler in his resolve. Speer later wrote that Hitler told him that the new plan arose because of the 'lack of understanding of the Reichs Economics Ministry and the opposition of the German economy to all large-scale plans . . .'.[125] There was indeed to be no discussion. On 4 September Goering reported to the Council of Ministers on the scope of the new powers he was to receive. He flatly rejected the economic strategy of Goerdeler and Schacht. He defended the policy of increased rearmament with the argument that

'Frederick the Great was in his financial policy a strong inflationist'. In justifying the extension of state power over the economy he explained that the danger from Russia and the general deterioration of Germany's world position made this imperative. 'All measures have to be taken just as if we were actually in the stage of imminent danger of war.'[126]

A week later Gauleiter Wagner announced to the assembled party leaders at Nuremberg Hitler's decision to set up a second Four Year Plan under Goering to solve Germany's raw material and trade problems.[127] In secret the leading authorities in the Reich were informed of the Plan's more important but unpublicised purpose: to prepare the German economy for war. The decree giving Goering full power was finally promulgated on 18 October.[128] On 28 October Goering spoke in the Berlin Sportspalast on the tasks of the Plan to an enthusiastic Nazi reception. 'The Fuehrer', he announced, 'has given me a heavy office ... I come to it not as an expert. The Fuehrer chose me only, simply and only as a national socialist. I stand before you and will complete this task as a national socialist fighter, as his plenipotentiary, as the plenipotentiary of the National Socialist Party.'[129] This was a clear statement of the Nazis' intention of bringing the economy directly under their control.

For Goering the Four Year Plan was a personal triumph. It brought him into the mainstream of economic and military policy, and promised much greater influence on foreign policy as well. Beforehand his intervention had been intermittent and restricted, his authority by no means secure. Schacht enjoyed widespread influence in the German business community at home and abroad. There were also challengers within the party, particularly Keppler and Darré, who had both expected to extract more from the political crisis for themselves. Keppler fought as best he could to maintain his privileged position within Hitler's circle, but Hitler had decided that the office of economic adjutant was now redundant. Goering repaid Keppler's help and advice by relegating him to an insultingly minor office in the Four Year Plan.[130] Goering did not intend to share his political spoils with anyone. Through a combination of good political management and ruthless self-advancement, Goering found himself once again in the political limelight from which he had been compelled to step back in 1934.

3

GOERING AND THE GERMAN ECONOMY

The establishment of the Four Year Plan with Goering at its head was the symbol of a sharp change of course for Hitler and the Nazi movement. It marked the point at which Hitler embarked upon a positive transformation of German and European life. Up until 1936 Hitler had required an economic recovery to guarantee the political stability of the regime and solve immediate social and economic problems. Political life had been in the service of the economy. Now the situation was reversed. It was the task of a healthy economy to serve political ends: to build up a powerful, autarkic military economy and to fight wars without regard for private interest or rational economics.

These moves towards a positive fulfilment of the Nazi promise co-incided with a fundamental change in the terms of the unspoken alliances made between the remaining conservatives and the Nazi movement between 1934 and 1936. During these years the army and big business were satisfied that the Nazi movement had not been as radical as they once feared. Nazis had been compelled to work with the traditional elites along lines they broadly approved of. Hitler of necessity left the economic revival in the hands of the bureaucratic and business groups concerned and rearmament and re-militarisation to the generals. This was very much the solution that Schacht and his military allies had looked for in 1932. The fact that the working class and the German left-wing radicals were controlled over the same period not by aristocratic coercion but by a mass movement itself drawn from the lower levels of German society was a fortunate and unforeseen bonus both for German capitalism and for the old ruling class. Yet it was the source of their miscalculation, to see the Nazi movement simply as a dependent but necessary instrument of repression in the service of the traditional holders of power.

This was not what the Nazi leadership expected. The Nazi Party achieved power not to subordinate itself to the existing power structure nor to share it with others, but to use the mass base of support it had mobilised to shift power downwards to those groups in German society which had rejected the older conservatives at the polls. The crisis over the Four Year Plan and the pace of rearmament marked the end of the phase that satisfied conservative hopes and inaugurated the phase in which the purposes of Nazism were made more explicit. The economy, now in the late stages of recovery, had to be turned away from expanding trade and increasing consumerism, which is what most businessmen wanted, towards preparation for war and a controlled level of consumption and exports. The armed forces had to be persuaded to accept a programme of continental expansion under Hitler's strategic guidance, based on a rearmament programme over whose tempo and cost they were to have less and less say. This implied quite a different position for the economic and military elites from that which they had enjoyed before 1914, or indeed during the Weimar Republic.

Such a change was essential if the Nazi Party were not to remain dependent on those groups it sought to replace, as Mussolini was compelled to be in Italy. Hitler and the Nazi leadership were well aware how political and economic power was exercised in Germany. Token or formal control was an insufficient guarantee that Nazi policies could be successfully implemented. It was necessary to take over direct control and establish a genuine authority, using the party elite for the task, and also to set up new institutions or 'Nazify' old ones. By 1936, with complete control over the civil and special police, it was possible to extend Nazi power directly into the citadels of the German establishment. This explains the significance of Goering's commission from Hitler and the rapid evolution of an economic administration more sensitive to Nazi requirements. The Four Year Plan was not simply a response to economic circumstances but was a consequence of a major shift in the political balance inside Germany. The shift itself was a gradual process, reflecting the usual Nazi tactics of patient infiltration, but it was a clear break none the less. By 1938 even Schacht and von Blomberg, both of whom were rightly regarded as Nazi collaborators by more critical generals and businessmen, were gone, as were a whole number of lesser officials, officers and ministers. In their place came Nazi placemen, either party members or sympathisers, or those too weak to resist. Actual power within both the economy and the armed forces was transferred piecemeal to the Nazi elite itself.

Some historians have explained this crisis in terms of economic or political necessity. It has been suggested that changing economic circumstances brought about by full employment and the threat of inflation compelled the Nazi movement to control the economy more than they would have liked in order to prevent any threat to living standards or the currency. Seen in this light the Four Year Plan was merely a continuation of the battle for bread and employment begun before 1936 in order to secure popular political support. To the force of economic circumstances was added the drive to foreign expansion, the perennial German solution to potential political dangers at home.[1] The difficulty with this argument is that the economic policy adopted after 1936 was the one most likely to exacerbate precisely those problems it was supposed to cure. If the Nazi leadership had felt the compulsion of economic necessity in this sense they would have adopted the strategy of Schacht, not Goering, for Schacht promised continued rearmament as and when it could be afforded, more trade, and balanced economic growth. Moreover such arguments suggest that the Nazis' political position was essentially negative and opportunistic, that the drive to war was the product not of deliberate intention, but was a by-product of unresolved political and social tension at home dressed up with imperialistic propaganda.

Nazi leaders could not, and did not, ignore economic and political pressures. But to make sense of the choices that they made during the period between 1936 and the outbreak of war it is essential to see Nazi ambitions springing from positive intention. These ambitions had to be tailored on occasion to fit the circumstances but they were not a product of opportunism or necessity. They were integral to Hitler's overall plan to re-shape German society and pursue racial imperialism. The period of compromise gave way to the period of Nazification not because Hitler had run out of alternatives but because that was the alternative to which his policy had been remorselessly progressing, regardless of circumstance.

From the mid-1930s Hitler began to move towards a more active foreign-policy programme to establish a German territorial empire in eastern Europe and to end the threat from Soviet communism, while at the same time creating at home the conditions in economic and institutional life to support such a programme of imperialism.[2] The key to making this possible was economic strength and massive rearmament which, while demanding present sacrifices, would guarantee racial prosperity and cultural hegemony in the aftermath of war. Goering's responsibility was to strengthen and expand the military economy and to alter the structure of the civilian economy to meet the needs of war. This was made clear shortly after the announcement of the Four Year Plan when he told an audience of German business leaders that 'The struggle which we are approaching demands a colossal measure of productive ability. No end to the rearmament is in sight. The only deciding point in this case is victory or destruction. If we win, then the economy will be sufficiently compensated.'[3]

The key to the rearmament effort was the construction of an economy sufficiently insulated against the actions of potential enemies as to be unaffected by blockade or economic warfare. Within such an autarkic economy highest priority had to be given to that core of heavy industries without which the war effort could not be contemplated; that is, iron and steel, fuels, chemicals and machinery. This was what the army economic staff called *Tiefrüstung*, armament in depth. Despite the army's fears that the Nazi leadership misunderstood the nature of this kind of preparation, everything that Goering involved himself with after 1936 suggested that his first priority was armament in depth, creating the necessary industrial sub-structure without which a sustained war effort would not be possible. 'The Four Year Plan', Goering later claimed, 'was a basic prerequisite for the entire building up and expansion of the armament industry.'[4] In all his speeches in 1937 and 1938 the emphasis was the same. Rearmament before every other priority; industrial and economic restructuring to free Germany from dependence on foreign supplies and to expand the output of capital goods and industrial raw materials.

Beyond rearmament and war lay the promised land. 'Our generation', wrote Goering, 'has the happiness and tranquil assurance that it has been chosen to make life easier and more beautiful for the coming generations.'[5] In the meantime Goering expected living standards to deteriorate, privately admitting that the Four Year Plan held out no promise of improvement.[6] The official view was later proclaimed that 'a higher standard of living is the ultimate goal, not the immediate object of the Four Year Plan'.[7] Nor could the policy of large-scale rearmament and economic restructuring have produced any different result. The emphasis in the recovery period before 1937 had been very much in favour of heavy industrial goods at the expense of consumer goods, either domestically produced or imported. This emphasis increased after the announcement of the Four Year Plan both in terms of the allocation of resources and the flow of investment. This suggests not that the Nazis trimmed economic and rearmament policy to meet the needs of the consumer but quite the reverse. A higher standard of living was the reward for sacrifices to be endured in the period of war preparation and war.

The Nazification of the German economy complied with a crude logic in Nazi ideology. From 1936 onwards leading Nazis started to revive the socialistic ideas that had circulated in the party before 1933. There was much talk about the economy serving the needs of the *Volk* and the nation rather than narrow economic interests. In the Four Year Plan memorandum itself Hitler wrote that 'The race does not exist for the economy nor for the economic leadership nor for economic and financial theories, but finance and economy, economic leaders and theories have to serve exclusively our people's struggle for existence.'[8] At a meeting of the Reich Chamber of Labour in April 1937 he explained that 'economic life may remain free only so long as it is able to solve the problems of the nation. If it cannot do so then it must cease to be free.'[9] At the Party Congress in September he returned to the same theme: 'the leadership of the people's community has the duty to give to the economy such directions as are necessary for the maintenance of the whole society.'[10] Goering defended the changes in economic policy on the same grounds: 'Just as I will be resolved to ignore the fate of individuals, if the well-being of the community demands it, I shall not show weakness in placing the interests of the *Volk* above the interests of individual businesses.'[11]

This emphasis on national over selfish interests was a defining characteristic of Nazi economic ideology. It was open-ended enough to permit a wide interpretation of what such interests were. It was the justification for the extension of state control, for what Goering called the 'managed economy' [*gelenkte Wirtschaft*], for the Nazi reorganisation of 'all areas of economic life'.[12] Goering and his officials argued that the Nazi economy was different from the liberal-capitalist economy that preceded it and the Marxist collectivist alternative. The Four Year Plan was designed to effect 'the radical adaptation of the former liberal national economy based on the principle of the international division of labour to the principle of military economic security'.[13] Priority for national military needs could only be met, it was argued, by taking decision-making away from producers and consumers, and giving it to the state through the agency of the party. Only the party leaders were in a position to know what the true interests of the people were. Private enterprise would be allowed to survive only in sectors which were not of vital interest to the state, and even these would have to be directed in accordance with the needs of the community. The 'undirected, liberal economy' was unacceptable because by definition it could not sacrifice its economic interest without ceasing to be capitalism.[14] In a Nazi economic system, Goering argued, 'Profits cannot be considered. . . . Calculations cannot be made as to cost.'[15]

Much as this economic view lacked sophistication, it was nevertheless the basis for justifying the extension of state control, for directing investment and finally for taking over significant sectors of the industrial economy into direct state ownership. The proof of the efforts to change the nature of economic life lay not in the unrefined *völkisch* ideology alone, but in the steps taken after 1936 to integrate the economy and its institutions with the Nazi state. In this respect the Nazi leadership had correctly judged the unwillingness of the business world to accept the principle of national interest where this did not obviously seem to coincide with self-interest. Capitalists had been willing enough to accept Nazi rule provided economic policy was directed by those sympathetic to its aims. Up to 1936 these aims were traditional; market expansion, protection of corporate or cartel interests, and profitability. Where state aid was needed it was only to overcome limited barriers to the fulfilment of these aims, to oil the wheels of the market economy. This was much more the kind of 'organised capitalism' that Hilferding had described in the pre-1914 era. The problem of Nazi economics in the era of the Four Year Plan was that all three of these basic aims were disregarded by the state in favour of its own defined goals. This did not mean that the profit motive or corporate interest did not still continue to function when and where they could, but they ceased to be the criteria whereby economic activity was ultimately judged, and were replaced by the criterion of community need. The period after 1936 was a period of transition, of 'disorganised capitalism' in competition with fascist economics.

The effort to extend state control brought fresh difficulties with it. Though Goering announced that 'In the years to come the Four Year Plan will determine the whole of Germany's economic and social policy',[16] it was quite another question to make good the claim. It is not clear that Goering himself knew from the outset how to approach the problem. Like so many

Nazi goals the broad parameters were set before the tactics had been fully worked out. At one level the problem was political. Neither Schacht and the big business allies of the Economics Ministry, nor von Blomberg and the army economic staff, favoured the extension of Goering's power beyond the level it had reached in the middle of 1936. Their resistance had to be overcome as a precondition for the exercise of Goering's unlimited authority. At another level the problem was administrative. Goering had to find a means of exercising direct control over German capitalism without which mere formal claims to authority would be meaningless. In order to make businessmen do what the government wanted them to do, close supervision and direction was essential.

The political problem had no easy solution. Quite apart from the contest over jurisdiction with the conservatives, Goering was only too aware of the growing influence of more radical Nazis around Hitler. The Nazi press was joining in the chorus for a more obvious break with the old system in line with Hitler's own thoughts on the economy.[17] Because Goering had made the economy his own special territory he could not afford to flout party opinion without forfeiting party support. The political context was also complicated by the fact that the army, having enjoyed considerable power in the military side of the economy since 1933, hoped to benefit from the economic crisis in 1936 by achieving a more prominent position in economic planning. Goering's role in the Four Year Plan threatened the army's special position in German politics and the conservatives' power to influence economic and military strategy.[18]

As we have seen, the army was sceptical from the outset of Goering's ability to solve the raw material question, or to contribute anything which the army could not usefully do itself. In December 1936 Thomas and Jodl prepared for von Blomberg the army view on the Four Year Plan Office and in February 1937 this was forwarded to Hitler. Von Blomberg demanded that three important principles be established: that only the War Minister had responsibility for overseeing war preparations and running the war economy; that Schacht, not Goering, should have responsibility for carrying out what was necessary for the preparation of the economy in peacetime; and that Goering's office should be abolished if war broke out, and should be confined in peacetime to a narrow sector of raw materials administration, supervised by the War Minister.[19] Short of this the army was not prepared to work with Goering. Hitler's answer was to ignore what von Blomberg said, leaving Goering room to extend his authority as far as he could without restriction.

In order to do this Goering chose the easier of the two avenues open to him by directly challenging Schacht to a test of strength. The contest was about both economic strategy and economic jurisdiction. The debate on economic policy had its formal origins in the crisis over foreign exchange in 1936, but it was ultimately derived from the way in which the German economy had developed since the beginning of the upswing in 1932. Economic recovery was based on a sharp increase in the rate of investment, helped primarily by government spending policies and subsidies to industry. Some concessions were made to help expand domestic demand but on the whole consumer demand and export demand grew more sluggishly than demand created through government investment in heavy industry and services. Building on trade and foreign currency regulations introduced during the depression, the government established after 1933 a comprehensive system of controls over all foreign transactions. The effect was to insulate Germany from the world economy while preparing domestic industry for renewed sales abroad. Price controls and wage controls were necessary to prevent inflationary pressures during the period of investment boom and to keep out imports.[20]

This economic policy was essentially Schacht's, supported by the heads of big business and the economic administration. By 1936 Germany was approaching full employment. The expectation was that government spending and investment would decline, while the brakes on foreign trade could be lifted because Germany would be able to sell larger quantities of exports, and earn more foreign exchange. The trade regulations embodied in Schacht's 'New Plan' were a temporary but necessary consequence of the severity with which the depression had affected Germany. In the long term Schacht rejected any idea of self-sufficiency. 'Autarky', he wrote, at the height of the conflict with Goering, 'cannot possibly be an ideal. It is opposed to the general principles of civilisation.'[21] Eventually Schacht and his private business associates hoped for the return of a more liberal economy and the successful pursuit of conventional economic growth.

Goering interpreted the economy very differently. Rearmament and more general preparations for war took priority. Exports were important only inasmuch as they promoted this goal directly by earning foreign exchange to buy strategic raw materials. Import-substitution was preferable to expanding trade. He argued for controls over all foreign trade and foreign exchange and for an extensive programme of domestic production of synthetics and other substitutes. What made this policy more difficult to fulfil, as Schacht pointed out to Goering on a number of occasions, was the high and rising level of government expenditure and investment. This had the effect of increasing the demand for labour and materials without compensating by allowing a higher level of foreign trade. Schacht expected the outcome to be a new inflation unless government expenditure were reduced. Goering was prepared to accept this risk, and to increase government spending substantially. This strategy was only possible with a more thorough regulation of the economy, which the Four Year Plan implied, and by reducing the growth of consumer expenditure. This was the real source of the division between the two views. Schacht wanted a growth in consumer demand and exports, which made economic sense; Goering wanted war preparations supported by higher levels of government investment, at the expense of both consumer and exporter.[22]

In the event it was Goering's policy that prevailed. Government expenditure rose steadily year by year from 1937, as did the public debt. Foreign trade did not expand as Schacht hoped. In 1937 exports were barely above the level for 1932; in 1938 they declined. Foreign trade accounted for 12.2 per cent of GNP in 1937 but for only 10.2 per cent in 1938. Gold and foreign exchange reserves, which had been unhealthy since the depression, fell from 529 million marks in 1933 to only 76 million in 1938.[23] The major economic indicators for the period are set out in Table 2.

Table 2   *Selected German economic statistics 1935–8 (bill. RM)*

	Govt expenditure	Govt investment	Public debt	Exports	Imports	Gold and foreign exchange reserves
1935	14.1	6.4	20.1	4.3	4.2	91.0
1936	17.3	8.1	25.8	4.8	4.2	75.2
1937	21.4	8.4	31.2	5.9	5.5	74.6
1938	32.9	10.3	41.7	5.3	5.4	76.2

Although Goering got his way with the economy, the economic disaster that the more conservative ministers feared in 1936 and 1937 was averted. This can be explained by Goering's willingness to extend controls and compulsion, against the wishes of many businessmen. As Goering himself confessed: 'Measures which in a state with a parliamentary government would probably bring about inflation, do not have the same results in a totalitarian state.'[24] Schacht had underestimated the ability of the capital markets to support government loans for rearmament in conditions where the government was in full control of the flows of investment. As long as the government controlled the main economic variables it was possible to expand public expenditures without risk of serious inflation. Neither Schacht nor the Finance Minister, Schwerin von Krosigk, nor the army, expected the level of military expenditure and government investment to expand after 1936 beyond a modest level. In fact the government was able to float loans totalling 3.1 billion marks in 1937 and a further 7.7 billion in 1938. This final figure exceeded the value of all the public loans issued since 1933.[25]

To make this economic policy work the Nazis introduced a number of important changes. Controls over the capital market and share issues were tightened up. The curtailing of consumer production and increases in taxation produced what was in effect a system of forced saving. To solve the problem of foreign exchange Goering announced two separate decrees giving the government the right to sequester the foreign assets of German nationals in return for payment in marks. Finally Goering embarked on an ambitious programme of synthetic and raw material production, together with a system of quotas for scarce materials, which allowed preference to be given to war preparations. Over all these policies Schacht raised objections; but because they were ultimately Hitler's own preferences, they could not be overturned.

Hitler's support for Goering over economic policy is an important part of any explanation of how he succeeded in destroying Schacht's influence and altering economic priorities. But the explanation is not as simple as that. Although Hitler was the highest court of appeal, Goering resorted to his judgment only seldom. The extension of Goering's power over the economy was the result of the gradual infiltration and subversion of economic institutions by Nazi supporters. This happened in Schacht's own ministry, and in leading businesses. At the same time Goering led a frontal assault by setting up rival offices to those of Schacht and challenging officials to ignore his demands, and those of the party, at their peril.

Not all of German business could be successfully subverted, but the exceptions proved vital in Goering's contest for control over the economy, for they undermined the strength of pro-Schacht business groups and made it difficult for industry or banking to adopt a common political front. One of the key institutions to fall under Nazi influence was the Dresdner Bank, one of the major German banks with widespread financial and industrial connections. Party influence in the bank was acquired gradually. A handful of pro-Nazi directors eliminated their opponents on the board one by one by one device or another, and replaced them with Nazi supporters.[26] The subordinate banks that the Dresdner controlled, particularly the German Aviation Bank, provided funds for rearmament channelled to it by the state. The parent bank was given the responsibility for handling many of the financial affairs of the Four Year Plan and its industries.[27] This situation allowed Goering effectively to by-pass the Reichsbank and other less sympathetic banks when it was necessary to raise money and distribute or hold funds. Karl Rasche, a Nazi promoted within the Dresdner Bank for just this purpose, became the intermediary between Goering's economic empire and the German banking world.[28]

A similar relationship grew up between the Nazi Party and the I. G. Farben chemical combine, Germany's largest private business. By 1936 the Nazis' initial distrust of I. G. Farben had evaporated. Carl Bosch, who opposed the persecution of Jewish scientists, was effectively excluded from the major decision-making in the concern he had established and those directors sympathetic to the Nazis increased their power and representation on the managing boards. This change was encouraged by the Nazi leadership because it was necessary to gain the co-operation of the company for the production of military goods and synthetic raw materials. Under the direction of Hermann Schmitz, Max Ilgner and Carl Krauch, I. G. Farben abandoned the position it had taken during the depression in demanding an expansion of exports and protection for agriculture in favour of German rearmament and autarky.[29] This shift in economic strategy was not effected without division within the firm's leadership but in 1936 the establishment of the Four Year Plan tilted the balance in favour of the Nazis on the board. The Plan promised significant benefits for I. G. Farben if it co-operated with Goering's industrial programme. Krauch was introduced into the administration of the Four Year Plan and was ultimately given control over domestic oil production, Buna rubber and explosives. The result of the final integration of I. G. Farben into the Nazi economic system was the exclusion of all Jews from the management boards and research departments, and the retirement of the directors who had opposed Krauch. All remaining directors became members of the Nazi Party and enjoyed increasingly close contact with Goering and his staff.[30]

Secure in the support of certain sections of the German business world, and of the party radicals who wanted to see an extension of state control, Goering established an administrative apparatus of his own with general jurisdiction over economic affairs. The foundation for this process of infiltration and usurpation was the Four Year Plan administration itself. Despite Goering's innocent claim that the plan required little in the way of new offices and personnel, it rapidly developed its own bureaucratic apparatus and its own executive agencies.[31] Indeed the scope of the plan was such that the administration established in 1936 resembled that of the Ministry of Economics itself. Not only did Goering acquire the power to take decisions in questions to do with foreign exchange and raw materials but he arrogated to himself responsibility for labour allocation, agriculture, price control, industrial investment and, through the foreign exchange section, ultimate control over foreign trade itself. The new offices were filled with those sympathetic to the aims of the plan drawn from the civil service, from informal party agencies such as the Keppler circle, and from the armed forces.[32] The central plan office was run by Erich Neumann and Friedrich Gramsch, who played a major role in co-ordinating the many strands of economic policy under the Plan's supervision.

A General Council was set up as the plan's co-ordinating body, but its executive powers were never defined or exercised. The individual departments, each with its own large staff, assumed the day-to-day planning and direction, reporting regularly to Goering in person. In order to ensure that the plan could be effectively integrated with the existing bureaucratic structure Goering chose as key departmental heads those who also held office in other ministries. Thus Backe was both commissioner for agriculture under the plan and also state secretary at the Ministry of Agriculture; Syrup was labour commissioner and state secretary in the Labour Ministry; Koerner, who became Goering's deputy for the Four Year Plan, was also his state secretary in the Prussian Ministry; and so on.[33] In this way the process of infiltrating other agencies and organisations could be carried out so that the key powers in the economy could ultimately be exercised legally by Goering. (See Chart 1 for the organisation of the Four Year Plan Office.)

It was this claim for jurisdiction outside the terms of the Four Year Plan

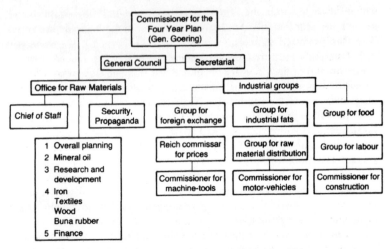

Chart I   The organisation of the Four Year Plan

commission that Schacht fought against. In the absence of any clearer definition of powers from Hitler the competition for competency turned on the ability of the two combatants to persuade other offices and authorities to obey them. Schacht had been uncertain at first about how to respond to the plan. He suggested to his staff that 'a friendly co-operation with the new agency was necessary and even possible', as long as the real decisions still lay with the responsible ministries.[34] But by the end of the year his attitude had hardened. Sensing Goering's purpose, he wrote a circular to all economic officials and major businesses making it clear that they should only take orders from the Economics Ministry, not from the Four Year Plan.[35] Yet in practice there was little he could do over questions concerning foreign exchange and raw materials. Nor could he exercise much influence over price and wage control, and the level of domestic consumption, since the resignation of his ally Goerderler as Price Commissioner and the appointment of the Nazi, Josef Wagner. The real testing-ground was finance. Goering acted from late 1936 onwards as if he were responsible for fixing the level of government funding and rearmament expenditure. Indeed von Blomberg addressed his request for a substantial increase in funds for 1937 to Goering, not to Schacht.[36] Goering was able to order the floating of loans and the large investment programmes under the Four Year Plan quite independently of the Reichsbank and the Ministry of Economics. This would have been more difficult for Goering had he not had the assistance of the compliant and weak-willed Minister of Finance who hesitated to oppose Goering openly, authorising the use of funds that Schacht was obliged to release. The financial weapon had been a very important one in Schacht's armoury. Goering's ability to finance his own economic policies gave him an independence of Schacht that rendered the latter's position untenable.[37]

Goering had no hesitation in intervening in areas of the economy in which his jurisdiction was by no means apparent. Throughout 1937 he took initiatives in trade, transport, manufacturing and investment. Gradually those offices and ministers who had been accustomed to taking orders from Schacht stopped doing so. The Council of Ministers, in which the conservative economic lobby had had, an important forum before 1937, declined in importance as a decision-making body in favour of Goering decrees and administrative discretion on the part of the Four Year Plan commissioners. Alongside the conventional apparatus of economic control Goering constructed an alternative apparatus, linked with the old through personal and institutional contact, governed by commissioners and special plenipotentiaries like himself.

It is important not to underestimate the significance of this change in the administration and supervision of the economy. Despite its excessive bureaucratisation and the loose definition of jurisdictional competency, Goering's economic empire effectively superseded the established instruments of economic control and overturned the policies of the recovery period. If the economic empire lacked a clear administrative centre distinct from Goering's personal office, that was a reflection not of its shapelessness or incoherence but of the style of leadership and organisation that Goering preferred, which matched fascist practice elsewhere. Historians have been equally loth to take Goering's own claims for power at face value on the assumption that they were mere propaganda boasts, or that he was too incompetent to deflect German capitalism from pursuing its own interests regardless. In other words that the much vaunted re-direction of the German economy brought about by the Four Year Plan was a façade, like the corporativism of Mussolini's Italy.

Had Goering been merely content with a nominal authority the Four Year Plan might well have become a façade, and the initiative in industrial planning been retained with large-scale private capitalism. But this did not happen, because Goering and those who worked with him realised that to make the plan work it was necessary to control, and in some cases take over, German industry itself. During the course of 1937 and 1938 Goering not only increased the degree of government regulation and the level of state investment, but took the important step of increasing direct state ownership. This was perfectly consistent with the aims of the commission that Hitler had given to Goering in 1936 because community interest was now put above the interests of private capitalism where the two did not coincide. Indeed by late 1938 Goering was speculating on the possibility of the complete nationalisation of heavy industry in order to complete the Nazi economic and military programme. 'The time has now come', he told an audience of industrialists, 'when private enterprise can show whether it has the right to continued existence. If it fails [I] am going over to state enterprise regardless.'[38] Hitler also hinted at this at the Party Congress in September 1938 when he said that the party's role was 'to protect . . . authority from the spiritless attitude of big business circles'.[39]

Some idea of how extensive Goering's direct influence on industry was can be gathered from changes in the pattern of industrial investment. In 1937 and 1938 investment through the Four Year Plan accounted for over 50 per cent of total fixed capital investment in industry. To this can be added investment in the aircraft industry which was directly under Goering's control as Air Minister, bringing the total figure up to nearly 60 per cent. Since the figures for the Four Year Plan exclude coal and energy investment over which Goering also had considerable say, the final figure for industrial investment directly controlled by Goering's economic offices was nearer two-thirds of the total.[40] There was a concentration of investment in heavy industry, primarily in iron and steel, chemicals and machine engineering, at the expense of consumer production and house-building. In 1939 total investment in the consumer industries was still lower than it had been in 1928 while investment in heavy industry was more than double the 1928 figure (see Table 3).[41]

Table 3   *Selected statistics on German investment 1936–42   (bill. RM)*

	Total industrial investment	Four Year Plan investment	Aircraft industry investment
1936	2.2	0.75	0.29
1937	2.8	1.50	0.49
1938	3.7	1.95	0.71
1939	4.4	2.10	0.87
1940	4.3	2.49	1.05
1941	4.6	2.49	n.a.
1942	4.9	1.97	n.a.

Source: D. Petzina, *Autarkiepolitik im Dritten Reich*, Stuttgart, 1968, p. 183; BA-MA RL3 46, Capital investment charts, fuselage and aero-engine industry.

The Four Year Plan provided the general planning framework for investment programmes and controlled as far as possible the flow of resources into particular industries. The same controls were extended over agriculture as well. The Four Year Plan assumed responsibility for the 'Production Battle' on the land, producing and distributing the tractors and fertilisers needed.[42] By 1939 there was no part of the economy that was not touched by the Four Year Plan. Businessmen were compelled to submit for approval all investment plans, were subject to regulations concerning the location of industry, could only sell products at a price agreed by the Price Commission, could not freely dispose of profits, and could neither import nor export without a licence. Both sources of capital and sources of raw materials were governed by a system of priorities arranged through the Ministry of Economics and the Four Year Plan in consultation with the armed forces. In this way it was possible to determine in advance what would be produced and what would be restricted, and to compel firms to adapt their output to the requirements of current Nazi policy.[43] Controls over labour were particularly important in this respect. The plan organisation undertook to train skilled apprentices, to retrain other workers and to compel workers who had changed their jobs from a vital industry to return to their original skill.[44]

In addition to these formal economic controls, Goering created special plenipotentiaries for individual industries to ensure that the policies were fulfilled and production targets met. The most important of these were for the iron and steel industry, the machine industry, the oil industry, for construction (under Fritz Todt, who later became the first armaments minister under the Four Year Plan), and for the textile and automotive industries.[45] The special commissioners were responsible for increasing industrial participation in the rearmament and heavy industry programmes by attracting smaller producers into the circle of contractors and also for encouraging rationalisation of production. The rationalisation drive was promoted by Goering as a way of matching the growing demands on labour and materials with the planned output of finished goods. Rationalisation – 'greatest output with the least resources'[46] – became a popular slogan with Goering during 1938 and 1939. Manufacturers were compelled to simplify and standardise production, and to improve the system of distribution. In late 1938 Funk was made special commissioner for rationalisation to get industry to think more seriously about what was involved.[47]

As the head of the Four Year Plan Goering also acquired powers for taking over Jewish firms into state ownership, a policy carried out to ensure that they would be used for 'national' purposes, and not for the personal gain of small businessmen. It has sometimes been wrongly assumed that Goering was an opponent of the party's extreme anti-semitism, expressed through events like the *Kristallnacht* pogrom in November 1938. Nothing could be further from the truth. His main concern was jurisdictional. He wanted the expropriation of Jewish firms to be carried out systematically under the exclusive control of the Four Year Plan. There was no question of his disagreement with the principle involved. He accepted the Nuremberg Laws restricting Jewish civil rights.[48] Indeed as Reichstag President he was closely involved in the passage of the laws through parliament, arguing in their defence that if God had intended men to be equal he would not have created races.[49]

Under the terms of these laws and the subsequent decrees on aryanisation Goering was already engaged on expropriation well before the disturbances in November.[50] His alleged 'distress' at the news of the pogrom on 10

November were crocodile tears, caused not by scruples over anti-semitism but by the fact that the pogrom had been arranged without him and that it interfered with the policies he was pursuing for the pseudo-legal takeover of Jewish firms. It was the random and destructive nature of the pogrom that alarmed him. He was particularly incensed at the fact that German insurance firms would be forced to pay out to compensate Jewish owners whose homes and businesses had been burnt down. To show his concern he announced on the day of the crisis that any measures taken over the Jewish question were the responsibility of the state authorities alone.[51] Hitler confirmed this, giving Goering wide-ranging powers to centralise the efforts to solve the 'Jewish problem'. For Goering this was 'in the main an extensive economic problem'.[52] The pogrom destroyed property. Goering wanted it taken over by the state to help with preparations for war. The pogrom encouraged local Nazis and businessmen to take the law into their own hands. Goering wanted aryanisation to be carried out solely through the Four Year Plan so that Jewish workshops and factories could be integrated into its programmes. The consequence of the *Kristallnacht* was the establishment of a more formal system for seizing Jewish property, under terms of Nazi law, and in the interests of the state.[53] The model for such a system was the work carried out by the Austrian Nazis in Vienna, who by November 1938 had detailed plans for the closing down of 14,000 Jewish shops and the sale of 3,000 more, and were awaiting Goering's authorisation to proceed. On hearing of these plans Goering's response was: 'I will produce the decree today!' Funk promised to implement similar plans in Germany. Goering did not conceal his delight that in a matter of weeks the Jews would be completely excluded from the German economy 'and this whole story really be cleared up'.[54]

Other opportunities for extending and consolidating state ownership were to be found in industries that were already dependent on state funds, particularly the aluminium and aircraft industries. It was a different matter altogether when Goering began to intervene in the iron, steel and coal industries, the traditional core of private German business, and a political force in their own right. For the large trusts that ran heavy industry it was important to have a government that was basically sympathetic to its corporate interests. When this had not been the case in the past, heavy industry involved itself in politics to secure more amenable conditions. To strengthen their political position the industrialists involved had forged close links with the military elite and with the banking and ministerial bureaucracy.[55] In the years after 1933 the Schacht-Blomberg axis in German politics had created conditions very favourable to heavy industry. When Goering undertook to undermine the conservatives and to overthrow conventional economic policy he inevitably invited the distrust and, eventually, the open hostility of the pro-Schacht industrial elite.

The issue between Goering and the iron and steel industrialists coincided with and was linked to the contest with Schacht and the crisis over the

Four Year Plan. Its origin is easily understood. Germany was heavily dependent on external sources of iron ore to supply the large German iron and steel producers. Table 3 shows how this dependence was distributed. Out of the 21 million tons of ore smelted in 1935 only 25 per cent could be provided from domestic resources, the bulk of the rest being provided from Sweden and France. To the Nazi leadership this situation was full of dangers. French supplies of ore could be used by the French government as a means of bringing pressure to bear on Germany.[56] Swedish supplies could, as Goering argued, be the victim of striking miners, unsympathetic to the Nazi regime.[57] In either case Germany was dependent in a way that she had not been during the First World War on outside supplies that would in all likelihood be cut off during any future war. Even as it was the supplies of ore from both domestic and foreign sources were insufficient to provide all users with enough steel. In 1936 the army regularly complained about the bottleneck in iron and steel supply and warned both Hitler and Goering of the consequences in the event of war.[58]

Table 4 *German sources of iron ore 1929–35*

	Total supply ('000 tons)	Germany	Sweden	France	Spain	Other
			(per cent)			
1929	21.280	25.8	32.8	16.6	11.3	13.5
1930	14.877	29.4	36.4	16.1	7.7	10.4
1931	8.453	26.7	36.4	17.4	6.7	12.8
1932	5.428	24.6	29.7	20.2	11.3	14.2
1933	7.376	27.5	35.4	20.1	5.0	12.0
1934	12.881	29.6	39.0	14.6	3.8	13.0
1935	21.170	25.3	32.1	31.1	4.0	7.5

Source: Nuremberg Trials, Case XI, Defence Document Book (Pleiger) 3, p. 270.

To Goering the solution was a simple one. Domestic sources of iron ore were to be exploited to the full to give Germany greater independence of foreign supplies. Keppler had argued this case since the early 1930s. Goering took over these ideas as his own. Keppler's technical research team had shown that it was feasible to smelt the low-grade ores in central and southern Germany, although with contemporary iron technology the process was costly and complicated. When it was discovered that similar ores were now being successfully smelted in England, at Corby, under the guidance of an American engineer, Henry Brassert, Goering determined to adopt the same methods in Germany. The question was whether the German iron and steel industry would respond to the plans for domestic ore production in the way that I.G. Farben had responded to the demand for synthetics.[59]

The attitude of heavy industry to Goering's plans was essentially negative. Encouraged by Schacht, who had opposed plans for domestic production all along, the major Ruhr industrialists rejected the proposals put to them.[60] The reasons for this opposition were largely economic. The industry had suffered from over-capacity during the depression years and was unwilling to sanction the large-scale investment programme involved in domestic ore production because it might seriously affect their capital position if the rearmament boom petered out. Goering's wild threat to build 'three times as many blast furnaces' as there already were in Germany was an invitation to massive over-capitalisation.[61] The second problem was to do with costs and markets. The domestic ore was much more expensive to produce and smelt than foreign ore for its iron content was much lower. To produce iron and steel at higher cost threatened the interest of the manufacturers who used it as a raw material and ultimately threatened Germany's export position.

If the arguments were economic, their effect was highly political. For the Nazis the rejection confirmed that the national aims of the movement and the purposes of German capitalism were no longer the same. Hitler wanted war and imperial expansion. Private capitalists might indeed benefit from the achievement of such an empire, but their immediate aims in 1937 were to gain a favourable capital structure for the industry and to expand markets and short-term profitability by strategies of their own. Schacht argued in their defence that 'the state should not run business itself and take the responsibility away from private enterprise'.[62] The Ruhr industrialists shared this view; jealous of the important position they enjoyed in German economic and political life, they wanted to reserve the final decision on initiatives in the German economy for themselves.

These arguments were lost on Goering. In December 1936 he warned leading businessmen that 'If someone cannot decide for himself on the exploitation of his mines, he must sell his property so that other people can do so . . . we are here concerned with the welfare of the whole German nation and not with the welfare of one individual enterprise.'[63] In March 1937 he argued that 'the state must take over when private industry has proved itself no longer able to carry on'.[64] In private he accused the Ruhr leaders of 'the crassest economic egoism', what he later called 'a toilet-seat perspective' on national affairs.[65] Spurred on by the more radical middle-class elements in his organisation, and by his own frustration and hostility to the Ruhr, Goering gradually moved towards the decision, finally announced at a meeting with the industrialists concerned in June 1937, 'to have a very large plant built under [his] personal influence'.[66] The industry and the Economics Ministry were caught by surprise. Within a month plans were complete for an industrial complex for extracting and smelting the iron of the Salzgitter ore-fields in Brunswick. Goering reported to the same industrial audience the foundation of the Reichswerke 'Hermann Goering'.[67]

This decision finally broke Schacht's political power in the economy, as it challenged that of the Ruhr. All their moves were monitored by Goering's intelligence network. In August the iron and steel industry drew up a paper

– the so-called Düsseldorf Memorandum – rejecting Goering's autarkic strategy. Alerted to its contents in advance by an informer, Goering immediately and characteristically ordered the arrest of the leading Ruhr industrialists. Pleiger succeeded in persuading him instead to telegram to all those concerned that he would treat all signatories to the memorandum as saboteurs. Krupp was offered a large arms contract at the same time in order to buy his support and to undermine any united front that the industry might set up against him.[68] With great reluctance the industrialists accepted defeat, frightened of the consequences for their businesses and their own persons if they persisted in overt opposition. Goering passed a decree for the compulsory purchase of the privately-owned ore claims in central and southern Germany, and compelled the private firms to invest some of their own money in the establishment of a state-owned competitor.[69] In triumph Goering told Voegler, the head of the Vereinigte Stahlwerke and a major opponent, 'Now I am no longer dependent on you. You have been leading me around by the nose for long enough!'[70]

The nature of the Reichswerke and its subsequent expansion provide a vital key to understanding the progressive 'Nazification' of the economy. Although it bore Goering's name, the Reichswerke in no sense belonged to Goering. Pleiger suggested using the name as an indication to others that the leading Nazi in the economy stood behind the new firm. It was only in this official capacity that Goering was linked with the business. What personal profit he made from it was incidental to its purpose. Nor was the Reichswerke in any sense a capitalist or 'state-capitalist' enterprise, despite the fact that it enjoyed the same legal status as private corporations. This was merely a juridical convenience. From the outset the Reichswerke was intended as a state-owned and state-run industrial complex, integrated into the Nazi-dominated economy as the industrial instrument for the fulfilment of war-related goals. Like the Four Year Plan and Goering's own economic offices, the Reichswerke concern was a typical product of fascist economics.

In fact once the Reichswerke had been founded it developed a character very different from its stated purpose. What began as a small firm funded by state and private industry together to help mine domestic iron ore was transformed by Goering's decision to develop the Reichswerke as a colossal state enterprise constantly extending its interests as the needs of the *Volk* dictated. Early in 1938 Goering authorised a very large increase in state funds for the Reichswerke, taking its capital from 5 to 400 million marks. The plan was to turn it into 'the core of the whole of German rearmament, of supplies for the arms industry in peace and war'.[71] Goering saw it at one and the same time as 'an economic and political instrument' designed to resolve the conflict of interests between the Nazi state and private business and to speed up the construction of a military economy. Like the Four Year Plan it was organised on the 'leadership principle', with Goering responsible for all questions of fundamental importance and a subordinate hierarchy of officials directly and personally answerable to him.[72]

As with the Four Year Plan office, the staff of the Reichswerke was chosen from among loyal party officials and small businessmen anxious to increase the influence of the party in the economy and to ensure the triumph of the Nazi ideal. Paul Pleiger was a small steel producer from a working-class background who used the state organisation to gain political influence over the large-scale companies that dominated the industry. Koerner, Goering's personal deputy, came from a similar small business background and was unsympathetic to large-scale capitalism. Other leading officials were drawn from among party stalwarts, many of whom had long associations with the party and were not simply post-1933 opportunists. Wilhelm Meinberg, who worked closely with Pleiger, was a Nazi peasant leader in the 1920s: Dietrich Klagges, another director, was an ex-elementary school teacher and an old party member: and so on.[73] The mushrooming organisation of the Reichswerke gave opportunity for the small business and official class to use the power of the state to impose their own political interests on the traditional capitalist elite, just as the Four Year Plan had proved a suitable means for undermining the influence of the military and financial conservatives. Goering was put in the fortunate position of being able to leave much of the routine work of establishing and running the Reichswerke to the enthusiastic party members appointed to its board.

The large increase in funds for the Reichswerke indicated the importance attached by the party to the successful completion of the project. The plan was to produce annually domestic ores totalling 21 million tons and to use the ores to supply a complex of blast furnaces and rolling mills to be completed by 1945–6 in three major stages, increasing the output of finished steel from domestic ore by at least 4 million tons.[74] By this single stroke the Reichswerke became the third largest enterprise in Germany, with unlimited access to funds. Goering's imagination became fired by the vulgar hugeness of the project, by the fact that he had cut through all the objections of a technical or economic nature and created from the ground up a giant industrial complex as a symbol of the regime's vitality and resourcefulness. The Reichswerke was a propaganda monument to Goering and the party.[75]

By the outbreak of war the Reichswerke had become what Goering intended it should be, the largest industrial enterprise in Europe.[76] The details of its structure can be seen on Chart II. Goering poured into the Reichswerke any industrial assets that came his way: Jewish firms compulsorily aryanised, coal mines taken over through the bullying and harassment of the Ruhr coal-owners, the bulk of the heavy industry captured in Austria and Czechoslovakia and state-owned armaments works in the Reich.[77] Building on the pattern of the private trusts he developed a whole network of dependent and ancillary businesses so that the Reichswerke was involved not only in extracting ore and coal, but in smelting and refining the iron and steel, manufacturing the finished metal in the form of armaments or

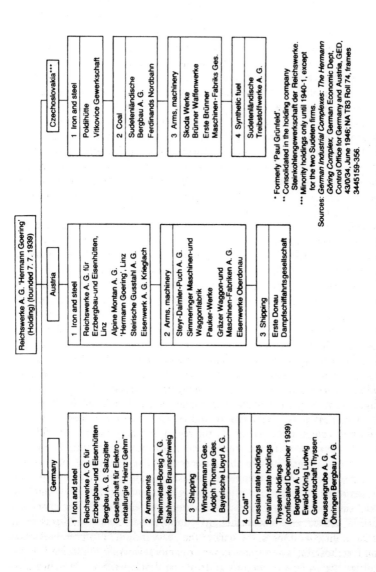

Reichswerke A. G. 'Hermann Goering'
(Holding) (founded 7. 7. 1939)

Germany

1 Iron and steel
Reichswerke A. G. für Erzbergbau- und Eisenhütten
Bergbau A. G. Salzgitter
Gesellschaft für Elektrometallurgie 'Heinz Gehm'*

2 Armaments
Rheinmetall-Borsig A. G.
Stahlwerke Braunschweig

3 Shipping
Winschermann Ges.
Adolph Thomae Ges.
Bayerische Lloyd A. G.

4 Coal**
Prussian state holdings
Bavarian state holdings
Thyssen holdings (confiscated December 1939)
Bergbau A. G.
Ewald-König Ludwig Gewerkschaft Thyssen
Preussengrube A. G.
Ohringen Bergbau A. G.

Austria

1 Iron and steel
Reichswerke A. G. für Erzbergbau- und Eisenhütten, Linz
Alpine Montan A. G.
'Hermann Goering', Linz
Steirische Gusstahl A. G.
Eisenwerk A. G. Krieglach

2 Arms, machinery
Steyr-Daimler-Puch A. G.
Simmeringer Maschinen- und Waggonfabrik
Pauker-Werke
Grazer Waggon- und Maschinen-Fabriken A. G.
Eisenwerke Oberdonau

3 Shipping
Erste Donau Dampfschiffahrtsgesellschaft

Czechoslovakia***

1 Iron and steel
Poldihütte
Vitkovice Gewerkschaft

2 Coal
Sudetenländische Bergbau A. G.
Ferdinands Nordbahn

3 Arms, machinery
Skoda Werke
Brünner Waffenwerke
Erste Brünner Maschinen-Fabriks Ges.

4 Synthetic fuel
Sudetenländische Treibstoffwerke A. G.

* Formerly 'Paul Grünfeld'
** Consolidated in the holding company Steinkohlengewerkschaft der Reichswerke.
*** Minority holdings only until 1940–1, except for the two Sudeten firms.

Sources: *German Industrial Complexes: The Hermann Göring Complex*, German Economic Dept, Control Office for Germany and Austria, GED, 43/0/34, June 1946; NA T83 Roll 74, frames 3445159–356.

Chart II The Reichswerke and main subsidiaries, September 1939

heavy machinery, producing synthetic petrol, running transport businesses and supplying building materials. Its size and the complexity of its operations gave the Reichswerke concern a key place in the German industrial economy. Perhaps if the private firms had co-operated with Nazi plans in 1936 and 1937 such a degree of state intervention might have been unnecessary. But to have done so would have been to compromise too much the corporate strategies and political claims of the large industrialists. Nor would it have satisfied the logic of Nazi ideology and populist economics, nor Goering's personal ambition.

During the course of the political crisis over the Reichswerke the balance of power swung firmly in Goering's favour. Distrusted by the party, and increasingly cut off from his military and industrial allies, Schacht's influence declined sharply. Although the army persuaded Hitler in July 1937 to effect a jurisdictional reconciliation between the two men, Goering ignored it.[78] Schacht responded by suspending his activities as Plenipotentiary for War Economy, a post that he had held since 1935, and when that had no effect, he left the office of Minister of Economics in abeyance as well.[79] Hitler hesitated to sack Schacht directly, because of his fear of the effect this might have on foreign public opinion. Instead both Hitler and Goering bided their time, waiting until Schacht's resignation would be politically acceptable. Hitler let it be known that his confidence in Schacht had gone. Goering harassed Schacht's officials and overturned his policies. He would accept nothing short of Schacht's complete subordination. In front of Hitler he told Schacht 'I must be able to give you instructions'.[80] In November Hitler finally accepted his resignation, satisfied that the political repercussions could be coped with. An anti-Schacht campaign orchestrated in the press had helped to persuade the public that Schacht had in some way betrayed the nation's trust. Goering became temporary Minister of Economics in his place. His first act was to ring Schacht from his erstwhile office in the Ministry: 'I am now sitting in your chair!'.[81]

The transfer of economic power from Schacht to Goering inevitably involved a renewed clash with the army which had no desire to see its economic affairs in the hands of the party. Goering was well aware of the army's attitude. During the long struggle with Schacht, von Blomberg had taken every opportunity to pull rank on Goering (who was in military terms his subordinate). He hoped to be able to use his position as Supreme Commander to bring the whole military economy under army control, employing Goering as a mere agent of the armed forces.[82] The ambitious head of the army economic office, Georg Thomas, supported von Blomberg's strategy and worked actively in the background to extend the power and responsibility of the armed forces' economic inspectorate which was instrumental in maintaining army control over military industries.[83]

The army was no more successful than Schacht in bringing Goering to heel. He remorselessly eroded the influence of the army in the economy. The oil industry came under his jurisdiction, to the complaints of the generals, in the course of 1936. The chemical industry, including the manufacture of explosives, came under his control in 1937 and 1938.[84] Construction of the western fortifications, after an acrimonious struggle with the army leaders, was taken out of their hands in 1938 and given to Fritz Todt, commissioner for construction in the Four Year Plan.[85] Finally, on the resignation of Schacht, Goering took over temporary responsibility for the tasks of the Plenipotentiary for the Economy, thus removing the army's main ally in the civilian establishment.

Nevertheless the army remained a major political force, preventing Hitler from exercising a free hand in the change of course that he had decided on after 1936. Goering shared Hitler's distrust of the army leaders. He was jealous of von Blomberg's influence and wanted the party more involved in military questions. During 1937 his distrust crystallised into a desire to become War Minister in von Blomberg's place. In the winter of 1937–8 he undertook a number of initiatives to elimate the army leadership and extend party power, using his contacts with the secret police and the SS to achieve it. He could be certain of Himmler's support in this because the SS had its own ambitions to extend party influence into the regular armed forces.[86] All Goering required was the opportunity to strike.

The chance came in October 1937. Von Blomberg approached Goering in search of a guarantee from the party that an affair on which he had embarked with a 'lady with a past' would not affect his official position. Goering was only too willing to help. Through the security services he was able to uncover the nature of the unfortunate alliance that the War Minister had made. Still posing as an ally he agreed at von Blomberg's request to go as far as to arrange the 'voluntary' emigration of one of the woman's other lovers. He was sent very much against his will to an economic post in Argentina.[87] Goering then agreed to allow von Blomberg to marry in January 1938 and to say nothing about the bride's background or the shady intrigues surrounding the marriage. Both Hitler and Goering were witnesses at the hastily conducted wedding. Within two weeks Goering, on the pretext that the police had uncovered evidence that von Blomberg's new wife was an ex-prostitute, a fact that he already knew, confronted Hitler with the information.[88] Hitler was outraged. Goering asked to be allowed to inform von Blomberg personally that the marriage should be annulled. But Goering's visit to von Blomberg became instead what he had clearly hoped and planned for: the opportunity to ask von Blomberg to resign his office on grounds of honour. To make doubly certain he spread the news rapidly among the other generals, who also insisted on resignation. Von Blomberg unwillingly did so, unaware that Hitler had not finally decided what should be done.[89]

Goering's duplicity was clear. So too, under the circumstances, was von Blomberg's personal ineptitude and political innocence. The affair was the culmination of a web of intrigue that Goering and Himmler wove together in the last two months of 1937. For not only had Goering prepared in advance to entrap von Blomberg and clear the way for his own assumption of the War Ministry, but he had conspired with Himmler to force the resignation of von Fritsch, the army commander-in-chief, who stood next in line to von Blomberg and was a firm opponent of Goering and the SS. It was Goering's good fortune that the Gestapo also had a file on von Fritsch, compiled in 1935, which alleged his homosexuality. Although the file had lain unused for two years, because the evidence was so suspect, Goering chose to re-activate it at the end of 1937 in order to complete his coup against the army leaders. It is unlikely that Goering knew at first how spurious the evidence was – it was a clear case of mistaken identity – for in order to present Hitler with firm proof of von Fritsch's unsuitability as army commander-in-chief he had him followed by secret service officers when he went on holiday in Egypt in December.[90] Although nothing new could be proved against him, Goering used the insalubrious file on von Fritsch to persuade Hitler at the vital moment not to appoint him as von Blomberg's successor. His efforts were rewarded. The mud thrown at von Fritsch stuck sufficiently to force his resignation. Goering then manoeuvred to obstruct a full military investigation of the allegations against von Fritsch, for it might well have exposed the full extent of his intrigue. By the time von Fritsch's innocence was proved beyond doubt it was too late for him to be reinstated.[91]

By this stage Goering had already achieved most of what he wanted. Indeed in the last week of January 1938 he was poised to become not only overlord of the economy but War Minister as well. Though Hitler was prepared to accept the first, he was not willing to grant the second. He argued that Goering was too involved in his other offices to cope with any more responsibilities, which was substantially true. Less charitably he argued that Goering was 'too idle' to make a suitable supreme commander. But he was not ungrateful for Goering's efforts for they resolved a growing tension between the armed forces and the party which Hitler had been uncertain how to handle.[92] In the wake of the von Blomberg crisis he took the opportunity to purge the upper echelons of the army of those elements least sympathetic to his strategic aims.[93]

Goering's intrigues against the army leaders have to be set against a background of renewed hostility and mistrust between the party and the remaining conservatives in government and military circles. The signs had been there throughout 1937. In February the Transport Minister, von Eltz-Rubenach, was forced to retire in favour of appointees chosen by Goering. Schacht followed in November.[94] Early in 1938 a wave of compulsory retirements swept through both the army and the upper reaches of the civil service. The most important victim was the Foreign Minister von Neurath, who was replaced by Ribbentrop. Von Neurath too was known to be unsympathetic to the foreign policy and military plans that Hitler had revealed during 1937. Behind all these moves lay Goering's restless desire to resolve the political disputes that surrounded his own position in the government, and to take revenge on those who had obstructed his ambitions in the past. By making it clear to Hitler that only Nazis could be trusted with the major offices of state it became the logical step that Hitler himself should assume, as he did on 3 February 1938, supreme command of the armed forces.[95]

Goering's own political stock rose substantially over the course of the crisis, despite the fact that his conservative opponents knew by the end of February 1938 that he had achieved his coup through a combination of bullying and shoddy intrigue.[96] He was rewarded by being allowed to take over the Ministry of Economics and reorganise it in such a way that it was tightly bound to the Four Year Plan organisation. Schacht's allies in the ministry were gradually excluded from influence and Goering's supporters, including his state secretary Friedrich Landfried, were pushed to the fore.[97] Goering was also successful in persuading Hitler finally, and ironically, to appoint Walther Funk as formal head of the Economics Ministry, despite the fact that Hitler had previously refused to do so because of Funk's homosexuality. Funk was barely qualified for the job, but for Goering this was an advantage for it meant that he could continue to exert a decisive influence on the ministry without having to take on more official duties. Funk, an 'old fighter' like himself, was inexperienced politically, completely dominated by Goering. His history of homosexuality gave him no room for manoeuvre in his political relationship with his domineering superior. For all intents and purposes the ministry was under Goering's control. Funk's appointment as Plenipotentiary for the War Economy was a similar sham, perpetrated in order to prevent the army authorities from using the office as a wedge to drive between Goering and the armed forces.[98]

Though Goering failed to get the War Ministry, he did become the highest office-holder in the armed forces. On the day that von Blomberg's resignation was announced Goering was promoted field marshal. This at once altered the power balance between Goering and the armed forces. As the highest ranking officer he was in a position to exercise a more decisive influence on military matters without having to take on more administrative duties. Between February and July Goering was able to complete the transfer of responsibility for the military economy from the army. At Goering's insistence the office of Plenipotentiary for the War Economy was made immediately subordinate to Hitler (and in practice to Goering) instead of to the army.[99] The army ordnance office was excluded from the vital planning of the explosives programme and, in effect, a large part of army production. In July 1938 Goering informed the army that its responsibility extended only to questions of 'armed warfare' and the placing of contracts, as in the First World War.[100] As 'the highest authority in the direction of the economy' Goering assumed the responsibility for all questions to do with rearmament, strategic resources and the preparation of the economy for war.[101] As if to rub salt in the wound he revived the defunct Reich Defence Council which had originally been established by Blomberg and Schacht in 1934, and from which he had been deliberately excluded.

What emerges clearly from the rise of Goering's economic empire is the comparative ease with which it was created. The defence put up by the conservative military and economic elites was feeble in relation to the national political role they were defending. Yet it is easy to see why the conservatives found it so difficult to keep Goering under control. The advantage that the party enjoyed was its base of popular support, and in particular the broad network of junior officials and managers it could call upon for carrying out party tasks. Behind this support lay Nazi control of the security services and the police forces, which were used indiscriminately against anyone who stood in the Nazis' path. Goering even had his own personal security service which provided him with a stream of intelligence information. The political moves of his opponents were monitored by extensive telephone-tapping so that Goering was always one step ahead in negotiation and argument. Lacking access to such an apparatus and lacking also a mass base of popular support, the German elites were peculiarly ill-equipped to play the Nazi political game.

Moreover it is clear that for some time the groups around von Blomberg and Schacht failed to understand what the terms of the political contest were. They heavily miscalculated the nature of Hitler's ambitions or the seriousness with which Goering would pursue Hitler's wishes. They were satisfied, as they had been since 1933, that their technical expertise and social standing made them in some sense indispensable to the Reich. Schacht relied to the end on his international standing to preserve his domestic position even when it had been clearly eroded from within. The conservatives themselves, so accustomed to operating in a political context governed by *Aussenpolitik* were increasingly cut off from the course of German politics which, like the self-sufficient economy, was turning away from the outside world to be governed by domestic forces quite beyond their control. Unable to grasp how to behave in this new and unpredictable political world they either abdicated, as did Schacht and von Blomberg, or retreated into silent defence of what was left of their interests. Thus the large iron and steel trusts abandoned Schacht in 1938 and salvaged what they could from the crisis. The army too fell back in defence of its political and social position and co-operated as fully as it could to prevent further erosion. This defensive strategy did little to divert Goering or the regime from their course but it did prevent anything worse from happening, leaving both the army and private capitalism with much of their substance more or less intact. But both had to pay the piper, caught as they were in an endless dance of their own making. Hoping to profit from collusion with Hitler, they found the tables turned and by 1939 enjoyed a less decisive influence on national politics than at any time since the founding of Bismarck's Reich.

The conservatives also failed to calculate the effect of Goering's ambition and the strength of his attachment to Hitler. Goering had a shrewd sense of how to exploit the gap between Hitler's fantasy and German reality, and with great tactical flexibility. Once he had achieved a foothold in the economy he determined to push on into areas over which he had no specific political claim but where he sensed political weakness and where he knew Hitler would not prevent him trespassing. It was this dynamic expansion, drawing its strength from Hitler's support and unpredictable in its scope, that undermined any attempt at concerted resistance from the elites affected. Goering was not to be restrained by the formal rights of others nor by established political practice. He had a great sense of the possibilities in political life, of where to move on and where to hold back. Because the initiative lay with him, he had the advantage of surprise over his more scrupulous or innocent protagonists. Because his restless ambition grew larger with each administrative success, it was difficult to find conventional political means to restrain him, or to know what he would do next.

Goering enjoyed, too, the advantage of widespread personal popularity, which was true of none of the conservatives. His exposure to the German public was carefully cultivated. He posed during 1936 and 1937 as the champion of national solutions against the corrupt self-interest of the old elites and big business. The press was largely on Goering's side. Goebbels's propaganda machine heralded the new direction in economic life. Under such circumstances there was no question of dislodging Goering. There were certainly other Nazi claimants, but they were either too weak to oppose Goering, as was Keppler, or too involved in jurisdictional battles of their own, as was Ley. Goering rode roughshod over them all, supported by an ever-growing circle of subordinate officials who could see which way the wind was blowing and hurried to identify their cause with his.

Among the Nazi leadership he was increasingly isolated and distant, able, as long as he enjoyed Hitler's support, to ignore many of the squabbles that went on around him. Other Nazi leaders were envious of his popularity and of his political revival after the disasters of 1933 and 1934. Hess became so obsessively jealous that he tried to suppress newspaper pictures of Goering that flattered his figure.[102] Rosenberg hated him for his threats to uncover what he had been doing in Russia between 1917 and 1919.[103] Julius Streicher published allegations that Goering's first child, Edda, born in 1938, had been artificially inseminated (though it cost him his post as *Gauleiter* of Nuremberg). More scurrilous still it was rumoured that Mussolini was the father.[104] Ribbentrop, who was jealous of Goering's popularity and social ease abroad, called him in public 'that Christmas tree', a reference to his bemedalled appearance.[105] Himmler and Goebbels tolerated him because he posed no threat to them, nor they to him.

Nor did Goering spare his colleagues, for whom he had scant respect or liking. Keitel and Lammers he hated – 'mere secretaries' – for worming their way between himself and Hitler. Ribbentrop he nicknamed 'Germany's no. 1 parrot' for repeating whatever Hitler said.[106] Only Heydrich, Himmler's deputy, impressed him. Later in the war he said that Heydrich had been 'one of the only real men in Germany'.[107] He had certainly been one of the few men able to play Goering at his own political game of conspiracy and encroachment with any success. The other leading Nazis he indulged and despised by turns.

There were, none the less, limits to the exercise of Goering's power. Some of these limits were self-imposed. The very speed with which the empire was built up, and its vast scale, imposed constraints. With every major advance the administrative apparatus had to be set up or reorganised. The state-run industries had to be built and managed within a very short space of time. Moreover the deliberate centralisation of all major decision-making in Goering's hands was a clumsy device, placing far too much of the responsibility for broad questions on to one individual and isolating him from other leaders. This was, of course, the way that Goering wanted it; but so rambling and extensive were his political domains that both Goering and his subordinates were frequently lost in them. On one occasion a hapless aircraft manufacturer was threatened with court-martial by Goering, in his capacity as head of the air force, for pursuing a policy that had been authorised by Goering as head of the Four Year Plan.[108] This was part of the price that the Nazis paid for the kind of centralisation implied by the 'leadership principle'. Though Goering had risen to high office he had done so not through displays of administrative competence but simply as a senior party politician, promoted on strength rather than merit.

There were limits imposed from without as well. Much of Goering's time was taken up with defending the frontiers of his administrative empire against marauding rivals. Robert Ley, for example, had ambitions of his own to turn the Labour Front into a major institution for the conduct of social and economic policy and found himself frustrated by Goering's pre-emptive programme for self-sufficiency and rearmament.[109] Despite Ley's objections even the Volkswagen plant, set up in 1938 under the Labour Front, was assigned on mobilisation to the Luftwaffe at Goering's insistence.[110] His relations with the *Gauleiter* were not particularly good either, and his exercise of authority over the whole economy gave rise to numerous minor conflicts with local party bosses who believed that in the provinces such power belonged to them. Moreover as economics overlord Goering found himself the victim of everyone's grumbles and became more enmeshed in the day-to-day operations of the economy than he had intended.

Nor did the army and business circles sit easily under his direction. Although the power lay firmly enough in Goering's hands there was plenty of room in the interstices of the economy for those less sympathetic to the Nazis to hide themselves. At the lower levels of administration, where bureaucrats and managers could take discretionary decisions, something could be done to divert the full impact of Nazi policies. The arguments with the iron and steel producers could be duplicated for many other sectors resentful at the spread of state controls and the over-bureaucratisation of the economy. This was particularly so among the manufacturing and export-orientated industries over which Goering's control was more remote. The car industry resisted the Four Year Plan efforts, orchestrated by the unenthusiastic General von Schell, to force the rationalisation of vehicle production.[111] Leading entrepreneurs in the electrical industry retained their early distrust of the Nazis. Even the aircraft industry, so closely under Goering's eye, was filled with small-scale businessmen who resented the degree of state intervention imposed on them. The manufacturing sector continued to champion the need for more exports and less control over the domestic market and by tactics of delay and concealment was able to lessen the impact of the Nazified economy.[112]

The supreme test of Goering's economic empire was still to come. The whole purpose of building it up was to make Germany economically and militarily powerful enough to build an empire outside the Reich. Once Goering had successfully resolved the political struggles between the party and the remaining conservatives in the economy and armed forces, the way was clearer for an active foreign policy. Indeed Goering's political triumph was a major precondition for starting down the road to war.

4
GOERING AND HITLER'S WAR

A number of myths surround Goering's place in the preparation and launching of Hitler's war. One can be dismissed at once: the idea that Goering was the man of peace, seeking reconciliation and coexistence, arguing with Hitler against war, favouring domestic consolidation against the ambitions of the hawks in Hitler's entourage. Goering had strong opinions about the timing of war, but there can be no doubt that he prepared for war and expected it to come.

The second myth concerns what *kind* of war Goering was preparing for. A great number of historians agree that the Nazis' war was to be a war of *Blitzkrieg*, short wars fought with the minimum of economic effort. Such a war would reduce the burden to be borne by the German people (who might otherwise rebel) and required only a small military economy to achieve what was wanted. This interpretation is linked with the view that Hitler's foreign policy was essentially opportunistic rather than programmatic; that the short war could be turned on and off as diplomatic circumstances allowed. In this interpretation Hitler's foreign policy goals are short-term and revisionist and are not the goals spelt out in *Mein Kampf*.[1]

Very little of this interpretation can be supported by Goering's history during this crucial period. From his role in foreign policy it is clear that neither Hitler nor Goering lost sight of the perspectives of *Mein Kampf*. From the preparations of the Luftwaffe it is clear that a large war with a variety of strategies was expected. From the role Goering played in the economy the evidence suggests that total war, not *Blitzkrieg*, was the end product of German preparations.

Goering's views on foreign policy coincided closely with those of Hitler. That Versailles should be overturned and Germany be fully rearmed he took for granted.[2] His real interest in foreign policy, like Hitler's, was a direct product of Nazi ideology. Foreign policy was strongly influenced by ideology, for it was the means whereby the prolonged struggle of races and world-historical forces, so central to Nazi thinking, could finally be resolved. To the Nazi mind it was not possible to predict exactly how the dialectic of racial and cultural struggle would develop. Hence the fact that Nazi goals were kept deliberately general in character, capable of sudden twists and turns in response to the changing nature of the struggle. But the central goal was clear: the creation of a new racial empire under German rule, dominating world affairs. Goering was as emphatic on this point as any other leading Nazi: 'We want an *Empire*' ('Wir wollen ein *Reich*').[3] Like Hitler, he believed that Europe and Asia should be transformed politically in Germany's favour, to take account of German economic power and cultural superiority. The chief barriers to such an ambition were the Soviet Union in the east and the British Empire in the west.

Regrettably, Goering left little written record of his ideas on foreign policy. His many private conversations with Hitler, exploring future strategy, mapping out the contours of the new German empire, were for the most part unrecorded. One striking piece of evidence has survived. On a number of occasions in 1937, in February and again in September, he confided at length about his foreign policy plans to a visiting Englishman with whom he had struck up a friendship before 1933, Group Captain Christie. Considering the circumstances the conversations were remarkably candid and indiscreet. Their subject-matter resembles so closely the ideas expressed by Hitler in November of the same year, at the conference recorded in the 'Hossbach Memorandum', that they are worth examining in some detail.[4]

Goering saw German imperialism unfolding in two complementary stages. The first stage was to achieve *Mitteleuropa*, the creation of a central European area dominated economically and politically by Germany, acquired without general war. Austria would be incorporated of its own free will. The Sudetenland and Bohemia (but not Slovakia) would be seized by force, if the Czechs did not voluntarily agree to the dismemberment of their country, and amalgamated with the larger German region.[5] The South Slav states were to become allied or dependent and Poland was to be 'reconquered' through military or economic pressure, or both.[6] The second stage of imperial expansion involved the other great powers. Goering hoped that Britain might offer Germany a free hand in the east to solve the Russian question and find 'living-space'. Soviet Russia was to be overturned. 'Economic living-space', he said, 'must at the same time be political living-space.'[7] In the west, in co-operation with Italy, France was to be reduced to a subsidiary status, Britain to be excluded from continental affairs. Goering shared the ambiguity felt by many Germans towards Britain, fascinated by the life of the British upper classes but resentful of the British claim to moral ascendancy in world affairs.[8] As German foreign policy became more active, the attraction rapidly gave way to growing hostility. He argued that if Britain failed to give Germany a free hand in the east she would become Germany's 'chief enemy'.[9]

There is little doubt that these ideas formed the strategic framework within which Goering worked. They show Hitler's strong influence, characteristically speculative and unrealistic, strongly Darwinian in tone. There is little reason to doubt that these views were held sincerely enough. In succeeding years this geo-political speculation was turned, or almost turned, into hard reality. If there was apparent ambiguity and change of emphasis, these were tactical rather than strategic changes, reflecting the general looseness of his arguments. Goering accepted Hitler's central commitment to a great conflict for racial hegemony and world power.[10]

Such a conflict was the final test of German strength. According to Goering it was to be a new war 'of great proportions'.[11] In 1936 he told an audience of economic leaders that 'Our whole nation is at stake. We live in a time when the final disputes are in sight. . . .'[12] In 1938 the same refrain: 'All the time my thoughts are circling round one thing – when will war come? Shall we win? What can we do? . . . only a nation that stakes everything on its armaments will be able to continue its existence.'[13] When war did break out in September 1939 Goering convinced himself that he had been right all along. 'Today's war', he warned, 'is a total war, whose end no one can approximately foretell.'[14] Reich authorities were ordered to 'direct all energies to a lengthy war'.[15] Throughout the period Goering uncritically accepted the probability of a second 'Great War' to resolve the tensions and contradictions of international life created by the first. In doing so he continually argued for the unrestrained use of all resources, not for the limited economic commitment of *Blitzkrieg*.

Goering's place in these romantic and unsophisticated plans for German empire was a crucial one. Hitler needed Goering's new political power to push the economy towards war and to prepare the German population for economic privations ahead. Without Goering it would have been much harder to overcome the resistance of the conservatives to more irrational and dangerous schemes of expansion. His activity was intended to neutralise this resistance and to bring the economy and the workforce under the more direct control of party leaders. Many businessmen and soldiers no doubt shared the more limited ambitions of Nazi foreign policy, which made it all the harder to resist Nazi pressure to go further. Some German conservatives found it difficult to take Nazi schemes for expansion very seriously, even after the destruction of Austrian and Czech independence, which was why Hitler preferred Goering to Schacht, Ribbentrop to von Neurath.[16]

While the plans for world empire matured, Hitler concentrated upon the immediate goal of domination over the central and eastern areas of Europe. The creation of this middle-European political and economic bloc was an essential prerequisite for the waging of major war. Goering's economic responsibilities made it necessary for him to take a leading part in these initiatives in foreign policy. Having been excluded from foreign policy in 1934 because of his diplomatic clumsiness and the hostility of the Foreign Ministry, he was allowed in again when caution and tact were no longer so necessary. His increasing involvement in foreign affairs was at the expense of Foreign Ministry officials, a fact in which he took some pleasure. 'If it were up to me,' he told the Polish ambassador, 'I would have cleaned up

the Foreign Ministry long ago.'[17] Goering did not involve himself in everything, nor could he. In Ribbentrop he was faced with a Foreign Minister
every bit as hostile as von Neurath, and one who enjoyed considerable
influence with Hitler. This was a barrier that Goering found it difficult to
get past. Indeed at Nuremberg after the war he regretted that he 'had not
gone into foreign policy a little more'.[18] Hitler reserved to himself most of
the major decisions on questions of diplomacy, bringing in Goering only
when and where necessary. Most routine diplomatic activity was carried out
by Ribbentrop.

Nevertheless the areas in which Goering took an interest were of vital
importance: in Poland, in Austria and Italy and, after the outbreak of civil
war, in Spain. In the case of Poland Hitler told Goering in April 1935
that 'independently of official Polish-German relations, he should take the
relations between the two countries under his special protection'. In Spain
Goering argued, against Foreign Office opposition, for direct military intervention on behalf of Franco. Having persuaded Hitler, as he later claimed,
to offer support 'to prevent the further spread of communism . . . and to
test my young Luftwaffe', he went on to provide military aid and economic
co-operation that contributed materially to Nationalist victory.[19] In the case
of Italy Goering's object was to keep informal lines of communication
open between Hitler and the Italian leadership over the crucial question of
Austrian independence and over lesser problems in the Balkans. While
Goering spent much time in 1936 and 1937 assuring the Italians that
Germany would not act precipitately and without prior consultation in
Austria, he was at the same time giving active encouragement to Austrian
Nazis to press on for union with the Reich.[20] His intelligence agencies
monitored closely what was going on in Austria, providing both Goering
and Hitler with detailed political information.[21] Both men believed that
Anschluss was inevitable, merely a matter of time and opportunity.[22] The
difficult problem was to find a way of achieving it without alienating Italy
and the western powers.

In the first place pressure was put on Italy to reach closer agreements with
the Reich as a safeguard against her growing isolation over the Ethiopian and
Spanish wars. The closer Italy drew to Germany, the harder it was for
Mussolini to object to German policy in Austria. Secondly considerable
pressure was brought to bear on Austria's leading politicians from the late
summer of 1936 onwards to be more accommodating to the Austrian Nazi
Party and to accept closer economic co-operation with the Reich. This was
where Goering came in. As commissioner for the Four Year Plan he
negotiated tariff and currency agreements with Austria. German firms with
Austrian contacts were encouraged to link Austrian firms in which they
had an interest with industrial programmes in the Reich.[23] Discussions on
economic affairs brought Goering into discussions on politics as well.
Through a number of collaborators and agents, including the Austrian
Foreign Minister Guido Schmitt, who was later given high office in the

Four Year Plan, he contributed directly to the growing climate of crisis in Austrian politics.[24]

By early 1938 this crisis reached a climax, coinciding with the army crisis in Germany and the elimination of leading conservatives from high office there. The heightening of internal tension in Austria also coincided with a favourable set of international circumstances for the Nazis. With neither Britain nor Russia willing or able to prevent *Anschluss*, and with Mussolini much more dependent on German support, Hitler began seriously to explore the possibility of resolving the Austrian question. Pan-German pressure in both countries was mobilised to capitalise on the situation. Goering hoped to make capital on his own account at the same time by thrusting himself to the front of the Pan-German movement, anxious to bring Hitler his dream of union. Since Ribbentrop, the new Foreign Minister, had not yet left London to fill his new post, Goering was left in full possession of the field in Berlin. While Hitler hesitated to take the risk of annexing Austria outright, Goering took charge of the negotiations on 11 March that led to the resignation of the cabinet of Chancellor Schuschnigg, the eventual resignation of the Austrian president and the invitation to Hitler to send German troops into Austria to restore order.[25]

Once he saw that the risk had paid off, Hitler took firm control of the situation again. The Austrian Nazis, in imitation of Hitler's seizure of power, supplied the rest. But through his determined assistance on the night of the crisis and his presence at discussions in the days that followed, Goering basked in Hitler's favour, as he had done on the day Hitler was made Chancellor. He was given a special commission by Hitler to integrate the Austrian economy into that of the Reich.[26] On 26 March he announced in Vienna a programme for the reconstruction of the country based around 'a decisive and important programme' of direct and indirect rearmament. 'Austria is free,' he told his audience, 'and belongs once again to the Reich.'[27] Those who might have seen a contradiction between these two statements were no longer in a position to protest.

The next stage was Czechoslovakia. At the 'Hossbach' conference in November 1937 Hitler had argued that the British and French would not fight for Czech independence, and that the break-up of the Czech state could follow rapidly the achievement of union with Austria.[28] With the *Anschluss* an accomplished fact, the Czech strategic position visibly deteriorated. Throughout the summer of 1938 the Nazi leaders mounted an open diplomatic offensive against Czechoslovakia, the 'inconceivable creation' as Goering called it.[29] He was at the forefront of efforts to isolate the Czechs diplomatically, as a prelude to bringing the Sudeten German areas of Czechoslovakia back into the Reich. To weaken Czech resistance he encouraged the claims of the other non-Czech minorities to autonomy. Despite Ribbentrop's objections that such affairs were properly the province of the Foreign Ministry, Goering took it upon himself to win the support of the Hungarian and Polish governments for joint action against Czechoslovakia to bring about its dismemberment. By August 1938 he had secured rather reluctant Hungarian agreement. Poland waited longer to see how the western powers would react, but eventually agreed to join with Germany on Goering's assurances to Beck, the Polish Foreign Minister, that the Sudetenland was Germany's last territorial demand.[30]

Goering's chief concern was that the Czech crisis, unlike that over Austria, might lead to general war. Though he recognised that 'the necessity will arise to act by force', he was anxious that 'international conflict should be avoided'.[31] Goering's greatest fear was not of the west, but of Soviet Russia. Hitler, however, was convinced that he could conquer Czechoslovakia without the armed intervention of either Britain or France. The Soviet Union, on the other hand, was an unknown quantity, exciting all sorts of speculation. Goering gravely told the Polish ambassador that 'Jews and the Third International would pull Europe into war'.[32] He sought reassurances from the Soviet Union's western neighbours that they would not allow the passage of Soviet troops or aircraft. Even with these assurances, Goering put pressure on Hitler to avoid any risk of general war which might bring Russia in on the side of the western powers.[33] This perhaps explains Hitler's determination to neutralise the Soviet threat a year later before the resolution of the Polish crisis.

Nonetheless, Goering was determined that Czechoslovakia should be brought into the German orbit by force or through economic pressure and irredentist agitation.[34] Only at the last moment, when there finally seemed a serious threat that Britain and France might declare war, did Goering, together with Ribbentrop's predecessor, von Neurath, press on Hitler at a critical meeting on the morning of September 28 the view that German aims could be achieved in two stages: acquisition of the German-speaking Sudetenland by agreement, and then further pressure on the rump Czech state to accept German domination. Unwilling to risk general European war Hitler reluctantly accepted. That afternoon the Munich conference was organised and two days later the western states gave Germany permission to occupy the Sudetenland, a move that left the Czechs militarily much weaker, open to the kind of pressure Goering favoured.

Goering immediately set about compromising what was left of Czech independence. The Polish ambassador told Warsaw that 'it was obvious that Goering was anxious to separate Slovakia from the rest of Czechoslovakia, in order to create a Czech state economically dependent on the Reich.'[36] Two weeks after the Munich conference Goering told the Slovak leader Durčansky that he supported Slovak independence because it left the Czechs 'even more completely at our mercy'.[37] In October 1938 he told the Czechs that he wanted a customs and currency union between the two countries to be followed by 'influence over the economy and budget, which is very important for our rearmament'.[38] Abandoned by Britain and France, the Czechs were compelled to comply. Numerous orders for war material and capital goods flowed into Czechoslovakia from the Reich. When rump Czechoslovakia was occupied and divided in March 1939 the economy was already closely linked with Germany's and it became only a question of choosing the most opportune moment for converting economic influence into formal political control. The opportunity came when in March the Slovakians, with German backing, demanded independence. Already dependent on the German economy, isolated internationally, the Czech government consented to the collapse of Czechoslovakia. To speed up the decision Goering, who had been hastily recalled from a convalescence in Italy, threatened the Czech president with the destruction of Prague from the air.[39]

The creation of this larger economic region was an important stage in founding the economic base necessary to carry out large-scale war. 'The incorporation of Bohemia and Moravia', Goering explained to his staff in July 1939, 'has taken place ... in order to increase German war potential by the exploitation of industry there.'[40] The German object was to bring the other countries of central and south-eastern Europe into closer economic dependence on the Reich as well, so that they could provide the food and specialised raw materials, including oil, that the newly incorporated territories could not provide. This economic plan was the answer to Hitler's fear of blockade and Germany's trade and currency problems. A closed trading bloc was the best guarantee that in the event of major war Germany would have access to economic resources beyond the level dictated by domestic supply on its own. This strategy certainly had its drawbacks. Austria and Czechoslovakia were by no means self-sufficient economically and required goods from Germany and from international markets to make up this deficiency. Their incorporation into the Reich economy brought additional problems of foreign exchange and trade. But they also brought the great advantage of additional labour, raw materials, finance and productive capacity, which allowed Germany to undertake larger long-term plans for war and which offset the temporary problems of economic integration.[41]

It is the very scope and length of these plans for economic preparation for war that raise serious doubts about the view that German war preparations were modest in scale, intended to maintain civilian consumption at a high level while a narrow and flexible arms sector was used to launch short and inexpensive wars. Whether judged on the basis of general economic policy or the detailed military plans, Nazi intentions are consistent with the idea of a large war to be fought in the mid-1940s at a time of Hitler's choosing. This required a complete transformation of the German economy to the needs of war.

'The Four Year Plan', said Goering in July 1938 'has the task of preparing the German economy for total war.'[42] This preparation called for major structural changes in the German economy which would take a considerable time to complete. The first stage of this transformation involved the setting up of an industrial sub-structure to support large-scale weapons production: that is, the building up of the raw materials, machinery, factory capacity and labour to cope with the military programmes. The steel plan and the oil programme were the central features of this restructuring, involving not only the establishment of large state-owned industry, but the integration of supplies of raw materials and labour from the captured economies to compensate for their shortage in the Reich. Both programmes were due for completion in the mid-1940s; the Reichswerke iron and steel programme by 1944, the synthetic oil programme by 1946. Neither of these schemes made sense for a war to be fought sooner than that, and neither programme was necessary for anything short of large-scale war.

In the domestic economy the objective was to keep living standards low, to hold up the expansion of consumption and to promote heavy, war-orientated industry. Goering's private admission that living standards would suffer under the Four Year Plan was confirmed by the slow expansion of consumer industries and the failure of German real wages to reach the levels even of the years of depression.[43] Changes in German wage levels are set out in Table 5. The declining quality of products and the high levels of taxation and forced levies meant that the German consumer was accustomed to making sacrifices on behalf of rearmament well before the outbreak of war. In 1928 consumption amounted to over 70 per cent of national income. By 1938 the level had fallen to 59 per cent.[44] In order to fulfil the needs of rearmament and industrial re-structuring, private construction was sharply curtailed in 1938, particularly housing. Wage controls were strictly applied and forced saving introduced.

Table 5 *German wage statistics 1928–38*

	Real wages (1913/14=100)	Money wages (1913/14=100)	Real earnings (1925/9=100)	Wages (as % of national income)	Consumption
1928	110	168	106	62	71
1930	122	180	114	–	–
1931	125	171	106	–	–
1932	120	144	91	64	83
1933	119	140	87	63	81
1934	116	140	88	62	76
1935	114	140	91	61	71
1936	112	140	93	59	64
1937	112	140	96	58	62
1938	112	141	101	57	59

Source: G. Bry, *Wages in Germany 1871–1945*, Princeton University Press, 1960, p. 331, 362.

These changes went hand in hand with stricter controls over the labour market, for which Goering had also assumed responsibility. As the last labour reserves were used up in 1938 he introduced strict systems of priority in the allocation of labour and set in motion re-training schemes involving large numbers of workers who were needed for skilled rearmament work.[45] At this stage Goering still favoured using more female labour to bridge the growing gap in labour resources. On mobilisation it was planned to draft an additional 3.5 million women workers into the economy and to take 2 million more out of the consumer industries. Goering instructed the chief of the *Ordnungspolizei*, Kurt Daluege, to set up a national register to make sure that all workers in jobs not essential for the war effort would be classified. With this information it was hoped that workers could be moved quickly to war-essential sectors as and when required.[46] This applied particularly to female workers who were to be introduced rapidly into the war economy on the outbreak of war to release men for the front.[47] Women came to play a very important part in the German war economy, providing 51 per cent of the native civilian labour-force by 1944.

In response to the labour shortages, certain consumer industries, notably textiles, were forced to move to short-time work. This was in line with Goering's stated objective to reduce what he called 'inessential industries' and to divert their resources to military preparations.[48] Goering hoped that the changeover to military production and the accompanying austerity would prepare the German people 'spiritually for total war'.[49] 'The Labour Front', he remarked sarcastically, 'should make more Strength and less Joy.'[50]

The creation of the 'greater economic region' and the re-shaping of the domestic economy all pointed towards a large war planned at some stage in the mid-1940s. German rearmament plans were moving in a similar direction, designed to reach enormous proportions by the middle years of the 1940s. Even by 1939 the scale of rearmament was substantial. In that year German military expenditure reached some 23 per cent of GNP, much higher than that of any other power.[51] According to General Thomas, the German economy was by May 1939 approaching the levels of output achieved towards the end of the First World War.[52] Far from avoiding the total economic commitment of the earlier conflict, the German economy was poised to exceed it. To call this 'limited' rearmament, as some historians have done, is thus historically misleading. Goering had no illusions about what was needed. In 1938 he called for the economy 'to be completely converted' for war. Hitler's remarks on the economy betray a similar intention.[53]

This total commitment to war economy was made necessary by the very scale of the rearmament plans themselves. In the aftermath of the Munich conference Goering announced to his staff Hitler's decision to increase armament production through a 'gigantic programme compared with which previous achievements are insignificant'.[54] Hitler wanted him to raise 'the level of armament from 100 to 300'.[55] This was particularly vital for the air force for which Hitler now demanded 'a colossal quantity of aircraft' and a quintupling of front-line air strength.[56] Army requirements, too, threatened to become 'a bottomless pit'. To the navy Hitler promised a huge building programme, the so-called 'Z-Plan', that would once again provide Germany with a large battle fleet and numerous submarines.[57]

The naval expansion indicated that Hitler was now thinking beyond the establishment of an eastern empire to embrace the possibility of war with the major naval powers, Britain and the United States. So important was the programme that early in 1939 he gave it priority over all other rearmament plans and even over exports.[58] But like the raw material base, the naval programme was not due to be completed until 1944–6. The time-table for aircraft production was the same. Moreover here too the plans went considerably beyond *Blitzkrieg*. Hitler ordered not only a battlefield air force but a strategic air force to defeat the major powers through bombing.[59] Goering followed this requirement in the technical and military development of the air force. From the outset Goering planned to incorporate a strategic bomber into German air force equipment. The original models selected rapidly proved to be obsolescent and in 1936 were cancelled. But this was not, as has often been argued since, the end of the German heavy bomber. The following year orders went out for the He-177 heavy bomber which was designed to fulfil air force requirements in the mid-1940s. In the interim the air force was to rely on the Junkers Ju 88 medium bomber.[60] Milch calculated that this programme alone would cost over 500 million marks, more money than Germany had spent on the whole aircraft industry in 1937 and 1938.[61] Goering's object was to build up by 1944 a force of 2,000 heavy bombers, suitable for war against Russia, Britain and even the United States, to be supplemented by a medium-bomber force of 5,000 aircraft. This fitted in with the general pace of air force preparations, which were due to be completed in 1942 for a large war to be fought some years later.[62]

Plans for the army were just as great, and followed the same time-table. Motorisation of the army began slowly during the 1930s. Even by 1939 there were only six motorised or partly motorised divisions and the motor industry was still concentrated much more on the civilian market.[63] The plan was to expand this core to over 20 divisions so that by the mid-1940s the German army would be much more mobile and less dependent on rail and horse.[64] To cope with any remaining transport requirements, Goering authorised the overhauling and modernisation of the German railways, the programme to be completed by 1944.[65] The largest programme of production, however was the explosives programme. This was begun under the Four Year Plan in 1936. In 1938, under the direction of Carl Krauch of I.G. Farben, the initial programme was expanded enormously to reach in peacetime the achievements of the Hindenburg Programme of the First World War.[66] The new plans, published in June and August 1938, called for the level of production shown in Table 6. The scale of these programmes required a 40 per cent increase in the output of heavy machinery, and 120,000 additional tons of steel per quarter. It was hoped that such a capacity could be created by 1942.[67]

Table 6 *German explosives production plans, 1938 (tons per month)*

	Carinhall Plan 30.6.1938	Schnellplan 13.8.1938
High explosive	17,100	18,600
Explosive filler	14,400	15,400
Gunpowder	18,100	18,100
Chemical warfare	9,300	9,300
Total	58,900	61,400

Source: Case XI, Prosecution Doc. Book 118A, doc.NI–7835.

In the light of all these programmes the conclusion is inescapable that the Nazi leadership sought to expand war preparations and production on a vast scale for a major conflict with some or all of the great powers in the mid-1940s. This is, of course, exactly what Hitler had said at the 'Hossbach' conference in November 1937.[68] It was also the time-table that Goering had revealed to the Italians throughout 1938 and 1939.[69] And it was also the impression that the armed forces in Germany were given from Hitler's specific instructions on training and expansion, and from what they could see of German war preparations all around them.[70] General Thomas, who had been so unwilling to concede the army's role in rearmament to Goering in 1937, was satisfied by 1939 that the Nazis had produced a programme for total war, uncompleted but nevertheless broad enough in scope.[71] The work of the army armament offices now complemented that of the Four Year Plan, helping to realise Hitler's call in May 1939 for an economy capable of sustaining a war of ten or fifteen years' duration'.[72]

A factor that linked all these many projects together was the need for time. Neither Hitler nor Goering took the Four Year Plan literally. The programmes set up in 1938 and 1939 could not from their very nature be completed by 1940, in the lifetime of the second Plan. In October 1940 Hitler extended Goering's economic responsibility by announcing a Third Four Year Plan, and there is every reason to suppose that he would have done so whether war had broken out or not.[73] Goering was all too conscious of this question of time. 'I am aware that many things are not ready,' he confided to the aircraft producers in the middle of 1938, 'I am aware of the many obstacles in our way, and I greatly regret that I am unable to do everything as quickly as I would like. It is a bad thing if a man has to confess, once the battle has started – "damm it, I should have done this before.".'[74] It is easy to see from the timescale of the rearmament programmes the root of Goering's anxiety. The first year and a half of the Four Year Plan had been taken up with arguments about jurisdiction and the political struggle with the conservatives. The main structure of the heavy industrial expansion was only started in 1938 and the large military plans for the navy and air force were only worked out in detail in the winter of 1938–9. By the middle of 1939 the projects were all in the early stages of construction. It was because of this that Goering advised against risking a general war over Czechoslovakia or Poland. Germany needed five more years before her military forces and economic system would be ready.[75]

There were a number of serious obstacles in the way of speeding up rearmament. Germany was compelled to rebuild the whole infra-structure of military life again in full after the period of disarmament under the Versailles Treaty. The 'secret rearmament' before 1935 went some way towards re-militarising Germany but not very far. The real work of training, building military installations, laying out airfields and constructing fortifications took place after 1935 and was still incomplete by the end of 1939.[76] Secondly rearmament was expensive. It was difficult for the Reich, because of the heavy commitment already made to military expenditure, to find the huge additional sums required by the Four Year Plan and the new rearmament programmes. Goering, for his part, refused to see this as a problem. He was happy to expand the money supply and, if need be, to increase the national debt to meet these financial needs. He told the first meeting of the Reich Defence Council in November 1938: 'I have nothing against it, if the internal debt increases. In the final analysis it is only an internal debt, one which the Germans themselves have given and from which they themselves again obtain enormous advantages.' He allayed orthodox financial fears by adding the rider that 'savings must be made where they can be made', through the running down of inessential projects not related to the war effort.[77] He also argued that the large rearmament programmes would bring with them economies of scale. The more military goods produced, the cheaper each one would be. Neither the Finance Minister, nor Schacht as President of the Reichsbank, was satisfied with this explanation. Schwerin von Krosigk pointed out to Goering that the expenditures planned by the armed forces if a war should break out in 1939 exceeded the entire German national income.[78] The army too became increasingly anxious about the inflationary threat from high party and military expenditure and lent its weight to the efforts to reduce the military budget for 1939. Schacht's continued opposition to extending funds for rearmament became so critical that in February 1939 he was removed from the Reichsbank as well, to be replaced once again by the more compliant Funk. In the end Goering was compelled to accept some reductions in expenditure: not enough to satisfy the conservatives, but enough to slow down the implementation of the more ambitious military programmes.[79]

A more serious constraint was the slow way in which the civilian economy accepted the transition to military production. It was difficult to divert

sufficient resources of labour and raw materials to military projects once
they had been earmarked for civilian use. This problem was exacerbated
for Goering by the inconsistent and contradictory policies pursued by other
elements in the party and the economy. Ley, for example, refused to accept
that the Volkswagen plant was a contribution to war preparations, insisting
that Hitler had detailed it as a peacetime project even to the point of
refusing to build air-raid shelters on the site.[80] Fritz Todt, while engaged
in building Germany's western fortifications, was at the same time constructing a new road network that served very little military purpose because
there were too few lorries to use it.[81] All Goering's efforts to halt inessential
construction were thwarted by party leaders who clung on to prestigious
schemes against his instructions.

The same problem existed with industry. Not only was there much
opposition to state intervention to contend with, but the additional problem
that many industrialists, together with others in the military and ministerial
elite, refused to believe that there was a serious prospect of major war in
the near future. In 1938 and 1939 their priority was to expand export
markets and increase domestic consumption. Serious preparation for war
was often carried out only when Goering's officials directly insisted. The
more indirect controls, via the labour market and capital market took time
to mature or were ignored altogether.[82] In the absence of any national plan
for labour mobilisation, war-essential firms found themselves in competition
for labour resources with civilian producers, who colluded among themselves and with sympathetic officials to frustrate Nazi economic strategy.

Nor did labour respond to the increasing effort to rearm with any
enthusiasm. Increasing absenteeism, indiscipline and camouflaged strikes
reflected the basic hostility of much of the workforce to the Nazi system.
Because of full employment some workers were able to bargain for higher
wages, and to move to more lucrative jobs against the government's express
instructions. This complicated labour planning still more and worsened
relations between Goering's officials and the businesses suspected of
poaching labour. But for most workers there were few advantages from the
system. Low wages, a lack of any effective bargaining machinery, rising
taxes and party 'contributions' created an attitude of resignation and unco-
operativeness that affected the overall productive performance of German
industry.[83]

Against the background of sluggish and expensive transition to a war-
based economy Hitler determined to resolve the Polish question. The
settlement of the Polish problem, the return of Danzig and Prussian Poland
to the Reich, was the final step in the creation of the greater economic
region, the military and economic springboard for the great wars to west
and east. As we have seen, Goering had already argued in 1937 that this
was the logical course of events. Now, faced with a satisfactory end to the
Czech dispute, he began to pursue new ambitions against the Poles. To
outward appearances he seemed conciliatory. In March he told the Polish

ambassador that both he and Hitler would always safeguard Polish-German relations; the Danzig question could be resolved by co-operation.[84] But Ciano, writing in April, was disturbed by 'the tone in which [Goering] described relations with Poland: it reminds me peculiarly of the same tone used at other times for Austria and Czechoslovakia.'[85] Ciano's instinct was correct. During March and April the Nazi leaders arrived at the decision to eliminate Poland by force if necessary, by coercion if possible. 'I remember', Goering later recalled at Nuremberg, 'that in the late spring of 1939, the Fuehrer announced to me, unexpectedly, during a walk in front of his study, that he intended to solve the question of the Polish corridor within the year of 1939.' The corridor, however, was a mere pretext. Hitler explained this to his generals in May 1939: 'Danzig is not the subject of the dispute at all. It is a question of expanding our living-space in the East and of securing our food supplies.'[86] Hitler favoured limited military action against the Poles. Goering preferred economic pressure and the threat of force, which had worked so well against the Czechs, but he was not opposed to the use of force if necessary.[87] Although Hitler laid down plans in April 1939 to attack Poland in the near future, all options were kept open. The important point for Hitler, as for other Nazi leaders, was to eliminate Poland without a general European war.

There were plenty of reasons why the Nazi leadership neither wanted nor expected a general European war in 1939. Even Ribbentrop, whom Goering thought ran unacceptable risks in foreign policy, argued that Germany needed three or four more years of peace.[88] The first problem was that the large-scale economic build-up, to which Polish resources were to contribute, was far from complete. Goering knew this, as did Hitler. Although German armaments had increased substantially between 1937 and 1939, Goering doubted whether they were sufficient as yet to take on the major European powers. The one consolation came from German intelligence reports which suggested that British and French rearmament was facing even greater difficulties. This encouraged greater risk-taking in 1939 on the German side. Hitler gambled on acquiring large parts of Poland by a swift *coup de main* without a major war, so that the economy would be given sufficient time to complete the programmes of the Four Year Plan.[89]

Some historians have argued that the political costs of this rearmament programme were too great by 1939; that Hitler launched a European war in order to avoid a domestic crisis brought about by deteriorating economic conditions.[90] There is little evidence to support this case. Economic conditions were expected to deteriorate while the large-scale war preparations were carried through. Economic pressure was all for postponing general war in 1939, not for speeding it up. Moreover there was little sign of domestic political opposition in 1939, except among the German upper classes, and they were as anxious as Goering to avoid any major international confrontation. The repressive state apparatus was sufficient to ensure political stability at home.

Moreover, Hitler was determined to create diplomatic conditions in 1939 to ensure that the conflict with Poland would remain localised. Under the growing influence of Ribbentrop, Hitler argued that the failure of the western powers to take action in September 1938, or in March 1939, or against the Soviet action over Bessarabia demonstrated the pusillanimous nature of western leadership. In the event of German moves for a violent settlement with Poland, Hitler believed that Britain and France would do nothing beyond some token of disapproval. Indeed he hoped that his action would produce internal government crisis in the democracies, whose political structure he regarded as more fragile than his own.[91] His arguments for war against Poland only made sense from this perspective. At a meeting in May 1939 he said that: 'Our task is to isolate Poland. There must be no simultaneous conflict with the Western powers.'[92] At the meeting called on 22 August, shortly before the planned invasion of Poland, he agreed that 'war between Poland and Germany will remain localised . . . England and France will make threats, but will not declare war. . . .'[93] Throughout the summer Hitler gave no hint of urgency in military preparations of a general kind. Major war was expected later rather than sooner, and was not to be brought about by the Polish crisis.[94] This conviction provides a central explanation for the decision to attack Poland.

To make the localisation of the Polish conflict more certain Nazi leaders sought during 1939 to reach an agreement either with the Soviet Union or with Britain, to avoid diplomatic presssure on two fronts. An agreement with either power would avoid a repetition of the dangerous risks that had been run during the Munich crisis. 'One must bear in mind', Goering told the Polish ambassador late in August, 'that Germany had to choose between Great Britain and Russia.'[95] From late 1938 onwards the German Foreign Office under Ribbentrop's close supervision had made efforts to reach a rapprochement between Russia and Germany, an initiative welcomed by many army officers and businessmen. Initial contact was based on economic co-operation, building on Goering's efforts since 1936 to reach a trade agreement between the two countries. During the summer of 1939 co-operation broadened out into military and strategic questions.[96] Once it was clear to Stalin that he was being offered substantial concessions over Poland he agreed to a German-Soviet non-aggression pact, which was signed by the triumphant Ribbentrop on 23 August. The pact convinced Hitler, and Goering too (whose main fear in 1938 was of Russian intervention) that the miscalculation of the July Crisis of 1914 had this time been avoided; that the neutralisation of the east would guarantee the non-intervention of the west.[97]

To Goering fell the second task of detaching Britain from France by the promise of economic co-operation and declarations respecting the integrity of the British Empire. Goering was assigned the task informally by Hitler, largely because of his many British contacts and his unmerited reputation as a friend to British interests. He conducted his negotiations side-by-side with, and sometimes in conflict with, the Foreign Ministry, which was pursuing the same aim.[98] Goering's main tactic was to lull the British into a false sense of security by the apparent willingness of the Germans to discuss the Polish question and the conciliatory nature of German demands. Germany's true intentions were deliberately camouflaged right up to the last moment. Only a few days before Poland was invaded Goering sent out invitations to both the British and Polish ambassadors in Berlin, asking them to select a date in the autumn when they would like to accompany him stag-hunting.[99] Goering hoped that Britain could be bought off with economic concessions as she had been in 1938. Close contacts were established between Goering's representatives from the Four Year Plan and British businessmen and politicians. Discussions on industrial and trading co-operation and economic spheres of influence, in which the British showed much interest, persuaded Goering that they might indeed have their price.[100]

His secret intelligence on relations between the British and Polish governments lent weight to this expectation. Until the very declaration of war he hoped, like Hitler, that the British could be used to put pressure on the Poles to abandon the struggle as they had pressured the Czechs in 1938.[101] It would be wrong to see Goering in this as a man of peace, offering, as some historians have maintained, an alternative foreign policy to that of Hitler and the Foreign Office. It was certainly true that he wanted the conflict localised and the risk of a general war eliminated, as, of course, did Hitler. But he was not prepared to make any serious concessions on the question of Danzig and the Polish 'corridor', a position always unacceptable to the western powers. The one theme that runs through Goering's efforts to detach Britain from her commitments was his belief that the British were being unreasonable in their reaction over Poland and that German claims, one way or another, had got to be fulfilled. Early in September a German foreign office official noted that Goering's real intention 'was to destroy and exterminate the Polish people'.[102] The British negotiators, or the industrialists who visited Goering on 7 August through the offices of his Swedish friend Dahlerus, were mistaken in their view of Goering as a man of peace and good sense. His reasonableness was a pose, designed to pretend to the British that the Polish question was less urgent than they supposed, and that German demands were both modest and justifiable.[103]

Goering's relations with the British were also governed by personal motives. He was increasingly jealous of Ribbentrop's influence with Hitler during 1938 and 1939. Ribbentrop took the credit for the German-Italian Pact in May despite Goering's objection that 'he was the true and only promoter of the Alliance'.[104] Goering was determined that Ribbentrop should not forestall him again. If he successfully detached Britain from France he would once again secure a predominant position with Hitler. He deliberately kept his negotiations secret from the Foreign Office, despite

Ribbentrop's objections, and made no effort to reconcile his approaches to
the British with those conducted through formal channels, a fact that made
the British government deeply suspicious of Goering's motives. This
personal ambition explains Goering's flurry of diplomatic activity in the two
weeks before the outbreak of war. Ribbentrop had been successful with the
Russians. Goering thought right up to the last moment that he might be
successful with the British.[105]

As the crisis moved to a climax ambition was tempered by a growing
anxiety. The *Forschungsamt* provided him with conflicting intelligence, but
there was certainly evidence of growing British intransigence.[106] Hitler also
became more cautious. When the British, against German expectations,
confirmed the guarantee of military assistance to Poland Hitler temporarily
postponed action against the Poles. He telephoned Goering with the
message that he would 'have to see whether we can eliminate British
intervention'.[107] Goering resurrected arguments like those he used before
Munich. If the British would concede Danzig and the corridor, Germany
should take those first and then through economic pressure and the threat
of force acquire control over the rest in due course.[108] Ribbentrop and the
other party radicals argued against this compromise, demanding that Hitler
take the risk of invading Poland. The German-Soviet Pact seemed to confirm
the wisdom of this course. It relieved Hitler of the fear of a general war,
and appeared to place the Poles beyond hope of direct intervention on their
behalf by the west.

Goering shared this sense of relief, hoping that the British would now
see sense. He nevertheless remained less sanguine than Hitler. 'This time',
he warned, 'you cannot play *va banque*.'[109] He redoubled his efforts to get
the British to accept the reality of events and the justness of Germany's
cause. The British Ambassador, Henderson, was among those persuaded
by Goering's guileful moderation that Britain should keep the peace. The
British government itself was almost convinced of Goering's good faith,
enough at least to put more pressure on Warsaw to make concessions on
Danzig and the German minority.[110] If German soldiers had not actually
crossed the Polish frontier Goering's tactics might perhaps have worked
and Poland have been brought effectively under German hegemony without
war. Certainly Goering could not see why the British wanted any longer to
fight for Poland. Hitler, relying on intuition, was convinced they would not.
He was sure that he had judged Allied leaders correctly, that they lacked
the moral courage for acts of international heroism. To the end he remained
convinced that he could isolate the Polish war and, when he had won it,
come to terms with the western powers from a position of strength.[111] To
his consternation Britain and France declared war upon his refusal to
withdraw troops from Poland. On hearing the news of the British declaration
Goering is alleged to have telephoned Ribbentrop and shouted into the
receiver: 'Now you have your damned war!'[112]

The military conquest of Poland, as Hitler had hoped, was rapidly completed. Goering seized the opportunity provided by the final defence of Warsaw to show Hitler how decisive a weapon the Luftwaffe could be. Hitler showed an exaggerated pleasure at the performance of the air force, a fact that Goering was later to exploit when his political stock was much lower. The air campaign was recorded in a full-length propaganda film, *Baptism of Fire*, which was shown to neutral diplomats *pour encourager les autres*. The real war for Goering lay in the west. With the defeat of Poland he resumed, with Hitler's blessing, the efforts which had foundered in the last days of August to reach agreement with Britain. It must be remembered that this was Hitler's object too. He had argued both before and after the Polish campaign that it would be 'a simple matter after Poland had been defeated, to come to terms with England'.[113] Goering acted as Hitler's go-between with the British, not on his own initiative. Using his Scandinavian contacts, among others, Goering conveyed to the British Germany's willing-ness to reach an accommodation. Dahlerus was used to transmit Goering's assurances that Germany only wanted to keep Danzig, Silesia and the Corridor, and hints of a German undertaking to disarm. The Vice-President of General Motors, William Mooney, brought the same conciliatory messages back to Washington. There was even widespread speculation in the West that Goering, if given encouragement by the Allies, would overturn Hitler's government and end the war.

It was certainly true that Goering, and Hitler too, would have welcomed a British diplomatic capitulation, particularly as Italy, to Goering's deep annoyance, had failed to come in on Germany's side.[115] Poland was defeated and her territory divided. The Allies would be humiliatingly excluded from the affairs of eastern Europe, while Germany would have four or five more years of military preparation. Goering was still hoping to outbid Ribbentrop in foreign affairs. Forcing a compromise peace on Britain would have improved his chances of doing so. He was also flattered by his impact on American opinion. Rumours circulated from Washington that the United States might propose a peace conference at which Goering would be welcome as head of a German delegation rather than Ribbentrop.[116] There was, however, no division between Goering and Hitler for the Allies to exploit. Goering worked to isolate the British and weaken their resolve as a political tactic approved by Hitler. Goering only wanted agreement from the British on Germany's terms, as he always had. The main condition for any negotiation was that Britain should grant Germany 'a completely free hand with regard to Poland'. Germany should also be allowed to resolve the Jewish question as she saw fit, and be granted economic hegemony in the Balkans.[117] While the British did not reject German advances out of hand, such conditions were unacceptable as a starting point for negotiation. Even Dahlerus finally realised that he had been duped by Goering, 'that his aim had been . . . to have the opportunity of occupying Poland without running the risk of being involved in a war with Britain and France'.[118]

Goering made his final efforts to detach Britain in October, accepting

Dahlerus's stillborn proposal that he meet with the British General Ironside 'as soldier to soldier' to initiate discussions on a settlement; and sending Dahlerus back and forth to London to see what terms were available.[119] By this time Hitler had tired of the effort, since the British government showed no willingness to reach an agreement on the terms that he and Goering had suggested. He was angry and surprised by the British reaction, but he could no longer appear to be too conciliatory to the west for fear of its effects on Russia, whose continued neutrality was essential. To safeguard this new alliance both Goering and Hitler had made it clear to the west that the future of Poland was a German-Soviet affair, not simply a German one.[120] Goering was allowed to persist not from any real expectation that British resistance would finally give way but because it gave the impression that Germany was genuinely seeking peace while the Allies were determined on war. This was useful propaganda with the United States, whose special emissary, William Davis, visited Goering in October 1939 and found him apparently moderate in his ideas and convinced of the need for peace.[121] This was the argument that Goering was still using six months later when he talked to the American Under-Secretary of State, Sumner Welles. 'The situation', he told Welles, 'was clear. Germany desired peace . . . whether there had to be any fighting did not depend upon Germany, but upon her opponents. . . . But before God and the world he could state that Germany had not desired the war.'[122]

No doubt Goering was disappointed with his failure to eliminate Britain from the war and improve his own political stock at the same time. But he knew when to stop once Hitler had lost interest in securing peace. He blamed Ribbentrop for sabotaging his efforts for peace by his uncompromising demands, believing that his tactics of 'moderation' might have averted further conflict.[123] But he could not have been surprised by the outcome since the peace offers that he made were in reality so one-sided. It was not Ribbentrop who undermined Goering's strategy, but his own refusal to entertain for a moment abandoning any of the territory occupied by Germany since March 1939. There was nothing in principle more attractive to the British about Goering's offers than about those of Hitler or Ribbentrop. The British rightly assumed that Goering was acting in bad faith. Indeed while Goering was talking peace he was simultaneously ordering the reconstruction of the Polish economy in Germany's favour, movements of Polish population, and a high level of military expansion at home with the additional help of resources seized in Poland. He was now much more confident of victory in the west after the successful campaign against the Poles. 'We shall be victorious,' Goering told the Swede Sven Hedin, 'and then Germany will be the greatest and strongest power in the world.'[124] In November he brought to an end the efforts of Dahlerus in London.[125] While always keeping open the possibility that Britain would shy away from the conflict, he set about the transformation of the German economy for total war, while Hitler prepared a military campaign to punish the Allies for declaring war too soon.

Nor did Goering have any realistic alternative but to press on with preparations for total war. German strategy had been based on the assumption of total economic mobilisation in any war with the major powers; it did not make sense to abandon this assumption, even though the war had come earlier than expected. On 9 September Goering announced that: 'the complete employment of the living and fighting power of the nation [must] be secured economically as well as otherwise for the duration of the war.'[126] Goering's leading officials in the Four Year Plan and the leaders of the army economics staff were at one with Goering on this. Meeting in November 1939 they together resolved that: 'All enterprises which cannot be furnished with work essential for the war are to be shut down.'[127] Hitler, contemplating the prospect of a 'Seven years war, or one even longer', told Goering that he wanted 'the complete conversion of the economy to wartime requirements' for a period of at least five years.[128] In November and December he reviewed the armaments position and ordered a very large increase in weapons output, 'a programme of the highest possible quantities'.[129] The explosives plan was increased under Hitler's orders to the levels originally intended for a war in the mid-1940s; from an annual total of 600,000 tons to over 1 million tons.[130] All the detailed plans for weapons and munitions were increased in the last months of 1939 by 200 to 250 per cent.[131]

The result of these efforts was a sharp and sustained increase in military expenditure. During the first two years expenditure expanded faster than at any other time during the war. The rate of increase is set out in Table 7. Both state and military expenditure expanded continuously over the period, to cope with not only the military side of the war, but to continue financing the build-up of the war economy initiated by Goering in 1938

Table 7 *Military expenditure, state expenditure and national income in Germany 1938–44 (billion RM)*

	Military expenditure	State expenditure	National income
1938/9	17.2	39.4	98
1939/40	38.0	58	109
1940/1	55.9	80	120
1941/2	72.3	100.5	125
1942/3	86.2	124*	134
1943/4	99.4	130*	130

*Figures based on revenue from occupied Europe and Germany together.
Source: W. Boelcke, 'Kriegsfinanzierung im internationalen Vergleich', in F. Forstmeier, H.–E. Volkmann (eds), *Kriegswirtschaft und Rüstung im Zweiten Weltkrieg* (Düsseldorf, 1977), pp. 55–6.

and 1939.[132] It is important to underline the significance of these figures because they demonstrate that the German economy was geared from an early stage of the war to large-scale mobilisation of economic resources.

This degree of commitment to war was made clear by the reduction of civilian expenditure after 1939. It was obvious to those in control of the German economy that something would have to be done soon after the outbreak of war to reduce civilian purchasing power. Schwerin von Krosigk had already indicated as much to Goering in May 1939. The latter author-ised the necessary cuts in living standards in September 1939.[133] The only argument was about how this reduction should be made. Ley, who provided the Finance Ministry with detailed information about consumer spending in 1938 and 1939, favoured a system of special taxes that would cut down expenditure on durables and inessential products and would have the effect of removing 10 billion marks of purchasing power.[134] The Finance Ministry and the Economics Ministry favoured an increase in income tax and forced saving.[135] The Four Year Plan leaders favoured a combination of these policies but were particularly attracted to the idea of forced saving because this did not lead to an immediate threat of inflation and could be geared by the government to match the reductions in the consumer industries already planned.[136] In the end taxes were increased on personal incomes and a limited sales tax on luxuries introduced. Tax revenue increased from these sources from 14.4 billion marks in 1938–9 to 29.5 billion marks in 1941–2, the highest increase coming between 1939 and March 1941. The internal debt funded by public loans increased from 10.6 billion marks in 1938–9 to 41.5 billion in 1941–2 to soak up what purchasing power had not been removed by taxation.[137]

The financial and industrial policies produced the desired effect on consumption. Early in 1941 state secretary Neumann of the Four Year Plan was able to announce that: 'all articles of daily use but also practically all other goods have become increasingly scarce in recent years – even prior to the outbreak of war . . . a higher standard of living is the ultimate goal, not the immediate object of the Four Year Plan. . . . The fact that consumer interests had to be put second is regrettable but cannot be helped.'[138] German living standards had been comparatively and relatively low before 1939, showing almost no increase between 1928 and 1938, even though national income had increased by 41 per cent. From the outbreak of war onwards standards continued to decline and private civilian consumption to be cut back severely. The extra capacity needed for war work was to be found on Hitler and Goering's express instructions 'in the idle factories'. Goering ordered resources to be diverted away from 'the vital industries which are of importance to the life of the people'.[139] So wide-ranging was the conversion to war needs that the Four Year Plan office calculated that the proportion of the workforce engaged on the economic war effort had in-creased from 20 per cent in 1939 to 60 per cent by the beginning of 1941.[140]

The first areas to feel the cut-backs were the consumer durables, cars, furniture and clothing. Car production declined from a peak of 276,592 in 1938 to a mere 67,561 in 1940 and 35,195 in 1941. Of these totals the armed forces took 42 per cent in 1940 and 77 per cent the following year. The civilian population was left in 1941 with only 2.9 per cent of the number that had been produced in the last full year of peace.[141] The other major sector affected was the building industry. The number of housing units completed fell from 303,000 in 1938 to 80,000 in 1941, with many of the latter also designated for military use.[142] There were corresponding reductions in the output of other consumer goods and services accompanied by a system of rationing that had started even before the outbreak of war.[143] Very large proportions of the surviving consumer production, as well as much of the additional food, went direct to the armed forces. By 1943 most consumer goods produced in the civilian economy were in fact divided between the military and the general public in roughly equal portions.[144] So high were military requirements for consumer goods and food, due in large part to the strict standards of dress and supplies maintained by the military authorities, that much less was available for the ordinary German consumer than might have been possible under even the strictest economic regime. Some of this loss was made up by exploiting stocks found in occupied Europe, but this was only a temporary alleviation and much was diverted corruptly to party officials or stayed in the hands of the occupying forces. Hitler was careful to keep a propaganda eye on levels of consumption, exploring the possibility of reducing military expenditure in the wake of the defeat of France. But such a reduction was never seriously contemplated. Military expenditure continued to rise throughout 1940 and 1941 and civilian consumption to decline.

The peak of *per capita* civilian consumption under the Nazis was reached in 1938. By 1941 it had fallen 22 per cent. The output of producer goods expanded over the same period by 28 per cent, reflecting the diversion of resources to heavy war industries.[145] Throughout 1940 the monthly reports of the Four Year Plan office on the current economic situation stressed the lack of essential supplies for the civilian population – shortages of work clothes and shoes, all kitchen and household articles, food and transport facilities.[146] In 1941 it was reported that even Germans made homeless through British bombing could no longer be supplied with new goods to replace what they had lost.[147] Goering was faced with producers and a public keen to reverse the trend of declining consumption, but even in the summer of 1940, when there developed a popular belief that the war was virtually over, Goering insisted that 'the restarting of consumer industry' could not be considered.[148]

What the German leaders wanted to avoid was another 'Turnip Winter' like the one Germany had experienced at the height of the blockade in 1917–18. To do this meant giving the population a sufficient amount of food and enough goods on which to survive. It did not mean keeping up high levels of consumption but the opposite, the establishment of a bare minimum below which conditions should not be allowed to deteriorate. Even this minimum was difficult to maintain. As early as October 1939 medical authorities reported to Goering that planned food rations for the German population were insufficient for adults and quite unsatisfactory for children.[149]

The general contours of economic and military policy – the increase in military expenditure and the financial policies to restrict consumption – disguised considerable confusion in the actual programme of mobilisation. The chief cause of this confusion was the fact that the German economy was caught half-way through preparations for a longer war. Much of the labour and many of the resources were committed to the building up of the raw material and machinery base for war and had to be hurriedly transferred where possible to the production of finished weapons. Some civilian industries were not yet incorporated into war planning. Thomas's organisation of firms for mobilisation was still only 60 per cent completed when war broke out. The ineffectual Funk had barely begun his work on the industrial conversion plan.[150] Firms did not know what they were supposed to be producing and for whom. Many, in the expectation that the war would only be a short one, kept their labour and refused to release it for the munitions factories. Even firms with special war-economic status faced problems of dislocation caused by the poaching of skilled labour by other armaments firms and by conscription. The army ignored many of the regulations and conscripted large numbers of skilled and unskilled workers indiscriminately, even from war-essential occupations.[151]

Goering and his staff shared in this confusion. It was difficult to change economic strategy in mid-course, yet they were now being asked to produce the finished weapons before the completion of the Four Year Plan programmes. Without the explosives, steel, fuel oil and aluminium it was impossible to produce the large number of weapons planned. Without the labour and resources devoted to weapons production it was difficult to complete the build-up of the basic industries. The contradictions in this situation were clear. Voegler and Poensgen took the opportunity to point out to Thomas the folly of continuing to build up the steel capacity of the Reichswerke, because it would take more steel to build its blast-furnaces than it could actually produce before 1943.[152] Yet when Goering was pressed to call a halt to the building programme he argued that 'the construction of the Reichswerke Hermann Goering in Salzgitter lies in the urgent interest of defence. The completion of its construction according to the schedule must be guaranteed.'[153] Fritz Todt, under pressure from all sides to provide essential building materials and labour, was forced to ration his resources at the expense not of the raw material factories, which were backed by the full authority of the Four Year Plan, but of finished armaments, which were not.[154] Confusion was made worse by the fact that central policies for economic mobilisation were often not communicated properly. Some four weeks after the outbreak of war it was discovered that through an administrative oversight many firms had not even been notified of an official mobilisation order so that arrangements for war conversion could not be formally implemented.[155]

The experience of the German motor industry during the period of mobilisation was typical. There was in fact no general mobilisation plan. One was published in January 1940 leaving a large part of the motor industry's capacity unused.[156] The M.A.N. truck firm was left out altogether and was only included after indignant representations from its owners.[157] The largest car manufacturer, Opel, was given no war orders at all at the outset, a consequence of Thomas's own hostility to the business. The original cause of the conflict was Opel's decision to close down a small army supplier on the mobilisation list in 1936, but it grew wider with the lead Opel took in resisting Hitler's plan for the Volkswagen.[158] In September 1939 it was Thomas's wish that the workers and machines from the Opel factories – the largest and most modern in Germany – would be dispersed among other producers who did have war orders and Opel closed down. Opel was threatened with nationalisation if it did not comply.[159] Civilian car production ceased almost immediately and for two months Opel was compelled to pay its workforce for doing nothing. Eventually the Four Year Plan over-ruled Thomas, but not until February 1940 did the works begin on war orders.[160]

The story of the Volkswagen works was equally bizarre. Ley only agreed with great reluctance to Goering's request that part of the works should be used for air force contracts if war broke out because Volkswagen was classified as a peacetime project. In September 1939 Ley hesitated to hand over control of the factories. When Goering insisted it was found that the buildings were not yet suitable for large-scale production, that the machinery was only partly installed and the workforce scattered. Moreover when Speer was asked to provide the necessary resources to complete the construction it was discovered that the works had not even been put on the list of war-essential projects entitled to a quota of steel and building materials, so that nothing could be supplied to complete it.[161] Had war broken out in the mid-1940s not only would the mobilisation preparations and rationalisation of the motor industry have been completed, but the Volkswagen works, the largest conveyor-belt factory in Europe, would also have been available. As it was the confusion produced by a sudden mobilisation in 1939 aroused, in General Thomas's well-publicised remark, 'ein Kampf aller gegen alle' – a war of all against all.[162]

For Goering the early months of war were taken up with organising not just armaments production, but all the major aspects of economic life, including finance, trade, agriculture and labour. Some of the work was carried on by the ministerial departments responsible, but most of the major decisions were referred to Goering. As a result he found himself faced with a constant round of conferences and discussions in which he had to listen to the complaints and problems of the various ministries. Financial questions were resolved with the increases in taxation and new government loans. Agriculture and labour were to some extent bound together since one of the main problems facing German farming was a shortage of labour following widespread conscription not only for the armed forces, but also for essential industrial projects. Temporary shortages were covered by drafting in compulsory labour from Czechoslovakia and Poland, but the system for allocating domestic German labour, worked out before the war, proved difficult to enforce.[163] At the end of September 1939 Goering published a decree on skilled labour shortages in which he announced that failure to release labour for war work or inflated demands for labour would both be treated as acts of sabotage. But some months later Koerner was still reporting that labour mobility showed little sign of improvement.[164] Orders for the conversion of industry to war, and the movement of labour to war-essential occupations, published in a further decree on the 'Transition from Peace to War Economy' in November 1939, filtered only slowly through the industrial structure because Goering still lacked a satisfactory apparatus to see that such orders were properly enforced.[165]

In this lay the source of Goering's difficulties in organising the war economy. Goering wanted central control over the whole war economy to lie with him, but he lacked a central administration and a national network of officials capable of executing economic policy at a local level.[166] As commissioner for the Four Year Plan and *de facto* head of the economy there was little political objection to Goering's claim to be economic overlord. His political position had been strengthened in the early weeks of war by Hitler's decision to declare Goering as his successor, confirming that he was subordinate to no one save Hitler. This declaration was a testimony to the much closer relationship between the two men that had developed since the Munich crisis a year before. Hess, who was Hitler's official deputy, had hoped for the succession, but was passed over by Hitler because he lacked Goering's feeling for art.[167] Goering for his part displayed his new position as conspicuously as he could. Like Hitler he had special trains allocated for his personal use – codenamed Robinson and Asia – in which he journeyed from conference to conference surrounded by a large entourage. His life-style became more Baroque, his surroundings more courtly. After the outbreak of war he met regularly with Hitler for a general discussion of economic and military affairs, usually once a week, more often during a period of crisis.[168] At this stage of his career he was able to exert more influence on Hitler than at any other time. Hitler's air adjutant later wrote that early in the war 'Hitler made no important political or military decision without previous discussion with Goering'.[169] Under these circumstances no one except Goering could effectively take the lead in running the German economy.

The problem was to find an appropriate instrument for exercising control. Hitler told Goering in June 1939 that the newly revived Reich Defence Council, which Goering chaired, should become the central agency for running the war economy.[170] The council had been re-established in September 1938. Its purpose, Goering said, was 'to gather together all the resources of the nation for the accelerated build-up of German armaments.' He intended it to be the main forum for discussing questions to do with general economic strategy and for arriving at firm decisions. Ministers and departmental heads were to be summoned before it and orders issued directly to them by the council.[171] On the outbreak of war the council was streamlined into a small ministerial committee for the defence of the Reich, composed of Goering as chairman, Hess, Frick, Funk, Lammers, Keital and Thomas. After a handful of meetings, poorly attended by those appointed to it Goering allowed it to lapse. He was unhappy about working through committee, so that the council quickly became simply a vehicle for passing information on to Goering for his personal decision.[172] This was something he felt could be done as easily through the Four Year Plan, and by the end of 1939 he revertd to the system of personal commissarial rule that he had used before the war. Decision-making rested solely with Goering, in consultation with the separate departments of the Plan and the state ministries. The General Council of the Four Year Plan became the main agency for passing information on to Goering. It was empowered, according to its acting chairman Koerner, 'to examine incoming material for use in the general Council and for the use of the Field Marshal, to settle differences of opinion and to ensure a uniform policy'.[173] Funk was compelled by Goering at the same time to abandon his role as Plenipotentiary for the Economy and to confine his activities to the Ministry of Economics and the Reichsbank, which he had taken over from Schacht in February 1939.[174] The organisation of local armaments inspectorates under Colonel Thomas remained in being, but it had little influence on central policy. No major decisions in economic affairs were supposed to be taken after December 1939 without Goering's prior approval.

The Four Year Plan thus became the instrument to control and run the economy in wartime, a situation formally ratified by Hitler in January 1940.[175] Even the Ministry of Weapons and Munitions set up under Fritz Todt in February 1940 was placed within the organisation of the Four Year Plan on the basis of a special commission from Goering, who had first asked Hitler for permission to tackle the urgent problem of army weapons by setting up a specialised department.[176] This satisfied the army which had grumbled about the poor state of mobilisation and lack of planning, and to a limited extent restored army influence over weapons production which it had lost when Goering assumed control of rearmament in the middle of 1938. Nevertheless the context within which Todt operated was dictated by Goering's wider control over the economy which was confirmed again by Hitler in October 1940 when the Four Year Plan had to be legally renewed. The decree of 18 October extended Goering's powers for a further four

years 'with the special assignment of adapting the economy to the demands
of war'.[177]

Under Goering's direction and the labour of his many departments the
almost complete confusion of the early months of mobilisation was replaced
by the slow but inexorable conversion of the productive economy for war.
He neither abandoned the raw material programme nor the plans for large-
scale weapons production, but tried to devise a system that would strike a
balance between the two. The result was disappointing. The large armaments plans could not be fulfilled, while the programme for synthetic fuel
and iron and steel fell further behind schedule. The price that the Nazis
paid for the premature outbreak of general war was confused economic
planning and a remarkably low level of military production. Even with the
widespread conversion of the economy for war and the cutbacks in civilian
output it proved impossible to produce the quantity of weapons that
this transfer of resources permitted. This was a problem not of resources,
but of efficiency. In this crisis of production lay the roots of what appeared
to post-war critics to be a deliberately low level of economic mobilisation.

Despite all the efforts to produce something approaching total mobilisation German armed forces were relatively under-armed for the early stages
of the war. The reasons for this paradox form the subject of a later chapter.
It is only necessary at this stage to point out the growing gap between
what Hitler expected the war economy to produce and what was actually
forthcoming. Aircraft production was a case in point. Hitler had asked
Goering to plan the production of 20,000–30,000 aircraft a year in 1938.
Mobilisation plans were drawn up for the aircraft industry to produce
20,000 aircraft in the first full year of war. Yet in 1940 only 10,200 aircraft
were produced and in 1941 only 11,700. By the summer of 1941 aircraft
production was running at more than 50 per cent below target, while the
current target was itself 30 per cent below what Hitler had asked for.[178]
The *Luftwaffe* had fewer aircraft for the invasion of Russia than for the
invasion of Poland almost two years before. Almost 40 per cent of all military
expenditure went on the air force, so that this was a costly failure. Because
of the low level of output each ton of aircraft equipment cost five times a
ton of equipment for the army.[179]

Nor were the army or navy much better off. The 'Z' Plan was shelved
and the navy left short of resources.[180] Great difficulty was found in meeting
the explosives requirements. Hitler's demand for 1 million tons of explosive
a year by 1941 had to be revised downwards, first to 850,000 tons, then to
600,000 tons by 1942.[181] The programme for vehicles ran into similar
difficulties. The initial mobilisation plan was based on an annual output of
80,000 heavy vehicles a year, but in 1940 and 1941 actual production was
25 per cent below target, while the target itself was well below what the
armed forces actually wanted.[182]

Nevertheless the German forces achieved remarkable victories in the early stages of the war. Goering was able to conceal the poor state of mobilisation behind Germany's rapid and forceful reconstruction of Europe. As a result of these successes Goering's reputation, and that of the air force, reached their highest point. Hitler became convinced that the air force was 'the most effective strategic weapon' available.[183] Goering too believed German air power to have been the decisive factor. Not even the failure to prevent the Dunkirk evacuation seriously challenged the high expectations of air strategy. Goering believed that Britain could be eliminated as as enemy after the Fall of France by a massive strategic air attack using fighters and bombers together.

The victories were not, of course, simply the result of large air superiority (in fact Germany had rather fewer aircraft than the Allies on the outbreak of war).[184] Nor were they directly the result of *Blitzkrieg* planning. The armed forces were for the most part unprepared for a major war in 1939. Anxious to avoid the mistaken optimism of 1914 the army in particular had become much more defensive in outlook. Its economic strategy was geared to the prospect of a long and total war to avoid repeating the poor mobilisation in the early stages of the First World War. The growth of a large air force and navy was part of this strategy too, to eliminate the threat of blockade and to carry a war of attrition to the enemy through submarine warfare and bombing. In 1939 none of this strategy could be undertaken without considerable increases in equipment and trained men. Instead the armed forces had to switch military strategy in mid-stream, with some difficulty; so much so that it took time and Hitler's own unorthodox military imagination to produce any plan of attack in the west at all.

The victories, and the campaign preparations that preceded them, were for the most part a product of the very high fighting qualities of the German armed forces and the weaknesses of Germany's victims. Even though German war preparation was incomplete and military production slow to expand, the armed forces made maximum use of the material available. In leadership, organisation, tactical appreciation and fighting skills the German armed forces, with its large corps of trained and devoted officers, had no equal. In this limited sense Goering's habitual claim that military heroism and skill was much more important than mere material superiority proved true. But it was also the case that the Allied forces against whom the German troops were fighting were weakened by an even lower level of preparation, either material or moral, and considerable strategic and tactical incompetence. Britain and France were defeated on the Continent against the expectations of the German generals and even of the Nazi leaders themselves who, like Goering, believed that the war would not be quickly over, though they hoped that it would. This was *Blitzkrieg* by default, and it disguised the different time-scale and character that German preparations before 1939 had actually had.

The early campaigns also disguised a considerable degree of strategic confusion and uncertainty. The pre-war planning was programmatic in approach. The changed circumstances of war, as might be expected, compromised the achievement of the programme, which had been mistakenly based on the assumption that Hitler would be given a free hand in eastern Europe. The reality of the international situation was that Hitler had to face a major war in the west earlier than he had wanted while remaining uncertain about Stalin's intentions in the east. There were now, in the middle of 1940, two alternatives for the Nazi leadership. Either to seek a compromise peace and to buy the extra time required for economic and military preparation, or to speed the whole process up and begin the larger racial war sooner than intended, fighting on both fronts at the same time.

Goering hoped for the first of these alternatives. Where a compromise peace failed to materialise in October 1939, it seemed much more likely after the defeat of France in June 1940. Goering once again acted as the chief intermediary but with even less effect or enthusiasm than before.[185] Part of the plan was to detach the United States from Britain, which would further weaken British resistance. To this end Goering ordered a German contact in Mexico City to incite the American Mineworkers' leader to call a general strike in the United States to prevent Roosevelt from actively intervening against Germany.[186] Hitler had little time for all this. The great success of German arms in 1940 encouraged him in the growing belief that German military strength might indeed be equal to a war on two fronts after all. In the course of July, following Soviet moves into the Baltic states and the Roumanian province of Bessarabia, Hitler began to explore the idea of a massive war of annihilation against the Soviet Union even though Britain (and behind Britain an increasingly less neutral United States) remained undefeated. To satisfy those critics who favoured a slower timetable, Hitler promised the economic wealth of Russia which could be used in time to complete the drive for world hegemony against the Anglo-Saxon powers.[187]

While Goering thought that the defeat of Britain was the more sensible strategic course, he appreciated how important the eastern campaign was to Hitler. His criticism of the idea of war in the east was deliberately muted.[188] Ribbentrop, on the other hand, was hostile to the plan until Britain had been defeated or compelled to seek a humiliating peace. Ribbentrop's own political stock was bound up with the success of the German-Soviet Pact and he was loth to see it torn up so swiftly. Hitler refused to be diverted once he finally issued the directive for Operation Barbarossa in December 1940. He argued that the defeat of the Soviet Union would remove the one chance remaining to Britain and doom her more surely to defeat. As Ribbentrop dropped out of favour, Goering took the opportunity to support Hitler's new ambitions while at the same time seeking a way to end British resistance, first in the Battle of Britain, then through the bombing of British cities over the winter of 1940–1. He was lukewarm when secret attempts were made to get Anglo-German negotiations started again in the summer of 1940, perhaps because he sensed an opportunity to raise the profile of his air force yet further with British defeat.[189] When this failed to materialise, Goering switched his efforts to preparing for war in the east.

German power was not yet equal to a war on two fronts. Many of the weapons that Hitler hoped to fight the new campaign with were still only on paper, while the German economy struggled with the constraints on a more rapid or efficient mobilisation. This lack of realism in Hitler's strategic assessment, finally confirmed by his declaration of war against the United States in December 1941, was the result of a number of conflicting pressures. Not least was Hitler's consistent unwillingness to assess seriously the consequences of particular strategic decisions. The conflict with Britain and France, which resulted against his expectations from the Polish crisis, gave the war a world-wide dimension because of the threat posed to western interests by Italy and Japan. This meant that Germany was compelled, even if British troops were driven from mainland Europe, to maintain a Middle Eastern and a Mediterranean strategy as well, and to devote resources to protect Germany from the threat of British bombing. The war against Russia that was supposed to expand the economic resources available for a future conflict in the west, instead accelerated the crisis with the United States and gave Britain a breathing space in which to build up forces for bombing and invasion.

The decision to speed up the programme of expansion must also be seen against a background of misrepresentation and poor intelligence on the level of German and enemy war preparations, for which Goering was largely responsible. Hitler, whose orders for the highest level of economic mobilisation were unambiguous enough, was never made sufficiently aware by Goering of the true state of military production. It was clear enough to Hitler that there were problems but the full implications for military strategy of poor economic performance was never spelt out to him. Goering had his own political interests to protect so that he presented Hitler with an unduly optimistic and unrealistic picture of economic life and levels of military output. The endless flow of charts and graphs showing the course of production planning were passed on to Hitler as if they in some sense represented weapons that were available for the front line. Goering could do this because Hitler deliberately kept away from day-to-day economic questions, telling Goering that he wanted 'to take as few decisions as possible'.[190] He was more interested in results than details.

This process carried on down the hierarchy. Goering's subordinates sought favour with him in turn by presenting an exaggerated picture of output possibilities or the performance of weapons. The Ju 88 medium bomber was promised to Goering in large numbers and with an over-estimated performance not only to win Junkers the contract, but to win political credit for the production staff who promoted it. The reality was a much lower rate of output than had at first been suggested, a greater use of resources than expected and an aircraft that failed to match in most respects the claims of its supporters.[191] Misrepresentation on this scale was a product of the Nazi political system with its emphasis on work for the 'community' and political publicity. Those who failed in their responsibilities, or who argued for more modest levels of achievement were treated by Goering as potential saboteurs, and were occasionally subject to exemplary punishment. It was in the nature of the dictatorship to discourage confrontation and argument and to promote expediency and self-serving. The effect was to reduce the amount of accurate information available and to render valueless much of the long-term economic planning.[192]

Goering was also responsible for passing on to Hitler much of the intelligence on enemy economic performance. There was much misinformation here too. Enemy states were often poorly researched and the figures for foreign military output assessed very uncritically, partly to show up German preparations in as good a light as possible. Thus in 1939 Goering demonstrated to Hitler that Allied air strength was very much poorer in almost every respect than that of Germany whereas in fact Britain was already at a state of parity in output and was better organised for defence than the *Luftwaffe*.[193] In 1940 and 1941 Goering gave support to Hitler's conviction that Russian military power was fragile by misrepresenting the economic achievements of the Soviet system. And Goering was also responsible for the fanciful view in 1941 that the United States could produce only refrigerators and razor blades. German air intelligence sources assessed American aircraft production potential at 16,000, only one third of what the United States actually produced in the first year of war.[194] Whether or not Goering was fully aware of these discrepancies is unclear, for he was given and believed the intelligence he most wanted to hear. When far less favourable reports were produced by the secret services in 1942 he made sure they were suppressed so that Hitler would remain in ignorance of Goering's mistakes.

Despite victory over France and over Germany's weaker neighbours, the realistic limits of German military preparation were demonstrated in the failure to defeat Britain in 1940. Had war in the west broken out in the mid-1940s then Germany would have possessed the naval strength and the strategic bombing force planned for the later stages of German expansion. As it was, in the summer of 1940 German forces lacked the means to defeat Britain so decisively as to eliminate her from the war. A large part of the explanation for this failure lay in the shortage of the right weapons or of sufficient preparation for this kind of conflict. Germany lacked the means to conduct decisive war against British trade, or to severely disrupt the British economy from the air, or to defeat the British air force as a preliminary to invasion. At the height of the Battle of Britain German fighter aircraft production was running at an average of 178 a month, while British output averaged 470.[195] The output of German submarines failed to match requirements by a growing margin. There was even a shortage of bombs for the winter attacks against Britain.[196]

In the following year Hitler greatly increased the fighting area over which German weapons had to be spread, still in the belief that large quantities of military resources were in the pipeline. By June 1941 German forces were committed in the Balkans, in North Africa, against the British at sea and in the air, and against the Soviet Union. This was a range of commitments originally intended, if at all, after years of economic preparation; and it ran well ahead of what the economy was actually producing. The failure to conclude any of these campaigns successfully (except in the Balkans) in the course of 1941 demonstrated to Hitler the full extent of Germany's failure to mobilise efficiently, and the consequences of speeding up the programme of imperialism. His decree for rationalising war production in July 1941 was the first signal that he intended to take over more responsibility for the economy into his own hands, and marked the onset of Goering's personal political decline.

While Hitler continually and impulsively extended the scope of German expansion, Goering clung on to the original plan of building up the first stage of empire, the consolidation of central Europe and the establishment of the Greater German economy. But in many ways this programme had already been compromised by Hitler's new strategic horizons. While Hitler moved towards the achievement of the final stage of racial imperialism, Goering was still busying himself with the first. It was on this ground that Goering was hesitant about war against Russia, wanting to fight a campaign later that Germany could be certain of winning. The contradictory nature of German strategy at this point of the war was evident in the decision to devote military efforts in Russia to the conquest of the steel, coal and oil-producing areas while Goering, with Hitler's blessing, was simultaneously devoting great resources in the Reich to the production of synthetic fuel and low-grade iron-ore which a successful Russian campaign would render redundant. Goering's programme placed highest priority on raw-material and capital-goods production; Hitler's programme required more manufactured goods and a greater light-industrial capacity. The fact that the economy was still, by 1941, being pulled in different strategic directions contributed to its poor productive performance.

There were also powerful political arguments for Goering's pursuit of an economic strategy based on the consolidation and exploitation of Germany's conquests in Europe. The apparatus under Goering's control was strongly imperialist. The development of a Nazi New Order in Europe was a policy of the highest priority. Goering could not afford to neglect the opportunity presented by the defeat of France to lead this reconstruction and to increase the influence and political power of his economic empire. The struggle for control in Europe was an extension of the political conflict at home, one feeding upon the other. Goering identified himself closely with the Nazi commitment to empire, and with the radical party plans that lay behind it. But unlike Hitler, he believed that what was achieved in 1939 and 1940 should be consolidated both as a foundation for more imperialism in the future, and to ensure the survival and extension of Nazi domestic power. Goering's difficulty was to achieve either of these things under the conditions of a continually expanding war, in which he was also in active personal command of a large section of the German armed forces.

5

BUILDING THE
NAZI EMPIRE

When Goering told Christie in 1937 that 'We want an Empire', he was expressing an ambition that was central to the political life of the Nazi movement. Not only did Nazi ideologists see history as a continuous struggle between racial and imperial forces, but they saw empire as essential for Germany and the German people at this particular stage of their historical development. Not only did empire promise living-space and economic resources to guarantee the survival of the race (and the high cost of being an imperial power) but it promised an historic framework within which Germanic civilisation and racial culture could survive and develop. Hitler argued that only through conquest and extensive control over territory could a superior culture demonstrate its superiority: thus had Rome, Spain and England achieved hegemony in the past.

In this sense Nazi imperialism differed from the economic expansionism of the pre-1914 elites. The leading military and business groups of the Wilhelmine Reich had been anxious to extend influence and gain markets in central and eastern Europe but not necessarily to enjoy full political rule. Nazi imperialism obeyed the more literal view of empire; formal military and political power exercised over conquered or dependent peoples. This was what the middle-class annexationists had demanded during the First World War and it was this political heritage that the Nazi movement absorbed, not that of the old Prussia.[1] Hence Goering's belief that economic living-space had simultaneously to be political living-space. This ambition drew its strength from the Nazis' own crude theory of racial struggle and the social opportunism of the movement's members. For the Nazi activists were drawn largely from those same social groups sympathetic to colonies or to European expansion before 1914, who had also been active annexationists during the war. For them a Nazi empire held out the promise of jobs and influence, pomp and circumstance. Not only did an empire mean economic opportunity, it was synonymous with a 'civilising' mission and a sense of greatness, and would have, as Goering argued, a moralising effect on those Germans involved in building it.[2]

Goering never hesitated in his efforts to establish such an empire. As we have seen, his main concern was to begin the programme of expansion at a time when Germany could be certain of victory, not only because of its military and economic strength, but because the German people had been prepared psychologically and intellectually for empire.[3] Goering also found himself at the head of those very elements in the party most sympathetic to expansion. His successful takeover of economic power between 1936 and 1938 gave him a key role in preparing for and carrying out the process of empire-building. In the Four-Year Plan organisation, in the economics departments, in the Nazified banks and businesses, and in his own entourage, Goering was the representative of the radical elements most influenced by Hitler's version of territorial expansion. Though he was certainly no puppet of the Nazi imperialists, he could not afford to limit or ignore imperial expansion without sacrificing his own political power and his control of the domestic economy. He accordingly made it his task to lead as much as follow, and to enjoy in the captured areas of Europe the same degree of influence that Hitler allowed him to have inside Germany. Once Hitler had provided the strategic context for a 'New Order' in Europe, Goering controlled a large part of its tactical accomplishment.

The primary purpose of empire was thus both economic and political. Economic, in the initial stage, to provide the means to fight the other major powers; in the long term to provide the means to maintain a permanently high living standard for Germans. Political in that empire was to provide the instrument for expanding and cementing party power and institutionalising German superiority. From the nature of his domestic power-base Goering was compelled to concentrate his efforts on the economic transformation of Europe. But in practice this put considerable political power into his hands as well since most of the initial policies pursued by the Nazis were to do with the ownership and control of foreign businesses, with the mobilisation of labour, food and raw materials and the expansion of war-essential production. Some of these responsibilities conflicted with those of the military authorities or the Nazi governors so that the building of the Nazis' economic empire was punctuated by the same sort of jurisdictional disputes and internal party power-struggles that had characterised Goering's ascent to power within Germany. Goering's methods were in both cases the same: to rely on Hitler's personal support for his position and to use the state economic and bureaucratic apparatus under his direct control as an instrument to extend his authority in the institutions and economies of the captured areas. The Nazi empire and Goering's own public empire thus expanded side by side.

The foundations of the new German empire were laid in the period between the *Anschluss* and the outbreak of war. This was the period during which the Nazi leaders hoped to construct a large German-dominated central European region extending into the Balkans and to the Russian frontier in the east. The primary object was to exclude British and French economic interests from the region and to establish a large protectionist block which could provide an extended food and raw material base for the purpose of building up a large war-orientated economy. Two countries were essential to the success of this programme: Austria and Czechoslovakia. Both contained substantial industrial regions, centred around steel and advanced engineering, and it was these that Germany wanted to secure complete control over in order to speed up military preparations and provide an economic substructure more nearly equal to that of the Soviet Union and the United States. Once this area was militarily secure the incorporation of the central European region was largely carried out through the Four Year Plan, using the Reichswerke as the state's holding company. Each time a new area was incorporated with the Reich, Goering extended the jurisdiction of the Plan and confirmed his own economic powers.[4]

By a variety of methods of coercion and confiscation almost the whole of the heavy industry of the area was brought under the direct control and ownership of the Goering combine. The programme of incorporation took time, partly because of Goering's desire to give the acquisitions a legal gloss by actually buying shares in foreign companies, usually at a low value and with a rate of exchange determined by the German authorities. Even the process of aryanisation, the forcible confiscation of Jewish or part-Jewish concerns, moved only slowly and continued long after the initial occupation. Goering was certainly helped in the process by the willingness of businesses, particularly in Czechoslovakia, to reach arrangements with German contractors on the supply of raw materials and finished goods from factories that could no longer effectively supply the western powers and their economic allies. Even before formal ownership passed to the Reichswerke, Czech heavy industry was already providing the armaments and raw materials that Goering wanted. Smaller firms and sub-contractors followed suit. Before the incorporation of Bohemia in March 1939 German firms took the opportunity to place extensive orders with Czech firms. This was particularly the case with the German aircraft industry which, on Goering's instructions, sought out sub-contractors for aircraft components throughout Czechoslovakia. When formal political control was extended the Czech economy was already closely integrated with the economic and industrial policy of the Reich.[5]

It is important to emphasise that industrial expansion into Europe was carried out primarily by the Reichswerke and Four Year Plan, and not by private capitalism. Chemical works, it is true, fell to the I. G. Farben combine, but even this ceased to be the case automatically with the incorporation of Czechoslovakia in 1938 and 1939.[6] It is necessary to stress this point because it is conventionally assumed that if big business did not much like what the Nazis were doing after 1936 it nevertheless profited widely and generally from the occupation of European economies on Germany's borders. In fact the German economic empire was not won and held by private capitalism on behalf of the 'monopoly capitalists' but was firmly under the control and in large part owned and operated, by the Goering economic apparatus. This was even the case in Silesia, Alsace-Lorraine and

Austria where firms were owned or part-owned by private businesses in the Reich.

It is obvious why this should be the case. The expansion in Europe was carried out on behalf of those bureaucratic, military and small manager groups around Goering, in order to extend the authority of the Nazi state and consolidate the power of its administrative elites. To have handed over the economic resources of Europe to private industry would be to deny the logic of Nazi economic policy both within Germany and in the empire. The European economy was to be geared in the first place for military tasks, and hence required the same degree of close supervision that Goering had obtained in 1938 in Germany, and secondly it was to be re-structured to produce an economy working in the national interest and the interest of the movement, but not to satisfy the private desire for gain. 'We did not fight this war', said Goering, 'for the sake of private economic interests.' Goering and the more radical Nazis did not trust big business to carry out the incorporation of the European economy. Indeed it is arguable if private business was capable of carrying any such programme out. There were areas where the interests of private businessmen and Nazis coincided but on balance the political and ideological impetus behind the empire lay not with the industrial elite, which had favoured more conventional market penetration and integration in the 1920s and 1930s, but with the new managerial, military and bureaucratic elites thrown up by the Nazi movement in its penetration of the German economy before 1939.

To ensure that private economic interest should be excluded from planning the new European economy Goering controlled not only the general context of access to capital, investment policy and trade but undertook to acquire the direct ownership of the means of production. This was the distinguishing feature of the Nazi economic empire. It was the point at which 'liberal' capitalism in Germany and the new fascist economy parted company. Goering authorised the setting up and expansion of the Reichswerke for just this reason, to guarantee the interests of the racial state and to secure the predominance of the party in the economic reconstruction of Europe. This was important from Goering's personal point of view as well. The Reichswerke had a greater permanence than the Four Year Plan, with its essentially temporary character. The plans for the state enterprises at Linz, which Goering hoped to turn into the largest industrial centre in the Reich, and the building of Hermann Goering-Stadt at Salzgitter were projects designed to outlast the war and the rearmament crisis. The Reichswerke, and the new cities to be built around it all over Europe, were to symbolise the transition from the old liberal economy 'to the principles of national socialist economic and social policy'.[7]

This preference for state over private interests was echoed by Goering's subordinates as the Four Year Plan and the Reichswerke extended control over the captured areas. Hans Winkler, Goering's trustee in Silesia, although no particular friend to Goering's political ambitions, condemned private capitalism with its 'contests of strength between individual enterprises' and 'the re-introduction of methods of colonial-style seizure'.[8] State Secretary Neumann argued that 'the un-directed, liberal economy and its very concept are at odds in too many respects with the primacy of policy demanded by National Socialism'.[9] Goering's deputy Paul Körner, defending the Reichswerke's acquisitions in 1940 to critics in the Finance Ministry, explained that 'superior national tasks . . . have given the Reichswerke proportions and characteristics which make it impossible to bear the participation of private and competing enterprises. . . . It would be an impossible situation should shareholders in a general meeting criticise measures taken, or put questions to the administration based on their own interests which might never concur with opposite national interests.'[10]

This central political principle was followed ruthlessly in every area under German control. In Austria the largest private-owned concern, the Alpine-Montangesellschaft was acquired by Goering after its owners in the Ruhr were subjected to a year of bullying and harassment.[11] The attacks proved to be too much for Fritz Thyssen, Hitler's erstwhile industrial ally, who fled from Germany and from his place on the board of the Vereinigte-Stahlwerke, which owned the Austrian firm. His considerable industrial holdings fell forfeit to Goering.[12] Under similar pressure Ernst Poensgen, Goering's most consistent opponent in the Ruhr, later resigned his position on the Stahlverein. Under the cover of the Dresdner Bank and the state holding company VIAG Goering's officials took over control of 33 other major Austrian firms while plans were laid for the establishment of large new businesses.[13]

An avenue into Czech industry was provided by the takeover of Austria particularly through the aryanisation of Jewish firms. Even the efforts of the Vienna Rothschilds to prevent such an eventuality by placing their shares in London was frustrated. The Nazis captured Louis Rothschild in Vienna and held him to ransom until his family would agree to hand over their Czech and Austrian holdings in return for his life.[14] In the Sudetenland the extensive industrial holdings of the Petschek family were confiscated on the same grounds and brought under Goering's direct control.[15] At Goering's instruction Karl Rasche of the Dresdner Bank and Hans Kehrl of the Four Year Plan proceeded to buy up all the available shares in the heavy industrial sectors in Czechoslovakia.[16] This was done either through compulsory purchase, or through 'persuasion'. Native Austrian and Czech banks and shareholders were invited to sell their shareholdings to the Reich on unfavourable terms, and few refused. Where majority shareholdings could not be acquired the German state expanded the share capital with loans from the Reich in order to secure a controlling block of shares, in most cases 51 per cent. By October 1940 the Prague-based Skoda works, one of Europe's largest armaments producers, was finally brought under the control of the Reichswerke after an eighteen-month search for enough of the pre-war shares to provide legal ownership. So too was the Czech

Armaments Works, formerly owned by the Czech state, the large machinery plant at Brünn and the Poldihütte iron and steel works. The latter was placed under the management of Goering's brother Albert. The other firms were run by boards of directors drawn from the Reichswerke organisation and the Four Year Plan.[17]

The same complicated pattern of expropriation was repeated with the Czech iron, steel and coal industry. The largest concern, the Vitkovice complex, owned for the most part by the Vienna Rothschilds through a London subsidiary, came under the immediate influence of the Reichswerke on occupation of the area in March 1939. From then on it was operated by the Reichswerke until the end of the war, providing almost a third of the raw steel and rolling mill products of the whole Reichswerke concern. The German government tried initially to buy the plant outright and was on the point of concluding an agreement to do so with the Paris Rothschilds when the war intervened.[18] The only way round the problem of ownership was to declare the London shares annulled and to issue new shares on behalf of the Goering concern. To make the seizure more formal Goering was advised to leave a sum of money in a blocked account as payment for the shares 'in order to make the compulsory nature of the transaction less conspicuous'![19] This arrangement proved unsatisfactory, for the Protectorate administration under von Neurath (who was no friend to the Nazis) refused to recognise the firm as German-owned. Instead a special operating treaty was signed with the firm's Czech managers and a final decision on ownership deferred until the end of the war.[20]

The Reichswerke ran, and planned for, the Vitkovice concern as if it were directly German-owned. It was only the curious legalism of the German administration, which compelled Goering to produce genuine proof of ownership, that marred what was a *de facto* acquisition. Goering's directors at the plant integrated production and investment planning into the programme of the Four Year Plan. The firm's report for 1942 stressed that 'business prospects no longer govern the process of the economy'.[21] Capital was provided by the Reichswerke and by German banks; product policy and distribution was in the hands of the Reichswerke organisation. Goering's plans for Vitkovice were considerable. It was to become a central part 'of the Eastern industrial pillar of the Reich', providing iron and steel for the finishing industries of the east after the war.[22] The rest of the region was to be integrated with these plans as well. The finishing industries were to take their steel from Vitkovice and turn it into the rails, girders and pipes needed for the creation of a new economic infrastructure in eastern Europe. For this reason almost the whole of Czech heavy industry and raw material production by the middle of the war had fallen under the control of Goering's industrial empire. Chart III sets out the details of these holdings.

Goering was helped in his policy of expropriation by the degree of integration and interdependence of the central European economy. Acquisition of banks and businesses in Austria gave access to share-holdings in

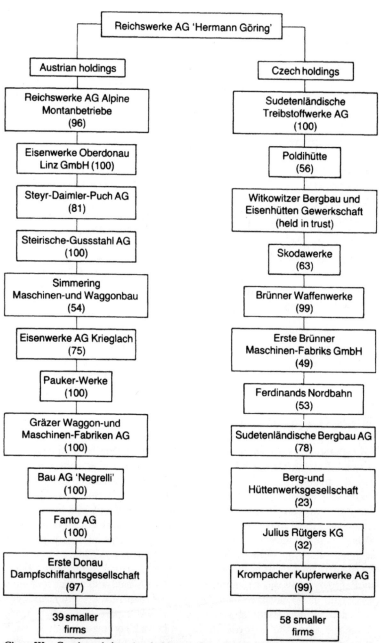

Chart III Czech and Austrian holdings of the Reichswerke 'Hermann Goering'
(% shareholding in brackets)

* Only the major firms are listed in full. There were many subsidiaries. The names by which they were known in German during the war have been used.

Source: NA T83 Roll 74 frames 3445227–362.

Czechoslovakia, Hungary, Poland and in Jugoslavia and was widened even further with the addition of Bohemia.[23] Moreover the incorporation of Austria and Czechoslovakia altered the economic relationship with south-eastern Europe. Before 1938 Germany had begun to expand trade with the Balkan region on a basis of providing industrial exports for raw materials and food. Payments were made by special clearing agreements which avoided some of the problems of finding sufficient foreign exchange. Under Goering's general direction contacts with south-eastern Europe increased and altered after 1938. Instead of relying simply on trade through negotiation Goering encouraged capital participation in selected eastern Europen industries as a way of influencing product policy in favour of Germany and of increasing pressure on foreign governments to accept German economic influence. In this way Germany could also bring greater pressure to bear on Britain and France (the main investors in south-east Europe) to grant a special position for German capital and trade. This strategy lay at the core of the plans devised by Krauch and Wohlthat of the Four Year Plan office for the economic hegemony of Germany in south-eastern Europe.[24]

The countries that most interested Goering in the south-east were Hungary, Roumania and Jugoslavia. From Hungary came agricultural goods in return for machinery, vehicles and arms. Goering viewed Hungary as a 'vassal state', closely linked through its military and foreign policy, as well as its economics with the Reich.[25] He looked at Jugoslavia in the same way. During the early part of 1939 for example, Goering promised a large credit for Jugoslavia to purchase German armaments in return for a political and economic policy favourable to German interests. This included not only a Jugoslav commitment to remain on friendly terms with the Axis powers but for Jugoslavia to provide raw materials, including concessions for oil, to help the German war economy. This relationship was extended and strengthened up to the German occupation of the country in April 1941.[26] It was oil too that attracted Goering to Roumania, though there was the added attraction of steel and engineering works, producing goods largely for the Roumanian domestic market. As in Jugoslavia Germany used political and diplomatic pressure to bring Roumania more closely into the German economic orbit, and indeed the Roumanian government became more willing, as the political balance swung in Germany's favour, to accept closer economic ties with Germany. King Carol suggested 'systematic co-operation for the development of economic relations' to Goering in November 1938.[27] By February 1939 this commitment had been turned into a firm economic agreement under pressure from Goering. In return for the promise of co-operation in investment and mining, and the export of German arms, Roumania agreed to tie agricultural output and raw materials production more closely to German needs. Goering insisted further that any material sent to equip the Roumanian air force was to be exchanged against petroleum products for Germany.[28]

The subsequent history of the economic and political ties between

Germany and Roumania, in which Goering was closely involved, provides a good example of the way in which the Balkans were brought into a dependent position in the German New Order in Europe. Roumania's position was a difficult one, for the Roumanian government while anxious to keep control over its own economy, was only too aware, especially after the fall of France, that it was dependent upon German good will. The oil companies directly owned by Britain, France and Holland were declared enemy property which brought them closer to Germany's direct control.[29] The Allies' shares in Petrol-Block AG were used by Goering to lever Germany into an important position in Roumanian oil production. By achieving an operating contract between Kontinentale Öl (Goering's state oil company) and the Dutch Astra firm, Goering acquired more than 50 per cent direct control of Roumanian oil output.[30] Another avenue into Roumanian industry was found through the holdings of Czech and Austrian firms in Roumania which were forfeit to the Reichswerke. The Czech Armaments Works had a limited share in the Resita iron and steel complex and the Roumanian Copsa Mica si Cugir mines. Although the shares had been deposited with the Westminster Bank in London, the Roumanian government was compelled to publish duplicates and to given them to the Reichswerke. In July 1940 Goering negotiated that three seats on the Resita board should go to Reichswerke representatives, and forced the resignation of the Jewish general manager, Max Ausschnitt.[31] In January 1940 the Reichswerke turned to the other major Roumanian heavy industrial combine, the Malaxa works. A technical aid treaty was signed with the company, under the terms of which German advisers were to be allowed to influence Malaxa's corporate policy in favour of German interests. After the overthrow of King Carol, Marshal Antonescu, who was on better personal terms with Goering, allowed still greater participation. After a summer of negotiations in 1941 a new company was formed called the Rümanishe-Deutsche AG für Eisenindustrie und Handel which divided the shares of Resita and Malaxa between Germany and Roumania, giving the former the right to control the technical, financial and commercial policy of the two firms, as well as influence in other sectors of the Roumanian engineering industry.[32] The Roumanian government later tried to regain its control over Malaxa but throughout the war Germany strongly influenced Roumania's industrial economy in her favour.[33]

It is possible to exaggerate the extent to which Germany was dependent upon the Balkans to fight Hitler's wars. Even by 1938 trade with the area constituted only 11 per cent of German trade, and there were limits to extending this much further.[34] Indeed the whole synthetic oil programme of the Four Year Plan was based on the assumption that supplies from Roumania could not be guaranteed in wartime, and even if they could be were insufficient for all Germany's military needs. There were other problems with Balkan trade too. The Balkan countries were reluctant to accept German economic hegemony on such unfavourable terms, particularly as they were currently in the process of industrialising and had no interest in perpetuating a semi-colonial economic relationship with their more advanced German neighbour. Moreover, Germany had a trade deficit with most of the countries of eastern and south-eastern Europe by the late 1930s. Germany refused to pay these balances directly, which discouraged the states involved even more from entering fresh agreements to supply Germany with food and raw materials for which there was no guarantee of payment.[35]

Germany hoped to get round this problem by offering generous credit facilities, and later on by offering captured Czech goods as a substitute for German. But it was impossible to disguise Germany's increasing inability not only to pay what was owed to the Balkan states, but even to supply them with the industrial goods necessary to cover essential imports. During 1939 both Hitler and Goering intervened to restrict the sale of German armaments and strategic goods, and then of Czech arms as well, arguing that they were needed more urgently by the Reich.[36] Those that were offered were over-priced (Jugoslavia was offered in 1939 a range of military equipment twice as expensive as that of Germany's competitors), or were held up in transit for long periods.[37] What drove the Balkan states into a closer dependence on Germany was not any advantage that this conferred but the fact that the western powers withdrew their political and economic support. By 1939 the Balkan states were compelled to recognise the changed political reality in eastern Europe and to see themselves as parts of a German economic sphere.

No doubt in the long run Germany could have extracted much more from the Balkans. The outbreak of general war in 1939 interrupted the systematic infiltration of German interests into the region and changed the circumstances governing German policy. Goering's original objective was to build up a German-dominated economic sphere to provide essential goods to prepare for major war in the mid-1940s. Now the region had to be exploited and utilised at once. Russia promised to make up for some of Germany's lost time by providing primary goods in return for machinery and military equipment, but this was a risky substitute. Instead Goering set out to secure the German grip on European economic resources to provide a broader base of resources for large-scale war production.

As each new area was conquered it was incorporated into the economy of the 'New Order' under Goering's direction. To do this he acquired new and extensive powers directly from Hitler which once again allowed him to extend the Four Year Plan organisation to all the occupied areas.[38] On 28 September 1939 Goering announced the scope of his new powers: uniform supervision of the new economic region, and the right to issue general and specific decrees on economic policy.[39] Poland fell to Goering in October 1939, Holland in May 1940, Norway in June, France in July; and so on.[40] This process culminated in the granting of wide-ranging powers to Goering in June 1941 to 'take all measures in the newly occupied Eastern territories for the greatest exploitation of all materials, stocks, and economic resources, and for the extension of economic potential.'[41]

In addition to this general right of economic control Goering also won further, more specialised, commissions that broadened his direct control not only in occupied Europe, but over trade and economic relations with the rest of unconquered Europe. The aluminium industry was placed under a special commissioner of the Four Year Plan, the aircraft manufacturer Heinrich Koppenberg, in order to integrate domestic production with the output of bauxite and aluminium in the occupied and neutral areas.[42] In 1941, following the crisis in the supply of coal for the war economy, Goering was charged by Hitler with the task of producing an integrated European coal basis. Goering set up the *Reichsvereinigung Kohle*, with Pleiger as its director, and thus acquired extensive control over an industry that was still largely private.[43] Finally Goering extended the rather ill-defined role that he enjoyed in the German oil industry by establishing a large European-wide organisation for oil production and processing, Kontinentale Öl, in January 1941, nominally directed by Goering, with Funk as his deputy.[44] These specialised functions gave Goering a more direct way of influencing decisions in areas of the economy where his contact might otherwise be too remote to be effective.

This system of collecting additional powers was evidence of the uncertainty with which Goering regarded his economic overlordship, and of the difficulties of enforcing his control. The extension of his influence in Europe was accompanied by a long series of political conflicts with the armed forces, other party leaders and institutions and private industry. In the scramble for political influence Goering could not afford to rely simply on his domestic authority. It was essential for him to join in the struggle for control of the European economy in order to retain his domestic power base and his own political position. In Nazi political life claims to power had to be diligently and regularly enforced; otherwise political power went by default. The establishment of the German New Order in Europe was a function not only of Nazism's ideological ambitions but also of its domestic political struggles.

The strength of Goering's position differed from region to region depending on circumstance. In areas still designated areas of military activity Goering was compelled to co-operate with the military authorities over questions to do with occupation costs, and the local provisioning of troops. In some cases the army took over local industries for the purposes of repair and front-line supply and these were run, in the first instance, by Thomas's armaments staff. Thus even in areas over which Goering had general jurisdiction, the actual mobilisation of local labour and industrial resources could be left to the armed forces. Where the Luftwaffe took over these resources, Goering's position was much safer. Because of the personal link between the air force and the Four Year Plan, the air force extracted a substantial share of local economic resources. By the middle of the war Luftwaffe orders on hand regularly exceeded those of the army.[45]

In regions under direct Nazi control, or in the hands of Nazi puppet governments, rather than military administration – in Norway, Bohemia, Slovakia, Croatia and Poland – it was easier for Goering to exercise economic control or arrange economic policy to comply with Germany's overall war requirements. Here the main difficulty was not so much military interference, as the jealousy of Nazi rulers. In the scramble to divide the political spoils of Europe Hitler saw fit to give responsibilities to Nazis whose role in the Reich was relatively minor, or whose influence had been eclipsed by more ambitious politicians. All these figures were determined to defend their responsibilities and not to allow the senior Nazis in the movement to encroach upon them without invitation. Frank in Poland, Seyss-Inquart in Holland, von Neurath in Bohemia, Rosenberg in the Baltic and Russia, Koch in the Ukraine all clashed at one time or another with the Goering empire. This was perhaps inevitable since Goering was the only Nazi leader given formal responsibilities in all the territories outside the Reich. What Goering wanted compromised the constitutional authority that they enjoyed, because he demanded the right to issue orders about economic affairs over their heads. This question of competency remained confused throughout the war. Goering thought he had the absolute right to take decisions on any question to do with the European economy. The army and local rulers believed that they had the right to veto anything Goering wanted which they did not like. All claimed Hitler's backing. This situation was complicated even more by the efforts of Ribbentrop and the Foreign Ministry officials during the first year of war to wrest from Goering the right to determine economic policy in all occupied areas not directly incorporated into the Reich. This contest formed part of the wider conflict over strategy between Ribbentrop and Goering and was resolved in this case in Goering's favour.[46]

Just as administration differed from region to region, so too did German policy. In the most extreme case, in occupied Poland, Goering directed that all resources that could be taken and used in the Reich should be seized and the population left with the barest minimum for subsistence.[47] At the other extreme, the Protectorate of Bohemia kept its substantial industrial base intact, together with much of its labour, and was integrated into the economic structure of the Greater German Reich. Goering reserved for himself decisions about the nature and level of exploitation in particular areas. Overriding priority was given to resources and production to help the German war effort. If the resources could be used more effectively in the country of origin they were; if not, they were transferred back to the Reich. Goering's immediate instinct was to take anything that could be moved: 'It seems to me', he said in 1942, 'that in earlier times the thing was simpler. In earlier times you pillaged. He who had conquered a country disposed of the riches of that country. At present, things are done in a more humane way. As for myself, I still think of pillage, comprehensively.'[48] In fact from early in the war the policy of looting was tempered with a policy of direct economic exploitation in the occupied areas. Even in Poland, where Goering at first ordered the dismantling and transfer of 'all enterprises which are not absolutely necessary for the meager maintenance of the bare existence of the population', he was compelled under pressure from Frank and the army to reverse this priority and restart industries in and around Warsaw for the German war effort.[49] In western Europe he accepted from the outset that the area should be exploited systematically 'in order to help German war production and to raise war potential for the fulfilment of the demands to be made in the interest of further warfare.'[50] This principle was eventually extended to the whole of conquered Europe.

While war production was a major priority, it was not the only one. While the war was still being fought Goering and his economic staff turned their minds to the question of planning the economy of post-war Europe. The starting point for the Nazi re-shaping of the European economy was the integration of the captured or dependent economies with the economic structure of the German area. Germany was to produce primarily high-value industrial goods, drawing labour and raw materials, compulsorily, from conquered Europe to supplement their supply within Germany. The surrounding economic regions would be allowed to produce only those industrial and consumer goods that Germany deemed necessary. Poland and the area of western Russia would be purely agricultural. The supply of raw materials from southern Russia and the Ukraine would be for German use only. France, Belgium, Holland and Scandinavia would enjoy, on the other hand, a higher standard of living and be allowed a mixed economy, complementing production in the Reich. European finance and European currency were to be arranged in Berlin on a European-wide basis.[51] To cement this control over the subordinate economies Goering proposed that as much as possible of European heavy industry and manufacturing be brought directly into German hands. In August 1940 Goering ordered a programme of direct capital penetration into occupied Europe, with the object of buying as many industrial enterprises (either in part or entire) as possible. The authorisation for purchase and the provision of the necessary capital Goering reserved to himself.[52] His aim was to take over into direct German ownership the bulk of Europe's heavy manufacturing industry and to control what could not be bought. In this way Germany's industrial predominance would be guaranteed, as well as the power of the party, and of Goering himself.

The policy of industrial acquisition was an important step beyond general control over economic policy. It stemmed partly from Goering's experience inside Germany where he had found that Nazi policy was best served by state enterprise and direct control. But it was also the most convenient method for controlling industrial sectors in very different parts of Europe on something like a uniform basis. The plans for the European textile industry show Goering's intention to run the European industrial economy as a single integrated unit. Drawn up in June 1940 by Hans Kehrl, Goering's deputy for textile production, the plans show clearly that the Nazis wanted to rationalise and reorganise the European textile industry, providing the raw material and controlling its distribution in favour of the Greater German economic area. All European trade in textiles, the location and provisioning of factories, and the distribution of the necessary labour was to be determined in German interests by German planners.[53] Similar and more far-reaching proposals were produced for the iron and steel industry in 1942 by the Reichswerke director, Paul Rheinländer. All iron and steel production was to be centralised and rationalised on a continental basis by Goering's staff, and in favour of German state interests. Since the Reichswerke controlled or owned almost all the European iron and steel industry by the middle of the war, it was a straightforward step to introduce industry-wide planning for the post war period.[54] Goering proposed the same solution with European oil. A large state-owned oil industry based on Russian oil and Roumanian acquisitions was to be set up and operated after the end of the war by the Goering empire. The same was true for the chemical industry, under the direction of the Four Year Plan and I.G. Farben together; and so on. It was not Speer, as he himself later claimed, who originated the idea of European 'production cartels', but Goering and the economic imperialists on his staff.[55]

This decision to run European industry under the control of the German state resurrected the conflict between the Ruhr and Goering that had smouldered on through the conquest of Poland, Scandinavia and France. The iron and steel producers at first welcomed the acquisition of Silesia and eastern France. They talked openly of *Repatrierung*, of the handing back of what had been theirs in 1918 but had been taken away at Versailles.[56] Goering, however, was unwilling to strengthen the Ruhr's political position and economic interests by giving it either Silesia or Lorraine. In Poland Goering set up a special trustee organisation, the *Haupttreuhandstelle Ost* which was given temporary control over all Silesian industry. Goering wanted Silesian coal in order to reduce his dependence on the Ruhr supplies and to complement his acquisitions in Czechoslovakia and Austria. Cutting through all the objections of the armed forces, the local Nazis and some, but by no means all, the Ruhr claimants, Goering took over the bulk of the coal mines (many of which were Polish state property), and a significant share of the iron and steel capacity not only of Silesia but around Warsaw as well.[57]

This was not done without some difficulty. Goering strengthened his political influence in the area by reaching a special agreement with Himmler over economic control in the Polish region which allowed him to circumvent most of Frank's objections.[58] The army withdrew from conflict only because their management of captured installations turned out to be so ineffective.[59] The Ruhr industrialists after some preliminary objections acquiesced in Goering's plans for the region, not because they accepted their validity but because, after June 1940, they were much more interested in regaining control in Lorraine where they believed they had a better opportunity of constructing an integrated and rational iron and steel sector within a convenient geographical area, and safe from Goering's encroachments. Nor could the Ruhr firms afford to become involved in a further legal and political clash with Goering. Instead the reorganisation of the east was abandoned in the hope that enough could be salvaged in the west.[60]

None of this reasoning was lost on Goering or the Reichswerke leaders. 'What is healthful for competition', Pleiger later argued, 'is dangerous to the Hermann Goering works.'[61] The addition of Lorraine to the expanded Ruhr firms would tilt the balance perhaps decisively in favour of private industry in the post-war reconstruction. Moreover it encouraged those who wished to see the whole Salzgitter low-grade iron ore project closed down in favour of more economical production in the west. The German acquisition of Lorraine not only threatened to improve the Ruhr's bargaining position, but also, through arguments on relative efficiency, to compel the Reichswerke, as the only high-cost iron producer, to abandon its political ambitions and to accept economic reality.

Goering of course had no intention of giving way to the interests of the Ruhr. In order to strengthen the position of the Reichswerke and his own plans for the European economy, as well as to ensure uninterrupted and secure production for the immediate purposes of war, Goering declared that the new region would be brought into the greater economic area and its economy run by the state.[62] The iron-ore deposits were placed directly under Raabe of the Four Year Plan as trustee, working under a special *Leifergemeinschaft* (supply company) based at Metz.[63] The organisation established did not take over direct ownership of the mines, but it governed pricing policy, investment and trade in iron-ore which was integrated with wider planning in Germany. Pleiger insisted that in any arrangements made in the area coal mines should be placed under a separate organisation and should not be linked up with particular steel-works. This, too, was designed to undermine the claims of the Ruhr firms and to help integrate the new region into central Reich planning for coal which came, in March 1941, under Pleiger's own control as head of the newly created *Reichsvereinigung Kohle*.[64] On the question of the steel works, and the wider problem of ownership that this invited, Goering's initial reaction was to demand that the state take over all the Lorraine firms without regard to past claims.[65] These could then be added, as had firms in Austria and Czechoslovakia, to the Reichswerke. In addition Goering hoped to integrate the industry of Luxembourg into that of the Reich, and in particular to acquire control of the Arbed trust, the largest Luxembourgeois iron and steel works. This interest had already been expressed by Goering's staff at the Four Year Plan Office in 1938, in their plans to strengthen German steel production against that of France. Now the interest was once more revived under very different conditions.[66]

The private firms, on the other hand, were not prepared to see their claims disappear yet again under pressure of arguments concerning the 'national interest'. Yet the response of the Ruhr firms was mixed when it came to the actual contest with Goering. Some shrank back again from a direct clash. Hoesch, for example, wrote to Körner in August 1940 that he was willing to give up an interest in the Arbed concern if the Reichswerke were interested in it at the same time.[67] More typical was the letter written by Flick to Goering shortly after the fall of France, in which he expressed the widely held expectation that the former owners of the Lorraine and Luxembourg plants would repossess them. Flick in particular wanted to gain a priority interest in Arbed for his own Harpener Bergbau company, as compensation for the loss of his coal interests to the Reichswerke early in 1940. Other Ruhr firms followed suit with their own shopping lists for Lorraine enterprises hoping to be compensated for losses in central and eastern Europe by rewards in the west.[68]

For six months after the fall of France the Lorraine region was operated under Reich commissars while the distribution of the spoils was argued over. Goering was compelled to modify his original desire for everything because the Four Year Plan organisation was already over-stretched. Pleiger and Körner restricted claims for direct absorption into the Reichswerke to the large de Wendel concern, which provided between one-sixth and one-fifth of all French steel; the Thyssen foundry of Hagedange; the Differdange foundry in Luxembourg; and a blocking minority shareholding in Arbed.[69] This list was impressive enough. The de Wendel concern had large holdings in Germany as well, valued at 200 million RM.[70] The Arbed, in which private firms were also keenly interested, could not be directly taken over as some 72 per cent of its share capital was scattered amongst numerous Luxembourgeois owners, but the 8 per cent of Schneider-Creusot's holding and the 20 per cent in the hands of Belgian banks was acquired to give the Reichswerke sufficient interest to influence the policy of the concern decisively.[71] Early in 1941, in the face of growing difficulties in getting the Lorraine industry going again, Goering issued a decree authorising a trustee system and allocating the remaining enterprises to the iron and steel industry in the Reich. The Reichswerke took over the firms listed by Pleiger, and organised them under a general holding company, Hüttenverwaltung Westmark. Goering thus succeeded not only in leaving the question of actual ownership still open (and dependent on the efforts of the private firms in meeting German demands), but also ensured that a sufficiently large part of the Lorraine and Luxembourg industrial base was transferred to the Reichswerke to secure its interests in future discussions.[72]

In some ways this was an ideal solution. It avoided a head-on collision with the Ruhr firms, while leaving the decisive questions of control and re-organisation as much in Goering's hands as before. But it did show that Goering was less able to ride roughshod over private ownership in the west than he had been able to do elsewhere. To some extent this reflected a wider problem. Goering's political influence in the western areas was much less than in the eastern economy, even though Hitler had given Goering 'authority with regard to the management of the whole French economy'.[73] Throughout the second half of 1940 Goering fought a jurisdictional battle with the Foreign Ministry over the economic negotiations with France. Goering claimed sole responsibility. Ribbentrop refused, and was able, with the help of those unsympathetic to Goering's economic policy, to ensure that decisive influence was exercised by the appointees of the Foreign Office.[74] The French themselves co-operated in this, preferring to accept what they could from Hemmen and the more moderate negotiators rather than suffer what the Austrian and Czech economies had experienced. Under any circumstances, France was intended to play a subordinate economic role; but without Goering's direct intervention French businessmen were able to salvage much more commercial and industrial autonomy than in the east. That this was Hitler's preference too made it harder for Goering to press his claims as forcefully as he might otherwise have done.[75]

It would be wrong, however, to underestimate Goering's power on the basis of conditions in France. If the western occupation showed limits to the expansion of Goering's empire it was to a great extent due to the fact that the whole unwieldy apparatus that Goering had constructed was losing momentum. There was a limit to the extent to which the Reichswerke could continue to absorb new firms, or the Four Year Plan provide commissars for European areas. While the arguments went on over Goering's French role, the Goering organisation was simultaneously involved in establishing hegemony in Silesia and Poland, in incorporating the industry of the Protectorate, in penetrating the Balkan and north European economies, as well as running large areas of the domestic economy. In the end Goering lacked a large enough party and administrative apparatus or sufficient pre-war contacts to push as far into France as he would have liked.

But for Goering's critics there seemed no frontier to his ambition. Just as the Ruhr firms had feared, Goering extracted enough from Lorraine to blunt their competitive edge. Poensgen bitterly remarked to his fellow industrialists that 'the Reichswerke is clearly only interested in the cherries in the cake.'[76] The mounting criticism of Goering and of the Reichswerke strategy was provoked on a number of grounds, and from a growing circle of officials and businessmen. The central cause for concern was the rising intervention of the state in the economy. It was not simply the Reichswerke, with its special privileges and state aid, that the private sector resented, but the whole structure of regulations and conditions that the state imposed on areas of economic activity that the industrialists believed were properly the preserve of private enterprise. Moreover much state intervention was not directly concerned with guaranteeing economic growth and economic stability, which the private firms might have accepted more readily, but with restricting growth and imposing Nazi policy on the strategies of the private firms. The right of the economy to determine its own course, which had apparently been confirmed between 1933 and 1936, was lost thereafter.

German capitalism still possessed a strong belief in economic liberalism. The state was useful in providing protection against particular threats, and in overcoming constraints on growth, but ultimately responsibility lay with the businessmen themselves.

Gradually the Ruhr firms came to suspect that Goering's ultimate goal was to gain 'majority' control of Europe's heavy industry, to contról, through ownership if possible, more than 50 per cent of the output of iron, steel and coal in the new economic area under German rule. The evidence suggests that the Ruhr was right. Goering and his political allies were becoming increasingly radical as the war continued and the opportunities for economic re-structuring opened up. In 1941 under pressure from Hitler because of the deteriorating coal situation, plans were prepared in the Economics Ministry for the nationalisation of all German coal mines. Goering supported the move, but was dissuaded from carrying it out by Pleiger on the grounds that the political crisis that it would produce in the middle of the war would be counter-productive.[77] To the Ruhr it was yet more evidence of the unpredictable socialistic tendency among the ascendant *völkisch* elements in Goering's empire. In iron and steel Goering's position was more favourable. Indeed by the time of the invasion of Russia Goering had already secured or had planned to secure direct ownership of or control over half the steel output of the new German empire.

The plans produced in the Four Year Plan office for the post-war European economy clearly show the breadth of Goering's intentions.[78] After a German victory the coal and iron-ore resources of Europe were to be controlled by the German state. The state would determine where the raw materials would be sent and how much to extract. Goering's planners regarded these resources as the property of the German people, which the owners would have to utilise as 'trustees'. It was planned to ration the extraction of the better ores and coking coal, or those that were more accessible, and to compel all the steel industry to use a mixture of high and low-grade materials, produced, if necessary, in high-cost mines. The industry's natural desire to produce the cheapest and best quality raw material first would thus be replaced by the 'people's' interest in preserving and utilising resources on a long-term basis regardless of cost. At the same time the manufacturers who used steel would be compelled to use the more expensive product, but not pass on the increased cost to the customer, who would continue to be protected by controls over prices and wage-levels.[79] The Ruhr itself would not be allowed to expand beyond its size at the beginning of the war. Additional steel capacity – which was reckoned at an extra 20 million tons a year in peacetime – would have to be built up elsewhere, in central Germany around the Reichswerke, but principally in the east.[80]

The whole weight of the industrial economy was to be shifted eastwards. This justified the ambition to create *Ostraum* for the German people. In Silesia and western Poland, in the Protectorate and around Linz large new economic regions were to be created, to produce and distribute the goods needed in the east. Vienna was to become the commercial capital of this vast area. In the long run the balance of output would swing against the Ruhr and in favour of the new, and largely state-owned, enterprises at the heart of central Europe.[81] The conquest of Russia would also ensure that the focal point of the Nazi industrial economy would lie in the centre and east of the empire. Goering was at pains to show that this kind of system was not collectivist in the Soviet sense, but even those close to Goering, including Funk at the Economics Ministry, found the distinction hard to grasp.[82] Goering did in fact harbour considerable respect for Soviet industrial achievements. On one occasion he told a meeting of armaments producers: 'You are just little repair shops beside the factories of Soviet industry. . . . In many cases the state has done things better, and Communism has unfortunately done things best of all. That is a pity, but it is so.'[83] The differences between Five Year Plans and Four Year Plans, between Stalingrad and Hermann Goering-Stadt became less clear-cut in Nazi plans for the new Europe.

The rapid restructuring of the European economy encouraged a growing radicalism among the Nazi imperialists. The speed and completeness with which European hegemony was achieved made it possible to push faster and further than might otherwise have been the case. Conquest and occupation broke down the more formal or legalistic barriers to German expansion and released Nazi leaders and officials from the constraints of peace-time politics. The swift seizure of empire and the dissolution of the European political structure created ideal conditions for consolidating and extending the political influence of the Nazi party. No Nazi politician could afford to ignore this opportunity and expect to remain at the centre of affairs. The leaders of the movement were carried along by an ideological and institutional momentum created by Hitler's expanding vision of racial empire and the political rivalry of those who struggled to fulfil it.

This acceleration of empire-building during the war was reflected in Goering's much closer contacts with the SS and his pursuit of Nazi racial policy. Goering's links with Himmler's organisations went back to the mid-1930s when the two had co-operated to eliminate the remaining conservative opponents to the movement's plans. Relations between the two remained co-operative, if not always cordial, until at least 1944. SS personnel were to be found on all the major boards of the Reichswerke industries;[84] Goering joined with the SS and the Gestapo in making judicial decisions in occupied Europe, particularly where the cases involved sabotage, or Jewish property. Goering needed this co-operation with the SS in order to carry out the full programme of economic imperialism. Although Goering enjoyed the authority to expropriate Jewish property, state property and any other wealth whose owners were defined as anti-German, it was the security organisations and the SS who did the necessary police work involved.

For Goering the Jewish question was by far the most important.

Throughout the war Goering's officials remorselessly carried out the policies of expropriation and aryanisation which he repeatedly authorised.[85] The Reichswerke contained numerous firms confiscated because their owners were Jewish or part-Jewish. Goering's home contained numerous works of art acquired on the same grounds.

Through his interest in the economics of aryanisation, and the use of Jewish concentration camp labour, Goering was inextricably caught up in the effort to find a solution to the 'Jewish question'. In the winter of 1938–9 he had acquired powers to organise the economic exploitations of the Jewish population. The wider question of what to do with the Jews thus excluded from public life he delegated to Heydrich and the SS, under his loose supervision.[86] Goering was attracted at first to the idea of expelling all German Jews, either to Madagascar or to the western powers. But he argued that it would only be possible to deal adequately with the problem in wartime because war released the Nazis from the constraints of international law and the pressure of public opinion.[87] After the outbreak of war the seizure of Jewish assets increased in scale, as did the exploitation of Jewish labour. It was during the 'cleansing' of the European economy that the Nazi leadership moved towards a final solution to the Jewish question.

In the summer of 1941 Goering ordered Heydrich to provide a plan for resolving the Jewish problem using any means available. Heydrich announced this at the Wannsee Conference on 20 January 1942, using it as a *carte blanche* from the movement's leaders to proceed to annihilation. Goering was not present at the meeting, but was represented by his state secretary, Neumann. It was his wish that he be kept closely informed about SS policy towards the Jews and it can be assumed that the SS carried out their tasks with Goering's knowledge and blessing.[88] He had for a long time, both in private and public, expressed his fierce hostility to the Jews. He saw Zionist conspiracies everywhere and, like Hitler, expected a final settlement of the scores between Jew and German.[89] The only reservations he had were expressed in terms of economic necessity. He insisted that Jewish labourers working on arms orders in Germany should not be moved eastwards while they could still work, but he removed even this constraint in August 1942. Otherwise he left Heydrich free to carry out his instructions 'for the achievement of the final solution to which we aspire'.[90]

Goering also co-operated closely with the SS on the establishment of joint enterprises and the recruitment and use of non-Jewish slave-labour. The reliance on forced labour was an inevitable result of the fact that much of the Reichswerke's operations lay outside the Reich. By 1942 the proportion of foreign workers and prisoners-of-war employed in the Reichswerke, including its German firms, was between 80 and 90 per cent, out of a workforce of more than 600,000.[91] The workers were drawn from all over Europe, some attracted from neutral or allied countries by the prospect of employment. The distribution of the workforce at the main Salzgitter works in June 1941 was as shown in Table 8. The average number of foreign workers in the rest of German industry at the same time was only 20 per cent. Not only did the Reichswerke take a large proportion of foreign workers, helped by the control over labour recruitment in Goering's hands, but it also worked with the SS to integrate concentration-camp slave-labour into the workforce. At Linz a special SS labour camp was set up to provide slave-labour for the Reichswerke. In Austria and Bohemia the SS and the Reichswerke set up joint enterprises, in quarrying, timber production and brick-making, which drew some of the necessary labour from neighbouring SS camps, including Mauthausen. Conditions of work were kept at a deliberately low level, producing, according to the SS economic office, a work efficiency only one-fifth that of a normal worker, thus increasing the demand for a regular supply of slave-labour.[92a]2.5

Table 8 *Distribution of the workforce by nationality, Reichswerke A. G. Salzgitter/Watenstedt (per cent)*

Germans	(pre- 38 Reich)	22.1
Germans	(greater Reich)	2.0
Italians		21.1
Poles		15.8
Czechs		11.0
Belgians		2.6
Bulgarians		1.3
Dutch		2.3
Others		2.7
POWs		17.4

Source: Salzgitter Archives, 12/141/1–2, company report, 2nd qtr 1941, p. 2.

After 1941 much of the forced labour came from the Soviet Union, but in order to maintain the slave economy Goering and the SS were compelled to spread the net widely. By the end of the war over 10,000 workers had died or been killed at the main Salzgitter plant, 6,000 of them French, the rest from the east.[93] The Reichswerke made special arrangements with the Gestapo for work-discipline, which, because of the high number of foreign workers and forced labourers, tended to be poor. Workers who were accused of slackness or indiscipline were sent to Gestapo 'work education centres' which one Reichswerke firm declared a great success. Very few workers, it reported, needed to be sent for a second time.[94] Saboteurs and propagandists were shot. Great care was taken to make sure that racial 'undesirables' and communists would not mix with other workers. The Watenstedt factory set up under joint SS/Reichswerke operation had a slave-labour camp attached to the plant and built in such a way that the slave labourers could be insulated from the remaining workforce. It was on these sort of grounds that Goering refused the offer of SS prisoners to work in mines because it gave the workers too great an opportunity for acts of sabotage or to spread communism and defeatism.[95] In all these enterprises Goering's officials relied upon the routine assistance of the SS and the security services in securing their grip upon European resources.

Nowhere was this growing radicalisation more completely demonstrated than in Hitler's intention to attack the Soviet Union in 1941 to complete the first major stage of racial empire. Goering did not oppose the idea of invading the Soviet Union as such, but he would have preferred to wait until more weapons were available and Britain eliminated from the war. At the Nuremberg trials he argued that war in the East was inevitable, but that he had expected it to break out in 1943 or 1944.[96] He proposed, in a rare moment of strategic insight, that German resources should be concentrated on driving the British from the Mediterranean by attacks on Suez and Gibraltar, before turning to destroy Russia. He also wanted more resources diverted to producing bombers to bring about defeat through a renewed strategic bombing campaign. Hitler on the other hand was convinced that Britain was powerless to damage Germany effectively and could be dealt with when Russia was defeated. He also argued that the Mediterranean theatre belonged by rights to the Italians whom he unwisely judged to be strong enough to contain British forces while he was occupied in the east.[98] Goering was compelled to accept the arguments. Nor could he do otherwise, for he had been among the foremost arguing for the final reckoning with Bolshevism. It did not make political sense to shrink from the conflict. The attack also gave him the opportunity to complete the programme of *Lebensraum* and to strengthen the hold of his organisation upon the new economic order in central and eastern Europe. By doing so the Four Year Plan and the Reichswerke could complete the process whereby they had become the chief instruments of economic and imperial expansion. The promise contained at the centre of extreme German imperialism, from the annexationism of the First World War onwards, was to provide Germans with the economic resources – labour, foods, raw materials – from the vast area of Eurasia. Not unnaturally there was considerable competition among the leading Nazi politicians for the honour of delivering such resources to Hitler and the German people.

For Hitler, as for many Nazis, Russia was the perfect geo-political complement for a vigorous industrialised Reich. Russia was rich in food and raw materials and would provide these resources, as well as labour, to satisfy the needs of the imperial German state; an agrarian hinterland for the more developed German-dominated area of Europe. An agrarianised Russia, cleared of all save a supply of slave-labourers, would also provide a vast area for German colonisation, from which the German farmers who went there could constantly replenish the German racial stock with Germans raised in the best racial environment. In addition the area would require large permanent garrison cities to prevent the renewal of any threat from the east, and an imperial bureaucracy drawn from the Nazi officials in the west.[99] In other words, Russia would give the Germans somewhere to rule. The circumstances of war made it necessary to acquire the raw materials and food as a first priority, but neither Hitler nor those directly in charge of the occupied area lost sight of the wider or more enduring purpose for acquiring *Lebensraum*. The trains that carried much-needed supplies to the German armies in Russia also carried settlers for the East, and the racial extermination squads.

Goering later claimed that he had not known of the proposed invasion of the Soviet Union until July 1940. In fact Hitler himself had only begun to explore the possibility of a campaign in July, and no final decision was taken until December 1940. Goering thus heard about the Soviet plans at the same time as other military commanders and party leaders, though it was also known from discussions in late 1939 that this was a possible option in Hitler's thinking.[100] Once Hitler issued instructions on July 30 1940 for planning a Soviet campaign, Goering authorised air preparations to that end, while he sought to protect and extend his own economic jurisdiction in the areas to be conquered in the east. For Goering the Soviet Union offered a reservoir of food, labour and raw materials to make up for the increasing shortages in these resources in the greater German area. The iron ore was of great importance for it promised to free Germany once and for all from dependence on the rich Swedish ores.[101] Most important of all it offered oil. Despite the efforts to produce synthetic oil and to increase supplies from Roumania, both sources failed to supply what was expected or asked for. Goering was more aware of this than most because the Luftwaffe lived only on oil of the highest quality. If war had been avoided in 1939 the synthetic oil programme would have provided a very large part of the military oil requirements by the mid-1940s. By 1941 it clearly could not. The acquisition of oil supplies from the Caucasus had become for Goering by June 1941 'the chief economic goal of the invasion'.[102] So much did the question of oil occupy Goering that Hitler, too, was influenced in 1942 to press on the southern front in Russia in order to get the oil necessary to complete the defeat of the Russian armies in the north.

It was because of the vital importance of oil, iron ore and food for the German war economy, faced with the prospect of war on three fronts by the summer of 1941, that Goering insisted on exercising complete power over the economy in Russia himself. Hitler agreed with Goering's view, granting him preliminary powers before the invasion and confirming them in the first decree on the exploitation of the Russian economy on 29 June 1941.[103] The decree gave Goering responsibility for the exploitation of all economic resources in the newly occupied eastern area without exception. At the end of July Goering published a general decree establishing his role in the east and setting out a list of priorities for the economic exploitation of the area; fats and oils, wheat, mineral oil and light metals. To carry out the necessary programme, Goering in co-operation with the Thomas office, established an economic supervisory office – *Wirtschaftsführungsstab Ost* – and an executive office – *Wirtschaftsstab Ost* – to co-ordinate and carry out the policies of the Four Year Plan.[104] The fate of individual enterprises was left under the immediate supervision of the front-line troops who needed the resources of local production for maintenance and repair of German *matériel*, but decisions on allocation were the ultimate responsibility of the Four Year Plan. The exceptions to this rule were the heavy industrial areas of the Ukraine and the Donetz Basin which were to come under the direct supervision of the agents for the Four Year Plan, and Soviet mineral oil production, which was directly under Goering's jurisdiction in Berlin.[105]

Goering approached the Soviet economy with a mixture of looting and direct exploitation. The looting began as soon as the troops moved into the Soviet Union. Goering had established special 'booty commands' whose job was simply to remove anything that looked useful for Germany industry and return it to the Reich. By the end of the first week in Russia over 8,000 machine tools had been transported back for use in the aircraft industry.[106] The retreating Red Army attempted to destroy everything that was left behind, but so swift was the initial German advance that this was not always possible. What the German troops did not want from captured areas was sent back to the Reich. Goering's orders were to leave the Russian population with as little as was necessary to keep a proportion of them alive to work for the new masters.[107]

Some things could not be looted. Goering had to decide on the question of how to exploit resources that could not be physically removed such as mines, or that could be used more usefully on their existing site, such as the iron and steel works of the western Soviet Union. The long-term plan for Russia denied these raw material resources to the native population, which was to be agrarianised or eliminated, and provided for their incorporation into the greater economic region. But under conditions of war, with great pressure on the domestic economy to produce more, Goering favoured exploiting the Soviet industrial base on an improved basis to underpin German war production. For once, the problem of ownership was uncomplicated. Since all property in Russia was owned by the state, it was transferred *en bloc* to the Reich. The system of collective farms was maintained organisationally in order to extract as much as possible, quickly, from the Russian area. Industry was transferred in trust to the Goering economic empire. The scope and nature of the trusteeship, and of the production contracts from the trustee office, was 'reserved for the consent of the Reichsmarschall'.[108]

In the early months of the campaign such trusteeship was exercised only loosely because the organisational form of the trustee offices had not been prepared beforehand. Until the jurisdictional question was defined, Goering allocated responsibility for industrial and raw material questions to three large state monopoly organisations set up for the purpose. These monopolies were in textiles, oil and iron and steel. Their common denominator was the direct authority of Goering as head of the Four Year Plan. The oil monopoly had been set up in January 1941 as the Kontinentale Öl

Gesellschaft. Although it had a private economic form, like the Reichswerke, it was a state-owned and controlled holding company. The block of state shares had multiple voting rights to ensure that under any circumstances the government would always have a 50 per cent controlling interest. By the time of the invasion of the Soviet Union, Kontinentale Öl had taken over the Belgian Confordia oil business, the French 'Columbia' concern, sections of the Roumanian-based Petrol-Block, and was negotiating with Standard Oil of America for acquisition of the Hungarian oil fields. When the Russian oil fields were finally occupied Goering intended to incorporate all of them into the oil monopoly and to keep its ownership permanently in the hands of the Reich.[109]

The other monopoly organisations were established on the same principle. The textile monopoly – the Ostfasergesellschaft – was set up under Hans Kehrl, the Four Year Plan official who had already helped to incorporate the Czech economy into that of the Reich. The iron and steel monopoly was set up at the beginning of September 1941 under Pleiger of the Reichswerke, with the title of Berg-und Huttenwerkgesellschaft Ost (BHO). The monopoly enjoyed by the BHO extended not only to iron and steel, but to iron ore, coal and manganese.[110] All Russian heavy industry was to be incorporated into the monopoly organisation. Its funds which totalled almost 100 million RM by the end of the first year, were provided by the state, the bulk of them through the Preussische Staatsbank and the Reichskreditkasse, Berlin.[111] The object of the organisation was the rational and integrated exploitation of the whole region under the firm direction of the state. Beginning with the industries of Nikopol and Krivoi-Rog, the BHO extended its operations to include the Donetz Basin and the industrial area of Dniepropetrovsk.

There were the usual objections to Goering's authority. The army was unhappy about the way in which the Goering monopolies operated in the east, urging Goering to be more flexible and to release industrial capacity for the use of the front-line troops as maintenance and repair depots.[112] Neither Gauleiter Koch in the Ukraine, nor Rosenberg, who was given ill-defined powers of jurisdiction in the east, were willing workers in Goering's efforts to take over the Russian economy. If Goering acquired the right to allocate and administer all Soviet property then the role of other party appointees in the Soviet Union was, as Rosenberg argued, superfluous. Rosenberg kept up a continuous correspondence with Goering over economic policy throughout the period of German occupation, which Goering chose to ignore. He was only given what he regarded as satis-factory powers when the German forces had been all but driven out of Soviet territory by the Red Army.[113]

Goering's main stumbling-block in reviving Russian industry proved to be one of resources. The capital goods and labour required were already in short supply in the Reich. The Goering administration was itself stretched to the limit of its managerial resources. The Russian monopolies were

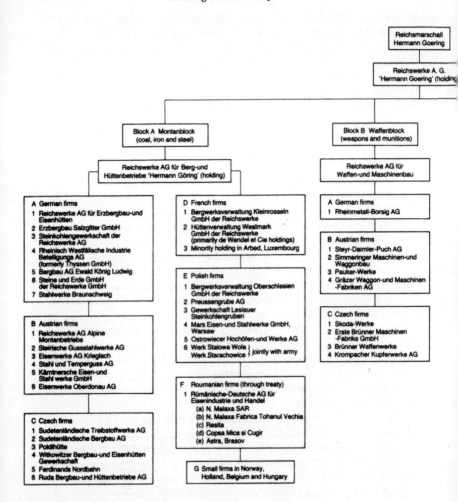

* In addition to the above the Reichswerke owned numerous smaller or subsidiary plants and held minority shareholdings in other larger businesses. The list here includes the major businesses in each country taken over by the Reichswerke. In the case of the Soviet Union it includes the major state-owned plants.

Source: NA T83 Roll 79 frame 3451540. Organisational Chart of Berg-und Hüttenwerksgesellschaft OstmbH. Dec. 1942; Roll 81, frames 3453364-6 Report on iron ore supply in Lorraine, 1944; IWM Speer Collection FD 264/46 Hermann Goering Works index of firms, 15.8.1944.

Chart IV   The Reichswerke organisation, 1942

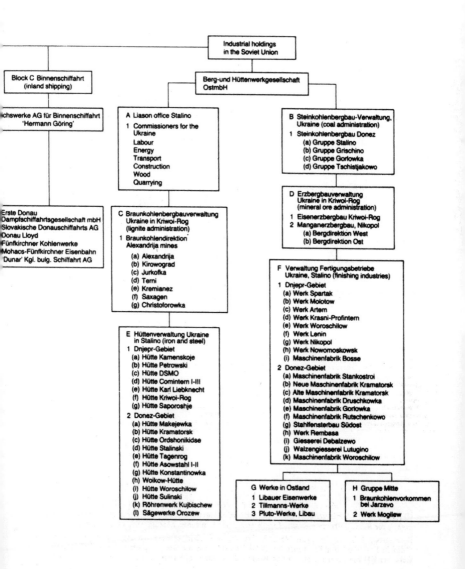

Industrial holdings in the Soviet Union

Block C Binnenschiffahrt (inland shipping)

...ichswerke AG für Binnenschiffahrt 'Hermann Göring'

Erste Donau Dampfschiffahrtsgesellschaft mbH
Slovakische Donauschiffahrts AG
Donau Lloyd
Fünfkirchner Kohlenwerke
Mohacs-Fünfkirchner Eisenbahn
Dunar' Kgl. bulg. Schiffahrt AG

Berg-und Hüttenwerkgesellschaft OstmbH

A Liason office Stalino
1 Commissioners for the Ukraine
  Labour
  Energy
  Transport
  Construction
  Wood
  Quarrying

C Braunkohlenbergbauverwaltung Ukraine in Kriwoi-Rog (lignite administration)
1 Braunkohlendirektion Alexandrija mines
  (a) Alexandrija
  (b) Kirowograd
  (c) Jurkofka
  (d) Terni
  (e) Kremianez
  (f) Saxagen
  (g) Christoforowka

E Hüttenverwaltung Ukraine in Stalino (iron and steel)
1 Dnjepr-Gebiet
  (a) Hütte Kamenskoje
  (b) Hütte Petrowski
  (c) Hütte DSMO
  (d) Hütte Comintern I-III
  (e) Hütte Karl Liebknecht
  (f) Hütte Kriwoi-Rog
  (g) Hütte Saporoshje
2 Donez-Gebiet
  (a) Hütte Makejewka
  (b) Hütte Kramatorsk
  (c) Hütte Ordshonikidse
  (d) Hütte Stalinski
  (e) Hütte Tagenrog
  (f) Hütte Asowstahl I-II
  (g) Hütte Konstantinowka
  (h) Woikow-Hütte
  (i) Hütte Woroschilow
  (j) Hütte Sulinski
  (k) Röhrenwerk Kujbischew
  (l) Sägewerke Orozew

B Steinkohlenbergbau-Verwaltung, Ukraine (coal administration)
1 Steinkohlenbergbau Donez
  (a) Gruppe Stalino
  (b) Gruppe Grischino
  (c) Gruppe Gorlowka
  (d) Gruppe Tschistjakowo

D Erzbergbauverwaltung Ukraine in Kriwoi-Rog (mineral ore administration)
1 Eisenerzbergbau Kriwoi-Rog
2 Manganerzbergbau, Nikopol
  (a) Bergdirektion West
  (b) Bergdirektion Ost

F Verwaltung Fertigungsbetriebe Ukraine, Stalino (finishing industries)
1 Dnjepr-Gebiet
  (a) Werk Spartak
  (b) Werk Molotow
  (c) Werk Artem
  (d) Werk Krasni-Profintern
  (e) Werk Woroschilow
  (f) Werk Lenin
  (g) Werk Nikopol
  (h) Werk Nowomoskowsk
  (i) Maschinenfabrik Bosse
2 Donez-Gebiet
  (a) Maschinenfabrik Stankostroi
  (b) Neue Maschinenfabrik Kramatorsk
  (c) Alte Maschinenfabrik Kramatorsk
  (d) Maschinenfabrik Druschkowka
  (e) Maschinenfabrik Gorlowka
  (f) Maschinenfabrik Rutschenkowo
  (g) Stahlfensterbau Südost
  (h) Werk Rembasa
  (i) Giesserei Debalzewo
  (j) Walzengiesserei Lutugino
  (k) Maschinenfabrik Woroschilow

G Werke in Ostland
1 Libauer Eisenwerke
2 Tillmanns-Werke
3 Pluto-Werke, Libau

H Gruppe Mitte
1 Braunkohlenvorkommen bei Jarzevo
2 Werk Mogilew

operated by men who already had wide responsibilities throughout the whole of Europe. Under these circumstances it took time to organise the new Soviet area, to supply the necessary materials, to establish a workable administration. By ruthless use of local labour, by the compulsory transfer of skilled personnel to the east, it was possible to get the least damaged plants working by the end of 1942. Indeed manganese ore production in 1942 exceeded that of the last year under Soviet control. But eventually Goering was compelled to order the large Ruhr firms to take over selected Russian installations and run them themselves under a system of trusteeship like that used in Lorraine. The Ruhr was, not surprisingly, unenthusiastic at the prospect of having to spend money and lose engineers and machinery which they argued could be used to much better effect at home. It was the concept of trusteeship, which left major decisions to the state and all the problems of production to the private firm, that industrialists so distrusted. Some of the more radical Nazis in the east disliked the idea of involving private firms at all, and accepted Hitler's orders to do so only as an act of expediency to cope with the problems of war production.[115]

With the re-establishment of Soviet industry the Goering empire, like the Nazi empire in general, reached its fullest extent. Within the overall compass of the Four Year Plan, the Reichswerke grew to become an industrial giant without rival, an integrated production organisation with central planning and policy control and linked finances. The full scope of the industrial empire and of the organisation that governed it is set out in Chart IV. The assets of the iron, steel and coal block alone by 1943 totalled over 5 billion marks with a workforce in the main plants of 400,000 by the end of 1943 and a total employment estimated at more than one million.[116] The Economics Ministry in March 1941 calculated that the Reichswerke was larger than all other state-owned enterprises put together.[117] By 1944 the Reichswerke provided 50 per cent of German iron ore, 20 per cent of all coal, one-eighth of all steel production, one-sixth of all tank output, 20 per cent of all shells. Its sales exceeded those of all the private iron and steel firms together.[118] To these figures must be added the enterprises that Goering controlled on behalf of the state in other key sectors, in oil, chemicals, aviation and non-ferrous metals, all adding up to a state industrial empire without rival or precedent.

This empire was built up through a process of what can best be described as legalised theft. By a combination of bullying,persuasion, seizure and bribery Goering acquired control over a large part of the economic and industrial resources of Europe. Not only was the structure that was set up linked organisationally in a pyramid with Goering seated at its point, but it was linked through its personnel as well. All the major branches of the industrial organisation were directed by Goering's deputies and officials, so that the same names recurred on managing boards all over Europe. Most of the new managers were also employees of the Four Year Plan or of its related offices or were members of the party's own economic circles. But like any imperial power, the German authorities were compelled to use the administrative and managerial skills of the conquered areas. In this way the Reichswerke could be expanded more rapidly, and the German managerial workforce be diluted without undue strain. For their part the local managers hoped to protect their firms, or the local workforce, or to improve their own standing with the occupying force. Of course no amount of prudent collaboration or careerism in conquered Europe could disguise the fact that the new German overlords were preparing to take over and control European capitalism, either through direct ownership or close supervision, just as they had done in the Reich. If Hitler believed war was too dangerous to be left to the generals, Goering believed the economy too valuable to be left to businessmen.

The New Order, in its larval stage under Goering's management, incorporated all the features of its Nazi progenitors. It was the material manifestation of the ideology of racial conflict and the imperative to conquest at the centre of Nazi thought. Through the conquest of Europe and the invasion of Russia the Nazis freed themselves from the constraints of the international political system as they freed themselves from the democratic system in 1933. In this way the racial policies of the more radical Nazis, and their economic policies too, could be carried into the very structure of the imperial apparatus, supported by a class of technical experts, bureaucrats, managers and soldiers, who believed in rule from above by the party. It was not of course just Goering who built the Nazi empire, but a significant minority of educated Germans who were also Nazis, and hoped to become a new ruling class, like that in Russia, that was neither capitalist nor working-class. This was difficult to achieve within the confines of the existing class structure in Germany before 1939 but was comparatively easy in the context of a German-dominated Europe. It was here that Nazi officials hoped to rule, that Nazi technical and economic experts hoped to make rational use of European resources to the permanent advantage of the master race and on the basis of a crude assertion of power. There was a place in this new empire for private capitalism, operating as trustees for the people's leaders, and a place for the German working class (in the long run) as the skilled and most advantaged workforce in Europe. But political and social power belonged to the party institutions.

6

THE ERA OF EGOTISM
AND INCOMPETENCE

Albert Speer, reflecting in Spandau prison on the lost opportunities of the war years, characterised the period between 1939 and 1941 as an era of 'incompetence, arrogance and egotism'.[1] For him it was the period when the German economy failed to respond to the demands of war, the period of political empire-building, poor co-operation and administrative mismanagement. It was inefficiency and ineptitude that kept the output of military material too low for the strategic tasks which Hitler set the German armed forces. Speer pointed the finger of blame for this situation directly at Goering, for throughout the early war years there was no one else with more authority and a wider range of interests in the economy. The crisis of the German war economy, already anticipated in the poor state of mobilisation in the early months of war, became increasingly obvious during 1941 and led early in 1942 to Hitler's direct intervention to exclude Goering from control over armaments production and to rely more on technical 'experts' and successful party administrators.

No one was more aware of the shortcomings of the war economy than Goering himself. Indeed the exploitation of Europe was intended as a substitute for the poor state of preparation in Germany itself, a direct result of the premature outbreak of war. From the occupation of Czechoslovakia onwards Goering made it a central feature of German strategy that resource bottlenecks and slow mobilisation at home should be compensated by continental resources. It could certainly be argued that this had always been an over-optimistic strategy, for it was premised upon an obvious contradiction: if the military economy could not reach the necessary level of mobilisation quickly enough in Germany, it could hardly do so in the conquered areas where the degree of dislocation and confusion was even greater. It was certainly possible, as Napoleon had once done, to take money, food and workers from Europe as tribute. But the more complex and delicate task of integrating the captured economies with that of Germany, utilising the resources in a rational way to meet Germany's technical and military needs, required not weeks and months, but years. Pre-war German strategy had originally been based on the idea that the new central European economic region, acquired without general war, would be carefully integrated over a number of years into German war programmes. Instead Goering was forced by circumstances to exploit the area almost immediately, before it was ready.

Goering's anxiety to utilise the European area for the war sprang, as we have seen, from the high level of demands for war material from the outbreak of war onwards. It is against this background that Goering's exploitation of resources outside Germany must be judged. Throughout 1940 and 1941 the demands of the services, in accordance with Hitler's own strategic intentions, expanded continuously. Following the defeat of France Hitler insisted on expanding, not reducing, the size of the army, with an initial establishment of 180 divisions to be completed by March 1941 and an additional large reserve to be fully established by 1943. In addition this new army was to contain a complement of 20 Panzer divisions and a further 10 motorised divisions. This was three times the number of mechanised divisions available before the outbreak of war. Hitler also intended that greater efforts should be made after the defeat of France to expand aircraft and naval armament, though not at the expense of the army but in addition to it. Indeed Hitler hoped to build an army that was as large as 'all enemy armies put together'.[2]

The same picture of escalating demands can be painted for all the armed forces. The so-called 'new priorities' for armaments in the summer of 1940 required, as Thomas wrote to Goering, 'considerable increases in war production, and with it additional materials, capacity and labour'.[3] The Flak programme, which had been run down during the actual fighting in France, was revived after July. Hitler was anxious that Germany should be sufficiently well-armed to deflect Britain from bombing attacks on Germany whose effectiveness he much exaggerated. The output of Flak shells had fallen to 122,000 in July 1940 from 274,000 in January. Hitler ordered output to rise to 400,000 by January 1941. A year later, in July 1941, he ordered output to increase to 2 million a month.[4] The planned output of aircraft, although it lagged behind Hitler's original pre-war schedules throughout 1940 because of production bottlenecks, was revised upwards again. Goering wanted it doubled in size.[5] Hitler ordered in the middle of 1940 that fighter production should be immediately increased by 75 per cent.[6] In the course of 1941, and in response to the failure of the aircraft industry to reach such targets, a renewed effort was made to rationalise production and expand output. Hitler now wanted a quadrupling of air force production.[7] The demand for naval armament (and submarines in particular) went hand in hand with the other demands, although submarine production, like aircraft production, fell behind the targets that the naval command regarded as essential if the submarine war were to have any real strategic effect. By early 1941 output had fallen to 10 per month, but Raeder and Dönitz had planned for a minimum of 25.[8]

None of this suggests a war-making machine that was deliberately wound down during 1940 and 1941 once the victories had been gained, and kept at a deliberately low level in order to preserve civilian consumption. Indeed what frustrated Goering, Todt and Thomas was the fact that from October 1939 onwards every effort had been made, sanctioned by decrees from either Hitler or Goering, to achieve the necessary cutbacks in civilian production. Over the whole period the so-called *Auskämm-Aktionen* (the combing-out operations) were in force, taking away inessential labour and redistributing it to the firms with special war-production status.[9] The corollary of this action on labour mobilisation was the cutting back (*Verdrosselung*) of civilian consumption in less essential and smaller firms. This intention was clearly stated in Goering's decree of 29 November 1939 in which he ordered that: 'Labour and capacity not engaged on the production of war goods or those essential for subsistence are to be freed in so far as they can be used to strengthen armaments output.'[10] The Thomas organisation and the Economics Ministry under Funk set about organising this task, with the less than willing co-operation of many firms, during the first half of 1940. In July 1940 Goering demanded further cuts in civilian consumption, ordering Funk to carry out a second wave of compulsory closures and re-allocation of labour.[11] In February 1941, prompted by Thomas's pessimistic reports, Goering ordered further fierce reductions not only in non-military production but in non-essential military output too.[12] By July 1941, in the face of new armaments programmes, Thomas and Todt calculated that 68 per cent of the industrial workforce was directly engaged on war production, and the remainder in areas such as mining, transport and energy that directly served the military producers.[13] There appeared to be no more resources or capacity left to be converted to war. Yet in his decree of 14 July Hitler called for 'further restriction of civilian production'.[14]

The impending crisis of war production explains why Goering established, through a network of decrees, the direct exploitation of the captured areas for war purposes. This continued the process begun with the regions of central Europe acquired before the war. It was here, in Austria and Czechoslovakia, that the highest level of exploitation was achieved. The major raw material producers, particularly the Alpine iron-ore business and Sudeten lignite production, were expanded and output increased to levels very much higher than they had been prior to 1938. The same was true for the manufacturing industries of the area. Either through direct contracts for war production with the large firms such as Skoda, or through sub-contracting for parts and components with smaller firms, the central European areas were tied closely to the production requirements of the Reich.

Outside these areas the situation was very different. It was certainly the case that a continuous flow of resources was extracted from all the occupied areas, but only after a considerable period of sharply reduced production, and throughout the war at a level well below capacity. In the French iron and steel region, for example, the plant was operated at only 40 per cent capacity even by the end of 1942.[15] By the middle of 1941 the war economy in Germany required some 36 million tons of iron and steel a year, but was getting only 24 million tons. Coal production even after the incorporation of Poland failed to match demands. Coal requirements were estimated at 280 million tons a year but actual allocation was 245 million tons. Of this total 220 million tons was produced in Germany so that the rest of Europe provided only 25 million tons. The gap was made good by government and military stocks.[16] The situation in aluminium production was the same. Requirements in 1941 were 480,000 tons but German and European production only 370,000.[17] Indeed aluminium production in Europe – which Goering planned to reach over one million tons by 1944 – never exceeded 450,000 tons throughout the war. In frustration Goering scribbled at the side of a report on aluminium production: 'Why is aluminium output not greater? and with the European area?'[18]

The list of extravagant hopes and frustrated production schedules could be extended for a large number of articles. Europe's aircraft capacity was consistently under-utilised.[19] The naval dockyards failed to compensate for the shortage of U-boat capacity at home. Even foodstuffs, which were easier to produce and procure, brought problems. If the food question never became as acute as it did in the winter of 1917–18 nevertheless by 1941 and 1942 rationing had to be more strictly enforced and it was found to be difficult to supply and distribute the extra rations for Germans engaged on heavy war-essential work.[20] Goering, against his better judgment, followed Hitler and other economic leaders in the argument that the conquest of Russia would ease all these problems. Iron ore, steel capacity, food, oil, light metals, coal and labour all were to be exploited in Russia to make up for the increasing gulf between the demands on the war economy and its actual capacity. But in the event Russia failed to provide any oil, only limited amounts of coal, iron ore and steel, and less food than had been counted upon. Moreover, some of the efforts devoted to extracting resources from Russia had to be diverted from essential work elsewhere, for example in Lorraine, and this further reduced its economic advantages.

It is not difficult to see why Europe's economy failed to come up to Goering's expectations. It was unrealistic to expect under conditions of war and occupation, with shifting and conflicting demands upon the occupied territories, that anything like a normal level of output could be maintained. But everywhere the problem was compounded through shortages of labour. The reason for this was simple. The needs of the Reich for labour took priority and from 1939 onwards a stream of foreign workers and prisoners-of-war was brought into Germany to make up for the loss of German workers to the armed forces. It is sometimes forgotten that the efforts of Fritz Sauckel after 1942 to recruit labour for the German economy did not initiate the flow of foreign labour, but completed it.[21] Well before March 1942, when Sauckel was given control of labour recruitment, Goering had ordered the mobilisation of non-German labour. By 1941 certain sectors of the war economy were already heavily dependent on the use of foreign labour. The Salzgitter works of the Reichswerke employed only 22 per cent Germans by the middle of 1941. The rest of the workforce was made up of foreign workers, with 17 per cent prisoners-of-war.[22] If this proportion of foreign labour was exceptionally high, most other armaments firms and heavy industry relied on a substantial proportion of non-German labour. By the middle of 1940 there were 2.2 million foreign workers and prisoners in Germany, by the end of 1941, 3.5 million.[23] Not only did this recruitment of labour fail to alleviate the shortages in the Reich, since demands for labour continued to escalate throughout 1941 and 1942, but it also created acute shortages of workers in the occupied or dependent countries when they were asked to provide a higher level of production to help the German war effort.

The problem of labour was symptomatic of the wider problems faced by the economic leadership in Germany in its approach to economic strategy. The fact that labour was recruited in large numbers at exactly the time that orders were beginning to flow out from Germany to the rest of Europe showed both the hurried nature of the whole programme and the failure to think through what kind of economic exploitation the Germans actually wanted. This in turn led back directly to the difficulties encountered in making strategic judgments after the premature outbreak of general war, for Goering had expected to have a longer period of armed peace within which to prepare the expanded central European region. The demands on German administrative and political resources through having to erect an empire at great speed made it difficult to produce a coherent economic plan for Europe along the lines of those suggested before 1939. The circumstances of war produced a real dilemma for German policy, which was never properly resolved. The European economy was regarded at one and the same time as a substitute for the heavy industrial 'sub-structure' which Goering had not had time to produce in the Reich, but also as a source of machines and labour to be forcibly brought into Germany for use in German factories, in the 'super-structure' of industrial production. This reflected the deeper conflict between Goering's emphasis on a raw-material based economic programme and Hitler's demand for more finished manufactured goods.

The outcome was that neither limb of the strategy worked satisfactorily. Insufficient resources were brought into Germany to solve the problem of materials for weapons manufacture, while insufficient resources were left in the captured or satellite economies to fulfil the demands for basic production there. This resulted in a continuous flow of money and materials and labour back again from Germany to the occupied territories to rectify the imbalance of resources. Investment programmes outside Germany were set up to make the captured economies produce more, made all the more necessary by the fact that much of the capacity taken over outside Germany was over-age or obsolete or based on a different technology. It might have been argued that even over-age machinery could be made to fulfil the temporary requirements of the war economy, but the German authorities insisted that where possible new machinery and higher technical standards should be used. Scornful of foreign methods of production, the German officials placed in charge of foreign production tried where possible to impose the methods with which they were familiar.[24] Some of the investment programmes were very large, particularly in Czechoslovakia, Poland and Russia, although in the latter case they resulted from the systematic destruction of Soviet economic installations by retreating Russian troops. The Finance Ministry argued against some of the more extravagant schemes, because they undermined efforts to cut back government investment.[25] But Goering insisted on carrying the programmes out, partly because most of the industrial structure outside the Reich was under his direct influence which was not the case inside Germany, partly because the whole economic strategy before 1939 had been geared to expansion into central Europe. Little attention was subsequently given to the advantages or disadvantages of cutting such a programme back once war had broken out.

The consequence was a series of unfinished projects, of money used to pay for capacity that could not be used in time for the military contingencies with which Germany was faced, of machinery and labour denied to the industries of the Reich and used unproductively outside it. The expansion of Skoda, Vitkovice and Brünner Waffenwerke was too ambitious to be realised within the time-scale set, although the resources were provided to carry much of it out.[26] In Norway, the expansion of aluminium production foundered for the lack of resources, and poor planning, so that those resources that were allocated were wasted.[27] In Austria the most notorious of failures occurred with the three vast aero-engine works sanctioned by Goering in 1938. Still uncompleted five years later, these vast factories soaked up money, labour and machinery for which no benefit accrued in terms of finished goods. When the first production lines were finally ready in late 1943 the Allies bombed the plant so successfully that all production ceased.[28] There was a similar outcome in Alsace where the Luftwaffe began work on a massive plant that was to produce all the air force's requirements of propellers, but which failed to produce anything before the Allied armies overran it.[29]

Nor did it prove any easier to revive existing industries. In the French aircraft industry, for example, the contracts placed by German firms could only be met with the help of German personnel, German machinery and, in some cases, the return to France of labour previously conscripted to Germany. Arguments about the allocation of French capacity, substantial duplication of administrative effort, the lack of clear policy guidelines, all conspired to hold up the restarting of French factories until well into the war. Many German aircraft firms used their French sub-contractors as additional research institutes, developing aircraft and equipment that they were prevented from working on in the Reich. French firms co-operated in this subterfuge because it gave them an excuse for keeping their design teams and labour force together. There was also much evidence of slow working, deliberate sabotage and passive resistance which held up the delivery of supplies for Germany. Such practices were less dangerous than they might have been because of the inefficient, muddled supervision of the French plants. The net result was that the French industry supplied only 2,517 aircraft over the period 1940 to 1944, the bulk of them trainer aircraft, 1,700 of them supplied in 1943 and 1944 after the occupation of Vichy France when German demands were more vigorously enforced. The capacity of the aircraft industry in France was approaching 5,000 a year by 1940, almost ten times greater than the amount Germany actually extracted.[30]

The difficulties experienced in France were repeated all over occupied Europe. The exploitation of European resources was poorly planned and was carried out in an atmosphere of administrative confusion. Because the economic empire had been built up so quickly, in a largely *ad hoc* way, its performance was often startlingly inefficient. The problems caused by improvised and un-coordinated expansion were clearly apparent in Goering's own Reichswerke organisation. The faster it grew, the more difficult became the task of managing it. By 1941 Goering's deputy, Körner, was compelled to spend almost two-thirds of his time on work for the Reichswerke instead of his more general responsibility for the Four Year Plan.[31] The amount of administrative and political energy that was required simply to construct and run the Goering empire diverted efforts away from the more urgent task of organising output to wage the war. At the height of the Battle of Britain Goering found himself involved in a bitter dispute within the Reichswerke over managerial efficiency which compelled him to spend days away from the battle zone where he was commander-in-chief.

The source of the crisis concerned two things. What limits, if any, to place upon the acquisitiveness of the concern; and how was such an unwieldy enterprise to be managed. There were plenty of critics outside the Reichswerke who pointed out its drawbacks. The Finance Minister, who was forced by Goering to continue to pay out Reich funds to subsidise the business as it expanded, tried to extract a price for the money with demands for greater rationalisation.[32] But the growing crisis in 1940 was brought about by the managers themselves who could see no method in Goering's madness. In April 1940 Pleiger wrote to Goering with a proposal for the reorganisation of the Reichswerke. He criticised the random way in which Goering had acquired the member firms of the concern and the tendency to vertical rather than horizontal integration. Pleiger argued that rather than try to produce the iron ore, the iron, and the manufactured product, the Reichswerke should get back to its starting point and aim to become 'the biggest mining industrialist and producer of iron' and through this 'the instrument of the economic policy of the state'. The processing and manufacturing plants should be abandoned.[33]

Goering's response was to defend the concern's policy of absorbing different kinds of firm and product and to strengthen his personal control over the whole enterprise. Since 1938 Goering's relationship to the enterprise had been ill-defined and, at times, tenuous. Although the broad strategy for expansion was worked out and approved by Goering, the running of the organisation had been left very much to the boards of directors involved. Pleiger's memorandum prompted Goering to reconsider his political position. Arguments and criticism within the concern had percolated outside the organisation, and this, Goering wrote, 'had contributed to endangering the reputation and effectiveness of the concern which carries *my* name'.[34] Goering resolved to increase the organisational unity of the regime and to institute his firm authority over it. Management consultants were brought in to instruct Goering on the proper way to manage large concerns, and during the summer of 1940 the idea evolved of dividing the many businesses up into three blocks on the basis of their primary economic function.[35] The three blocks were to be organised through the *Führerprinzip* in such a way that all managers were linked in a chain of responsibility and authority that ended with Goering and the organisation's central office under Körner. Goering insisted that in every firm, however small, there should be one man responsible directly to him for carrying out policy that was in the general interest of the whole concern. In this way a balance would be struck between decentralised responsibility and a highly authoritarian command structure. Pleiger caustically commented to Goering that the proposed structure would operate 'according to the pattern of the structure of the Armed Forces', with Goering performing the role of the supreme commander.[36]

This was indeed exactly what Goering wanted. In the letter sent to all concern managers on 15 August 1940 announcing the setting up of the block organisation Goering emphasised that 'it is now necessary that an effective and purposeful management which will follow my orders must be secured as quickly as possible'.[37] In a personal letter to Pleiger Goering explained that 'the leading men of the Reichswerke "Hermann Goering" and its subsidiary companies must at any time be in a position to bring my orders to bear, even within the smallest companies of the concern'.[38] To ensure that the political arrangement of the concern conformed to the new military pattern of organisation Goering dismissed a number of influential managers and directors and demoted others, including Pleiger himself. The managers who remained were given three months to carry out the reorganisation which was formally set up in January 1941, after much discussion and internal argument. Three blocks were established, for coal, iron and steel, for arms manufacture and for shipping. Over them all sat an umbrella organisation with Goering at its head which carried the responsibility for general policy and decisions on the expansion of the concern for which Goering already had considerable plans. Although Pleiger continued to be critical of the new structure, since he believed it undermined managerial responsibility, he and the remaining directors had to accept Goering's ambition 'to create out of the concern an economic and political instrument that must at all times be ready for action on behalf of the Reichsmarschall'.[39]

This solution by no means ended the difficulties for Goering continued to increase the demands made upon his managerial resources by pressing his claims in France, Poland and later in the Soviet Union, so that the organisation was never still enough to benefit from the effects of the rationalisation of 1940. Goering's dilemma was encapsulated in this situation. Anxious to defend his own political position, unwilling to concede the initiative in economic and industrial affairs outside the Reich to anyone else, a great deal of Goering's time and effort had to be devoted to setting up the organisation and defending its borders while trying to expand domestic output of armaments at the same time. These two major and very different tasks produced problems faced by none of Germany's enemies, who could concentrate their administrative energies on extracting as much as possible from an integrated domestic economic structure.

The belief that the conquest of Europe could make up for the deficiencies of Germany's domestic economy was an illusion. Under conditions of peace, and with a much longer span of time, much more might have been obtained. But the problem was that the economic empire-building was conducted against a background of war, resistance and occupation. Goering's difficulties thus assumed a Napoleonic dimension. The New Order, like the Continental system, brought as many disadvantages as it brought benefits. Germany enjoyed the advantage of money and labour extracted from the occupied regions to help pay for the war and increase the size of Germany's forces, but the establishment of the New Order itself persuaded Hitler to gamble further by attempting the defeat of the Soviet Union and placing excessive demands on the German economic structure. Moreover, the Germans were faced in all the occupied areas with active and passive resistance. Like Napoleon before him, Goering was to discover that even the collaborating forces in the occupied countries were basically unenthusiastic about the prospect of permanent imperial control. In some areas collaboration was hard to establish at all; the difficulties experienced in Norway, Jugoslavia, Russia and France owed much to the work of resistance fighters in sabotaging and undermining efforts to reconstruct industrial life. Europe's economic resources used for the German war effort were by no means negligible, but the military and administrative effort needed to extract them compromised the efforts to mobilise the economy within Germany. Germany's new empire had its share of Bernadottes as well. The jurisdictional and political contest among the new imperialists diminished the rewards of empire still more.

The failure to extract sufficient from Europe in the first two years of war highlighted the difficulties faced by Germany's domestic economy. Escalating military demands, the wide-scale conversion to war, the efforts to complete the expensive projects of the Four Year Plan placed a growing strain on German resources. Goering became overwhelmed by resource problems between summer 1940 and the battle for Moscow late in 1941. He blamed his difficulties on disappointing efforts in Europe but there was no disguising the fact that the problems ran deeper than that.[40] There was a growing awareness that Germany was not making the best use of the resources at her disposal, that the problem was not so much a shortage of economic resources as the inefficient way in which they were mobilised. The clearest evidence of this was to be found in the mobilisation of German labour.

In mobilising labour there were a number of different though closely related questions. The first was how to prevent the armed forces from mobilising any worker whatever his skill or the importance of his work. This was a particularly acute problem in the armaments and metal-working plants where much of the workforce was in the younger age groups and liable for conscription.[41] Efforts were made to produce a classification scheme for firms on the basis of the degree of priority they should enjoy for the war economy, but even such protection was on occasion ignored by the armed forces while firms with less essential tasks spent great efforts trying to win privileged status and hang on to their labour. The second problem was that of the volume of labour. There were no unemployed labour reserves available on the outbreak of war. The armed forces drew some 4.4 million men out of the labour market in 1939 and apart from a brief work leave in the summer of 1940, the armed forces continued to expand in size at the expense of the economy.[42] The war industries then had the responsibility under the guidance of the Economics Ministry and the Four Year Plan of absorbing labour from the agricultural and inessential industrial and tertiary sectors to compensate for losses to the armed forces. This was done with mixed success by the middle of 1941 when almost all industrial labour was registered as working on war economic tasks or on work essential for the survival of the home population. In addition labour was recruited or coerced from outside Germany and from the prisoners-of-war. The main movements in the German labour force are set out in Table 9.

The demand for labour rose steadily over the first years of war. In February 1940 the current requirements of new labour totalled 250,000; in February 1941, 1,100,000; early in 1942, 1,300,000.[43] Many of the demands from the factories or from the armed forces were deliberately inflated in the efforts to compete for labour. But the high level of demands also stemmed from the failure to mobilise additional labour resources satisfactorily enough or to use existing labour more efficiently. Additional female workers were not mobilised at all for the war effort because of Hitler's insistence that women should stay at home to boost the men's morale. Nor, initially, were many of the prisoners-of-war put to work. By 1942 only 2 million out of 5 million were at work.[44] There is no doubt that the absence of a central authority for labour with sufficient power exaggerated the competition between labour users as well. Throughout the war the effectiveness of additions to the workforce from outside Germany was reduced by

Table 9   *Distribution of labour in Germany 1939–44   (millions)*

| Date | Civilian labour force | | | | Armed forces | | |
	German men	German women	Total	Foreign labour and POWs	Total mobilised	Losses	Active strength
31 May 1939	24.5	14.6	39.1	0.3	1.4	–	1.4
31 May 1940	20.4	14.4	34.8	1.2	5.7	0.1	5.6
31 May 1941	19.0	14.1	33.1	3.0	7.4	0.2	7.2
31 May 1942	16.9	14.4	31.3	4.2	9.4	0.8	8.6
31 May 1943	15.5	14.8	30.3	6.3	11.2	1.7	9.5
31 May 1944	14.2	14.8	29.0	7.1	12.4	3.3	9.1
30 Sept 1944	13.5	14.9	28.4	7.5	13.0	3.9	9.1

Source: N. Kaldor, 'The German War Economy', *Manchester School*, XIV (1946), pp 27, 32.

the simultaneous withdrawal of more German labour into the armed forces. All Goering's efforts to reverse this process and to treat foreign labour reserves as a net addition were frustrated by the priority enjoyed by the armed forces for military labour.[45] This would have mattered much less if German labour had been efficiently used, but in fact under the pressure of wartime conditions and a confused wartime administration the productivity of German labour remained static or in some major industries, such as aircraft, actually fell considerably during the early years of war. Later in the war much more was produced with the same or even less labour, much of it unskilled and unwilling, because the shortage of skilled German workers had increased the pressure to introduce more mechanisation.

The inefficient use of labour reflected the general inefficiency of the German war economy in 1940 and 1941. Throughout the period 1939 to 1941 the quantity of labour, raw materials and factory capacity made available for war expanded at a faster rate than output. Aircraft production, for example, rose only 30 per cent between 1939 and 1941 while the resources made available for it increased by almost 100 per cent.[46] The scale of this failure can be illustrated by the fact that German leaders planned to increase aircraft output by between 200 and 400 per cent over this period. The central explanation for the low level of weapons output in the early part of the war lies in the extraordinary degree of inefficiency and wastefulness in the German war effort.

The answer to the German economic difficulties was rationalisation. Speer later claimed that it was he who was responsible after 1942 for transferring resources from civilian to military production and rationalising the German war economy.[47] In reality the transfer of resources had largely taken place by 1941. Speer himself later admitted that 'in the middle of 1941 Hitler could easily have had an army equipped twice as powerfully as it was. For the production of those fundamental industries that determine the volume of armaments was scarcely higher in 1941 than in 1944.'[48] Nor did Speer begin the rationalisation of the economy. Improved productivity had been a major government priority even before the outbreak of war. The Todt ministry had been set up specifically to improve productive performance, and Todt himself had recognised at once the deficiencies of the procurement system and set out to rectify them. Other critics pointed out how inefficient the railway network was, how poorly labour was distributed, how badly co-ordinated and interest-ridden the procurement process was.[49] Even Goering was aware, though he did little about it, that the economy he controlled was full of muddle and waste.

But so hastily had the economy been mobilised that it took time before a clear picture could be formed of what the problems were. Hitler only became aware of the dimensions of the economic problem towards the end of 1941. Indeed his initial response was to assume that the war programmes he had set were too high and ordered the armed forces to make fewer demands and to make their programmes match the scale of available resources.[50] But by October Hitler, too, was persuaded by Todt, Thomas and Milch that the real problem was rationalisation and his subsequent decrees reflected this realisation.[51] By this time the first efforts had already been made to change the administration of the war economy and raise the level of industrial efficiency. Todt introduced a series of special committees for separate groups of weapons, involved industrialists more in decision-making, and streamlined the administration of army production. Success was partial, but it laid the foundation for the more rational production programmes later in the war which Speer was to administer.

In aircraft production, which was independent of the Todt ministry, it was Milch, Goering's deputy, who organised production along more rational lines. Goering gladly accepted the proposed rationalisations because he had the task of explaining to Hitler why aircraft production was lagging so far behind target. Under cover of two new aircraft programmes, the 'Elch' programme and the 'Goering' programme, designed to bring the Luftwaffe closer to its production targets, Milch and Udet transformed the aircraft economy from the peacetime programmes and pattern of mobilisation, in which it was still stuck, to a more rational wartime structure. Milch introduced more industrialists into planning with a special 'Industrial Council' set up in May 1941. The council recommended a wide range of reforms, the most important of which were the introduction of a system of industrial committees and 'rings' linking together the producers and contractors for a particular aircraft type, and the insistence on modern methods of factory production.[52] The committee system anticipated the one that Speer was to make more general in 1942 and the introduction of new production methods laid the foundation for the rationalisation drives of 1942 and 1943. There were limits however, to what could be done at this stage of the war. Much time had been lost in misdirected or undirected planning during mobilisation, and the efforts made in 1941 could not hope to bear immediate fruit. The German air force never made up the lost ground of the first two years of war; Germany produced considerably fewer aircraft than any of the major Allied powers and not significantly more than Japan which was much less generously endowed with industrial resources. Goering and his deputies laid plans in the middle of 1941 for aircraft production to match that of the United States and Britain, with figures in excess of 50,000 aircraft a year, but such figures were never remotely realised, despite the fact that resources for them existed in the economy.

Nevertheless a considerable amount was achieved. Using the same quantity of labour, and fewer raw materials, the German aircraft industry produced 31 per cent more aircraft in 1942 than in 1941, and in 1943 111 per cent more.[53] By 1944 output of all weapons was three times greater than in 1941, while the amount of additional labour, materials and factory space had increased by very much less or, in some cases, not at all.[54] Production later in the war was based on the level of resources already employed before 1942, but used to better effect. The bottlenecks that had so worried administrators before 1941, particularly labour, became much less serious with the more widespread application of modern production methods and the rationalisation of resource distribution. What had appeared to Thomas and Goering as an absolute restriction on war production placed by the level of available resources, became, through their more effective utilisation, merely relative. From 1941 all the major armaments firms reported substantial improvements in efficiency in the use of labour and capital, achieved by a combination of better production planning, more advanced work methods and the elimination of wastage. In many sectors output per man hour rose by 200 to 300 per cent between 1941 and 1944. For the first time planning and actual output began to converge.[55]

There were plenty of scapegoats for the inefficient mobilisation of the German economy. Goering blamed individual administrators, especially those in his own organisation; he blamed industrial firms with their company egoism; and he blamed himself for not taking a firmer grip on the central control of the economy. There was certainly something in all these explanations, particularly the last. There was a close and recognisable relationship between Goering's personal political fortunes and those of the economy. Overall economic performance was critically affected by Goering's own position in the political structure and the power relationships that this generated. Yet personal failure is not a sufficient explanation on its own. Goering's technical incompetence certainly made the problems worse than they might have been. The real problem was a structural one, the failure not just of Goering, but of the movement as a whole to alter institutional and social structures in Germany in such a way that the fullest use could be made of German resources for waging war. In the end this was a political question, not an economic one.

To understand the difficulties facing those who ran the German war economy it is necessary to go back to the political crisis of the mid-1930s. During this crisis the reintegration of the military, industrial and political elites, achieved during the first few years of economic recovery and rearmament, came to an end. Under the pressure from the party to adopt a more dirigiste economic policy and to prepare for expansion in Europe the integrationist alliance gradually broke up. The direction of economic and military policy became a predominantly party affair, although the armed forces and the heads of industry were still expected to bear much of the responsibility for carrying Nazi programmes out.

The Nazis provided an alternative apparatus, bureaucratic and coercive, designed to transcend particular interests and impose the primacy of Nazi political goals. The aim was to produce a new integration, based on the political interests of the party. In this attempt Goering played a central role. Through his wide use of patronage, and the large new institutional structures that he created, he not only saw to it that Nazi supporters were given positions of responsibility in the existing military and economic administration but established new agencies like the Four Year Plan. Some, indeed, of the new Nazi officials were themselves soldiers or businessmen but they were often of low rank and were genuinely committed, unlike the more senior officers or the Ruhr industrialists, to establishing a new integration of political forces under the directing influence of the Nazi movement. For this generation of Nazi officials there was little to be gained from the restoration of the pre-1914 conservative political system.

Indeed many of them had become Nazis in order to avoid a restoration of social and political power to the old elites. Paul Pleiger regarded the old trusts and cartels of the Ruhr as politically bankrupt, incapable any longer of pursuing the interests of the people as a whole.[56] What the new, and predominantly middle-class officialdom wanted, was a redefinition of social power in their favour, derived from membership of the Nazi movement. As in Stalin's Soviet Union the long-term aim was to create an 'integrated' community dominated by the political power of the party, controlling its own military and bureaucratic apparatus. Between 1938 and 1942 Goering assumed the responsibility for constructing and running this alternative apparatus. By excluding the military and industry from decision-making, the Nazis hoped to create a new political consensus, and to pursue policies that would be identified much more with the party and not with the old ruling classes.

The problem was that it proved impossible under the circumstances to overturn the reality of social power altogether. Because neither of the major elites could afford to come out in full opposition to the party their response to the loss of political influence was a defensive one. The armed forces, and particularly the army, joined in the jurisdictional struggle in order to maintain their historic role in determining questions to do with military affairs. In this they were only partially successful. Hitler and the party leadership despised the political pretensions of the officer corps but respected their technical competence. Although Hitler took over the determination of all grand strategy into his own hands (and later in the war much battle strategy as well), the technical and administrative role of the armed forces was left intact. Goering insisted on his right to give orders to the armed forces' own economics staff under Thomas, but accepted the technical role that Thomas's armaments inspectorates played at factory level. As head of the Luftwaffe Goering could direct its main strategic development, but left the routine work of technical procurement and organisation to the military experts. In this way the armed forces cemented their grip on the lower levels of decision-making as a way of saving their traditional social and political role from extinction.

The industrial leadership became equally defensive, like the armed forces, and used the cartel structure and the dominant position it enjoyed at the local level of the economy to secure its interests in the face of state controls or uneconomic state policies. The centrifugal nature of the industrial economy contrasted sharply with the Nazis' own preference for a strongly centralised machinery. It reflected a strong desire for an autonomous economy in which the major businesses could shape economic strategy in a way that best suited their long-term economic interests. The armed forces' desire for a similar degree of autonomy produced a situation not unlike the period of political crisis before 1932 when particular political interests were able to undermine any attempt at producing an integrated and workable political system.

The problem for the conservatives was that the Nazis were now the masters, centralising control and determining the nature of the political system. This led to a perpetual contradiction between the centralising tendencies of the party apparatus and the defensive strategies adopted by those whom the Nazis sought to control. The army and industry pulled in an opposite direction, favouring more devolution of responsibility, in defence of their interests. This political centrifugalism could only be combated by the effective exercise of central authority, which placed much more emphasis upon the competence of those like Goering who wanted to exercise it. It could be argued that this tension between Goering's political claims on behalf of the party, and the social and political reality with which he was confronted were never satisfactorily resolved during this period. Believing that greater control was required over the armed forces and the economy in the period of war preparation, Hitler and Goering in fact encouraged the disintegration of the very political alliance that they needed to carry the war programme out. Only the early victories disguised the consequences of this shift in the political system. The growing economic crisis in 1941 showed the extent to which Goering had proved incapable of providing a satisfactory party alternative, and how unwillingly the military and industry tolerated his authority.

It is in this respect that Speer's charge of personal incompetence becomes important. It was not that Goering's alleged incompetence could not have been mitigated by the industriousness of his subordinates for indeed it could be, and was, during the 1930s. The problem was that Goering had actually created, in his efforts to supplant the conservatives, a political and administrative structure in which his personal political role assumed a critical importance. Other Nazis interpreted this as simple ambition but it was more complicated than that. Nazi insistence on the *Führerprinzip* made it imperative that the lines of authority should run vertically from the top of the administrative structure down to its base. In order to effect the political shift after 1936 Hitler moved away from cabinet and committee government to government by special commissioners and leaders. Goering was the chief of these. The special role of such plenipotentiaries was to bridge the gulf between the disparate parts of the economic and administrative apparatus, acting as the means whereby Nazis could directly co-ordinate national policy. This meant in effect that all the major decisions of policy that involved one or more major departments had to be taken by the figure at the top on his own personal responsibility. Hitler acted like this in foreign policy; Goering was expected to do the same in economic affairs and in a large number of military questions. The effect of this was to discourage co-operation between departments at a lower level, leaving them isolated and dependent. At the same time such a system placed a much higher premium on the strategic and administrative capabilities of particular individuals than was the case in any other country with a corresponding degree of industrial and institutional modernity.

Was Goering equal to such responsibilities? The short answer would be no, were it not for the fact that during the 1930s he showed himself to be a cunning and determined politician. In a very short space of time he became Hitler's immediate successor in the Nazi hierarchy. Many of his contemporaries were impressed with the massive energy and organisational effort that went into the building of the Luftwaffe before 1939. It was precisely because of the promise contained in such efforts that Hitler chose Goering, rather than another party leader, for the tasks involved in the Four Year Plan. Goering's main problems derived from the nature of the political empire that he established and the wide range of structural and institutional constraints that it imposed, rather than from straightforward incompetence. Of course it would be impossible to deny that Goering lacked any real strategic vision. When forced to make a judgment about priorities or the direction of overall military or economic policy Goering's instinct was to favour anything that strengthened his political position first, and to ignore advice that conflicted with his personal view of events. This intellectual waywardness was then magnified because of the organisational context in which he worked.

The most obvious constraint was the sheer size of the political empire that Goering tried to rule. Discounting his many minor offices, Goering was responsible for the Luftwaffe, for Prussia, for the Four Year Plan (and most economic policy after 1938), for rearmament, and for certain areas of justice. In addition there were party obligations, and an informal role in

Hitler's own field of national policy. To cope with so many offices, in most of which Goering was the highest responsible authority, some kind of cabinet structure might have been appropriate. But instead Goering tried to run them all, simultaneously, on his own. Not even Churchill, nor Roosevelt, attempted so much without a regular cabinet structure and routine consultation and delegation. Goering certainly relied on his chief administrators to take decisions in his absence – if he had not his empire would have collapsed – but in every office he insisted on taking the major decisions, formulating strategy and, in a great number of cases, dealing with the day-to-day routine when he could. The trivial nature of so many of the problems that his staff presented to him for a decision has echoes of Napoleon and Frederick the Great, who would trust no one to take the responsibility for small decisions. It was no accident that the portraits of both men could be found in Goering's study at Carinhall. But the result of such efforts was to dissipate the time Goering could devote to each area, and any pretence at central policy-making was lost in the mountain of administration required to keep Goering in direct touch with the farthest frontiers of his organisation. His staff records show an unceasing round of interviews, meetings, receptions and speeches.[57] During the war the routine became even more frenzied. In between the regular administration Goering visited Hitler at his headquarters as often as he could and made a general 'progress' through Europe on his special train once or twice a month to keep in touch with front-line troops, and to review local economic policy.[58] As a result Goering found himself continually seeing trees instead of the wood.

A second, and more damaging constraint, was provided by the widespread failure to devise a satisfactory means of central control. Goering was not blind to this necessity but failed to produce it. This was partly due to the unwillingness of other officials and senior authorities to work with Goering but it also reflected an unwillingness on Goering's part to accept a position as mere chairman of a committee. He preferred to keep the parts of his empire distinct, so that the centre point achieved greater political significance by maintaining the balance between them. Thus in 1939 he established a new administrative structure for the Luftwaffe which separated the functions of military and technical staff still further and reduced the possibility of useful co-operation between them. His solution for the crisis in the Reichswerke was not to create greater co-operation between its component parts but to divide it up still further along quasi-military lines with himself firmly in command. The two more formal structures for consultation, the Reich Defence Council and the Economic Council, set up during the early months of the war, met only infrequently and became merely vehicles for information rather than centres for deliberation.[59] Goering, like Hitler, preferred to give orders directly rather than to arrive at a policy through a process of discussion and argument, bringing all the competent authorities together to assess strategic goals and the most rational way of achieving them.

The structure of control was further weakened by Goering's political vanity. When he had to delegate he preferred to choose people whom he could dominate easily. Although this increased his personal power it meant a progressive weakening of the top echelons of his administration. Walther Funk at the Economics Ministry was Goering's creature, manipulated unscrupulously by his patron. No match for the intrigues around him, he let much of his formal responsibility fall into desuetude rather than do battle. 'In order to put up with all this', he confided to von Hassell, 'one has to be either crazy or drunk. I prefer the latter.'[60] Ernst Udet's career bore a striking resemblance to Funk's. Unsuited to his responsibilities, anxious and suffering increasing ill-health, he was bullied and manipulated by everyone around him. His office became notoriously ill-run. In November 1941 he committed suicide, scrawling on the wall before he died that Goering had betrayed him to the Jews in the Air Ministry.[61]

Goering's personal ambition, the size of his empire and the administrative weakness at its core, combined to encourage those very centrifugal pressures that the political contest had already thrown up. Goering's political victory was made hollow by the difficulties experienced in enforcing that victory on other influential groups in German society, including sections of the Nazi Party itself; and it had the effect, as we have seen, of making both the armed forces and the major industrialists defend their entrenched position in German society rather than abandon it to the centralising power of the party. These were problems that faced the Nazi movement as a whole and not just Goering. The social environment with which the party was confronted – the pervasive influence of the military, the large and inert bureaucracy, a distrustful and conservative capitalism – constantly frustrated the efforts to mobilise German society for war. Nor was the party itself sufficiently homogeneous to present a united front against the structural barriers to mobilisation.

Goering had a major problem in his relationship to the party. Since his own power ultimately derived from this source he could not afford to disregard party interests lightly. His place in the party was not as secure as, for example, that of Goebbels or Bormann because he did not hold high party office and had not earned his place in Nazi politics through routine party work. His relations with other senior Nazis were often strained because of this. Goering was never free of jurisdictional conflict with the party throughout the period from 1936 to 1945. It was at its most acute in the early years of economic empire-building and in the contest for control over the conquered areas of Russia. His main advantage was his control over large areas of patronage. This made him a more attractive political ally or master for other ambitious Nazis and secured for him a major role in setting up the imperial apparatus outside Germany in which party interests were paramount. But this also had the effect of diverting Goering's political activities from the central issue of fighting the war to the domestic problems of party conflict and administrative expansion.

Goering's most delicate conflicts were with the regional party leaders, the *Gauleiter*. In the first place the *Gauleiter* regarded themselves as the guardians of economic life in the areas over which they ruled. Goering found resistance among them to his proposals for the more rational dispersal of contracts or the siting of new capacity away from areas in danger of bombing because this benefited some areas at the expense of others. Where Goering's authority over the national economic structure was constitutionally clear, his constitutional relationship to the local party was poorly defined. A powerful local leader could challenge Goering's authority by appealing to Hitler and the party leadership directly, as did Erich Koch in the Ukraine, or Fritz Sauckel in Thuringia. Other local party officials found a host of minor disputes through which to extend *Gau* influence at the expense of the centre. This they could do because the local party organisation contained many of the more radical elements in the movement. Central authorities found it dangerous to be seen to ignore ideology too openly, while local zealots could make political capital in their own city or region by exposing policies that were ideologically unsound or threatened particular local interest. Thus Goering was compelled in the course of 1938 to take the *Handwerker* organisation into the planning of war production and to distribute contracts to small businesses and workshops away from the main industrial centres. He was also forced to modify the claims of big businesses where the local Nazi leaders had vetoed them in defence of small firms.[62] The *Gauleiter* could, and did, make things difficult for businessmen who had the backing of Goering's ministries but who would not co-operate with the local party. The aircraft producers Heinkel, Focke-Wulf, and Henschel failed to establish satisfactory relations with local Nazis and suffered intermittent harassment as a result.[63]

Finally the *Gauleiter* felt themselves to be in the front line of the party in its efforts to win political support in the German population and were as such much more sensitive to questions of morale than those more remote from day-to-day affairs. Unpopular policies from the centre had to be justified at a local level by the party's representatives. Goering aroused hostility for his policies on cutting consumer output and spending and local officials refused in some cases to institute the cuts or delayed them as long as possible. The shortages of coal in 1941 brought widespread recrimination as did policies on labour conscription.[64] Both were unpopular with the local populations and provincial Nazis made efforts to resist them. Goering regularly spoke to meetings of party leaders to justify specific policies and explain strategy. The hostile reception he sometimes received stemmed from this conflict between economic necessity and local politics. When later the Luftwaffe failed to stem the bombing offensive, the *Gauleiter* sided with the bombed population against Goering, whom they personally blamed for the failure.[65] These conflicts lit up the tensions between centralism and local interest within the party, and affected the scope and speed of economic mobilisation.

Problems such as these could be found throughout the entire bureaucratic apparatus, of which the party itself provided an extensive part. It should be said at the outset that the German problem was not bureaucracy *per se* but the particular role that it played in German society during the period of Nazi rule. The German civil service at a local and national level was very large by the standards of other major industrial powers. Its virtues were widely known, and it was from the permanent bureaucratic officials that the Nazis recruited the experts required to run much of the government machine. Many bureaucrats at a more junior level either were Nazis or had voted Nazi in 1932, and filled the posts in new party offices or in non-Nazi institutions where party supporters were needed. But because of the over-representation of bureaucrats and administrators in the new Nazi elite, the party was encouraged to establish an ever-growing army of officials. This led to excessive duplication and widespread jurisdictional confusion. The offices themselves were run efficiently enough. In fact part of the problem was that officials knew their job only too well. Every time a new office was set up it immediately invited the introduction of the entire vertical apparatus of under-secretaries, secretaries and departmental heads together with all the ancillary paraphernalia of bureaucratic life. The *Amt für deutsche Roh- und Werkstoffe* set up under Goering in anticipation of the Four Year Plan produced an organisation with 121 departmental heads within six months.[66] The Air Ministry was notorious for its intense compartmentalisation and sprawling administration. Even Goering despaired of it. 'All of a sudden', he told Milch, 'you find there is this department that has been ticking away there for a dozen years and nobody knew about it.'[67] Once such offices and departments were constituted they defended their independence from other departments and hid behind excessive protocol to do so. The effect was bureaucratic inertia and the stifling of co-operation and initiative.

Once established the bureaucratic structure was difficult to dismantle. When the Russians were on the borders of the Reich in 1944 the officials of Goering's eastern economic empire still functioned in Berlin over a territory long since vacated by German armies.[68] Not only was it difficult to dismantle but separate administrative hierarchies fought with each other for the right to administer policies where the jurisdictional question was unclear, rather than give way and reduce the number of offices. Much effort was wasted on trivial questions of precedence and procedure and on the mere duplication of the same labour by separate offices, on what Thomas called 'Parallelarbeit'. Yet because the executive was itself fragmented among competing leaders and institutions so, too, was its bureaucratic foundation. Despite complaints from all sides, particularly from those in charge of technical departments who were frustrated by the competition of party and semi-official agencies, there was little effort to reform the system. In fact the number of officials increased during the early stages of the war with the introduction of rationing and the occupation of Europe.[69] The New Order required an army of new officials who, by accepting such offices, could both avoid war service and increase their career prospects. The result was an unnecessary diversion of scarce educated manpower and the production of a slow-moving wartime administration in which decisions were delayed, information misdirected and co-operation almost impossible to achieve. The bureaucratic world, favoured by many Nazis, and deeply entrenched in traditional German public life led not to an efficient totalitarian machine but to isolated, decentralised, competitive hierarchies, politically powerful enough to defend themselves against efforts at rationalisation.[70]

No organisation was so guilty of excessive bureaucratisation as the armed forces themselves. There were several reasons for this. First of all the armed forces wanted to avoid the problems of the First World War by smothering the country with military controls in the event of another. When war broke out in 1939 military offices expanded to meet all the new organisational needs even where a civilian alternative existed. The second factor was military protocol. Excessive emphasis on a formal structure of military administration both behind the front and at home multiplied the number of people required to run the military machine. By 1943, only 25 per cent of the 8 million in the German army were at the front.[71] The army explained this by military tradition. Every military unit required its complement of adjutants and officials. So too did every military department. 'That', complained Speer later in the war, 'is military thinking, that absolutely stubbornly runs offices exactly as if they are a regiment at the front.' Goering called these military bureaucrats 'Papierkönigen' – paper kings – and blamed them for simply churning out reports and statistics instead of taking initiatives.[72] His own Air Ministry was full of such departments. The result for the economy was that yet another layer of administration was imposed on it next to the civilian and party offices. Its cost was considerable. By 1941 the administration's salaries and wages took some 60 per cent of all military expenditure, denying the funds for more urgent economic projects. In 1940 only 8 per cent of the military budget was actually spent on the procurement of weapons.[73] It also meant the loss of considerable manpower both at the front and in the factories. Despite efforts to reduce the size of the armed forces administration or to get the forces to run their rear services on managerial lines, the problem tended to get worse rather than better with the establishment of military spheres of occupation. Moreover the armed forces, in defence of their traditional position in German society, argued that it was militarily necessary to deploy so many non-combatants: not to do so would impair the smooth operation of the military machine and the maintenance of military standards.[74]

In this argument lay the core of the problem. The military establishment needed little prompting to insist on high standards, on widespread controls, on an all-pervasive militarisation of German society. Not only was this an endemic feature of German life but it gave the military elite an area of political and technical influence that not even the party was successfully able to breach. By emphasising the necessity for doing things the right way and the dangers of ignoring military procedure, and by stressing the importance of participation in military life (and of the status derived from it) the military authorities were able to salvage much from the changing political world of the 1930s. If Hitler was dismissive of orthodox and timid strategy, he was full of an NCO's respect for military values and organisation. Nor could, or would, Goering restrict the impact of military life since he was himself a high-ranking officer and the Luftwaffe was as culpable as any of the services for hoarding labour and for maintaining a vast officialdom. Indeed the existence of a separate air force created conditions of inter-service rivalry that only fuelled the growth of a military administration to back up the claims of the three services. Like the civil service the separate parts of the armed forces thought as much in terms of conflict as of co-operation. All too seldom did Hitler resolve the conflicts with clear jurisdictional decisions.

The claims of military life affected the war economy in two crucial respects. The armed forces encouraged the growth of an arms industry that was an exceptionally inefficient user of economic resources: and they insisted upon treating industry as if it were merely an extension of the military world rather than a civilian partner. What linked these two factors together was the existence of a large number of technically competent officers who lacked industrial experience. The officers who selected and developed weapons were highly educated, critical and demanding. The result was that the armed forces expected the best military equipment they could get. Not only did they expect it to be of the highest quality in terms of the materials used and its technical efficiency, but they insisted that the weapons should be constantly changed and modified to keep abreast of current research and the demands of the front-line soldiers. The effect was, of course, to produce weapons of remarkably high standard. But this faced the economy with difficulties. It meant that the weapons took a lot of development work and research, and were very expensive. During 1940 Germany spent an estimated $6 billion on weapons where Britain spent only $3.5 billion. Yet Britain produced 50 per cent more aircraft, twice as many heavy vehicles, twelve times as many armoured cars, considerably more naval equipment and almost as many tanks and artillery pieces. Even by the end of the war the actual cost of British weapons per year did not reach two-thirds of the amount spent in Germany in 1940.[75]

The high standard of German military equipment meant that the armed forces enjoyed excessive control over production, constantly interrupting manufacture to insist on the introduction of modifications or new materials. This in turn made it impossible for industrialists to plan long production runs and, in many cases, to move very far beyond the level of traditional handwork. Goering complained later in the war that industry 'could never get itself organised because every few minutes something new was called for'.[76] The army's own preference for small skilled workshops reflected this emphasis on closely controlled quality at the expense of quantity. This preference increased the demand for highly skilled labour to meet the specifications for design and finish from the armed forces' design offices. The forces despised mass-production, preferring to use craftsmen who could respond flexibly to design changes and modifications and who could be trusted to produce weapons and equipment of exemplary standard. A policy of high-quality production also involved a heavy demand for scarce raw materials for specialised components. The military officers in charge of procurement found it habitually difficult to modify demands for valuable raw materials in favour of cheaper substitutes for fear that military efficiency at the front would suffer. But in fact the more sophisticated weapons were harder to maintain at the front, requiring higher maintenance times and a larger stock of spare parts. The failure of the armed forces in Russia in the winter of 1941 stemmed in many cases from the shortages of spares and the impossibility of maintaining a satisfactory service organisation with a rapidly shifting front line.

Goering had planned to avoid this situation in the air force by insisting well before the war on the construction of a narrow range of high-quality aircraft which could be built easily in the new factories.[77] But the actual outcome was the development of aircraft that were so technically compli-cated that they took years to produce, as in the case of the He-177 heavy bomber, or were so sophisticated that they were regularly grounded for want of minor parts and were impossible to produce with rational factory methods. The aircraft industrialists all blamed excessive military interven-tion, particularly in demands for a constant stream of aircraft modifications or prototypes, for slowing up aircraft production dramatically and postponing the introduction of mass production methods until late in the war. 'The industrialists', Hitler told Jodl in August 1942, 'were always complaining to me about this niggardly procedure – today an order for ten howitzers tomorrow for two mortars and so on.'[78] Hitler only came to recognise the problem fully during the campaign in Russia. Through Keitel the armed forces were ordered in September 1941 to abandon the idea that only the best, highly finished and most modern weapon was acceptable and to make more use of 'simple and robust construction'.[79] All the services were asked to produce weapons 'which simplify the production flow and benefit mass-production. Besides a saving in production time, this course can save not only essential raw materials but also skilled labour for other important equipment. Oversophisticated machinery and equipment is unusable in war.' Goering was still echoing Hitler's instructions in 1943: 'not every wish from the front line has to be respected. I have set up whole institutions so that this over-sophistication should be reduced and the most primitive tech-nology taken up.'[80]

This situation certainly improved over the course of the war with a greater insistence on quantity and standardization, but it never disappeared. And the change came too late to much affect the war before 1943, by which stage the German forces were on the defensive against enemies where mass production under civilian control was the norm. The military preference for its own technical administration and close control over industry was a product of the general attitude of the military leadership towards civilian life, and the unwritten assumption that military interests came first. For the military authorities there never was any question about the conversion of civilian life to serve the needs of the war economy, nor that such conversion should be as far as possible under the control of the armed forces. Industry was cast in the role not of partner, but of handmaiden. The officers believed that only they were competent to judge questions relating to weapons production and excluded the industrialists from any real role in decision making. Within the services themselves the engineering officers were looked down upon by the combat soldiers, who stressed military endeavour as the highest social duty. The complicated structure of military snobbery served to reinforce the role of the military in economic life at the expense of those with managerial and production experience. Fritz Todt complained in 1941 that he was never allowed to talk to Hitler without the presence of military adjutants to press the armed forces' viewpoint; and that officers frequently by-passed civilian departments altogether in arriving at technical decisions.[81] Under Todt and Milch in 1941 some effort was made to loosen the grip of the military on industry and to bring together manufacturers under centralised civilian control; but these efforts were only successfully completed in 1944 in the imminent prospect of defeat.

The effect of the military control over industry was to reduce the initiative for planning and technical innovation on the part of the industrialists, to place design above production needs, to increase administrative particularism. It also demoralised many managers who felt that their efforts to improve production and meet Goering's high targets were jeopardised by military short-sightedness. The Opel works blamed its poor productive performance during the war on incompetent instructions from the military procurement agencies.[82] The leader of the economic group representing the aircraft industry blamed military intervention for sabotaging the rationalisation drive initiated in 1941.[83] The military organisations also directly restricted resources by insisting on the priority of conscription. Although many firms were protected by special status, how this status was assigned and how effectively to enforce it were not satisfactorily resolved until well into the war by which time hundreds of thousands of skilled men had to be hunted out from the armed forces or replacements found for them. Raw materials became more restricted than they should have been because of the high standard of general equipment demanded for the troops, and the high level of demand for military construction. Not until 1941 did Thomas alert Goering to the wastefulness of much so-called military production, which were simply consumer goods now designated as military necessities.

Even Goering, the least abstemious Nazi leader, expressed his surprise at the degree of luxury enjoyed in many army kitchens. The failure of the china, leather, paper and textile industry to contract faster after 1939 bore witness to the large-scale production of inessential military equipment.[84]

From the German businessman's point of view an inefficient, high-cost military machine was an unmixed blessing. As long as the contracts were made and paid for, and a reasonable rate of profit could be maintained, there was little incentive to produce along more rational lines. Some manufacturers did so from a genuine desire to improve wartime efficiency, but many concurred with military priorities and produced high-quality goods with slow production methods and wasted resources. Small firms were all too happy to establish a special relationship with the services for fear of being closed down under wartime regulations. Other firms in the armaments sector were managed and led by designers who preferred to direct energies towards development of new and better weapons rather than to concentrate on production questions. Indeed many German managers were conservative in the face of demands for new factory methods and rationalisation. General Bauer, responsible for industrial rationalisation in the air force and a firm believer in Taylorism, despaired of persuading the industrialists, particularly the small-scale ones, to adopt modern production methods.[85]

Under the circumstances, industrial conservatism was only to be expected. Firms preferred to encourage policies that benefited their financial position and to circumvent restrictions on profits, dividends and investment decisions. Speer found in 1942 that shift-working was almost non-existent in many arms firms, not because of labour shortages alone, but because, instead of adopting shift-working, the firms had persuaded the government to finance additional floorspace and machinery as a boost to their assets.[86] In this way the defensive distrust and uncertainty that characterised much of industry's response to Goering's war measures prevented the best use of available resources by diverting labour and materials to basic construction, away from weapons output. Not only was private industry safeguarding its interests against state power and the Nazi Party in particular, but the implicitly junior role assigned to it by the military establishment left industrialists with little choice but to retreat to the sanctuary of the firm or the cartel and criticise the performance of the war economy from the outside. When Goering was compelled by circumstances to introduce businessmen for the first time into the running of the war economy in 1941 the effect, though subdued by the accumulation of months of poor and unco-ordinated planning, was significant.

There was little else, under the circumstances, that Goering could have done. The Nazi party depended upon the support of the armed forces and the bureaucracy even after the victory of the party in the 1936–8 crisis. It was possible to win political ascendancy over traditional social groups and institutions but it was neither possible nor desirable for the Nazis to transform them altogether. For their part the armed forces and the administrative

1. The party's military hero. Captain Goering wearing his decoration 'pour le mérite'

2. Goering relaxing with Hitler in Bavarian dress. Ernst Roehm is standing behind Goering

3. Hitler, Goering and other party faithful visit the house where the poet
Dietrich Eckart lived

4. Goering in uncharacteristic hat and coat, shortly before the seizure of power in 1932

5. Goering the politician, photographed here at his desk as President of the
Reichstag

6. Goering the soldier, in full military dress. A popular picture-postcard of the 1930s

7. Hitler's 'first paladin' greets his leader

8. Commander-in-chief of the air force. Goering talking with pilots and air force personnel

9. The two faces of Goering. The civilian leader and economics overlord. 'Dining with the Warden of New College', remarked the British Ambassador, 'General Goering might pass as almost civilised'.

10. Goering the fanatic, seen here saluting Hitler at a Party rally. 'I have no conscience,' declared Goering, 'Adolf Hitler is my conscience.'

11. *Left* Captain Ernst Roehm, victim of Goering's vengeance on 30 June 1934, the 'Night of the Long Knives'. Roehm had ambitions to set up an SA air force

12. *Right* Hjalmar Schacht, Minister of Economics, 1934-7 until forced to resign by Goering, who took over as supreme authority for the economy

13. *Left* Field Marshal Werner von Blomberg, War Minister 1933 to 1938, until forced from office by Goering and Himmler's intrigues

14. *Right* Joachim von Ribbentrop, Reich Foreign Minister from 1938. A jealous rival of Goering, he tried to outbid him in foreign policy during 1939 and 1940

15. *Left* General Ernst Udet, head of air force procurement from 1936 until his suicide in 1941. Goering later blamed him for the failure of the Luftwaffe

16. *Right* Fritz Todt, construction head under the Four Year Plan and Minister of Armaments from 1940 to 1942, when he was killed in an air crash. At the time Goering was intriguing to become armaments overlord himself

17. *Left* Field Marshal Erhard Milch, Goering's second-in-command. Goering was jealous of his organising abilities, but needed him to revive air production after 1941

18. *Right* Albert Speer, War Production Minister from 1942 to 1945. Promoted over Goering's head, he gradually took over most of the work in the economy previously controlled by Goering

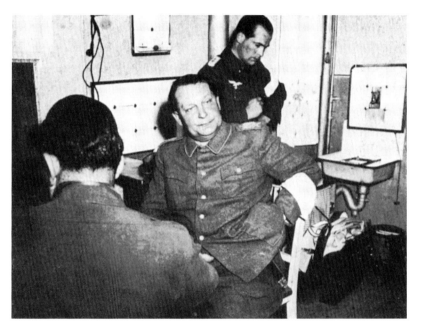

19. Goering in captivity. Here he is being relieved of his ornate dagger by American de-briefing officers

20. Goering at the Nuremberg Trials, where he re-asserted his authority over most of the other prisoners and found himself at last the 'leading man in the Reich'

departments jealously guarded their traditional social position and values just as the industrialists defended the interests of private capitalism. Under the hegemony of the party this was the last line of defence. Thus Goering was faced with groups whose relationship to the Nazi war effort was highly ambiguous, and all of whom, for one reason or another, pulled away from the centre both politically and administratively.

This centrifugal pull the party did little to alleviate, and through the growth of party bureaucracy actually encouraged. Goering was personally unable to hold the different groups together, for while he favoured greater centralisation, his own organisations contributed to undermining it. The Nazis that made up Goering's own rambling organisation were as interested in constructing the New Order as they were in running an efficient war machine so that a territorial decentralisation was added to a functional one. Goering himself hoped that the balance of political forces at home would tilt in favour of the party, and of his organisation in particular, by taking over the administration of conquered Europe and integrating its economic resources with those of the Reich. But this took him further from the central task of mobilising the domestic German economy. The efforts of the Nazis to establish an alternative apparatus for running the war economy and directing the nation's energies for war foundered on the imperialist ambitions of its leaders, and left an ill-defined administrative structure, resting on a balance of forces drawn from both the traditional and the more radical elements in German society. Neither side was strong enough for its version of the war economy to prevail and the consequence was economic stagnation and inefficiency, under an administrative structure that constantly threatened to break up under the conflicting claims of its component parts.

7

THE FAILURE OF
THE LUFTWAFFE

While Goering attempted to bridge the gap between expectation and reality in the economy he tried simultaneously to fill the role of commander-in-chief of the German air force. This in itself says much about his eventual failure in both enterprises. Most other men found high military command intellectually and physically exhausting enough. But to Goering it was a characteristic of the new breed of German leader to be part soldier, part governor. And it was in his capacity as soldier that he was most anxious to excel because it seemed to him that here true virtue lay. His heroes were the great warrior kings who were both rulers and fighters: Charlemagne, Frederick the Great, Napoleon. When he ordered a genealogical tree of the Goering family to be drawn up, its architects happily discovered that its roots could be traced back to the Carolingians, and to Charlemagne himself.[1] Goering always preferred to be known by his military titles, General-Feldmarschall or, after 1940, Reichsmarschall rather than Minister-President. The very title of Marshal of the Reich conjured up the vision of a man who embraced the whole spectrum of public life.

This romantic longing for military distinction was of the highest importance to Goering. Throughout his career he glorified military life. Honour, heroism, obedience were for him the hallmarks of man's real nature, the criteria of historical and human value. To some extent this merely reflected his own narrow military background and the pervasive traditions of German military life. Yet here, as in other areas of German society, Goering sought to supplant the traditional elite and transcend its values by providing a military leadership that was characteristically national-socialist. For Nazis, military endeavour was a reflection of the spirit of the race, a sign of a healthy people, aware of the historical necessity for struggle and willing to fight for its rewards. Neither Goering nor Hitler was willing to trust such an important aspect of the national 're-awakening' to the conservative and defence-minded Prussian establishment. From the outset the tone of military life under Nazism became more aggressive, while the population was bombarded with propaganda on the virtues of military duty and sacrifice. The revival of German military life became closely associated in the popular mind with the party rather than with the old military elite.

Goering's role as commander-in-chief of the Luftwaffe thus served a number of different purposes at the same time. It provided the party with a direct role in military affairs, through building up what was popularly regarded as the 'Nazi service'; it provided a means of circumventing the traditional military leadership and reducing its influence on strategy; and it gave the Nazis an opportunity of parading the union between party ideology and military life. Goering would have liked to command the army as well, and used the Blomberg-Fritsch crisis of January 1938 as a means to achieving it. Instead Hitler took over the supreme command for himself, leaving Goering free to develop the air force on his own, a fact that only encouraged Goering's growing isolation from the other services and his strong desire to prove that the air force, as a result of its national-socialist leadership, was the most decisive element in a future war. This view of air power was shared widely both inside Germany and abroad, but it assumed a distorted significance under Goering because of his broad political powers. Air strategy in Germany became a function of Goering's political position as much as a function of military strategy in general. Under his guardianship of the air force it was difficult to co-ordinate the plans of the three services or to arrive at a critical appreciation of air strategy.

The ultimate failure of the Luftwaffe later in the war can be traced back to Hitler's decision to give absolute control over the air force to Goering. At the time his lack of military experience in high office was assumed to be an advantage. Uncluttered with questions of military protocol and free of the military conservatism of the generals, Goering was supposed to bring fresh perspectives to the waging of war. In fact the claims of Goering's many civilian offices made it impossible for him to devote sufficient time to the air force even if he had been a capable leader, which he was not. Yet his fear of political encroachment made it difficult for others to take over his responsibilities. Thus, while he depended in practical matters throughout the period of the Third Reich on officers and engineers who were technically versed in air force affairs, he refused to relinquish his ultimate authority and the right to shape air force strategy. So much so that he hesitated to appoint officers of distinction who would expose his own shortcomings, and preferred to appoint officers or party comrades whom he could successfully dominate. This situation gave rise to a permanent tension between the commander-in-chief and his subordinates, many of whom would have waged air warfare very differently, but most of whom feared to speak out directly against Goering. For his part their commander took every opportunity to disguise his own inadequacies from Hitler, whose ideas on air warfare he slavishly followed for political advantage.[2]

Despite such drawbacks, Goering was not oblivious to the debates surrounding air strategy. Indeed his real weaknesses were exposed in the more technical aspects of air warfare or in co-operation between the services. When it came to providing political protection for the infant air force, Goering's help was invaluable. There was never any serious question of subordinating the air force to the other services once Goering was its commander. This protection, combined with Hitler's anxiety to build up air strength as a diplomatic weapon, meant that the air force grew very rapidly, certainly faster than the army and War Ministry would have liked. Air power promised immediate dividends, while holding out the prospect of new strategies for the future. With great energy its commander set about establishing an air force capable of sustaining such strategies. But there was always a gap between wish and fulfilment. Goering's vision of the future use of air power tended to be uncritical and impressionistic. He was aware of its importance but was much less sure in his grasp of the strategic and technical complexity of the service. He was not an ignoramus in air matters. His main difficulty lay in translating his views on air power into strategic and operational reality, and in the proper performance of a command function.

There were two basic objectives in air force planning. The first was the development of a close-support capability for the army in the field. The second was to construct a force capable, in the long run, of strategic bombing. The first function was accepted by most German air theorists. Germany's geographical position made it essential to be able to provide air cover for the army's activities. Although air units were designed to be operationally independent of the army units they were protecting, they were integrated closely into the plans for army operations.[3] As most of the air staff was made up of ex-army officers this was perhaps unsurprising. But Goering, too, was content to see the Luftwaffe as the leading spearhead in any projected attack by combined air and land forces. Over the question of the bombing role for the air force there was more confusion. Not all air force officers accepted the feasibility of truly strategic air operations, of attacks from the air designed to achieve a military victory on their own. But Goering, supported in this by Hitler himself, did believe that the bomber had a crucial part to play in air force strategy. He foresaw two main purposes for bomb attack. The first was a complement to the main army/air assault, attacking the enemy rear and supply services and if necessary attacking key industrial and administrative targets to speed up surrender. The second was strategic bombing. From 1935 onwards the Luftwaffe worked to create a strategic bombing force to attack the economic and military targets of the enemy or enemy morale, independent of army operations.[4]

It is worth looking at the German decision to plan for strategic bombing in more detail because this was an area of particular failure during the war. In fact so unsuccessful was it that most historians have dismissed altogether the idea that the Luftwaffe prepared for bombing in the same way as the Royal Air Force or the United States Army Air Forces. Yet at the Nuremberg trials Goering protested that his intention had been from the outset to create an air force for independent bombing operations, and that tactical army support was secondary.[5] The basic decisions for such a strategy were taken before 1935 under the influence of the first Luftwaffe chief-of-staff,

Colonel Wever. On his death in 1936 Goering cancelled the orders for the heavy four-engined aircraft known as the 'Uralbomber' because it was obsolescent but almost immediately approved trials for its successor. In June 1937 the Heinkel heavy bomber He 177 was chosen as the Luftwaffe's strategic bomber for the mid-1940s and from the end of 1938 it was integrated into all air force production plans. It was supposed to enter front-line service in 1941 and 2,000 were to be produced by early 1943. In addition, plans were laid for the development of a range of super-bombers to replace the He 177, capable of reaching the United States.[6] As this was a peacetime production schedule the Luftwaffe worked on the assumption that these figures would be substantially increased under conditions of war. To bridge the gap between 1938 and the creation of the heavy-bomber force Goering approved the building of a large fleet of medium bombers with a high performance and chose for the purpose the Junkers Ju 88. Until the He 177 could be produced in quantity the air force planned to produce by 1942 between 5,000 and 7,000 medium bombers.[7] Given Goering's belief that major war would not break out until at least 1942 or later the programme made considerable strategic sense. The Ju 88 promised to fulfil all the likely needs before then, and could be used either as an army support bomber or a long-range bomber should the need arise. Goering argued that smaller bombers also had the advantage of being cheaper in raw materials; the production of heavy bombers depended on building up the heavy-industrial base of the new central European economic region.[8]

In practice this programme was not very different from that of Germany's enemies. Neither Britain nor America produced their major four-engined bombers in quantity until 1942, and neither could mount a serious bombing offensive until 1943. The difference was that Germany's strategic bombing force never materialised, while the medium bomber fleet was provided in insufficient numbers and with lower-quality aircraft than had been intended. This was due partly to the time factor. The Luftwaffe was built up from nothing in a very short space of time and required much longer to be fully prepared for waging strategic air warfare. The premature outbreak of war caught the air force only part of the way towards completing the bomber programme and denied it the four or five years of peace that Goering had counted on to prepare for a major conflict. The lack of time was exaggerated in its effect because of deliberate efforts to shield Goering from the truth about air preparations. The Junkers Ju 88, for example, was promised for service far sooner than was in fact possible, while its performance was considerably overstated by the Junkers concern in their anxiety to win the order for the new medium bomber.[9]

To add to this problem was the slow development of the weapons, infrastructure and personnel necessary to mount a bombing campaign. The choice of the He 177 as the only heavy bomber for the Luftwaffe meant that any technical difficulties experienced in its production would delay the whole programme. This is exactly what happened. The aircraft was plagued with such grave development problems that it never saw service in any number. The training of personnel, the provision of airfields capable of handling heavy aircraft, and the tactical preparation for a bomber force had barely been started by 1939. Not until early 1939 did the Luftwaffe produce contingency plans for long-range attacks, and these were unenthusiastic about the prospects of success before the right weapons were available and the build-up completed.[10] The stage that the German bomber force had reached on the outbreak of war was an intermediate one. The medium bombers were only capable of inflicting selective, local damage in support of army activities and to attack undefended areas in the rear of advancing armies. They were not capable of strategic bombing on any scale. It was at this stage that the Luftwaffe remained stuck throughout the war.

The fate of the German strategic bombing plans illustrates very clearly that the German air force was much less well prepared for war in 1939 than her enemies believed. It was certainly true that the first stage of the build-up, begun by Milch some five years before, was complete. Germany possessed in 1939 a large number of advanced fighter aircraft to support army attacks, and a large fleet of medium bombers to carry out tactical bombing attacks. But the number of aircraft available to Germany in the last years before war was exaggerated by the Germans themselves for the purposes of diplomacy, in order to make strategic gains without actually using the air force in a major conflict.[11] In fact in 1939 German air strength was slightly less than the total strength of the Allies. The bulk of German aircraft produced since 1934 had been trainer aircraft to allow Germany to catch up with the numbers of trained personnel abroad, or converted civilian and transport aircraft designed to fill a temporary role as bombers in case Germany were pre-emptively attacked.[12] In 1939 Allied monthly aircraft production passed that of Germany. Moreover the policy of putting every available aircraft into the front line, authorised by Goering in order to meet Hitler's high targets for air force size, meant that there were few reserves available to Germany. The Allies by contrast pursued a policy of large-scale reserve-building.[13]

At the outbreak of war the German air force was in the early stages of a second five-year period of expansion and development begun in 1938, designed to bring the Luftwaffe up to full preparedness by 1942–3. The air force itself thought in terms of a major war, if at all, in the mid-1940s and Goering did nothing to suggest that this was not his time-scale too. Until then the provision of pilots and aviation fuel in sufficient quantities could not be guaranteed. Pilot training was a cumbersome affair. The air force staff planned the training programme in slow stages which the training facilities could cope with, and to avoid swamping the force with commissioned officers. Only by the mid-1940s would the air force have satisfactory numbers of trained personnel with lengthy air-force experience and a primary loyalty to an independent air strategy. In 1939 the German air force lacked this experience and degree of commitment. Many of the senior commanders were seconded from the army and by inclination favoured a role for the Luftwaffe closely tied to that of the other services. They brought to the air force a pattern of military life that was based on army needs, and although some were sympathetic to the idea of an independent air strategy the failure to pursue it with any urgency by 1939 must in part be explained by the links between army and air force personnel.[14]

The situation for the Luftwaffe was exacerbated by the divisions, encouraged by Goering, between the military and technical branches of the air force. The determination of air strategy and the development of aircraft to meet the strategy were deliberately kept apart. Goering reorganised the Air Ministry in February 1939 making the air staff fully responsible to him for the conduct of air warfare and the formulation of aircraft needs. The technical and engineering staff were made separately responsible for producing and developing the aircraft and had to report directly to Goering rather than discussing requirements with the air staff. Neither side had the right to trespass on the work of the other, which had the effect of leaving the soldiers in ignorance of what industry might produce if asked and the engineers in ignorance of what direction air strategy might take.[15] It was in the midst of adjusting to the new top-level organisation of the air force, with the unsatisfactory division of functions and a shortage of trained air staff officers sensitive to the needs of air warfare, that the Luftwaffe was faced with the prospect of a major European and world war.

The Luftwaffe was fortunate in that it faced enemies much weaker than itself for the first months of war. The Polish campaign was ended with a *coup de grâce* provided by the bombing of Warsaw which gave Goering the opportunity to claim that, in a way, the air force had brought victory in Poland. Once again he found himself in the position of handing over to Hitler the prize that he most wanted. Against Poland the air force did what it was designed to do up to 1939. In Norway, Holland, Belgium and northern France it played the same role, acting as aerial artillery for the army, providing fighter cover for the battlefield, harrying the enemy forces and bombing their supplies and formations. With good internal communications, numerical superiority and a high level of army-support training, the Luftwaffe won air supremacy over the whole of occupied Europe in a matter of weeks. The Allies had failed conspicuously to mass their air forces together, or to co-operate effectively in working out primary targets and battlefield tactics. The Luftwaffe was thus able to destroy one air force at a time and to overcome the numerical disadvantage that it might otherwise have suffered.

The effect of the German victories was to disguise the actual weaknesses of the Luftwaffe and to encourage in Goering an over-optimistic estimate of the air force's contribution to victory. Later in the war Goering rebuffed all his critics with the argument that the air force had been responsible for turning the tide of victory in 1939 and 1940.[16] Goering was more encouraged than ever in his conviction that the air force should remain completely independent, even though victory had in fact been largely won by the army, skilfully deploying the air force to provide extra fire power. There is no doubt that Goering distorted the strengths and capabilities of the air force in order to bask in Hitler's favour. If the air force had proved so valuable a weapon in 1940 it was only because, as Goering insisted to Hitler, it was operated and led along true national-socialist lines. Hitler accepted this interpretation uncritically at first, and even later in the war when the air force was on the point of defeat, still argued Goering's case that the air force always counted as the crucial factor in turning a battle in Germany's favour. When, in July 1940, he appointed Goering Marshal of the Reich he justified the title on the grounds that Goering had 'created the preconditions for victory'.[17]

Goering and Hitler's exaggerated opinion of the air force was regularly confirmed by the poor intelligence reports they were given on the strengths and nature of enemy air forces. Before the outbreak of war German intelligence provided figures on Allied strength far below the true picture. Aircraft production figures were dismissed as well below what was expected from German factories on mobilisation, and the new air defence system of the RAF was misunderstood and its potential minimised. Despite repeated warnings from the technical departments of the air force on American and British production potential, air intelligence insisted until well into 1943 that British production figures were exaggerated.[18] On the basis of the early, easy, victories Goering was more inclined to believe the intelligence reports, for they conformed with his own version of events.

Yet at the time when the Luftwaffe, and its commander, were at the height of their prestige the real limits of German air power were clearly demonstrated. If Luftwaffe preparations were sufficient to support the army in continental campaigns they were far from adequate to defeat Britain. Indeed the kind of air strategy necessary to overcome British resistance was at best only in its formative stage. The decision to attack Britain from the air taken in July 1940 was taken in the absence of any clear strategic alternative, and not because the Luftwaffe had been prepared for such a campaign. The generals saw it only as a necessary prelude to an invasion by the army, and thus simply an enlarged version of the combined operations in the Battle of France. Only Hitler and Goering half hoped that the Luftwaffe might be able to inflict on Britain an air attack whose intensity would persuade the British government to sue for a humiliating peace.[19]

In the Battle of Britain the Luftwaffe faced for the first time an enemy with well-organised air defences and a clear view of air strategy. British air preparations before 1939 had been geared (though late in the day) to just such a contingency. The advantage lay very much with the defending force for its equipment and planning had been specifically designed to prevent enemy air attack. Luftwaffe preparations were by contrast at a rudimentary stage. There was no heavy bomber capable of carrying large loads over a long range. Fighter cover could only be provided for very short periods over a small part of the enemy's territory because they could carry only small quantities of fuel. German dive-bombers were unsuitable, being too slow for attacks on well defended air targets. Little was known about British radar and the defence communications system or how to combat it effectively; even less was known about British strength and production. It was over the question of aircraft numbers that the Luftwaffe made its greatest miscalculations. German intelligence assumed that the RAF would be supplied with only 180 fighters a month, and expected this figure to drop once air attack had begun. Yet actual British production was 496 in July, 476 in August, 467 in September.[20] The Luftwaffe on the other hand had suffered heavy losses throughout the European campaigns. From 10 May to 31 July the Luftwaffe lost 2,630 aircraft of which 1,764 were totally destroyed. The additional aircraft supplied from the factories barely made good these losses. During September 1940 almost 1,000 aircraft were lost. Yet the monthly output of German fighters over the summer averaged less than half that of Britain. By August 1940 the German fighter force was only 69 per cent of its strength before the Battle of France while the number of serviceable aircraft fell even faster.[21] Throughout the Battle of Britain German forces suffered an attrition rate of aircraft and pilots that could not be satisfactorily covered by the factories and training schools in the Reich.

The Luftwaffe might well have suffered even more during the Battle of Britain if it had not had the advantage of better combat training and experience and better fighter tactics. As it was these advantages were soon overcome and were more than offset by the rapid decline in German strength. It seems clear that Goering himself did not understand at first why the air force could not defeat the RAF, for he believed the British to be on the point of collapse. Indeed he spent some of the time before the opening of the battle in re-establishing contacts with intermediaries who could persuade the British to abandon war and accept a peace treaty, since a diplomatic solution seemed to be to Britain's advantage given her military isolation. The first reports on the air conflict seemed to confirm Goering's view. By 20 August German intelligence estimated that 644 British aircraft had been destroyed in the first week of fighting and 11 airfields permanently destroyed when the true figure was 103 aircraft and one airfield temporarily put out of action.[22] By mid-September Goering, who left much of the routine running of the battle to his staff, had to accept the growing exhaustion of the Luftwaffe and search for some alternative. The choice of the Blitz, of independent bombing attacks against British economic and military targets, was a final attempt to force the British to submit with the weapons that Germany had to hand and suffered from the start from its improvisatory nature. The Luftwaffe lacked a sufficient number of aircraft to carry out an effective bombing campaign. The bomb-loads of the medium bombers over a long range were too small to inflict the level of damage likely to have any strategic effect. At its peak the bombing attacks involved no more than 9,000 tons in a month and declined to a mere 1,000 tons by the end of the winter. These figures were only a fraction of the quantities dropped by the Allies in 1943 and 1944. In November the German radio navigation beams were jammed by British counter-measures, removing an important tactical advantage, while bomb attacks were spread over a very wide variety of military and war-related targets. Anxious to conserve air strength for the attack against the Soviet Union, and aware of the failure to achieve anything decisive by air attack, Hitler ordered an end to the Blitz in the spring of 1941.[23]

The failure of the Luftwaffe to contribute anything decisive to the efforts to defeat Britain in the autumn and winter of 1940 marked an important turning point in the German air effort. Although both Goering and Hitler consoled themselves with the belief that Britain could be finished off later in the war after the defeat of the Soviet Union, by the development of massive air superiority, the shortcomings of the Luftwaffe were clear. At the very highest level there existed considerable confusion about the nature of air strategy. Both Goering and Hitler treated air power as if it conformed to the laws of land warfare. As long as the air force was engaged on combined operations in support of the army such an attitude was not out of place. But when the attempt was made to defeat Britain through air attack Goering showed that he still thought in terms of a single short battle, concentrating all forces against the enemy front line aircraft. In fact air supremacy over Britain could only be achieved over a considerable length of time, and through continuous air warfare rather than a single sharply defined battle. Given Germany's material resources in 1940 it was not possible to attack more than a small part of the enemy's territory effectively, thus allowing time for the RAF to regroup outside the range of German attack. Nor did Germany possess the means to destroy the British aircraft industry and halt the permanent flow of new aircraft to the British air force. Hence Goering's frustration and incomprehension at the continued resurrection of an air force that his staff assured him was defeated. The same confusion arose over bombing policy. Goering failed to decide on priority targets and greatly exaggerated the impact of bomb attack. Later in the war he continued to insist that London and Coventry had 'disappeared' under Luftwaffe attacks in 1940.[24] The fact was that Goering did not know what his bombing force was capable of nor what targets should be most profitably attacked. These were problems that the Luftwaffe had only begun to consider in 1940, in contrast to the years of internal service debate over bombing in the RAF.

German air power in the early years of war was compelled through circumstances to accept a limited role. The obvious success of co-operation with the army and the lack of strategic preparation for other types of air warfare made such a situation inevitable. Indeed the air force by 1940 had barely begun to develop the independent bombing strategy that Goering ultimately wanted and had ignored naval air power and aerial defence altogether. Here again Goering betrayed his lack of strategic vision. Since 1938 the navy had pressed for an air force of its own or for a Luftwaffe policy of air–naval co-operation. In 1940 Raeder convinced Hitler that a campaign against British shipping and imports was the most effective way of bringing about victory as an alternative to a costly invasion. Goering, on the other hand, had refused to give up significant numbers of aircraft to help the navy or to work out any strategy for co-operation with the navy and an air war against shipping. This was partly through his fear of losing control over such units to the navy, for he was not opposed in principle to the idea of a trade war carried out by aircraft. But, as with strategic bombing, Goering's sins were sins of omission. Too little effort was devoted to working out the advantages of air-sea warfare or to giving any sense of urgency to the material preparations it required. Goering eventually found himself in the unenviable position of having to purchase torpedo fuses from the Italian navy.[25]

The lack of a substantial air defence system reflected the same uncritical attitude to air power that Goering displayed elsewhere. The Luftwaffe was primarily an *Angriffswaffe*, designed for aggression. During the 1930s Goering developed a large anti-aircraft system based on the new heavy anti-aircraft guns and searchlights. Until the advent of acceptable radar aids the system relied on observers to give advanced warning of attacking aircraft. Hitler favoured the use of anti-aircraft defences against bomb attack. Goering followed suit. So optimistic was he of the effectiveness of ground defence that he boasted that not a single enemy bomb would fall on German soil, a boast that held good until the second day of the war.[26] Other air officers favoured aerial defence. The lessons learned from the Battle of Britain showed the need to copy the British defensive system in order to combat possible bomb attack. But Goering refused to sanction such measures until 1942 and did not allow a full aerial defence strategy to be developed until the middle of 1943. Until then he refused to believe that the British were capable of mounting any serious bomb threat, or one that could not be fought effectively with anti-aircraft guns. As a result too little attention was paid to communications systems, night-fighting and defensive tactics and the weapons and fighting methods had to be forged in the midst of the bombing offensive under rapidly deteriorating conditions.

Goering's failure to predict and prepare for the bombing offensive can be well understood. Under conditions of peace in the early 1940s many of the gaps in German air preparations would have been gradually filled. In the middle of a victorious war, with a leader who insisted, literally, that defence meant defeatism, there was little pressure to establish aerial defence. It seemed unlikely that Britain could mount a sustained offensive from distant air bases. The Luftwaffe itself had learned how little such bombing could do during the Blitz and the air staff gave Goering little indication that he should anticipate an attack of any strategic significance. Once again Goering was ill-served by his intelligence sources. Neither the scope of British or United States preparations was discovered nor the nature of Allied strategy. Goering regarded the attacks as terror attacks, revenge for the Blitz, and failed, perhaps excusably, to see what the British bombing strategists were after.

Admittedly Goering was given little room to manoeuvre by Hitler. From the winter of 1940 onwards, when confronted with the reality of failure against Britain, he came to play an increasingly influential role in the shaping of air strategy and the conduct of air operations. The campaigns of 1940 were the last ones in which Goering and the air staff were given any real operational independence. The lessons that Hitler drew from the early campaigns, and with which the army-minded air force generals agreed, was that the air force should primarily be used as a close-support weapon for the army.[27] Jeschonnek, chief of air staff, greeted the conflict with Russia as 'a real war at last'. Preparations for the invasion against Russia were left to Hitler and the army. The air force was made to fit in with overall strategy. Goering's role was to agree with what Hitler had decided the Luftwaffe should do. This period marked the beginning of Hitler's systematic encroachment on air force policy. By 1943 Hitler gave the day-to-day orders to the air squadrons and had copies of them sent to Goering.[28]

Goering's own unorthodox style of leadership led, perhaps inevitably, to this situation. Although Goering showed in moments of insight that he was capable of making rational strategic judgments, these tended as often as not to be the product of hindsight. Yet he was loath to delegate the tasks of discussing and elucidating strategy to those with more technical competence and more time. As a result there were almost no regular conferences on the broader questions of the air war; very little top-level evaluation of priorities and alternatives. Strategy emerged at best tangentially from Goering's decisions. One line of strategy was seldom related to another. The serious evaluation of air power was undertaken at a much lower level in the air force technical and research departments. If these reports reached Goering or not was a matter of luck. In the absence of clear strategic guidelines the air force leaders themselves concentrated on tactical questions, and small air units. This path led directly by default to a policy favouring army support and Hitler's view of air power.

There can be no doubt that the air force lost strategic direction in 1941. Little effort was given to evaluating the advantages and disadvantages of particular strategies, or of drawing lessons from the failure over Britain. During 1941 the air force was asked to fulfil a number of roles in the war at sea, in the Mediterranean theatre, and in the bombing of Britain, for which insufficient preparations had been made. The momentum of preparations for a bombing offensive petered out in the face of these diversions, to be revived only later in the war. Goering talked vaguely about future objectives, giving too few clear guidelines for those who had to arrange the training and equipment necessary for future operations. Lack of obvious success in the war at sea, or on the southern front, only served to strengthen the strategic inertia of the Luftwaffe. When, later in the war, it was called upon to defend the Reich against bombing attack, and to mount strategic attacks on Britain and Russia, it could do neither satisfactorily because of the way in which Goering had allowed air strategy to drift after the Blitz. Not knowing what Goering wanted them to prepare for, the air force leaders marked time, willing to accede to Hitler's requests for tactical air power.

Thus it was that during 1941 the Luftwaffe abandoned any pretence of a general air strategy. In the Balkan campaigns and in the invasion of Russia the air force units behaved as they did during the Battle of France. Their initial success vindicated the army view of air power. Against the demoralised and tactically inferior Russian air force the Luftwaffe made substantial gains in the first three months of the campaign, winning air superiority in the main battle areas, and retaining it with decreasing confidence during 1942.[29] Yet despite a qualitative and tactical advantage over the Soviet air forces the Luftwaffe failed to defeat them in the way that the French air force had been defeated in 1940. The main reason lay in the shortage of aircraft and crews and the poor level of aircraft maintenance. This problem of supply plagued the Luftwaffe throughout the war, decisively so between 1940 and the middle of 1943. During this crucial period of the war Luftwaffe air strength stagnated while that of all Germany's enemies substantially increased. Table 10 shows the figures of Luftwaffe strength from September 1939 to September 1943.

Table 10   *German air force combat strength 1939–43*

Date	First-line aircraft*	Serviceable aircraft (%)	
September 1939	2,916	2,292	(78.6)
March 1940	3,692	2,509	(68.0)
September 1940	3,015	2,054	(68.0)
March 1941	3,583	2,479	(69.0)
September 1941	3,561	1,907	(53.5)
March 1942	2,872	1,627	(56.6)
September 1942	3,967	2,449	(61.7)
March 1943	4,420	2,741	(62.0)
September 1943	4,254	2,605	(61.2)

*Includes fighters, bombers, dive bombers, fighter bombers and night fighters.
Source: C. Webster, N. Frankland, *The Strategic Air Offensive against Germany* (4 vols, HMSO, 1961) iv, 501–4.

It was at this point that Goering's economic and military responsibilities coincided. The failure to mobilise the German economy effectively enough restricted the growth of the air force. It was the poor supply position that made it impossible to pursue either an independent air strategy or effective army support after 1941. During 1942 the re-grouped Soviet air force was able to win back control over selected areas of the front and to withstand

Luftwaffe attacks elsewhere through sheer weight of numbers. During 1943 the Luftwaffe was overwhelmed by a vast numerical disparity. For every German aircraft her enemies produced six.[30] In the west the Luftwaffe never again regained the initiative and the British and American air forces were given the opportunity to build up an invasion air force ten times greater than the German forces that opposed it. Moreover by the middle of the war the qualitative lead that the Luftwaffe had enjoyed was eroded as the allies replaced ageing aircraft with new models more appropriate to the strategy adopted and with a much higher technical performance. Goering suggested to the assembled *Gauleiter* in November 1943 that material superiority made no difference, that one German flyer was worth five Russians.[31] The stark evidence of the contracting air fronts proved the contrary.

The question of aircraft production was of fundamental importance. With larger numbers of aircraft German air strategy, like that of the RAF, could have coped more effectively with an expanding series of strategic tasks and air fronts. In Russia, where the Soviet air force depended for much of the war on crude numerical superiority, large numbers might well have secured air control for the German air force and have slowed down the progress of Soviet armies. This does not necessarily mean that greater numbers on their own would have solved the problems of premature war and muddled strategy, but it would have allowed much greater strategic flexibility and would have prevented the initiative in air warfare from passing to the Allies at such an early stage in the war.

How is this failure to be accounted for? One explanation might be derived simply from the more general production failure. But in fact aircraft production expanded even more slowly than the rest of the military economy. Between 1940 and 1941 aircraft output rose by only 7.5 per cent. The output of tanks increased 123 per cent, that of ships 172 per cent and of army weapons and explosives 42 per cent.[32] Aircraft production cannot be explained just in terms of the general problems of mobilisation. It might be argued that insufficient resources were available for aircraft production, but this too was not the case. Indeed very large resources were diverted to aircraft output, more than for the army. The air industry took the most labour, the most raw materials and enjoyed the lion's share of research and development. The amount of resources allocated to the German air force during 1940 was greater than that available to the British air industry in 1944, and not much less than that available to Germany in the same year. Yet in 1940 Germany produced only 10,000 aircraft while Britain produced 15,000. In 1944 the figures were 36,000 and 26,000 respectively.[33]

Nor can an absolute shortage of pilots and aircrew be used to explain the poor production record. Pilot training was adjusted to the number of aircraft planned. The Allies had no great pool of skilled pilots to draw on, but embarked on an urgent and large-scale training scheme when the production plans were finalised. This was well within Germany's capabilities too. The fact that insufficient pilots were trained was a reflection of the wider lack of urgency and imagination in the formation of future air strategy, not of a shortage of training facilities and volunteers.

Finally it has been argued that aircraft production remained low because the German leaders had not planned to produce more until forced to accept total war in 1942 and 1943. But this too, cannot be supported by the facts. The necessity for large numbers was assumed from the outset. Mobilisation plans laid as early as 1937 foresaw an output of 15,000 aircraft in the first year of war, increasing steadily thereafter. Mobilisation plans a year later called for an output of 21,000 aircraft during the first year of war, to be achieved by introducing double shift work throughout the aircraft industry.[34] These figures were not in fact realised until 1942 and 1943. Hitler and Goering both worked on the assumption that large numbers of aircraft would be forthcoming. In 1938 Hitler ordered an air force strength of 12,000 by 1942 and annual production of from 20–30,000. During the early months of war similar demands were made, supported by suggestions from industrialists and air ministry officials that figures of 3,000 aircraft a month or more were necessary to prosecute a major air war.[35] By 1942 Milch was working on the assumption that an output of 80,000 aircraft a year would be both necessary and possible by 1945.[36] Yet in spite of the plans the output of aircraft remained far below expectation, so much so that aircraft production became a special area of crisis.

We are left with only one satisfactory conclusion. The failure in aircraft production was a direct result of German militarism in general, and Goering's military attitudes in particular. There were, to be sure a number of important economic and organisational constraints that aircraft production shared with the rest of the military economy. But these problems have to be seen in a context in which military questions and military values were allowed to take precedence. In this lay Goering's most serious strategic misjudgment. In its simplest terms Goering favoured the strictly military branch of the air force at the expense of its services and production. For Goering air warfare was a moral rather than a material question. 'Personal heroism', he believed, 'must always count for more than technical novelties.'[37] He kept to this principle throughout the war. When defending the air force at a party meeting late in 1943 he argued that 'numerical superiority does not come into the question as far as I am concerned. For us the man has always been of most value. If you look at the American and English prisoners, you really have to say: the superiority of the German is still very great. And that, too, gives me great hope.'[38] Goering did not ignore questions of supply and production but saw them as subsidiary to the main task of actually fighting. This attitude was that of the front-line fighter from the First World War and betrayed Goering's lack of military experience. For in air warfare above all there was a very real unity between production, supply and air fighting. Air strategy relied on the development of new weapons and the large-scale output of aircraft as much as it did upon purely military questions.

Goering's military attitudes were reflected in his general preference for the soldiers in his service at the expense of civilians and engineers. Throughout the war he blamed industrialists and researchers, or his own ministerial staff, for the failures in air warfare. His relations with the aircraft producers were poor, for he was arrogant and bullying in their presence. His respect for those who had to develop new weapons was scant, leading on one occasion to frenzied efforts to get some of his own research personnel executed for delaying projects.[39] The whole tone of his orders to civilians who had to work for the Luftwaffe was militaristic and vicious. His decrees were notorious for the threats of punishment that civilians would incur for failing to provide what the military wanted.[40] This dismissive attitude towards those who did not actually fight became institutionalised. He deliberately kept the soldiers and producers apart through the creation of a separate engineering officer corps and the strict separation of military and production organisations within the Air Ministry. This reinforced the existing hostility between the two sides. The engineering officers were regarded as second-class citizens by the regular soldiers. The new ministerial officials, like Milch, who had been given military titles as well, were despised as parvenus and every effort made to exclude them from military decision-making. The regular soldiers never got used to the fact that men like Milch could achieve high military office without having followed the career of a regular officer.[41] The producers found themselves subordinate to the fighters, ordered to provide what it was that the soldiers required but unable effectively to influence strategic decisions. Goering further reinforced this separation and the subordination of the non-combatant branches by giving absolute priority to the demands of the front-line airmen and refusing to allow engineers to visit the front. Thus aircraft production was at the mercy of junior officers whose view of the problems was from below rather than above.[42]

This championship of the front at the expense of the rear services was extended to the air force staff officers themselves. Most staff officers had to have front-line experience which resulted in the loss of almost a quarter of all trained staff officers in combat from a service already suffering from a shortage of experienced and intelligent officers. Goering also insisted on appointing airmen who had distinguished themselves at the front to administrative jobs or high military office for which they had not been trained. He himself preferred the company of junior officers, and mixed regularly with them throughout the war.[43]

Goering's relations with his ministerial and production staff was by contrast formal and often hostile. This would not perhaps have mattered if Goering had allowed the aircraft producers the opportunity to supply aircraft without interference. But in fact Goering not only gave preference to his air staff in discussions over production and procurement but insisted on exercising his authority regularly over technical and economic questions as he did in the economy as a whole. Thus the non-military branches of the service became the victims of Goering's lack of technical understanding and basic lack of sympathy for the material side of war. Army armament was, from 1940 onwards, given a prominent ministerial and administrative apparatus, strengthened still further under Speer. Air armament, on the other hand, remained confined within the narrow administrative and intellectual framework forced upon it by Goering.

The effect of this failure to grasp the particular importance of supply, and the need for a strategy that closely integrated production and military requirements, was to reduce the urgency to expand aircraft production and to increase the demoralisation and frustration of the producers. The supply position was made even worse by other military misjudgments that stemmed in the end from the poor relations between the two sides. The air staff, and Goering too, miscalculated the rate of loss to be expected in air warfare. In fact from 1939 onwards it soon became apparent that losses whether in combat or not were much higher than had been allowed for.[44] The rate of attrition was a crucial variable in calculating future aircraft needs yet it entered hardly at all into Goering's discussions of air policy. The figures for aircraft production were accepted as gross additions rather than net additions once allowance for losses had been made. The same attitude was betrayed with reserves. The Luftwaffe failed to build up reserves before 1939 and continued through the war to supply aircraft straight to the front line in preference to reserve-building.[45]

A policy of reserve building, like a proper appreciation of loss rates, would have made necessary a much greater production effort. This was at its most obvious with aero-engines. Many aircraft remained grounded during 1941 and 1942 because, although the fuselage was still airworthy, there were too few reserve engines. Only at the end of 1942 did Milch insist on increasing the stock of engines as replacements when reserves were only 30 per cent.[46] In Britain and the United States 100 per cent reserves were built into the production programme. The same problem emerged with repair and maintenance of aircraft. Insufficient attention was given to the services necessary to keep the air force flying. Shortages of technical personnel or sufficient spare parts, and the lack of a large enough organisation reduced serviceability levels for the Luftwaffe throughout the war. Only when industry was brought in by Milch to solve some the of the maintenance problems did the situation improve, though many of the basic deficiencies remained. Serviceability in the German air force was well below that of the other major air forces. As with aircraft production as a whole, the supply and repair services failed to attract sufficient attention or to enjoy enough priority from the air force leadership.[47] Not only did the Luftwaffe suffer from a low supply of aircraft but it could not make the best use even of those it was given.

The growth and development of the German air force was governed in the end not by any realistic appreciation of future needs, which implied giving much greater prominence to questions of supply, production and organisation, but by the pace at which the military leaders were willing to build up the front-line units. This encouraged a natural conservatism. To expand the air forces faster meant disrupting the careful pattern of military build-up which was traditional to the German armed forces. It also implied bringing in officers from outside or relying on civilians in uniform. Instead the Luftwaffe generals allowed the shortage of officers to hold up the growth of air units. This in turn reduced the number of pilots that needed to be trained, and the number of aircraft to be produced. These attitudes reflected a basic acceptance of the principle that the quality of personnel counted for more than the quantity. Goering believed this to the end of the war. It was indeed true that in the early stages of the war German pilots were better trained and showed higher fighting standards than their enemies; but as the rate of battle attrition rose, so the pool of highly-trained pilots dwindled to such an extent that in 1943 even the training schools lacked instructors of sufficient experience. The prejudices of the professional airmen made it difficult for the engineering and technical officers to persuade their colleagues of the need for large aircraft and pilot numbers, of quality balanced with quantity. When Jeschonnek made his remark to Milch that he would not know what to do with 360 fighter aircraft a month, he was stating the view of a defensive and conservative staff unwilling and unable to circumvent the traditional structure and attitudes of the military even in the face of a growing wartime crisis.[48] Although Goering asked for large increases in output, and talked of doubling and tripling air force strength he allowed himself to be persuaded by the military staff that military organisation and standards, more than production, should be the most important influence on air force size.

Under these circumstances aircraft production was very much the junior partner in the air force effort. This was reflected in the subordinate position of aircraft production agencies within the overall organisation of the Luftwaffe, and in Goering's choice of inexperienced or low-ranking technical staff often chosen because of some past association with him, or because they were party supporters.[49] The irony in this was that Goering's political position in the economy at large allowed him to allocate a very great quantity of resources for aircraft production, and to defend such allocations against other predatory services. Yet having acquired the resources, he then established an organisation to use them which had insufficient political weight and enfeebled leadership. Characteristically, he did so because of his fear of losing control over the air economy to more competent administrators. The effect of deliberately reducing the organisation of aircraft production to a small branch of overall air force administration was to magnify the special problems involved in aircraft manufacture. Aircraft were the most complex and rapidly changing weapons of the Second World War. Their production involved striking a balance between the needs of industry for secure guidelines on production and sensible engineering choices and the needs of the armed forces for aircraft of high and improving quality. Aircraft had to be planned many years in advance of their eventual battle-use: industry took from a year to two years to produce new models in quantity. Few of the main air powers during the war succeeded in achieving such a balance without some major mistakes, but all of Germany's enemies established at the very least a separate, large-scale department or ministry for aircraft production. These ministries were given high priority, negotiated as equals with the air force and were heavily dependent upon the advice and assistance of manufacturers.[50] None of these things was true of the technical department of the German air force.

The organisation of aircraft production came under one section of the Technical Office of the air force, department LC III, until February 1939. At first technical questions were handled by Milch, Goering's state secretary. In 1936 Ernst Udet was appointed to head the Technical Office and Milch, whose success in helping to create the Luftwaffe was unpopular with Goering, was effectively demoted, losing his responsibility for questions of aircraft development and production.[51] In 1939 Udet's position was strengthened against Milch at Goering's instigation, with the creation of the post of *Generalluftzeugmeister*, (GL), a post equivalent to that of army quartermaster-general. Udet held the post until 1941. The GL-Office was responsible for the research, development and production of aircraft equipment and differed from the Technical Office that preceded it by the fact that the GL had direct access to Goering, thus by-passing the state secretary, and that he was deliberately separated from any military questions. Goering's choice of Udet was of great significance, for unlike Milch he posed little threat to Goering's authority in the air force. He was chosen for his weaknesses rather than his strengths. With his appointment Goering's influence with Hitler over air matters was restored and the resentment against Milch shown by the regular officers mollified.[52]

The choice of Udet surprised those who knew him. Heinkel wrote that he found it 'extremely difficult to imagine him as a chair-borne colonel and head of a planning office. . . . He was a bohemian, an artistic, light-hearted and frivolous man. . . . He was weak and sensitive and very easily influenced.'[53] On accepting office Udet allegedly told a friend: 'I don't understand anything about production. I understand even less about big aeroplanes.'[54] He had spent his life since the First World War as a stunt-flyer, making money from films and his cartoon drawings. His only technical qualification was a part share in a small aircraft firm that collapsed in the early 1920s. Goering told him that his lack of any relevant experience did not matter – indeed his own career had been very like that of Udet until 1933. Udet took him at his word. On his appointment to head the Technical Office he told his staff 'I will tell you . . . straight away that you cannot expect very much office work from me.'[55] From 1936 until 1941, when Udet committed suicide as a desperate release from his impossible position, the major decisions about production and development were taken by Udet and Goering, neither of whom had any experience or detailed knowledge of either aeronautics or production. The lower levels of the Technical Office were filled with young engineering officers and officials whose experience was in many cases similarly restricted, and whose rank and status was too junior to win out in competition with other military officials or to earn the respect of the industrialists and researchers.

The result of the lack of seriousness with which Goering was seen to treat production matters was reflected in the deprecating attitude of regular airmen and civilian officials towards the GL-Office and the unwilling co-operation of the aircraft industry. Udet's political and administrative weaknesses encouraged industry and other air force departments to set up rival offices that duplicated the work of the GL. Thomas interfered in air force production through the local inspectorates, giving contradictory orders and advice to manufacturers. Individual manufacturers such as Koppenberg of Junkers or Messerschmitt were given special powers to press the claims of their firms outside the influence of the GL-Office.[56] Udet himself was bullied and influenced by contractors, airmen and researchers so that the primary influences on production came from those with local or particular interests and not from above. The decentralised and confused administration of aircraft production reflected a similar structure in the economy as a whole. In both cases Goering created a nominally centralised system in which he was responsible for taking all the necessary decisions but without creating an adequate means for evaluating policy. Udet feared to show Goering quite how inadequate the system was and learned from his master the art of dissimulation and concealment when called to account.

From the Luftwaffe's point of view the most serious result of administrative inadequacy was the failure to involve industry in the planning and organisation of production. Industry was expected to take orders from the military authorities without question. It was not involved in the administration of aircraft production. Its responsibilities were narrowly confined to the factory where it was policed ineffectually by low-ranking engineering officers from the air force. In response the firms confined themselves narrowly to their own interests, competing fiercely with each other for contracts and resources, leaving all the broader questions about the air force economy to Udet and his staff. Knowing too little about industrial practices, and lacking a large competent staff to see what aircraft firms were doing with the resources at their disposal, Udet unwittingly permitted the industrialists' individual interests to dictate the pace of aircraft production, just as the air staff under Goering allowed front-line officers to dictate the technical demands made to industry in the first place.

This situation only encouraged the firms to do as little as was necessary to meet the demands made on them. Since overall policy was not their responsibility (for they were specifically excluded from any say in the matter), and since they were working on guaranteed state contracts there was no incentive for efficient production. The result was that the aircraft industry became one of the least productive areas of the German economy. Part of the reason for this lay in the nature of the industry's development. From the outset in 1933 the industry had been subsidised by the state. Its contracts all derived from state orders, its finance was provided where necessary by the state-owned Bank der deutschen Luftfahrt. None of the firms was subject to the pressures of the market or to serious attempts by the air ministry to place priority on a high productive performance. This lack of pressure for rationalisation conformed with the interests of many of the leading aircraft entrepreneurs. They had begun a business career in many cases – Heinkel, Messerschmitt, Tank of Focke-Wulf, Dornier – as designers rather than producers. After 1933 design remained a primary interest at the expense of production questions. Junkers proved to be the exception only because after its nationalisation it was placed under the control of a manager who had distinguished himself as a producer rather than a designer.[57]

Because of the design and research priorities of the entrepreneurs, the instructions from the Air Ministry to confine the work of the firms to particular aircraft types was ignored with Udet's connivance. All the major aircraft firms, except the state-owned Junkers concern, worked on a whole range of projects throughout the pre-war and war period. Heinkel, instructed to produce bombers, spent time designing jet fighters; Messerschmitt, ordered to produce fast fighters, devoted much effort to winning the heavy-bomber contract.[58] The result was an unnecessary amount of inter-firm competition, a deliberate effort not to exchange research information, and a stream of projects thrust at Udet year after year for his uncomprehending evaluation. It also meant that a large amount of skilled technical personnel was involved in the perpetual struggle to win design contracts by designing an aircraft for every occasion, instead of diverting the technical effort to questions to do with efficient use of resources and production. The complete failure of the Me 210 heavy fighter, on which Udet based the expansion of the Luftwaffe in 1942, was a direct result of the failure to relate design and production questions together.[59]

The rapid growth of the aircraft industry from a scattered number of single workshop businesses to the largest manufacturing industry in the Reich by 1939 brought additional strains. The managerial staff were compelled to adjust over a short space of time to the special needs of large-scale industrial organisation. This encouraged managerial conservatism as small-scale industrialists struggled to cope with the implications of changes in scale. The aircraft firms that grew as offshoots of heavy industry found this adjustment much easier, but they were deliberately restricted in scope in favour of the original small producers as a concession to ideology.[60] Later efforts to introduce large-scale firms into aircraft production met the same hostility from smaller and financially weaker producers. The main effect of such conservatism was to slow up the introduction of more advanced factory methods. When General Bauer, who had responsibility in the Wehrmacht for industrial standardisation, addressed the aircraft producers in 1934 on the importance of new production methods he found that his recommendations were too difficult for them to understand.[61] To both the designers and the military authorities 'mass-production' was associated with large-scale capitalism and shoddy goods.

The prevailing ethic in aircraft production remained that of the craftsman. Before 1933 aircraft were built one at a time or in small groups. Each aircraft was assigned a team of workers under a foreman who would do all the work on one aircraft, since the apprentice engineers were trained in at least four specialist skills.[62] Even when much larger numbers were built during the war the habit of building in single units persisted since it matched the skills of the workforce and the demands for high quality from the forces. There was relatively little mechanisation, control of the production flow, rational organisation of the distribution of materials and labour. Line production was introduced slowly and partially. The standardisation of parts was achieved only by the end of the war. The Ju 88 bomber was designed with 4,000 different types of screw and bolt and had to be rivetted by hand instead of with the automatic machine-tools available for the purpose.[63] Indeed aircraft production was characterised by a high degree of handwork and hand finishing. The air ministry was regularly alerted to the widespread survival of handwork but did little about it until 1942.[64] Bauer complained bitterly of the firms that preferred the 'unco-ordinated old-fashioned craft-bound unit production with all its consequences such as delays in delivery, lack of the right production equipment, lack of standardisation, confusion in the supply of components. . .'.[65] The American and British intelligence officers who surveyed German industry at the end of the war found the aircraft industry riddled with old-fashioned practices, well behind not only standard American factory practices but even those in British factories.[66] The bombing of Germany only served to encourage the survival of such methods for it led to widespread dispersal into smaller units and scattered workshops and reduced the possibility of full rationalisation.

The inefficient and conservative factory practices encouraged a poor level of resource use. This was at its most notorious with raw material and labour. Lacking any overall view of raw material requirements the individual firms argued for as much as they could get. Udet did not know, and failed to elicit, what was really necessary for production and complied with the firms' demands. Thus a stream of resources was fed into an unrationalised industry without effective control. When Milch led the drive to improve efficiency in 1941 he discovered that Udet had authorised the allocation of 16–18,000lbs of aluminium for every aircraft irrespective of its end weight (a fighter weighed some 4,400lbs fully equipped).[67] Firms had simply hoarded the surplus to protect themselves against future losses or had wasted the material. Although the industry took over half all aluminium in weight, by the time the weapons got to the front they contained only a third.

Over 1,500lbs of aluminium was wasted on the production of a single aero-engine. Messerschmitt developed sidelines in the production of aluminium barracks and ladders.[68]

Traditional work methods also encouraged excessive demands for skilled labour and inefficient labour-use. The workers themselves understandably did little to undermine this situation. Many workers had been recruited from the declining craft trades after 1933 and were anxious to safeguard their traditional skills. The master-craftsmen and foremen drafted into the aircraft factories brought with them the spirit of the artisan shop, and a resentment at new methods and the anonymity of the large-scale production process. This showed itself in a preference for the single unit assembly method, instead of the division of the workforce along a production line. The master-craftsmen, the *Meister*, retained control over individual work-teams and a range of specialised hand tools. When some firms attempted to alter this situation and pay bonuses according to individual rather than group effort at points calculated along the production life of an aircraft there was strong resistance and the old system was reinstated.[69] The approach of the older skilled workforce was very easily passed on. The workforce in the industry contained a high percentage of young workers, which gave the older and more experienced men an important role in organising and educating labour. The Air Ministry encouraged this for political reasons, arguing that apprentice schemes should be run by the traditional *Meister* because they were more reliable national-socialists.[70] The apprenticeship system, with its four-year period of specialised training, survived into the war. All attempts to by-pass it or to shorten apprenticeship times were resisted as an attack on skills and a path to labour dilution.[71] The firms themselves came to match production methods to suit the workforce. A highly skilled workforce reduced the need for expensive labour-saving machinery and complicated re-organisation. Such a workforce was also essential to cope with sudden changes to design, of which the air force demanded a great number, and the flexibility and high standards of the skilled workforce were used as a defence for poor productivity. The outcome was wasteful use of resources but a very high standard of finish on all German aircraft.

The degree of industrial inefficiency was exposed only later in the war when Milch began the slow process of reform. Yet the results were startling. With virtually the same quantity of resources the industry increased output from 10,000 in 1940 to 39,000 in 1944. Had it not been for the impact of bombing and the accumulated years of ineffective supervision of aircraft production the latter figure would almost certainly have been very much greater. There were of course, genuine resource problems, not those that derived from the ineffective mobilisation of existing resources. Industry was only concerned with the utilisation of resources once they had been allocated by Udet's office. The responsibility for coping with shortages at a national level was the concern of Udet or Goering, not the concern of individual firms. Udet's primary failure was his inability to define the main areas of need. Indeed he became so strongly influenced by all the firms' complaints about labour and raw materials that he ignored the major constraints on production from a shortage of factory capacity and specialised machinery. Even when Milch began to tackle the problem of inefficient resource use he was still left with a legacy of insufficient preparation for large-scale, mechanised production.

Goering placed great confidence in the ability of the aircraft industry to increase output by two- or three-shift working on the outbreak of war.[72] This was a cheap and effective way of increasing capacity without building new factories. But it failed to work largely because the firms were too wedded to traditional work methods and skilled labour. There were not enough skilled workers to operate three shifts and there was considerable resistance, as in Britain, to night-shift work on a prolonged basis. Milch was sent in 1937 to investigate the shadow factory scheme operated in Britain, but was unimpressed by the policy of setting up additional factories, ready tooled up, waiting to be used if war broke out.[73] Although some effort was made to expand the floor-space of the industry, the plans suffered from the excessive demands made upon the construction industry by other projects and Udet's poor bargaining power on behalf of aircraft production. Goering, at least, had some vision of the great demands that aircraft production would make upon factory space, but Udet had very little. Aircraft production from its very nature made very great demands on floor-space. Moreover, to achieve the necessary economies of scale in aircraft production large factories were essential. Only in this way could shortages of skilled labour be circumvented by standardised large-scale production and the use of semi-skilled labour. Russia, Britain and the United States all coped with the peculiar problems of aircraft production with an imaginative view of the scale involved. Later in 1943 Milch complained that no one in Germany before the outbreak of war had ever seriously considered the scale of wartime requirements.[74] Indeed investment in the aircraft industry for factories and equipment declined from a peak in 1937–8 until the middle of the war. Investment in the final assembly industry declined from 59m RM in 1937–8 to a mere 12m RM in 1939–40.[75] Yet by the outbreak of war the aircraft industry was fully utilised, already beginning to complain of a shortage of floor-space. The answer that Udet devised was to disperse production among small sub-contractors and suppliers drawn from the idle consumer industries. The effect of this was to reduce still further the efficiency of the industry for the firms were given no help from the ministry in the recruitment and organisation of suppliers. This produced extensive competition with the army and navy for the spare firms and aggravated the tendency to non-standardised and inefficient production through the use of small businesses.

The second major problem faced by the aircraft firms was the shortage of specialised machine tools. This was a particular hardship for the aircraft producers because they relied heavily on special machinery. There was no shortage of general purpose tools. These were in such generous supply that the authorities used this as an argument against increasing the output of more specialised equipment.[76] The high reliance on skilled labour also obscured the shortage, for the skilled men worked largely with general purpose tools operated by hand. But in fact one of the major constraints on the extension of aircraft production capacity was the failure to produce sufficient specific-purpose tools. Milch regarded this 'as one of the severest bottlenecks' during the war, for it held up the introduction of mass-production for which special tools were needed.[77] By 1941 aircraft firms were sending back standard tools supplied by the Plenipotentiary for the Machine Industry because they had too many, but week after week complaints were sent to the air ministry of delays caused by the lack of special tools. By 1941 the delivery delays for a whole range of such tools stretched from two to four years.[78] The labour necessary to build such machinery was in short supply, as were designers competent to cope with their design. The machinery industry never devoted more than 8 per cent of its total output to specialised machines and proved as inflexible and conservative in approach to engineering questions as the skilled master-craftsmen.[79] Yet the savings that such machinery brought were very substantial. At the BMW plant in Augsburg, the introduction of special flow-production machinery in 1944 cut production costs by half, raw materials used by 49 per cent and reduced worktime per engine from 3,150 hours to 1,250 hours.[80] Reliance on general purpose tools and skilled labour, encouraged by dispersal of contracts to small firms throughout the war, and the shortage of special machinery and large production units, placed a severe restraint on the growth of the industry that the more efficient use of raw materials and labour could do little about.

What emerges from the history of aircraft production is a picture in which industrial initiative was stifled and the effects of ministerial incompetence magnified. Udet aimed to extract the minimum from industry, never the maximum, and continually pretended to an uncritical and preoccupied Goering that more would be produced presently. Any subsequent failures Goering blamed on industry so that relations between both sides remained poor. Excluded from industrial planning, yet blamed when the planning went wrong, the industrialists retreated, demoralised and frustrated, to the confines of their own businesses. Goering then blamed them for excessive *Firmenpatriotismus*, for putting the interest of the firm before that of the air force. One major reason for the poor relationship between Goering and the manufacturers was the suspicion constantly in his mind that the aircraft firms put financial and private interests before that of the state. The manufacturers for their part resented his ignorant and bullying exhortations, his lack of technical competence, his poor judgment.[81] Although it was difficult and dangerous to say so directly to Goering, the constant criticisms of Udet and the technical office of the air ministry were an implied criticism of

Goering. When, at the end of the war, the head of the aircraft industry
group looked back at the failures of aircraft production, he blamed the
ministry for its failure to provide 'a clear, constant line in the development
and evaluation of air force equipment'.[82] Messerschmitt accused the ministry
of total confusion and incompetence: 'the greatest difficulty in the way of
a rational output of aircraft and equipment lies in the first place with the
planlessness with which the air ministry works. . . .'[83] A special commissioner set up to study the problems of the aircraft industry in 1943
concluded that over the war the greatest explanation for lost production lay
with the lack of 'clear planning' and 'precise allocation of tasks' in the
ministry.[84]

The entrepreneurs were by inclination hostile to ministerial interference
because it replaced their own initiative and responsibility with that of military
bureaucrats whose technical competence they questioned. Resentment at
state interference extended to a fear on the part of the private manufacturers
that the Nazis planned to nationalise the arms industry. The industry was
divided between those firms that had been taken over or set up by the state,
including the largest, Junkers, and those that had grown out of small
private firms in the 1920s. Messerschmitt championed the cause of private
enterprise, buying back shares from the state out of retained profits, and
making desperate efforts throughout the 1930s to free the firm from reliance
on state aid.[85] The ministry practised a policy of favouritism for state firms
in awarding contracts and had much closer links with the managers in state
factories. The pro-Nazi managers in the state sector tried to encourage a
spirit of corporatism in the industry which only served further to undermine
confidence in the long-term prospects for private business.[86] The fear of
the state merged with a more general distrust of the party and its role in
industry. Tank, Heinkel and Messerschmitt found themselves harassed by
their local *Gauleiter* and on bad terms with Goering as a result. The
chairman of Messerschmitt was imprisoned later in the war for his antipathy
to the state, and Messerschmitt, whose firm Bormann had under scrutiny
for its alleged employment of Jews, was himself sacked in 1942 from all his
managerial jobs in fulfilment of Goering's threat to remove unco-operative
businessmen.[87] Heinkel wrote after the war of his 'rather ingenuous belief
that I was master in my own home and the conviction of the party that it
had the right to meddle in all matters not strictly technical and influence
them according to its own political tenets'.[88] Another industrialist explained
the antipathy in terms of the fact that the Nazi movement signalled 'a *lower-
middle class revolution*'.[89] It was the turn of the clerks to rule the managers.

What the Nazis lacked was the goodwill of those who produced the
aircraft. It was not that the aircraft industrialists were unpatriotic; far from
it. Many of them had fought through the First World War or produced
aircraft for it, and many looked forward to German rearmament and the
overturning of the Versailles settlement. During the Second World War
they made clear again their desire to defend Germany against attack,

especially from Soviet Russia of whom the industrialists had a particular fear.[90] What created the lack of goodwill were the shortcomings of Goering's system of government. As engineers the entrepreneurs resented controls on their creativity from those who knew no engineering. As producers they resented the dull and complex administrative apparatus with which they were increasingly burdened. As capitalists they feared the socialising ambitions of Goering's ministry and the parvenu and ineffective minions who ran it. Goering returned their distrust. The resulting lack of mutual understanding placed a severe strain throughout the war on the ability of the Nazi planners to get the aircraft they wanted.

During the course of 1941 the failure of aircraft production could no longer be hidden. By the middle of 1941 output was below the monthly level for 1940 and plans for future production were conservative and uncertain. First Goering, and then Hitler, saw the need for urgent changes. For Goering this meant making political concessions. He was compelled to reintroduce Milch into production planning, first as an assistant for Udet and then, during the summer of 1941, as his effective replacement.[91] Goering hesitated to sack Udet outright but was saved from his predicament by Udet's suicide in November. Milch used the opportunity of Udet's political decline to replace poor administrators in the ministry with competent officials of his own choosing. Goering tolerated Milch's activities because he had no other alternative. He could not rescue aircraft production himself but feared the consequences with Hitler of allowing it to languish. Milch was thus given a freer hand than he might have expected.[92]

Milch began from the outset to plan aircraft production on the largest scale. Unlike Udet he worked on the basis of what the war required, not on the basis of what industry said it might produce. As his yardstick he used the large production figures which it was now known that Britain and the United States were planning. Goering never fully grasped the relationship between future needs and the current war situation. Later in the war he chided Milch for always thinking in terms of what the enemy might produce.[93] The conclusion that Milch drew was that industry should aim in the first place for 3,000 aircraft a month in late 1943 and 1944 rising to 7,000 aircraft a month by 1945. When he assumed responsibility for production in mid-1941 output was running at less than 1,000 aircraft per month. Goering agreed to Milch's arguments and on 20 June announced a quadrupling of all aircraft equipment production.[94] In order to achieve an immediate increase Milch altered the plans for new models which were to be introduced slowly in 1942 and replaced them with much larger quantities of existing types. To the Chief of Staff he insisted that 'Serial production has priority' and ignored the military demands for more advanced and specialised equipment.[95] Milch realised that it would take time for the new programmes to materialise. Even in 1942 production did not reach the levels originally planned for the first year of war. It proved to be impossible to undo quickly the five years of poor planning and ineffective mobilisation in the midst of a large-scale conflict.

From the middle of 1941 onwards aircraft production was reformed as far as it was possible to do so. The industry was reorganised into a system of production 'rings' and committees responsible for each aircraft model. The sub-contractors were carefully organised so as to reduce the time for the delivery of components and to rationalise their production and allocation. A new system of so called 'F'-orders was established so that all the firms involved in aircraft production would know from week to week what they were supposed to be producing, when and where it was to be delivered.[96] A new Industrial Council was set up for the aircraft industry in May 1941 charged with rationalising the industry.[97] Milch himself reorganised the distribution of raw materials, reducing the quantity allocated for each aircraft and utilising the scrap materials more effectively. Every effort was made to introduce standardisation, to eliminate excessive handwork and to modernise factory methods. Thus the construction of the Ju 88 with its 4,000 types of bolt was simplified and the number reduced to 200. The number of types of cylinder produced was reduced from 3,232 to 1,138.[98] Most important of all Milch guaranteed that the factories would have long production runs that would make it worth their while to introduce new production methods and special machinery and to adopt more semi-skilled work practices. The number of unskilled and semi-skilled workers was increased and the apprentice scheme reduced in scope. This in effect compelled the larger firms to reduce their reliance on skilled craftsmen and to modernise production processes.

The results of the rationalisation scheme were uneven, for it took time to organise the changes and the shortages of factory space and special machinery were difficult to overcome. Nevertheless all the major factories reported significant gains in productivity. Messerschmitt reported that after the introduction of flow-production methods construction time on the Bf 109 was cut by 53 per cent during 1942 and a further 15 per cent in 1943.[99] At the Siebel works the mechanisation of wing assemblies for the Ju 88 brought an increase of 250 per cent in output using the same labour and floor-space.[100] BMW reported a drop in production time for each engine of 60 per cent, Henschel of 50 per cent.[101] The savings in resources used meant that less aluminium was supplied in 1942 than in 1941 but produced some 50 per cent more aircraft. Firms demanded from 600,000 to 1 million new workers to complete the Goering programme but discovered that with more rational labour use the plans could be fulfilled with virtually no labour increases at all.[102] Junkers aero-engine factories increased output by 80 per cent between 1941 and 1942 but added only 2 per cent more labour. At Messerschmitt and Junkers main assembly plants numbers of workers actually declined between 1941 and 1942 while the output of aircraft increased almost 50 per cent.[103] Moreover the number of skilled workers fell away sharply during 1942 and 1943. At Henschel the number of skilled

German workers declined from 45 per cent of the workforce in 1939 to only 11 per cent in 1943.[104] The workforce was compelled to accept dilution and de-skilling. The forced foreign labour that was drafted into the aircraft factories proved to have a better productivity record than the skilled German workforces because of the new production methods.

The remarkable change in productivity levels was a testimony to the very poor level of mobilisation that existed in the industry before 1941. Some of the constraints, however, could not be removed; and new bottlenecks appeared, particularly in transport and fuel. Moreover the changes that many firms made after 1941 were of an elementary kind, or were simply the result of better ministerial organisation. There remained large areas of the industry that either could not be mechanised in time or resisted its introduction. The dispersal of orders forced by bombing from 1942 onwards made rationalisation difficult to maintain. Smaller firms were unable to meet the demands of the large firms on time and many aircraft were left with parts missing at the factories for weeks because of wide differences in productive performance between the assembly plant and the suppliers. Bombing also had the effect of throwing the carefully planned production and delivery schedules out of gear, which again prevented the larger firms from fully benefiting from modernisation. Schemes for substituting wood or steel for scarcer materials achieved poor results. Standardisation took time to enforce, largely because of the specialised demands made from the front for modifications to existing aircraft types. Finally the air force was compelled to compete for resources with the army. Goering's loss of influence in the economy after 1942 meant that Milch had greater difficulties in acquiring resources, for the army enjoyed the support and political power of the Speer ministry.

The period of reforms brought about a substantial change in the political structure of aircraft production. The industrialists were invited by Milch to participate much more in aircraft production planning while the influence of the civilian side of the air ministry was increased at the expense of air staff. Many industrialists welcomed such a change. By 1941 they were reluctant any longer to take the blame for Udet's shortcomings. Milch offered them more direct control over production as well as responsibility for the rationalisation drive. Milch was less sympathetic to private interests than the firms might have expected but he did respect the technical judgment and organising ability of the managers. At the same time Goering was excluded more and more from the day-to-day business of production and development, so that production was affected less after 1942 by Goering's uninformed interventions and military bias. The air staff and the air force generals were also forced to accept that the civilian organisation should enjoy both greater prestige and greater influence than it had done under Udet and some, at least, of the officers were sympathetic to Milch's efforts to boost production.[105]

The only serious difficulty that remained between the soldiers and civilians was the problem of aircraft quality. Milch's productionist approach threatened the monopoly enjoyed by the air staff in the formulation of demands for new aircraft and the qualitative modification of existing types. This had considerable implications for air strategy since the air staff firmly believed in the principle of qualitative superiority as a key to victory and the absolute right of the combat airmen to choose the appropriate weapons. Goering sympathised with this view. Since 1938, when he acquired wide authority over research for air warfare, Goering championed the idea that in new weapons and improved performance, rather than mere quantity, lay the strength of the German air force.

One of the legacies of Udet's stewardship was the bankruptcy of this principle. Air research was scattered among a large number of separate institutes. It remained unco-ordinated and confused. There was little rational allocation of research resources, duplication was widespread and the exchange of information limited. Individual researchers jealously guarded their projects either from other academics or from industry. Industry developed its own research apparatus, duplicating the work of the academic institutes. The fierce competition for contracts between the firms discouraged co-operation on basic research and left all the firms pursuing an undisciplined range of research goals without any effective control from the Air Ministry.[106] The Junkers concern alone spent some 246m RM on research and development between 1939 and 1943, a great deal of which was spent on aircraft that never saw service.[107] It was Udet's job to sort through the wide range of projects and to match them with the demands made by the air staff for new aircraft. The evaluation of new aircraft was left to a man who openly confessed his distrust of novelty and was ignorant of even the most basic changes in aeronautical theory.

Neither Goering nor Udet fully grasped the principles of technological change in the air force, for this was an extremely complex question, one that no air force during the war got entirely right. Though they appreciated the need for new aircraft and equipment, they lacked the understanding to plan successfully the phasing out of old types and the introduction of new ones of observably superior quality. They failed to grasp the implications of the fact, spelt out in indignant memoranda from the aircraft firms and research stations, that new aircraft took five to seven years to develop from the gleam in the designer's eye, and that much forward planning was, from its very nature, speculative.[108] Instead the Luftwaffe leaders assumed that aircraft could be got into production much faster than was in fact the case, were sceptical of more novel developments, and tended to put too much emphasis on one chosen model instead of keeping a range of projects in being in case one should have been misjudged. The evaluation process itself was fractured by the rivalry and mistrust between the ministerial officials and engineers on the one hand, and the regular officers who formulated future requirements on the other. Udet proved incapable of overcoming such conflicts and imposing a clear set of guidelines and an appropriate administrative structure for evaluation. Final decisions rested with Goering, and these could be influenced by factors as arbitrary as the judicious presentation of aircraft replicas in silver and gold by competing firms.

Thus it was that in 1942 the new generation of aircraft that Goering had hoped to use for a major air war failed to materialise; Germany's qualitative superiority evaporated with it. The He 177 heavy bomber was dogged by technical problems caused by Udet's insistence that it should be able to dive-bomb. The Ju 288 similarly failed to match the expected performance and was plagued with design problems. The Me 210 heavy fighter was scrapped in 1942 because it consistently failed to match the necessary technical performance and was dangerous to fly.[109] Udet had placed the Luftwaffe's eggs all in one basket. The failure of all three projects, and of other less essential development, forced Milch to insist in 1942 that the old aircraft types should be kept in quantity production and new projects be confined to a minimum. This the air generals accepted with great reluctance.[110] Throughout the war the stream of new projects continued while the air staff insisted on making substantial modifications to existing models to make up for the loss of new ones. Production schedules thus continued to be disrupted since the front-line soldiers still enjoyed priority in making technical demands at any stage in the production life of an aircraft. Milch improved the evaluation system, and brought in more competent engineers to do so, but he was still compelled throughout the war to accept specifications and demands from the air staff that were in his opinion strategically unnecessary and wasteful of resources. As late as October 1943 Milch calculated that there were 425 different aircraft models and variants in service, a product of excessive demand for refinements from the front.[111]

The changes in aircraft production and arguments about quality took place against a changing background. During 1942 aircraft losses continued to mount. Air superiority was lost over the whole Mediterranean theatre and large parts of the eastern front. The disparity in production between the Allies and Germany reached a peak in 1942 and 1943. In 1942 the Allies produced 100,000 aircraft, Germany and her allies 26,000. In 1943 the figures were 151,000 and 43,000.[112] Milch's efforts to revive air production came too late to cope with the downward spiral of German air strength. Even the 50 per cent increase in 1942 and the 75 per cent increase in 1943 could not prevent the massive attrition of the air force which her enemies' numerical superiority ensured. The reform of aircraft production only averted a yet greater disaster. In 1942 and 1943 Germany was also faced with the threat of large-scale bombing aimed at still further reducing her economic strength. Milch's conclusion was that the only hope for the Luftwaffe lay in concentrating all efforts on home defence and on producing large numbers of standard, technically sound aircraft until Germany was in a position to take the initiative again. Within the air staff itself there developed a growing criticism of the failure to link strategy and production in the past and growing support, particularly among younger officers, for this strategy of defence and large numbers. The General of Bombers himself wrote to Milch admitting that the policy of using medium bombers for everything had been a strategic mistake.[113] The fighter generals arrived at the same conclusion as Milch that air defence was crucial. Slowly the air force accepted what the industrialists and officials had recognised much earlier, the link between a successful air strategy and a high level of output. Some officers went as far as to accept the need for standard, easily produced models in favour of over-sophisticated aircraft that were difficult to maintain.[114] Under General Kammhuber and General Galland the first steps were taken to strengthen the air defence of the Reich as an essential first step for the development of new air strategies.

The two main obstacles to building up such a defence were the persistent shortage of fighter aircraft and the opposition of Hitler. Hitler's view of air strategy was very different. He insisted that anti-aircraft fire could cope with the bombing attacks. Aircraft were of most use in offensive operation, either fighting with the army or on bombing attacks. By the end of 1942 and throughout 1943 Hitler took all the major decisions in air warfare, assuming virtual tactical control over air units on the eastern front. The only independent operation of any size that Goering controlled was the Stalingrad airlift, which had disastrous consequences both for the future of the Luftwaffe and Goering's own reputation. Goering's loss of genuine command over the air force allowed the air staff greater say in running day-to-day affairs, and freed the fighter generals for building up the Reich defences in defiance of Goering, but it also meant that they had the additional and much harder task of persuading Hitler to gamble on defence, something against which he was strongly prejudiced. Indeed the Stalingrad airlift had come about largely because of Hitler's rigid insistence that no German army should retreat when it could still stand up and fight.

Goering's bizarre generalship was replaced in reality - though not in name - during the middle of the war by Hitler himself, who remained basically hostile to the drift in air force thinking in favour of defence and quantity production. In arguments about air strategy he placed uncritical faith in the quality of weapons, arguing that the air force in particular could be rescued by the invention and development of fantastic devices which would defeat sheer weight of numbers. He intervened more regularly in air force discussions, urging on the production of the new weapons that he had been promised before the war. Together with new weapons Hitler wanted to renew the bombing offensive against Britain. Here he had many allies in the forces for it was widely believed that revenge bombing would end the Allied attacks and give the Luftwaffe time to regroup and gather strength. These allies included Jeschonnek, the Chief of Air Staff, who went as far as to beg Hitler to take on the leadership of the air force as he had done that of the army in 1942.[115]

Goering was faced in all this with a dilemma. He could support Milch and those who argued for a defensive strategy, openly admitting the failure of the air force (and at first he had seemed inclined to do so).[116] Or he could agree to Hitler's proposals for an offensive strategy based around bombing with new qualitatively superior weapons, which he knew the Luftwaffe was not capable of carrying out in 1943. Goering finally chose the latter course out of expediency. While he made it widely known that he blamed Udet and the ministry, the industrialists and the research institutes for the failure to provide the air force with the weapons it needed earlier in the war, he identified himself closely with Hitler's strategy on air warfare.[117] He ordered preparations for a new bombing offensive and a more frantic search for new weapons hoping to rescue his failing military fortunes by taking cover behind Hitler's own ideas. The result was that Goering found himself working against the tide of Milch's efforts. Air force generals sympathetic to the idea of bombing and anxious that it should remain a powerful independent element in the air force, and aircraft industrialists with a vested interest in bomber production, supported Goering's efforts.[118] The air force officers who believed in qualitative superiority welcomed Goering's search for new weapons and continued to disrupt Milch's production programmes in pursuit of them. The contradiction was complete. Unable to cope with the consequences of such a contradiction Goering's chief-of-staff, Jeschonnek, committed suicide, leaving behind him a written indictment of Goering's feeble generalship.[119]

Goering set out in the autumn of 1943 to provide Hitler with a 'new Luftwaffe'. Its purpose was to attack rather than defend, like the air force of the 1930s. The central feature of the new air force was the build-up and preparation for a new bombing offensive against Britain and attacks on Russian industry. Hitler believed that the British would stop bombing Germany only if they thought that Germany would retaliate in kind. Hitler planned to create a force capable at first of attacking with only 40–50 aircraft a night on a continuous basis to force the British to stop, achieving the desired effect as much through demoralisation as through actual destruction.[120] Goering accepted this view despite the fact that the evidence in Germany suggested that small attacks had very little effect on morale: 'Go and make the first attack on London with 150 aircraft and only with 150, and then just read the English press.'[121] On 1st December 1943 Hitler ordered the new campaign to begin. In the east, where Hitler demanded heavy bomber attacks 'in horizontal flight, by night against long-distance targets', the IV Air Corps was withdrawn from the front 'in order that it might be prepared for strategic operations against Soviet Russian industrial targets'.[122]

The precondition for both these campaigns was an increase in the number of bombers available, and improvements in the quality of both aircraft and bombs. Goering reversed Milch's priority for fighter aircraft, set up in 1943, in his discussions with those sympathetic to a renewed bombing offensive. Actual production of bombers had fallen to only 329 a month by September

1943. With the support of the bomber commands Goering demanded 600 a month, rising to 900 a month as soon as possible. Of these new aircraft a number were to be the redesigned He 177, insisted upon by Hitler in May 1943, and a fast jet bomber, the Arado Ar 234.[123] At the same time Goering ordered the speeding up of bomb development so that the promised new incendiary devices would be ready for the new offensive. He had grasped the importance of fire-bombing some years before: 'if a machine drops one or two large bombs', he told an audience in May 1942, 'and these don't hit the target precisely, then the whole attack has failed; were many incendiaries to be carried then the greater spread of bombs would create more damage. . . .'[124] Finally the Luftwaffe staff was given the task of drawing up plans for a bombing campaign. General Peltz was instructed to prepare for a new Blitz against Britain, while for the eastern front a report was drawn up, based on target research by the Air Ministry and the Speer Ministry for 'the Campaign against the Russian Armaments Industry' in November 1943.[125] Hitler delightedly confided to Goebbels that the Luftwaffe would 'regain air mastery in two or three months'.[126]

The strategy might well have had important results if it has been developed over a period of time with the appropriate tactics and weapons to hand. It was substantially the strategy that Goering championed in 1938 when the plans for heavy bombing were laid down. But in the conditions of late 1943 the offensive was doomed to failure. The bomber forces had suffered a high rate of attrition of skilled pilots and aircraft during 1943. By the late summer bomber forces on all fronts had fewer than 600 serviceable aircraft, while production was running at the rate of 350 a month, only a little above losses. The rate of serviceability averaged between 30 per cent and 50 per cent in the second half of 1943. This was less than half the number of bombers available during the attacks on Britain in 1940–1, yet they were to be directed against three major fronts.[127] The aircraft available were also inadequate, consisting of medium bombers of limited range and bomb-capacity. The few heavy bombers produced were so dangerous to fly and so unreliable that the squadrons were never able to put more than a handful into the sky, and in some cases refused even to do this because pilot loss was so high.[128] The technical problems with all heavier or faster bombers remained a permanent restriction on the expansion of Germany's strategic bombing forces. Moreover the air defence available in Britain and the Soviet Union was considerably greater than that available during 1940, while the British also enjoyed a lead in radar counter-measures and radio communications. The operation against Britain petered out after a few ineffective, small-scale attacks. Attacks against Soviet industry were never attempted. Goering's 'new Luftwaffe' was a fantasy conjured up to disguise from himself the real demoralisation and ineffectiveness of the air force. 'The zero hour', Goebbels complained, 'is being postponed again and again. If we could only strike back at the English soon. But look where you will, no such possibility is to be seen.'[129] Instead of renewing the bombing

Goering was forced, against his will, to accept the criticism of the party radicals and the anxious *Gauleiter* and prepare for a more active air defence.

Hitler's other gamble was on the discovery of new 'terror' weapons, capable on their own of turning the tide of war against the Allies' conventional equipment. In 1942, when Speer and Milch were turning the economy towards effective quantity production of standard weapons, Hitler argued that 'for us today it comes to this, maintaining the lead in the area of war technology, which has made possible up till now our great victories.'[130] Goering took up the theme and hounded his researchers and the industrialists for not producing advanced equipment: rocketry, wooden aircraft, jet bombers, advanced air armament.[131] In some cases this was a direct result of the poor evaluation system, in others simply a failure of technical imagination, as much Goering and Udet's responsibility as that of the scientists. Neither Hitler nor Goering could easily conceive of the long time that such developments required and the resulting frustration produced a stream of urgent requests that often made the research and development process slower rather than faster. Those that were selected as priority projects, the V1 and V2, were hardly war-winning weapons. The jet aircraft was still in its technical infancy and was unlikely on its own to turn the tide of any campaign. Only nuclear weapons would have had the kind of effect that Goering was looking for because it was the only qualitative leap that could have bridged the growing gulf between Germany's economic potential under the threat of bombing, and that of the Allies. Yet Heisenberg and Planck, Germany's leading atomic physicists, did not begin to interest the air force seriously in nuclear research until the middle of 1942, and then presented their case so modestly in the light of other research demands that it was never taken seriously enough as a project that might produce a war-winning weapon in time.[132]

The search for 'wonder-weapons' was understandable enough in the light of Germany's fading military fortunes. In the Luftwaffe even more so because of its association with modernity and Hitler's conviction that 'in the final analysis it was always the Luftwaffe which had turned the scales. . . .'[133] Yet there were no secret weapons of the kind that Hitler hoped for. The Luftwaffe even lost the qualitative lead in conventional air weapons that the Nazi leaders took for granted in the early years of war. The performance of the best Allied aircraft was considerably higher than that of German aircraft available in 1943 and 1944. In more specialised fields such as radar, radio and air weapons Germany spent much of the war trying to catch up. This qualitative crisis reflected not only the general weaknesses of the air force procurement system, but a more fundamental problem with basic German scientific research.

No one in the Nazi leadership was more closely involved in research questions than Goering. From an early stage he linked the research institutes to the air ministry so that they would have ample funds and feed new research directly into the air force apparatus.[134] Under the Four Year

Plan he assumed more responsibility for research in the synthetic materials programme and agriculture.[135] Research, like everything else, was infected by the political system. Many of the best researchers either fled from Germany or were excluded from public life because they were Jewish. Other scientists worked unenthusiastically for the Nazis, seeing them as enemies of scientific enquiry. The ignorance of the Nazi administrators allowed much basic research to continue that was unimportant to the war effort or led to the exclusion of research that contravened the new definition of 'Aryan science'.[136] Scientists who rose to high positions did so because they were Nazis, not because they were good scientists. This still further alienated the scientific community, while it restricted the supply of militarily useful projects because of the limited vision and egoism of the Nazi scientists. Nor was scientific research immune from the more general problem of excessive bureaucratisation, institutional rivalry and unco-operativeness. The large numbers of research institutes jealously guarded their own research and duplicated much that was done elsewhere. When Heisenberg tried to alert Milch to the possibilities of nuclear research he was prevented from seeing him in his official capacity because his institute was directly responsible to the Education Ministry, not the Air Ministry.[137] The lack of centralisation and the excessive compartmentalisation with its strict adherence to protocol suited many scientists who were thus able to carry on their work without compromising themselves by inventing weapons for Hitler's war. In addition the competition for scientific labour and resources between the Air Ministry, the SS, the Education Ministry and the firms undermined efforts to recruit science more effectively for the German war effort.[138]

Late in 1942 Hitler proposed to involve scientists more fully in the military economy. Goering had already taken steps towards this some months before. He had been under pressure from the Air Ministry to create a national research organisation in which air research would have greater access to new ideas. In the spring of 1942 he had already authorised the establishment of a research council for the air force to replace the jumble of separate institutes and authorities responsible for the various aspects of air research.[139] Those who pressed Goering to reform the research programme pointed out that the main weaknesses lay in the lack of centralised review of scientific work and the failure to develop basic research once it was available. The development problem was made worse by the fact that many researchers preferred to work in industry where they were paid more, but where commercial rivalry prevented the widespread dissemination of ideas or work on unprofitable experiments. The intervention of the military at every level of research and development tended to stifle initiatives that did not fit in with the armed forces' own technical judgment.[140] The new air research council was designed to overcome some of these problems and to free scientists for wide-ranging research, while retaining a flexible review system to avoid duplication and wastage.

In practice the reforms of the research system in 1942 came too late and were difficult to enforce. There were too many interested parties involved. The chairman of the research council, Seewald, hesitated to take his appointment because it was clearly so political in character, requiring him to balance the interests of industry, the armed forces and the scientific institutes.[141] Industrialists co-operated half-heartedly with the scheme because they were committed to the developments already embarked upon. The other armed forces competed with each other for research personnel and resources and refused to co-operate with the air force. Within the air force itself the engineers continued to pursue their own research and to give orders to the scientists rather than accepting and evaluating what the scientists had to offer.[142] Seewald and the other research leaders were demoralised by their task and unable to secure enough power to make the centralisation effective. In October 1943 he resigned, still voicing the same criticisms he had made a year before.[143] The people who had the power were unsympathetic to academic scientists, and were too technically unschooled to be able to arrive at sound scientific judgments themselves. Goering and Udet prided themselves on their amateur qualifications. Radar, for example, Goering considered 'simply a box with wires'.[144] Udet could not understand, for he had never heard of it, how Heinkel's experimental jet aircraft could fly 'with no engine'.[145] Even Milch for all his organisational skills was basically unsure of himself with more sophisticated equipment and was uncertain how to extract the most from the research establishment. This scientific philistinism earned the leadership the animosity and ridicule of the researchers. War-winning projects got lost in the system and the political effort of resurrecting them was often more than the researchers were willing or able to supply.

Nevertheless, Goering, as in so many things, was aware of the problem even if his own leadership was a permanent barrier to its solution. When Hitler ordered that scientists should be more involved in the war effort, Goering's air force organisation, which was widely regarded as the most advanced of those of the three services, was used as the model for creating a new national research organisation. At Speer's suggestion the *Reichsforschungsrat* (Reich Research Council), founded in 1937 under the auspices of the Four Year Plan, was taken over by Goering as an instrument for centralising and directing all German research. Goering saw its role in finding out 'who researches what, where, how, under whose orders and with what results'.[146] A small central committee was set up to streamline the organisation consisting of Goering, as President of the Council, Speer, Voegler and Rust, the Education Minister. Below the council were representatives of the armed forces and the civilian researchers in a special research 'Senate'.[147] The other two services accepted this with great reluctance, and never abandoned their own claims to independent research. The 'senate' became like so much of the wartime apparatus, simply a talking shop where serious decisions could not be arrived at because its members lacked sufficient authority and were present as representatives of specific interests.

In its haste to increase communication between researchers details of every project, whether germane or not, were sent to every department and research bureau so that from a shortage of contact scientists found themselves submerged beneath a flood of technical reports too great to be of real use.[148] In the end the research organisation lacked the voluntary support of its founders so that it in practice changed little. By 1944 of its 800 research projects on hand over 70 per cent were for agriculture and forestry, and only 3 per cent for physics.[149] Moreover the SS took over much research in 1944, subjecting German science to its increasingly eccentric demands, while the army clawed back half the 5,000 scientists that had been rescued from the ranks during 1943, leaving the research institutes as starved of skilled personnel as ever.[150]

The story of German research has echoes throughout the German war effort. There was no shortage of scientific talent and resources for research. But the scientific effort, like the production effort, broke down through the accumulated weight of Nazi policies, military interference, an understandable lack of commitment and professional pride. The prickly and exclusive character of the German professional elites combined with the ignorance, mistrust and inexperience of the petty-bourgeois Nazi politicians to prevent the rational use of Germany's civilian resources. That is not to say that much was not achieved as the war continued and the urgent need for better weapons became more apparent. The problem for German forces was that these achievements were insufficient either to achieve the great qualitative leap in technology that Hitler wanted or to keep abreast of Allied military developments.

The 'new Luftwaffe' and the secret weapons needed to equip it evaporated in the face of the military reality of 1944. Yet Hitler and Goering were reluctant to accept the collapse of the final efforts. Hitler was determined to use the air force for attack in the west. If the expected jet aircraft could not be used to bomb mainland Britain, then they should be used to throw the Allies back from the landing beaches.[151] Goering supported Hitler in this. He ordered that the Me 262 jet fighter should be converted to a fighter-bomber role, and insisted that the stocks of fighters that were being built up in the Reich to combat the bombing offensive, should be used for a massive offensive strike against the invasion forces, and not for the role of combating the Allied bombers.[152] Goering chaired a series of meetings in the early part of 1944 in which he outlined the possible routes of attack for the Allies and the number of bombers and fighters available to resist them. This planning showed the uncertainty in the minds of the German intelligence departments, for he was given evidence that the Allied attack would come in Portugal, or through Norway and the Baltic, or through Turkey and the Balkans.[153] The Luftwaffe, with its dwindling supply of serviceable aircraft, was compelled to plan for all and any of these unlikely contingencies and to forego its defensive role. Both Milch and Speer combined to impress upon Goering the importance of keeping aircraft in the Reich, but Hitler was determined that attack alone would bring the necessary strategic dividends. When the invasion came the fighter forces of the Reich were drafted into the invasion battle and were eliminated, leaving the Reich close to the point of defencelessness in the air from the middle of 1944 onwards.[154]

When Hitler finally agreed to give absolute priority to air defence in late June 1944 it was already clear that Milch's strategy of defence and large quantities had been undermined by Goering's efforts to build the new attacking air force.[155] Large numbers of aircraft only began to appear during the spring and summer of 1944, at almost exactly the same time as the Allies finally produced a combination of bombing accuracy, long-range fighters and effective target selection to fulfil the promise of the bombing offensive. As a prelude to the European invasion the Allies had agreed to neutralise the German air force first. This was done by a systematic attack against the aircraft industry begun during 'Big Week' in February 1944, and was completed by the attacks against the oil producing plants in the summer of 1944 that reduced the amount of aviation fuel available to a mere fraction of overall needs.[156] Thus many of the aircraft produced in 1944 under the auspices of the emergency 'Fighter Staff' set up in the Speer Ministry, were destroyed at the factories and in transit, or were held up for want of vital components destroyed in bombing attacks.[157] Those that were sent to units in the course of the summer were starved of fuel, spare parts, and pilots with sufficient training. The long-term attrition of the German air forces could not be reversed by the so-called 'Production Miracle'. The downward spiral of Luftwaffe fighting strength which had begun in 1942 was never effectively reversed. Milch's revival of aircraft production took too long to mature to halt the pattern of attrition during 1943 and 1944, and those aircraft that were supplied were asked to perform a number of conflicting roles that reflected the divisions on strategy among the air force leaders.

Characteristically Goering blamed the collapse of the air force on poor morale among his pilots. He argued that the officers had failed to get pilots to fight either energetically or intelligently. The decline in enthusiasm for combat Goering attributed to the spreading of information about combat losses among the troops, and to officers who refused to send men out on impossible missions.[158] Goering retained naive confidence in his own ability to inspire the troops. 'I believe,' he announced, 'that if I finished a tour in which I had spoken to every fighter group, we would soon see an undoubted victory.'[159] Frustrated at his officers' alleged timidity, he refused to wear his war decorations until 'the German Luftwaffe starts to fight with the kind of dedication it fought with when [he] won them'.[160] Goering always identified himself with the front-line fighters, and became increasingly blind to the fact that it was his shortcomings as supreme commander that so demoralised his pilots. He was able to say of his own air commanders that they were 'ageing, overweight, cockatoos' without a trace of irony.[161] In the illusory world which he inhabited he was still the young airman fighting over Flanders, encouraging his troops to acts of heroism.

The truth was that loss rates were particularly high for German pilots and that the missions which they were ordered to fly made increasingly less strategic sense to them. Unfortunately Goering's public admission of declining war-willingness was taken up by the party and used as a popular explanation for the failure to stem the bombing. The general climate of resentment against the air force was reinforced by the army troops which complained that the Luftwaffe was nowhere to be seen over large parts of the front. Shortly after Goering's accusations of cowardice a civilian commission was set up to remove large numbers of troops and workers from the Luftwaffe and send them into the army. The Chief of Staff wrote to Milch that the proposed loss of 430,000 men would mean 'the dissolution of the Luftwaffe', and that to give such a task to civilians impaired the very nature of military authority.[162] The conclusion he drew was that Goering was responsible: 'The commanders and leaders must assume that their supreme commander does not trust them any more.'[163] Although Goering hastened to save face with his own forces, he was unable to prevent large numbers of airmen from being drafted to the eastern front. During 1944 attacks on the air force became more widespread and bitter. Himmler's proposal to establish an SS Luftwaffe to replace the regular air force reflected the feeling among the party radicals that the air force was much less national-socialist than they had been led to believe.[164]

Goering could not escape from the recriminations that he had helped to set in motion. Indeed his own lack of confidence in the fighting qualities of the air force did lead to widespread demoralisation, and yet further accusations of cowardice and corruption.[165] The airmen in turn blamed Goering for strategic errors and unfulfilled promises. Some even blamed Hitler. Koller, the last Chief of Air Staff, wrote that 'the Führer himself . . . made some of the greatest mistakes.'[166] Even Goebbels found it difficult to accept that the supreme commanders should abandon their responsibility and blame military defeat on the soldiers. In his diary he commented that 'it is no good the Führer saying today that he had wanted the right thing but had not insisted on it'.[167] Yet Hitler was able to shelter behind the popular backlash against the air force, blaming its architects indiscriminately for their failure to provide him with the terroristic war-winning weapon that he had sought in the 1930s and that Goering had rashly promised him. Hitler had long suspected that the air force was a prime example of the inflexibility and officiousness of military life: 'The Luftwaffe are a lazy bunch, nobody does any work, with red tape everywhere.'[168] Hitler's disappointment was expressed in threats to shoot or hang all the air force commanders.[169] In September 1944 he informed the Chief of Staff that 'The entire air force is incompetent and yellow.'[170] On 3 September he finally reached the decision to disband the air force altogether and to replace it with an army-controlled anti-aircraft ground defence force. Goering was compelled to beg Hitler to leave the air force in being. Hitler agreed but let it be known for the rest of the war that he blamed the air force, and Goering in particular, for what had gone wrong.[171]

'Everything the Führer says about the Luftwaffe is one long indictment of Goering,' wrote Goebbels.[172] Within the air force there grew a strong movement to replace him and to reorganise the air force command. The Chief of Staff wrote to Goering in January 1945 about the officers' 'lack of confidence in the Luftwaffe high command with regard to armament, concentration of forces, personnel policy and leadership of the air force generally.'[173] Conspiracies among the Luftwaffe officer corps dated back to 1943. Goering's reaction was to punish all complaints as insubordination, thus depleting the air force of competent officers and replacing them with more amenable ones.[174] The army encouraged the criticisms, happy to profit from the discomfiture of the 'Nazi service'. The failure to persuade Hitler to replace Goering completed the force's demoralisation. Aircraft production was taken out of the hands of the air force completely. The Air Ministry was by-passed in favour of the SS-dominated armaments staff.[175] The increasingly tenuous grip that Goering held on the air force during 1944 marked the end of his pretensions to military greatness.

The historian might conclude that this was always a forlorn pretence. Goering lacked the intellectual and administrative capacity for his task, but he also lacked, and this was of crucial importance, the willingness to delegate the command to others. 'Goering will not tolerate a personality of any importance around him,' Goebbels noted.[176] The qualities that were admired in Goering in the the 1930s, his energy, enthusiasm and ruthlessness, were qualities suitable for the daring front-line pilot. They were even appropriate for the initial task of building the Luftwaffe, which was largely left in its routine aspects to others. But because they were not also complemented with sound judgment, strategic vision, a grasp of administrative and command method, Goering was a poor wartime leader. He failed to establish a wider sharing of responsibility for strategy that could mitigate his own lack of judgment, and was on poor terms with some of his more important commanders and officials. His time was taken up with a wide range of responsibilities so complex that one man could not hope to fulfil them all. His view of air power was rhetorical; he remained trapped in the romance of early air warfare and the exaggerated hopes of aircraft and air warfare that this generated. The quick victories of 1939 and 1940 only strengthened this view. As the sole source of all authority in the air force he imposed his uncritical and heroic visions of air power on the whole system. Those Luftwaffe officers who were critical of Goering's leadership, and of Nazi strategy in general, remained in General Koller's words, 'voices crying in vain in the wilderness'.[177] It was Goering's political authority rather than his military capabilities that prevented any change in this situation. The air force was inextricably bound up in its military fortunes with the political ambitions of its commander. If Goering was forced to give up the economy, he was bitterly determined to retain the Luftwaffe to the end, and with it the mirage of victory in the face of defeat.

In military terms the German air force was of much less value than Goering pretended. If the period of planned expansion had been completed without war then a more satisfactory relationship between strategy, production and training might have been possible. As it was the air force was only well prepared for one limited task, army co-operation. The failure to expand aircraft production or to plan alternative strategic tasks seriously enough, left the air force committed to this limited role throughout the war. Even this task was compromised in the end by the production crisis and the multiplication of tasks after the onset of war against Russia and the United States. Efforts to redirect air strategy to cope with this mounting crisis foundered on Hitler and Goering's resistance to defensive plans. The resultant split in the air force destroyed any prospect of reviving German air power even on the basis of improved production. By 1944 the new output was rendered ineffective in any case by the massive numerical superiority enjoyed by the Allies and the success of the bombing campaign. Although aircraft production took over 40 per cent of all resources and large numbers of men, German forces got little advantage from air power after 1941. In terms of military effectiveness the German air force was an expensive liability that brought far less strategic benefit for the costs involved than was the case with the Allied air forces. Goering, however, staked everything on the survival of an independent air force, denying the allocation of resources to the army and to home defence which made more strategic sense. The price was the loss of both his military reputation and his political credibility.

8

THE DECLINE OF
THE GOERING EMPIRE

Military failure alone does not explain the gradual decline of Goering's political empire. The failure of the Luftwaffe formed part of the overall failure to maintain the political ascendancy Goering had won after 1936, but only part. The disaster of Stalingrad came in the second winter of the Russian war by which time Goering had already lost considerable influence and prestige in the formation of strategy and the running of the war economy. Yet it would be a mistake to see Goering's political fall as either sudden or complete. His jurisdictional position remained intact for most of the war, and he still enjoyed authority, and some power, even by its end. Throughout 1942 the economic empire over which he ruled continued to expand into conquered Europe, while his overall responsibilities for economic activity declined only in the area of direct arms manufacture. In the wider sphere of the domestic economy Goering was still the final court of appeal and he carried on his administrative duties in this and many other fields well into 1944. The power that drained from Goering's empire after 1942 did so slowly and imperceptibly, seeping away to other political leaders and institutions through that very same process of stealthy attrition that Goering had employed against his own rivals during the 1930s.

Goering's political position was fatally weakened by the manifest failure to supply an effective national socialist alternative in running the military-economic apparatus. This was not all Goering's fault, for the sharp twists and turns of strategy had largely been Hitler's. Nevertheless he was an easier political target than Hitler and the failure of the Luftwaffe against Britain, the continuing crisis of economic resources, and the confused and bureaucratised system of economic mobilisation were ultimately Goering's direct responsibility. Although Goering remained too powerful a figure to criticise openly in public, the lack of co-operation and goodwill shown to him by industrialists, party officials and army officers gave more silent testimony to the fact that his strategic misjudgments and political egoism were isolating him from the rest of the wartime administration. His virtual exclusion from the top-level preparations for Barbarossa marked a new direction in Goering's political relationship with Hitler.[1] Increasingly Hitler relied on his own strategic intuition and supervised more closely what the home front was doing. As a result Goering became more of a mouthpiece for Hitler, with correspondingly less influence on strategy.

The turning-point for Goering's political career coincided with a major turning-point in the war. By December 1941 it was clear that Germany had failed to defeat the Soviet Union in the opening campaign. Goering shared with others the belief that the Soviet Union would be easily defeated in 1942.[2] Yet this prospective success was overshadowed by the entry of the United States into the war and the imminent defeat of the Italian forces in the Mediterranean. Goering, from a combination of poor intelligence reports and ignorant illusion, minimised the impact that the United States would have on the war, a fact that may well have influenced Hitler's decision to declare war.[3] Even as late as 1943 he continued to rank Britain as Germany's second most serious threat behind the Soviet Union.[4] He consistently maintained that America could not convert her economy from the manufacture of cheap consumer goods to the mass output of armaments quickly enough to help the British and Russians. Nevertheless Goering was realistic enough to see that the changing character of the war required a massive output of German armaments and it was against this changing strategic background that he increased his efforts to concentrate the central running of the war economy in his own hands.

Goering based his efforts to rationalise the war economy on the successful outcome of the Todt reforms for army armaments and the re-organisation of aircraft production carried out under Milch and Udet. By the autumn of 1941 he was talking openly of taking over Todt's responsibilities himself, becoming overlord for all military production.[5] Thomas had become convinced of the need for a central planning agency and the central co-ordination of the war economy and encouraged Goering, whom he now regarded somewhat naively as an ally, to implement them.[6] On 7 November Goering called a major conference on the war economy and its reorganisation. Goering directed Todt to take new steps to increase productivity while the Four Year Plan was designated as the instrument for the newly proposed central planning office. Reichsleiter Bouhler was appointed as Goering's special plenipotentiary for rationalisation. On 17 November the leading Reich authorities were notified of Goering's decisions and the first steps taken to put the new regulations into effect.[7]

Yet unknown to Goering, who saw the urgent economic changes as the final opportunity to consolidate his economic power, those with whom he worked were trying to find a way of improving the performance of the economy by circumventing him. The more Goering insisted upon the extension of his powers, the more his subordinates shrank from implementing them. What turned the tide against him was the increasing unwillingness of the armed forces, industrialists and officials to accept Goering's direction. Milch, Todt and Funk began to co-operate more fully in the last months of 1941 in an effort to get round the departmental fragmentation developed by Goering.[8] The army became more openly critical. Keitel blamed the failure to defeat Russia on the poor mobilisation under Goering's authority in 1940 and 1941.[9] Relations between Todt and Goering were poor and this adversely affected the output of army weapons. The conflict between Goering and the leading Ruhr industrialists led to continuous complaints and recriminations from industry on the inefficiency and maladministration of the economy. By the beginning of 1942 much of this changed political situation had become apparent to Hitler.

It has been argued that it was at this stage of the war, some time between early December 1941 and the middle of January 1942, that Hitler changed the economy from *Blitzkrieg* to total war.[10] This is to misinterpret the whole nature of the crisis. Hitler's decision on 3 December to order the 'rationalisation' of the economy was not a last-ditch effort to save the concept of a narrow arms base and limited war, but was part of a more general move in the second half of 1941 to overcome the problems posed by the evidence of widespread inefficiency.[11] It was a means to improve the performance of an economy already committed to large-scale mobilisation, not a means to avoid it. The December decree must be set side by side with Hitler's orders to convert the civilian economy to war, which did not start in the winter of 1941–2 but stretched back to December 1939. The last of these had come in July 1941 when he ordered significant reductions in the non-military sectors of the economy, bringing to an end, not starting, the period of conversion to war.[12]

Hitler's subsequent instructions, including the rationalisation decree in December and the Führer directive 'Armament 1942' of 10 January, were efforts to achieve earlier production targets by improving the productive performance of German industry, through rationalising the organisation of war production and overcoming the confusion in economic policy-making.[13] Todt had already promised Hitler in November and December that he would rationalise as far as he could, though Goering so resented Todt's ambitions that the latter was close to resigning in January 1942, thus bringing the whole crisis to the surface.[14] Thomas, too, supported Hitler's resolve to change the way in which the economy was managed. His urgent memoranda to Hitler have to be seen in this context. They were not about converting to total war and ending *Blitzkrieg*, but suggested new ways to achieve the high targets set for military output in the heavily mobilised but inefficient military economy at Germany's disposal.[15] Hitler gradually recognised these problems. His initial solution was to involve industry more in the running of the economy. His directive on this dated from September 1941, and although Goering hesitated to go as far as Hitler wanted, since it was likely to expose his own shortcomings, changes were already under way to do just this months before the crisis over economic management in December.[16] There was thus no decisive break in economic strategy in January 1942. The changes set in motion during the winter of 1941–2 were designed to improve economic performance and overcome the political crisis growing at the centre of wartime administration brought about by Goering's mismanagement.

The growing crisis of confidence in Goering came fortuitously to a head in February 1942. On 7 February Todt was killed in a mid-air explosion flying from Hitler's headquarters back to Berlin.[17] The accident came at the end of a month of growing uncertainty over the future direction of the war economy. By chance Albert Speer was staying at the headquarters on his way back from the eastern front, and had been the last person to talk at length with Hitler before Todt's death. The following morning Hitler summoned him to a formal interview and appointed him as successor to Todt as minister for armaments and head of wartime construction. Speer was given to understand that he enjoyed Hitler's complete confidence for the task and that no other authority, including Goering, could overrule his decisions in the area of weapons production. Shortly after Speer's appointment Goering arrived at Hitler's headquarters on a routine visit arranged some weeks before, and not, as Speer later maintained, in reaction to the news of Todt's death. He offered to take over from Todt as the single and central authority for the economy.[18] Hitler curtly rejected the offer. Five days later Hitler confined Goering simply to the detailed tasks of the Four Year Plan and publicly announced that Goering had been replaced in what responsibilities he had enjoyed for the production of armaments other than those of the air force.[19]

Why did Hitler choose Speer instead of Goering? Goering had already prepared a draft of a Führer decree giving him complete control over the economy and appointing him as a Minister for war production with absolute powers over all branches of the armed forces, but he had not yet submitted it to Hitler.[20] Goering had almost certainly been intriguing since November or December 1941 to take over Todt's position, which no doubt accounted for his consternation at Hitler's spontaneous appointment of Speer. Milch later recalled that Todt's political enemies had planned to overthrow him in the winter of 1941–2. In the last weeks of January Goering was involved in an unusual flurry of conferences with other senior Nazis, with Himmler, Heydrich, Goebbels, Bormann (with whom he was temporarily reconciled), as well as regular meetings with Thomas and Milch.[21] It seems likely that Todt was set to suffer the same fate as von Blomberg and Schacht before him.

Although it is doubtful if Hitler knew of these schemes, he was influenced by the fact that Goering already enjoyed wide power which he had not used well and that it would be unwise to give him yet more. This was ironic, for Goering's complaint since 1939 was that he had not been given enough central control to cope with the decentralising pull of the armed forces and the administration. A further irony arose from the grounds upon which Hitler based his criticism of Goering. In the first place Hitler believed that Goering was too identified with the military to be given further tasks of technical importance. He could see that it was military control over armaments that had led to so much rivalry and confusion in the granting of contracts, and he encouraged greater participation by the party at the expense of the armed forces. Secondly Hitler came to identify Goering's empire as a prime example of the kind of military–industrial bureaucratisation that stifled the economy.[22] In January 1942 he turned down Goering's request for new deputies to supervise the rationalisation of the administration on the grounds that it would simply be an excuse for creating more bureaucrats. To have given Goering more political power would have solved nothing. Hitler told Speer later that 'the capacity for increased production was available' but that under Goering, 'things had been mismanaged'.[23] To achieve the renewed arms targets set down in January for the army and the air force would mean a more rational use of existing resources. Goering's poor record before December 1941 was a scant recommendation for the task of reform. By contrast Speer's performance as the party's tame architect and Todt's deputy for wartime construction, had been competent enough.

There were also important political considerations. The decisions taken in February 1942 were designed to give Hitler himself much more say in the running of the economy, just as he had acquired exclusive control over military affairs in 1938. The appointment of Speer, who was a member of the immediate entourage, with privileged evening access to Hitler, represented a strengthening of Hitler's direct control over armaments affairs, confirmed by the regular Führer conferences that Speer later instituted.[24] Speer himself only succeeded as a political figure because of Hitler's personal support in his early months of office, and his power declined when Hitler began to make fresh appointments in the economy of men who also derived their power directly from him. On the military side Hitler achieved a further centralisation by insisting in his decree of 2 April 1942 that armaments requirements could only be formulated and sent out by his own headquarters staff, the OKW.[25] Hitler's belief that in the end only he was capable of making correct strategic and technical decisions led inexorably to a situation where he dominated economic decision-making as well.

At the same time Hitler was at great pains to bring the economy once again under the more direct influence of the party. It had been his intention with the founding of the Four Year Plan to achieve exactly this. Though Goering had been loyal to the initial intention he had failed to involve the party sufficiently. His own apparatus was filled with party members, but drawn from a narrow circle which included many ex-officers and officials. This had always been a danger for Goering, and he had at times made efforts to cultivate wider support in the party. One of the strengths of his position was his evident public popularity, confirmed by Hitler's decision in 1939 to make Goering his immediate successor. By the end of 1941 that popularity was fading, though it was still an important factor in his political survival, and party leaders took advantage of this fact to tie the economy more closely to party control. Goering's main rivals in this respect were Bormann and Himmler. Goering's relations with Bormann were generally speaking poor, while Bormann's personal influence with Hitler was growing rapidly. The close ties between Himmler and Goering in the mid-1930s had been replaced by a more distant and formal link. Both Bormann and Himmler, for different reasons, were radicals in the economy, anxious to extend state or SS control, and to involve industrialists of similar conviction in economic organisation.

Speer's links with the party were, on the other hand, much closer. To some extent this had been an accident. Speer's work as Todt's deputy for construction work gave him close contacts with the local Nazi authorities in areas where roads and buildings were sited. As an architect Speer was able to offer local party leaders a glimpse of buildings and constructions which would enhance the prestige of particular cities and their Nazi dignitaries.[26] Speer was also a member of Hitler's own inner circle – to which Goering never belonged – and though he had to endure the long evening monologues and the banal life of Hitler's entourage, it was this kind of dutiful sycophancy that helped Speer to realise his ambitions. This fact made Speer an ideal choice at a time when Hitler was under increasing pressure from the party radicals. Himmler, too, who spent considerable time with Hitler in the last weeks of January 1941, expected Speer to be a more pliable instrument than Goering and it was for this reason that both he and Hitler were prepared to give Speer open political support at a time when Speer, like Todt before him, would otherwise have been compelled by Goering to accept subordination.[27] Speer himself remained for several days after his appointment at Hitler's headquarters, with Himmler and Bormann in attendance, discussing the political implications of the new office.[28] Shortly afterwards Speer took the opportunity to gather together the *Gauleiter* and explain his willingness to co-operate with the party. Many of the posts in this new administration were filled from *Gau* offices, and Speer expressed a tactful desire to 'inform the *Gauleiter* directly of any general questions that involved all the *Gaue*', and to remain personally available 'to discuss any special questions that concern a particular *Gau*'.[29] These party links were strengthened still further with the appointment of Sauckel as Hitler's deputy for labour problems in March 1942. Sauckel was ex-*Gauleiter* of Thuringia and a friend of Bormann, chosen as a party hardliner to solve the labour problems that Goering's Four Year Plan office had failed to solve.[30]

Speer was thus a creature of the Nazi party, gaining political authority from Hitler's desire to acquire a firmer grip on military and economic policy in the early months of 1942. Speer brought with him an important advantage for Hitler, as Todt before him. Speer was a highly competent organiser where many Nazi leaders were not. He had a grasp of technical problems and arguments. Most important of all he was a popular choice with businessmen. Hitler was anxious that experts from the economy should be used much more in organising war production. Goering was unpopular with most manufacturers, including his own aircraft producers, for his bullying ways, technical ignorance and excessive intervention. Speer, following Todt's early efforts, favoured greater rationalisation in the economy using the industrialists to carry out the necessary changes themselves. Speer called the new strategy 'the self-responsibility of industry' and with it won support from influential areas of German industry anxious to escape from Goering's political embrace.[31]

Speer's appointment thus brought industry and party closer together in a mutual desire to increase output and involve the producers more fully in war work. This was confirmed by Hitler on 13 February 1942 when he addressed a gathering of business-men on the necessity of working closely with the Speer ministry and participating more fully in achieving the new armaments goals.[32] The decree that followed on industrial self-responsibility formed the basis of the new war economic organisation that removed some areas of state intervention and allowed industry some initiative in organising production and distribution. Much of this policy was not very different from that preached by Goering, Milch and Todt before 1942 but it benefited from the crucial fact that many businessmen preferred to work with Speer, seeing him as being both more amenable and more sympathetic than other leading Nazis. Under pressure of war the alliance between business and party that had flourished before 1936 was temporarily, though only partially, restored. Speer's variety of rationalisation benefited, too, from the increasing exclusion of military interference in the economy implied by Hitler's decrees. Thomas's influence declined rapidly after February 1942 and the armed forces were compelled to accept more and more that technical and industrial questions were the responsibility of civilians.[33]

The political shift implied by Speer's appointment took time to mature, and many of the problems it was designed to overcome were not eliminated completely throughout the war. Much of this was due to Goering, who manoeuvred during 1942 to retain his powers and to reverse the political humiliation experienced in February. If Speer had won the battle, he had not yet won the war. Goering's initial reaction was to find a device whereby Speer would become, if only technically, his subordinate. Since Goering himself could not so openly undermine Hitler's authority, he used the growing demand for an economic overlord as a cover by proposing the appointment of his state secretary Milch for the job. On 12 February Milch took Speer to meet Goering, who took the opportunity to remind Speer that his responsibilities only covered army armaments as had those of Fritz Todt before him.[34] The following day a major conference was scheduled at the Air Ministry, to which leading industrialists, economic officials and soldiers were invited. At this conference Milch's name was officially put forward as Goering's deputy for the whole economy. Speer had taken the precaution of seeing Hitler beforehand to explain Goering's manoeuvre and secured a promise of unequivocal support. In view of this Milch backed down and agreed instead to support Speer in his efforts at rationalisation. Funk, who chaired the meeting, followed suit. Not only did Goering fail to override Speer, but the obvious shift in Hitler's support away from Goering encouraged Goering's own senior deputies to transfer allegiance.[35] Since neither Funk nor Milch had good personal relations with Goering the move was understandable, but it contributed to Goering's isolation.

On 18 February Speer's new appointment was formally made by Hitler. The following day Goering threatened to resign his economic posts and break up the Four Year Plan.[36] Speer was not yet powerful enough to cope with the political implications of such an open breach and agreed to hold his office formally within the Four Year Plan organisation as had Todt. The new plenipotentiary office was approved by Goering on 1 March and by Hitler on 16 March.[37] In reality the powers that Speer enjoyed as plenipotentiary derived from Hitler and Goering's victory was merely nominal. During March the reality of the changing political situation was confirmed by Hitler's appointment of Sauckel as his deputy for labour. Goering complained bitterly at the fact that the appointment had been made without consulting him in a key area of his jurisdiction and again was mollified only by his right to confirm Sauckel's appointment himself within the Four Year Plan.[38] The loss of control over labour was a major loss, greater than the loss of power to Speer. Goering had never exercised much direct influence over army armaments, but he had taken the lead since 1937 in labour allocation. The appointment of Sauckel was a clear indication of Hitler's loss of confidence in Goering's position. Of great significance, too, was the loss of some of Goering's powers over raw materials, the very heart of the Four Year Plan. During March Thomas revived the earlier idea of a central planning agency to co-ordinate the distribution of raw materials. Goering was sympathetic to the move because at first he assumed that this would strengthen the position of his own organisation.[39] Indeed Speer approved of the idea of a planning agency 'gathered round the Reichsmarshall to direct central planning policy'.[40] The new agency, known as *Zentrale Planung*, took control over all raw materials except coal (which was organised by Pleiger) and synthetic fuel and rubber. Goering's deputy Körner was a member, as were Milch and Speer.[41] In fact *Zentrale Planung* became an agency designed to complement the new office acquired by Speer who immediately took a prominent part in its proceedings. Körner was an ineffective member, and Milch was now no longer obviously in Goering's political camp. Although Goering continued to refer to the organisation as 'my central planning' the move represented yet further centralisation at the expense of the rambling Goering empire.[42]

While Goering was fighting to maintain his central jurisdiction he was also faced with a new crisis within the Reichswerke, fuelled both by critics within the organisation and the hostility of big business. The 'block' reorganisation of 1941 had proved to be only a temporary solution. In November and December 1941 two of Goering's most senior managers wrote in detail to him showing once again the problems of over-extending the size of the organisation and of co-ordinating the very different kinds of production in the two main blocks.[43] Moreover the growing demands for more rationalisation from Todt and the army made it increasingly difficult to justify the Reichswerke's control over a large section of army production in the Weapons-Block. Pleiger recommended re-privatising the armaments sector of the Reichswerke and consolidating the iron and steel sector as the core of the organisation. In this Pleiger reflected the attitudes of those who ran the weapons side who were themselves unhappy about the organisational structure and about the continuous extension of state power and ownership. Roehnert, who was chairman of the board of the Weapons-Block, was closer to the Ruhr industrialists and had been himself a private manager with Rheinmetall-Borsig before its takeover by the state. His sympathies lay with the private capitalists and he enthusiastically accepted Pleiger's proposals.[44]

Goering accepted these arguments with an ill grace. He was nevertheless compelled to accept some reduction in the scope of the Reichswerke because Hitler, through Speer, had approved it. Early in 1942 his subordinates met together to work out a list of manufacturing firms to be sold back to the public. Goering, who was present at the meeting, angrily declared his intention 'to have nothing to do with this jumble-sale'.[45] To save face he justified the move as part of his wider strategy for cutting consumer spending. By placing the new shares on the market he hoped to absorb surplus purchasing power, while at the same time freeing some of the Reichswerke from the excessive control of the Finance Ministry.[46] But it was also an indication that Goering was no longer willing, or able, to continue the fight for state ownership with the same vigour. The changing climate in favour of more industrial participation in the war economy gave added weight to the pressure to alter the scope of the Reichswerke. Roehnert quickly moved from Goering's organisation to Speer's, taking the major arms firms with him. Rheinmetall-Borsig was de-nationalised and brought into the production rings for army weapons. Skoda and the other major Czech producers formed a new Waffen-Union and also joined Speer's organisation. In July 1942 Speer formally took over from Goering as the minister responsible for armaments production in the Protectorate.[47]

The change in the Reichswerke was not a crippling blow. The iron and steel sector was still expanding in 1942 and Goering's authority over it was every bit as secure as it had been before. The state retained a substantial shareholding in the reprivatised businesses and Goering appointed General Bodenschatz, his personal adjutant, as his representative on the new boards of directors. The capital involved in the Weapons-Block was a fraction of the capital of the raw material sectors.[48] Moreover the firms proved very difficult to sell to the public, in part, no doubt, because of the uncertainty surrounding the future should Goering change his mind. Even in 1944 Roehnert was still attempting to get the operation completed.[49] Some firms simply continued to use state money and operate loosely within the Reichswerke for lack of any positive alternative.[50] Yet in a sense the change was symbolic of the decline in Goering's political fortunes. Private industry was involved much more in production and could safeguard its interest much more easily than had been the case before 1942. Though nothing could be done to prevent the spread of Goering's influence in Poland, Russia and the western European ore regions, no further encroachments were made on domestic capitalism. Re-privatisation represented the beginning of a more co-operative, if brief, relationship between party moderates and industry, at the expense of the armed forces and Goering's economic empire.

Although there were cosmetic attempts to shield the reality, Goering lost substantially in the political crisis over production in 1942. The initiative in improving efficiency and removing military influence was taken by Hitler. The beneficiary of the new policies was Speer. The discovery of how inefficiently the total mobilisation of the economy was proceeding in 1941 made such a shift inevitable. But this change should not be exaggerated. Goering had been at the height of his power in 1941. Speer did not achieve complete control over even the armament economy until 1944. To describe the Four Year Plan in 1942, as one historian has done as a 'minor intermediary organisation closely controlled by the Ministry of Armaments and Munitions' is to miss the very wide powers that Goering continued to enjoy in the German economy.[51] Speer was able to persuade Thomas to abandon an independent army organisation for the economy and to merge his armaments office with the new ministry.[52] With Goering there was never any question that his functions would be taken over by Speer, and the latter was circumspect enough to recognise the fact. Goering retained and exercised his powers over general economic policy. These had never been clearly defined and in the absence of any economic 'cabinet' Goering continued to play the leading part in policy-making. Thus it was Goering and not Speer who took decisions on taxation policy, price policy, food and agriculture, foreign trade and much non-weapons production. He also retained control over transport, which was reorganised at Goering's insistence in 1942 under Milch's energetic supervision.[53] Nor did he relinquish control in March of the essential raw materials, fuel, synthetic rubber and coal. Labour was controlled by Sauckel, in noisy competition with Goering, who used every opportunity to pull rank on him.[54] To this Goering could add his direct control over industry, not only in the Reichswerke organisation, but more significantly the aircraft industry. Although Speer gained the active co-operation of Milch, Goering made it clear from the outset that air armament would remain under his control.[55] Since this represented some 40 per cent of all armaments production by value it gave Goering a still formidable say in the direction of the war economy.

The crisis also had the effect of stinging Goering into action. Over the following twelve months he became once again involved in all his economic endeavours, taking decisions, calling conferences, isolating the problem areas and searching for apppropriate remedies. While it is true that his judgment had not improved, and his interventions were sometimes ill-timed and poorly thought-out, he did not disappear as a major political figure but stayed (as far as he could) at the centre of events. It was thus unfortunate for Goering that the remaining areas for which he held responsibility proved so troublesome. The large increases in weapons output which resulted almost immediately in 1942 on the basis of initiatives taken in 1941 redounded to Speer's credit instead of his. The major constraints on expansion were all areas outside Speer's main jurisdiction.

The first of these problems was the question of prices and wages that Goering had first tackled early in 1940. Schwerin von Krosigk recommended to Goering that either prices or taxes should be raised in 1942 to cope with the excess purchasing power that had built up since 1939.[56] Goering's initial reaction was sympathetic. Hitler, on the other hand, was determined to keep prices and wages stable to maintain confidence in the currency and efficient war production, and to avoid the political repercussions of rising prices. In a secret decree issued in March Hitler ordered Goering to control all price rises and to penalise those who sought to profit from war by raising wages or prices.[57] This left Goering with the unenviable task of finding a way to control consumption while at the same time maintaining popular morale by keeping prices stable. Rationing was tightened up, which was unpopular with the local party, and taxes raised. But the real source of the problem by 1942 was the shortage of food and basic consumer goods, which encouraged speculation and black marketeering.[58]

Goering thus made it his own responsibility to increase food output to keep prices down and improve the morale of the home population. The solution appeared to lie in increasing the level of exploitation abroad and in drafting more labour into domestic agriculture. Sauckel made objections to the latter course, although Hitler finally insisted that eastern workers take the place of workers on German farms who had been conscripted.[59] Goering negotiated with the army occupation authorities and Germany's allies for larger contingents of food, which revived some of the problems of the 1930s about foreign exchange and food imports. Germany's allies and the neutral states were increasingly reluctant to expand food exports to Germany because of the difficulty of getting payment and the shortage of German industrial exports.[60] By August 1942 little progress had been made. There was growing criticism of Backe who was commissioner for agriculture in the Four Year Plan, and by implication, of Goering. The *Gauleiter*, meeting in Berlin early in August, demanded renewed efforts in food procurement and complained of declining morale.[61] Goering called together the various officials who were responsible for food production in occupied Europe and insisted that a solution be found within three months to meet the express demand of the Führer for adequate supplies.[62] By browbeating the local authorities into releasing food stocks a critical situation was made less critical but this was not a permanent solution.[63] By the following spring the situation had deteriorated again and it was impossible for Goering not to suffer the consequences. This was one of Hitler's most urgent priorities, to ensure that conditions at home remained better than in the First World

War. Because it was largely Goering's own organisation that was responsible for the inefficient distribution of food and the plethora of petty regulations to which Hitler took such exception, Goering had to take the blame.[64]

It was again unfortunate for Goering that he was so closely identified with transport and fuel. Goering's allies in the transport Ministry came under heavy fire from Hitler in 1942. Both Dorpmüller, the minister, and Kleinmann, the state secretary, had been closely associated with Goering when he manouevred to remove von Eltz-Rubenach from the post in 1937.[65] Now the manifest failure of the two came home to roost. The transport system, which had clearly needed a longer respite before the outbreak of war, threatened to come to a complete halt in the middle of the second year of the campaign against Russia. By 1941 the production of locomotives was running at only 1,300 a year, instead of the 2,8000 required. Production of wagons had fallen to half was was needed to maintain the railway network. Goering had volunteered to tackle the transport question before the invasion of Russia but had done very little. Hitler now took the responsibility away from Goering and appointed Speer and Milch as transport dictators, with a new state secretary in the ministry.[66] Even more damaging for Goering was the oil crisis of 1942. Roumania failed to provide enough to satisfy industrial and military needs during 1942, and was becoming less willing to supply Germany with unlimited amounts of oil. The synthetic oil programme suffered from the shortage of construction workers and materials and the installations already completed could only supply 6 million tons of the 13 million tons planned.[67] Hitler gambled on acquiring Russian supplies to solve the problem and gave Goering a special commission to carry exploitation out.

Although Goering had approved the Russian strategy and knew of its economic purpose, almost nothing was done to prepare for the exploitation of the Russian oil supplies in the Caucasus. There were too few drills and too little oil-producing equipment. What drills could be found were in use in Germany and Austria in the search for domestic sources of mineral oil.[68] There were too few skilled workers available as well, and the training programme established at Celle could only promise a third of the necessary experts by 1944.[69] The few preparations made had been undertaken by OKW even though it was Goering's responsibility, and the clumsy efforts late in 1942 to organise Russian oil supply were reduced to squabbles between the Four Year Plan and the army as to who had responsibility for oil in a front-line area. The army even refused to allow the oil engineers into the area, arguing that it was reserved for uniformed personnel only.[70]

Reliance on Russian oil for future campaigns had thus been an ill-thought-out strategy for it depended crucially on the German ability to extract the oil quickly. Yet economic and labour conditions in the oil industry were such that it would in practice take several years before a satisfactory supply of oil could be produced. For all Goering's energetic intervention there was little improvement between July when Goering first demanded full preparations and October when German troops were on the edge of the oil-producing region.[71] By December the fifty drilling machines needed at Maikop were still in the Reich and could not be transported. For the workers on the oil installations there was no food.[72] The subsequent failure to hold the Caucasus region forced a reversal of the preparations that had been carried out, at the expense of domestic production in Germany. Not only did Germany get nothing out of the Soviet Union, but home exploration and extraction was dislocated at a crucial stage of the war.

The failure to capture the Caucasus was not Goering's fault. The failure to make anything like adequate provision for oil extraction had the area been captured clearly was. Goering's uncritical belief that the capture of Soviet resources would solve everything damaged the domestic oil programme and arguably weakened the German military position in Russia by concentrating on the southern flank. Goering discovered the true state of preparations too late to reverse the strategy, while Hitler remained in ignorance of how little could be extracted from the Soviet Union, until Goering reported to him in December. From 1943 onwards the only hope of expansion lay with the synthetic fuel programme which suffered both from the constraints on the growth of heavy industry during wartime and the effects of bombing.[73]

Finally Goering was compromised by the fact that aircraft production, although it improved during 1942, still suffered the after-effects of years of bad planning and procurement policies. This did have a much more decisive impact on strategy. At the beginning of the second year of campaigning in Russia the Luftwaffe was no larger than a year before, but its tasks had substantially increased with the first serious bombing of the Reich and the extension of the war at sea and the southern front. With rising loss rates Milch found himself in the position of having to run simply to keep still. Any significant expansion of the overall size of the air force could only be met by a very much greater increase in output. Despite the efforts at reform carried out in 1941 there were still many constraints on aircraft production and the productivity of the aircraft firms. Military intervention remained at a higher level than in the production of army and naval weapons and aircraft firms were much slower to adopt labour-saving methods and standardised production.

Moreover in 1942 the Luftwaffe experienced the full impact of Goering and Udet's poor policies on development and replacement. No satisfactory replacement could be found for the old medium bombers. The heavy bomber He 177 which Hitler wanted for his revenge attacks against Britain was a casualty of Udet's insistence that it should have a diving capability and was never produced in numbers. The replacement for the Me 110 heavy fighter, the Me 210, was a technical and production disaster. Hitler had to be informed that the failure of the Me 210 had cost 192m RM and the loss of up to 1,400 aircraft in 1942 and 1943.[74] Firms that had planned to take the new range of aircraft and new engines for production in 1942 found themselves tooled up for aircraft that were no longer to be produced and forced to convert back again to older types. The result was growing animosity between the aircraft industrialists and Goering. In September Goering called them together and harangued them about the failure of aircraft production, warning them that if there were no improvement the industry would be completely nationalised and all the leading managers sacked. A month before he had threatened with court-martial any manufacturer caught falsifying statistics on output and resources.[75] The result was the opposite of what was intended. The aircraft makers remained as demoralised as ever.

Thus every area of jurisdiction that Goering defended against Speer during 1942 contained a potential crisis for which Goering directly or indirectly bore the responsibility. He adopted the function of fireman, intervening sporadically and energetically at critical points in the war effort, but failing to put out the fires. The great strength of Goering's relationship with Hitler since the early days of the movement had been his ability to provide Hitler with what he knew the Führer most wanted. By 1942 this could not be provided by brief bursts of administrative energy and barrack-room bullying and Goering sacrificed his political credibility in efforts for which he was by then completely unsuited. His staff became similarly demoralised by what they could see was happening and either took the initiative and went behind Goering's back to Speer or Milch or else stuck rigidly to their bureaucratic prerogative and left Goering to settle everything. As a result Goering became more and more immersed in trivial questions, while his ability to control the more general questions gradually evaporated. In November he complained bitterly to his oil staff of this dilemma: 'It is completely mad that I must involve myself here and there in details . . . that I must be called in to protect every little battalion, to approve every improvement in rations, to authorise every train journey. For God's sake, are you doing anything at all?'[76] The answer lay in the fact that despite the increasing complexity of wartime organisation, Goering was still trying to do too much. To make matters worse the Speer crisis early in 1942 had made him so anxious to defend his authority that he became more watchful and suspicious than ever.[77] Thus the more Speer succeeded in cutting through red tape and improvising, the more Goering became swamped by it. As long as Goering was willing to continue to play a major political role and his administrative apparatus remained intact, he continued to act as a drag on the efforts to reform wartime administration, increase output, and assess economic strategy rationally.

Goering wore himself out by these last administrative efforts. By December 1942 his powers were still intact on paper but in reality the decisions that affected overall economic policy and military strategy were taken at Hitler's supreme headquarters or by other special plenipotentiaries. Hitler's growing disillusionment with Goering was fuelled by Bormann and Himmler for their own purposes. Yet this estrangement was completed not through Goering's administrative failure, which could be, and was, blamed on bad subordinates, but by military failure. Anxious to restore his fallen stock by successfully ending the crisis of the Sixth Army at Stalingrad, Goering took the step, against all the advice of his staff, of promising to supply Stalingrad from the air and turn the tide in favour of the German army in the south.[78] It is doubtful whether even a successful supply operation would have halted the Soviet armies in the south for very long; but Goering was anxious to improve Hitler's view of the Luftwaffe, whatever the strategic implications. Most of Goering's staff were convinced that the proposed airlift was impossible under the circumstances. Goering himself in more realistic mood had rejected a similar proposal in July when the Luftwaffe was asked to supply German troops advancing into the Caucasus: 'My Luftwaffe cannot break itself up in some great transport scheme.'[79] Yet in the face of the poor weather conditions, poor transport, a shortage of large aircraft and of skilled pilots to fly them and a poor maintenance system, Goering was prepared to take the military gamble in order to save political face.

The Stalingrad airlift proved to be a disaster. The Luftwaffe around the city was poorly organised, morale was low for what seemed an impossible and pointless task. Not even Milch, whom Hitler once again trusted to fulfil the boasts that Goering could not, was able to salvage anything from the crisis. The necessary equipment and technicians were only supplied to the front when General Paulus was on the point of surrender, almost two months after Hitler had first asked Goering to undertake an airlift.[80] Goering was made to take the blame for Stalingrad, though Hitler had been equally determined not to allow Paulus to retreat. Instead of the 500 tons a day that Goering had promised the Luftwaffe delivered only 100, and far less than this towards the end of the battle. Over 1,000 aircrew were killed and the transport and bomber squadrons heavily disrupted.[81] Evidence was supplied to Hitler from the army that low morale in the air force had led to a situation where the crews refused to take risks or to over-exert themselves to supply the Sixth Army. For some days Hitler would not allow Goering's name to be mentioned.[82]

Goering's slow loss of political influence was reflected in his own physical decline, caused not by drug addiction, but by overwork and depression.[83] At conferences his subordinates noted his flushed, excitable appearance. He became confused and forgetful on occasion and at one conference with the leaders of the iron and steel industry he fell abruptly asleep in the middle of his haranguing discourse. His life-style became yet more bizarre. He received guests for discussion or conference at Carinhall dressed in elaborate mock-medieval costume and expensive jewellery. He increased in weight through a combination of anxiety and high living. He surrounded himself with a small circle of acolytes who shared in the extravagance, nicknamed by other air force officers the 'Kindergarten'.[84] But for much of the time he chose to withdraw from contact with outsiders, paralleling his political isolation with a personal one. In his administration he became punitive and vindictive, blaming his own political and military failures indiscriminately on manufacturers, air force officers and his own officials. Under such circumstances he became an easy target for those around Hitler who wished to fill the very large political vacuum created by Goering's slow withdrawal.

There was much for Goering's critics to report to Hitler. The bombing was a permanent reminder of the hollowness of his military claims. His failure to visit bombed areas caused additional resentment and accusations of bad faith. 'The most outlandish rumours have been spread about Goering,' noted Goebbels in his diary. 'It is claimed he has fled, committed suicide.'[85] Sensitive to such insinuations of cowardice, Goering ordered his staff to write all his correspondence with the heading *Hauptquartier* (Headquarters) instead of his Berlin address, to give the impression that he was always on duty at the front.[86] His life-style too was a constant source of friction with the more puritanical Nazis. His corruption in the acquisition of works of art from abroad and from Jewish collections could not be openly suggested because Hitler was doing the same; but in many other ways Goering's unorthodox style of living was reported unfavourably. To Goering's discomfiture Hitler became increasingly obsessed with a fear of corruption. In 1943 he decided to separate the political from the economic sphere as a safeguard against venal temptation.[87] Goering was a conspicuous example of a figure who held both political power and wide industrial interests at the same time. Although he survived Hitler's new regulations, his deputy Koerner and a number of other Reichswerke directors were compelled to resign from the organisation because they were also Reichstag deputies.[88] For Hitler it had become a point of racial honour that his officials should not make personal gain from offices that crossed the boundaries between industrial and political life.

To make matters worse, in autumn 1942 Goering's intelligence-gathering network, a great source of his own political strength, was suddenly brought under close scrutiny with the discovery of a communist spy-ring, the so called 'Red Orchestra', in the Air Ministry itself. Its ringleader, the aristocratic intelligence officer von Schulze-Boysen, had already been known for his communist sympathies, but was appointed by Goering none the less.[89] Other unfortunate appointments were uncovered in the ministry in the ensuing investigation. Soon a European-wide network was exposed with its links traced back to the German Air Ministry.[90] Under the circumstances Goering was fortunate in securing from Hitler permission to conduct the investigation and arrange the trial. The SS carried out its own investigation and placed Luftwaffe officers and officials under closer surveillance. The armed forces, sensing an advantage at Goering's expense, exerted pressure for the trial to be conducted along military lines before the Reich Court-Martial. This raised for Goering the uninviting prospect that those caught might not all be condemned to death as Hitler wanted, which would in turn throw more suspicion on to the motives of all those involved. To minimise this risk Goering appointed an SS legal expert in the Air Ministry, Röder, as the prosecutor and together with the help of the SS-dominated judicial system was able to overturn the lenient sentences of the military court in favour of death for almost all those involved or implicated in the plot.[91] But from 1943 onwards the Gestapo kept the Luftwaffe and Air Ministry under close watch.

Goering, the victim of his critics, also became immersed once more in the wider political conflicts of the regime, incapable any longer of taking the political initiative as he had done in the 1930s. Even while the Stalingrad airlift was drawing to a close Goebbels and Speer, who were both committed to undermining the influence of Bormann, Keitel and Lammers (the 'Committee of Three'), discussed the possibility of using Goering as an ally to restore the political balance in favour of the excluded ministers. Goebbels recruited Milch, Ley and Funk as prospective members of a revived Reich Defence Council under Goering, drawing its strength from Goering's nominal authority and wide administrative powers.[92] Goebbels visited Goering early in March to test his response. Goering spent much of the time railing against his political enemies (Ribbentrop, Rosenberg and the army generals) but willingly accepted Goebbels's proposals about reviving and consolidating his domestic leadership. Goebbels and Speer then awaited a satisfactory occasion to present the idea to Hitler. This caused some delay because in the aftermath of Stalingrad and with the mounting success of British bombing Hitler would scarcely allow Goering's name to be mentioned. Not until April 1943 did an opportunity arise to put the influence of Bormann and Lammers to the test.[93] The issue chosen was the permanent conflict with Sauckel over labour. A special meeting was arranged at which it was planned that Sauckel, who was regarded as Bormann's close ally, would be faced with the evidence of his own falsification of labour data and an effort be made to establish an alternative apparatus for labour allocation as a prelude to re-activating the Reich Defence Council. The intrigue was a complete failure. Goebbels did not attend through illness. Goering backed down at the last moment and instead supported Sauckel against Speer and Milch, blaming them for making difficulties at the party's expense. Bormann and Himmler had already made it clear that they would not tolerate a move back towards the political situation of 1941.[94]

Goering's abrupt change of support was understandable. He always hesitated to oppose the SS openly. While intriguing with Goebbels and Speer, Goering was simultaneously trying to improve his relations with Himmler. Goering was contemptuous of Lammers and Keitel – 'nothing but the Führer's secretaries' – but he was much more cautious with Himmler and Bormann, whom Goering did not yet regard as proven political enemies. Because Sauckel was Himmler's ally, and enjoyed the strong support of Hitler, Goering was loth to tilt at him too obviously.[95] Milch, less charitably, attributed his change of heart to the fact that the Gestapo had firm evidence of drug addiction and that Goering feared the consequences of its exposure.[96] This is an unlikely explanation. Hitler, Himmler and Goebbels, while highly critical of Goering's political behaviour, were agreed that his authority had to be maintained. Though there was talk in April and May of a crisis over Goering's political position, the SS could not have involved him in a drugs scandal as long as Hitler believed for his own reasons that Goering was 'indispensable to the supreme leadership of the Reich'.[97] A more obvious explanation was Goering's distrust of the leading conspirators, since most of them had been involved recently in the process of reducing his political power. Milch had suggested to Hitler some four weeks before that Goering be relieved of his command of the Luftwaffe and had said as much openly to Goering.[98] Goebbels and Ley hoped to use the episode to improve their own political standing by exploiting Goering's remaining political authority for their own ends. He was too adept a politician not to recognise this. During 1943 he drew closer to Himmler and the SS appointees in the economy in order to revive his fortunes by association, judging, perhaps rightly, that this was a surer way of rehabilitating himself with Hitler.

Yet by so doing he left himself much more exposed to Himmler's growing political acquisitiveness, as he had done in the contest for control of the police force in 1934. Himmler wished to create an SS economy which would be at the disposal of the party for essential economic tasks, just as the Reichswerke and Four Year Plan had been under Goering. As long as Goering retained Hitler's confidence and exercised his wide powers in person, it was difficult for the SS to extend economic activity. But when the momentum of Goering's economic direction slackened in 1941 the SS began systematically to penetrate economic organisations, to recruit sympathisers and agents within other ministries, and to embark upon a programme of industrial expansion under SS control. These were exactly the same methods that Goering had used in the 1930s and they were now turned against him. Himmler's purpose was not that different from Goering's. Both wanted to increase party control over the economy, to extend state influence over private industry, to build up a 'Nazified' industrial base. Both hoped to be able to win the war by providing a party alternative to the traditional economic and administrative elites.[99]

The great advantage that the SS enjoyed in these efforts was a widespread organisation at a local level and Himmler's control over the central apparatus of repression. The weakness of Goering's position was this lack of a large organisation of local party members personally loyal to him. Goering made the mistake of relying too much on officials in other departments and of not establishing a large formal ministerial department of his own. While this apparatus was sufficient to run the Goering empire when its leader was in a powerful position in the hierarchy, as soon as Goering's patronage became less valuable its worth was much less. Officials loyal to Goering found their places on committees and in the ministries usurped by SS appointees. Many, including Funk and Landfried in the Economics Ministry, effectively abandoned Goering and gave their support to Bormann or Himmler in order to retain favour with the party.[100]

Nor could Goering fall back on his links with industry as a means of defence against encroachment. Industrialists disliked Goering and by 1942 had the opportunity of sheltering under the Speer ministry with officials whom they could respect and who respected private capitalism. Those industrialists who were enthusiatic party members went in a different direction and joined ranks with the group around Himmler. For them the links with Goering's Four Year Plan had been a stepping stone to a more radical restructuring of German society. Goering's military and administrative failure, and his wider political failure in exerting a real central control over industry or the armed forces between 1939 and 1941 excluded him from benefiting from the party's further radicalisation through the SS, although he still had ambitions to be a part of it. He had joined forces with the party radicals in demanding coal nationalisation in 1941 and with Bormann to demand the nationalisation of insurance companies in 1942.[101] As the SS began to undermine Goering's organisation in occupied Europe, and to achieve more covert or open influence over areas of economic administration, Goering responded by trying to reach a closer association between his own organisation and that of Himmler.

Goering was particularly dependent upon the supplies of SS slave-labour. The more the Reichswerke and the synthetic fuel programme came to depend upon foreign and slave-labour, provided either by Sauckel or Himmler, the more enmeshed Goering became. In the aircraft factories, too, much more forced labour was needed and supplied by 1943 and 1944. As the aircraft factories were forced to disperse more during 1943 to avoid bombing so the SS was able to extend its influence. When Messerschmitt was finally sacked in 1942 it was Croneiss, an SS officer, who was promoted to his place.[102] After the affair of the *Rote Kapelle* the Gestapo and SS compelled Goering to accept greater surveillance in the Air Ministry, while he himself, not to be outdone, established witch-hunts of his own to root out 'defeatism' or incompetence. In this wartime situation of constant change, of the turnover of personnel, shifts in jurisdiction, denunciation and intrigue the SS flourished and Goering hoped to salvage what he could of his political reputation by putting no obstacles in its way.

After Stalingrad Goering became a political 'outsider' where before he had been one of the inner group of Nazi leaders, with regular discussions with Hitler, and the opportunity to take his own initiatives. Most of his contemporaries considered with Speer that he had 'sunk into his lethargy and for good'.[103] Historians, too, have for the most part dismissed Goering in the last two years of war. It is indeed difficult to form a clear picture of Goering's political position against a background of extravagant living, medical decline and corruption. Certainly his qualities of leadership became submerged beneath a growing incompetence and irrationalism. Goering's fear of the truth reflected his underlying belief that the war was now lost.

Yet despite all this he did remain part of the political picture. Although he was an 'outsider', most leading Nazis had become so by 1943. Goering traded his position as the second most influential man in the Reich for the status of one competitive minister among many. Moreover, Hitler never seems to have seriously entertained the idea of dismissing Goering, despite strong appeals to do so from all quarters.[104] To have humiliated Goering publicly was for Hitler a public admission of conflicts within the party and of his own misjudgment in giving Goering high office. Among the public as a whole Goering remained a more attractive figure than many other Nazis and the full extent of his corruption and negligence was shielded from them. On one of Goering's rare visits to the bombed cities in 1943 the local population flocked to see him, and to insist that they could bear the hardships involved.[105] Goering was thus carried along by his own momentum, by what remained of his accumulated powers and prestige.

There were also many tasks for which Goering had not been replaced. In occupied Europe, which included northern Italy after the fall of Mussolini, Goering still had extensive controls. In 1943 German industry was slowly dispersed away from the endangered bombing zones into southern Germany and the conquered regions. Goering was required to sanction these moves and he made the dispersal programme, which he had long favoured, one of his own priorities.[106] The Luftwaffe enjoyed a special place in this programme as Goering fought, at Milch's instigation, for a more favourable position for air armament in the continuous struggle for resources. To avoid the damaging implications of such competition Speer succeeded in August 1943 in getting Hitler to grant him complete control over the productive economy, including those areas previously covered by the Four Year Plan, but excluding labour. Goering, who had ceased to take any real interest in anything but aircraft production and research, concurred and approved Speer's new powers on 4 September.[107] In October he finally gave up his economic power in eastern Europe to Speer as well on the grounds that a more rational and integrated economic administration was required.[108] In economic affairs he devoted himself to aircraft and to the Reichswerke, an organisation that still employed over 600,000 people.

At the same time the Luftwaffe took up much more of Goering's attention. This was in contrast to 1942 when he was still widely occupied elsewhere. The senior Luftwaffe officers and the Air Ministry staff under Milch had reached the stage where they happily by-passed Goering in making most general and tactical decisions. During the second half of 1943 and into 1944 this became much harder, so much so that Goering's chief of staff, Jeschonnek, committed suicide rather than continue the unequal struggle in reconciling a declining military position with an incompetent commander-in-chief. Other senior airmen and officials were equally open in their condemnation of Goering but there was nothing to be done as long as he remained their commander. His high military office of Reichsmarschall gave him a permanent seniority. Brought up in the tradition of excessive regard for military protocol Goering's position was grudgingly respected. An unforeseen circumstance also made it harder to circumvent Goering. During 1943 Hitler took much more personal interest in Luftwaffe affairs as well, making more of the important decisions and controlling the way in which it was used at the front. Goering saw in this a final chance of resurrecting his reputation with Hitler by adopting Hitler's strategic obsessions as his own. Gradually Goering deluded himself into believing that a revived Luftwaffe would turn the tide of war.

The new Luftwaffe, as we have seen, was to contain a large complement of fast bombers. Hitler was determined on revenge for the 'terror' attacks of 1943 by the RAF. If Hitler wanted revenge attacks, so too did Goering. In the autumn of 1943 Goering ordered General Peltz to prepare a new bombing attack on Britain codenamed Operation Steinbock. The results were negligible. The aircraft were lacking and could not be provided in large numbers until Milch's new programme for bomber aircraft could be undertaken in 1944 and 1945. There was a shortage of pilots and the much-improved British defences to reckon with. Goering persuaded himself that an attack with only a handful of aircraft would have the desired effect, arguing that the British had grown soft in the two years since the Blitz. This was wishful thinking. Germany lacked the ability to mount a strategic bombing offensive against either Britain or Russia in the winter of 1943, and did so largely because of strategic and technical decisions taken earlier in the war. Goering recognised by late 1943 that what he needed was a 'giant air force' produced along the most economical, mass-production lines, but by then it was too late.[109]

Hitler's second obsession was with secret weapons. Goering, too, promised to find them. He urged on the production of jet aircraft, particularly of the Me 262 which Hitler wanted as a fighter-bomber, and rocket research. Like Hitler he laid inordinate and uncritical faith in the V1 and V2 weapons, and in the ability of jet aircraft to turn the course of the war even by such a late date. As a result of his desperate search for a wonder-weapon Milch's production schedules and research priorities were disrupted and the manufacturers and researchers harried by Goering for their failure to produce them. It was a considerable irony that Goering only discovered the necessity for long-term planning in the air force when long-term planning was no longer feasible. The decisions that might have produced a numerous and qualitatively superior air force by late 1943 and 1944 were not taken in 1940 and 1941 when they would have had much more effect. Goering blamed his subordinates, remarking bitterly to his staff: 'In future say about everything; it will appear at the front in series production in the year 1958.'[110]

Goering's borrowed priorities were particularly galling for the air force staff because they were the very opposite of what was required and were dictated by political interest rather than strategic necessity. Milch's efforts in 1943 were directed largely at producing large numbers of solid, technically

competent aircraft to meet the very large numerical superiority enjoyed by
the enemy on all fronts. Secondly Milch and the leading air force generals
wanted much more emphasis on home defence against bomb attack than
on the search for a new bombing capability. This required an emphasis on
fighter aircraft and a priority of defensive over offensive aircraft. It required
the complete failure of Peltz's offensive and the massive damage sustained
during the Big Week raid on German aircraft production in February 1944
to finally persuade both Goering and Hitler that Milch had been right.

Goering's attitude to the bombing was also conditioned by what Hitler
and the 'inner circle' of his supporters agreed. Hitler's stubborn racialism
persuaded him that the German people could accept bombing without a
collapse of morale.[111] Goering followed this judgment. To Speer, Sauckel
and Milch in October 1943 he presented the surprising conclusion that it
did not matter if Germany's towns were destroyed, for the German people
was older than its towns. 'If Berlin disappears from the face of the earth
that is frightful but not fatal. The German race already existed before
Berlin.'[112] For Hitler and Goering the remedy for the effects of bombing
was to be found not in a massive air and anti-aircraft defence, which Speer
and Milch were in the process of creating, but in the creation of an
underground economy.

The background to the decision by Hitler to move Germany's armaments
production into underground factory facilities was complex. Faced with a
widespread anxiety among the *Gauleiter* as to the fate of their regions
through the combined effect of bombing and industrial dispersal, the underground programme promised to halt the industrial collapse and gave the
Gauleiter the prospect of retaining control over at least some of the industry
of their *Gau*. In the spring of 1943 Hitler expressed the desire for a long-
term programme of underground construction, instead of a programme of
dispersal.[113] In August 1943 Himmler took up Hitler's request, for he was
anxious to do the necessary construction work using the new SS building
industry and the army of SS prisoners and slave-labour at his disposal.[114]
Goering was equally anxious to oblige, because the underground programme
promised a quicker and easier alternative to building up an extensive air
defence system, and gave him a chance of rehabilitating himself with Hitler.
The idea of underground production was no stranger to Goering. Proposals
along these lines had been circulating in the Air Ministry some months
before. So anxious was he to profit from this initiative that on one occasion
in the middle of a conference he jumped up to telephone Speer so that he
could confirm that Goering had been responsible 'for the first suggestion
that industrial installations go underground and into tunnels'.[115]

After much inter-departmental argument Goering won the right to
instruct Speer in October 1943 to begin work on a number of massive
underground aircraft plants. Speer refused to co-operate and contrived to
hold up their construction for some months. Private industry resisted the
scheme as well, preferring the dispersal plan that Milch and Speer had

already drawn up. Their main argument against underground factories was the lack of construction materials and labour, and the unsuitability of underground factories for both machinery and labour on any permanent basis. Goering, Himmler and Hitler were persistent. The underground scheme became the test of party loyalty as autarky had been in the 1930s and Speer, who had become increasingly critical of the section of the party around Hitler, undermined his own political power through his opposition to impossible schemes.[116]

In the first half of 1944 the political balance altered again as a result of the crisis over construction. Hilter agreed to Goering's demands for six to eight large underground areas each of 100,000 square feet to house essential aircraft production. The SS proposed to build large additional factory capacity for army armaments. Both Goering and Himmler, who met at length in March to discuss tactics in the affair, agreed that Speer should be removed from his responsibilities for construction and Kammler and Dorsch, both SS men, the latter a veteran of the 1923 Putsch, be given responsibility for the task.[117] While Speer was lying sick in an SS hospital Dorsch was appointed head of the Organisation Todt under Goering's direct jurisdiction in the Four Year Plan. Both Dorsch and Kammler were given special powers to carry out the programme of re-siting the bulk of German weapons production. Goering, taking advantage of Speer's illness, revived his claims to become armaments overlord in his place, but he was no more successful with Hitler than he had been in 1942.[118]

There was little that Speer could do about the changed political situation. The SS was entrenched in the economy by the winter of 1943–4, using the growing crisis of the war as the excuse for acquiring extraordinary powers. Wherever slave-labour was being used the SS claimed the right to share in the supervision of the plant. Factory managers who failed to accept SS conditions were bullied or replaced. Protection by Speer or Milch was ineffectual and industry found that Goering's unpopular dirigisme had been in the end exchanged for one even more uncompromising and ambitious. The moderates were gradually excluded. Speer returned from his period of illness to find that his ministry had been taken over by the energetic Saur who was much more sympathetic to Himmler. Milch was dismissed for continuing to insist that fighters should take precedence over bombers.[119] Goering did nothing to protect him. He accepted the centralisation of production and even the loss of direct jurisdiction over the aircraft factories in June 1944 because only by identifying with the SS and the new organisers could he avoid Milch's fate.

Though these tactics may have helped Goering to avoid anything worse, they did little to halt the stream of criticism directed towards him because of the Luftwaffe's failure to halt the bombing. Most of Goering's remaining political energy was directed towards combating these criticisms. Bormann wrote to his wife in August that Goering was 'fuming with rage' and 'was taking note of all those who pissed on him, or just lifted a leg'.[120] But there was little that he could do. Himmler began in 1944 to encroach upon air force territory as well. Both he and Bormann had access to the numerous SD reports on the political effects of the bombing. To replace Goering was from their point of view not just a military necessity, but was essential in order to safeguard the party's local political position.[121]

The SS was successful in its efforts to win influence over, and finally to control, air armament.[122] Himmler went so far as to propose an SS air force, though the proposal came to nothing. To resist these encroachments Goering was forced to demonstrate to Hitler at every turn that he was making loyal efforts to revive German air power and turn back the Allied bombing. In March he accepted the establishment of a special Fighter Staff to speed up essential fighter production for home defence. In April and May he turned from fighters to bombers, promising revenge attacks against Britain and planning large new bomber fleets to do it. He supported Hitler when he wanted the Me 262 jet aircraft to be a bomber, against all the advice of his staff. Then when Hitler changed his mind in June, making the Me 262 a fighter after all, Goering changed his mind as well, following Hitler's failing tactical and strategic judgment like a shadow.[123]

The bombing of Germany during the summer of 1944, the failure to stem the Allied invasion in June, and the reconquest of German-occupied Europe succeeded in destroying Goering's remaining sphere of influence and in exposing his military failure to the full. In the last months of war he was the victim of numerous conspiracies to remove him from office. Hitler refused to agree to this on political and sentimental grounds. The Luftwaffe had anyway virtually ceased to be a serious force after the autumn of 1944 so that there was little left for Goering to organise. Hitler took most of the decisions on air fighting himself and ridiculed and insulted the air force officers, fed as he was on a diet of unfavourable gossip by Bormann. Goering spent much of his time reminiscing; exploring past mistakes and recriminating against those who had worked in his empire and failed him. Of his major lieutenants only Pleiger remained, doggedly producing shells and iron and steel until it was no longer possible to do so. Goering was gradually allowed back into Hitler's company as the war drew to a close, sharing memories of past battles and fuelling false hopes of victory.[124] To the end he chaired committees and ordered the movement of air force troops, but his political power evaporated as the Reich suffered the full consequences of his military and administrative failure.

At the end of the war Goering was captured by advancing American soldiers. He asked immediately to be taken to see General Eisenhower.[125] He hoped that the Americans would accept him as a spokesman for Germany. Instead he was made a prisoner and brought to trial for war crimes at Nuremberg. The death of Hitler, Goebbels and Himmler meant that Goering was the most senior Nazi indicted. He expressed an ironic pleasure that he had at least become Germany's leader in succession to Hitler.[126] Against the background of the trial he tried to assert that leadership over the other prisoners. Some resisted his efforts. Speer and von Schirach rejected his call for a united front in the face of Allied accusations and confessed both their own guilt and that of the movement. Schacht and von Papen ignored him. But the remaining Nazis were too frightened or indifferent and Goering exercised an influence over them that reproduced the power relationships of the Third Reich itself.[127] Even Speer confessed a certain uneasiness at Goering's threat to bring him before a kangaroo court for confessing his treachery against Hitler and exposing the other leaders of the movement.[128]

Goering conducted much of his own defence. He argued that many of the things for which he was indicted were internal political questions and were no business of the court. He openly confessed his involvement with the Gestapo and judicial violence, and his role in German rearmament. 'Of course we rearmed,' he said, 'I am only sorry we did not rearm more. Of course I considered treaties as so much toilet paper. Of course I wanted to make Germany great.'[129] For Goering it was not simply the Nazi leadership that was on trial but Germany itself. He justified his actions on the basis of patriotism and loyalty to Hitler. 'If I cannot convince the court,' he said, 'I shall at least convince the German people that all I did was for the German Reich.'[130] He refused to criticise Hitler and repudiated those Nazis who did. After the showing of atrocity films at the trial, and the presentation of detailed evidence on racial persecution he shifted the responsibility for them on to Himmler and Bormann. He argued that neither he nor Hitler knew how literally the SS was taking the orders for the final solution.[131] Even the evidence that proved his own complicity in persecution and slave-labour left him far less moved than the other prisoners. His moral sensibility was non-existent. He displayed more open anxiety over revelations about his corruption and ostentation than over Nazi policy.[132]

Goering's rejection of the validity of the trial must be taken together with this belief that the German question could not be solved through the exemplary punishment of German leaders. Although the trials could be seen as a declaration that a decisive period of German history had come to an end, Goering maintained in a romantic and unhistorical way that Germany would still fulfil the destiny promised by Hitler. 'My people have been humiliated before. Loyalty and hatred will unite them again. Who knows but that in this very hour the man is born who will unite my people . . . to avenge the humiliation we suffer now.'[133] Goering clung to rumours of disunity among the Allies as an indication that Germany could still play a part in combating Bolshevism side by side with the western powers.[134]

Towards the end of the trial, however, as the evidence mounted against the Nazi leaders, Goering became less confident. His manipulation of other prisoners turned to squabbling. Whatever his long-term expectations for Germany, the shield of illusion which he used to protect his reputation and to give his role at the trial an historical importance was gradually destroyed.

His hope that he could achieve martyrdom was frustrated by the evidence of general revulsion and anger in the German population against Nazi crimes. Even Goering finally made concession to reality. As he awaited the verdict of the court he told the prison psychologist that the Allies no longer had to worry about the Hitler legend: 'When the German people learn all that has been revealed at this trial, it won't be necessary to condemn him: he has condemned himself.'[135] On 1 October 1946 Goering was sentenced to death. On the night before his execution he was denied the last rites for showing no sign of repentance. During the night of 14 October he committed suicide by taking cyanide. [136]

9

GOERING AND THE POLITICS OF THE THIRD REICH

One puzzle remains from the history of Goering's rise and fall. Why did Hitler allow him to stay in office for so long? He was only relieved of his offices, and his claim to the succession annulled, at the very end of the war when he attempted to take over the government of the crumbling Reich in the belief that Hitler was no longer in an effective position to govern.[1] Part of the answer can be found in the circumstances of this last exchange between the two men. What so angered Hitler about Goering's action was the fact that it finally broke the bond of loyalty that had linked them together since 1922. Goering, for his part, took days searching his conscience before he plucked up sufficient courage to take over from Hitler, for his oath of allegiance was not to be lightly broken even in the last hours of Nazi rule.[2]

This loyalty was the central feature of the political relationship between them. It was the source of Goering's own power. It was one factor that protected Goering from the insistent demand of his critics that he should be replaced by men more competent, for the loyalty flowed both ways. Hitler respected the way in which Goering had worked in the years of 'struggle' for the movement, and his subsequent efforts after 1933 to do everything to fulfil Hitler's ambitions. Goering in turn recognised, as well he might, that his political influence and authority derived solely from the special relationship he enjoyed with the Führer. This took the form not only of a political dependence, but of a personal one as well. He was sustained by Hitler intellectually and emotionally. 'I have no conscience,' Goering claimed, 'my conscience is Adolf Hitler.'[3] When the relationship between them become more distant and strained after 1943 Goering could hardly bear the ordeal of meeting Hitler. His staff watched him as he emerged from interviews in tears, a stark contrast to the brutal and bullying figure that he portrayed to his subordinates. If he did not always believe that Hitler had adopted the most sensible choice open to him, he accepted his word as law. Hitler was the prophet, Goering the disciple. The only thing he would not accept, according to Diels, was an order from Hitler forbidding him to believe in God.[4]

Hitler, for his part, saw in Goering an example of the new generation of German leaders. He spoke of Goering as a 'second Wagner', as an example of the Renaissance man, with interests alike in culture, war and politics.[5] Where Goering's flamboyance of dress and behaviour horrified the sombre and snobbish bureaucrats and soldiers who had contact with him, Hitler indulged him precisely because he was so different from the conventional upper and middle classes.[6] Hitler, while so thoroughly bourgeois in his own behaviour, claimed to have little time for the unimaginative and conformist life of the German middle classes. Goering's behaviour was tolerated as a crude statement of the gulf between the Nazi elite and those that it sought to replace; a reminder that where bourgeois life had stifled German develop-ment, the Nazi movement was liberating German culture by reuniting Germany with its history. In this sense Goering was both a modern and a Renaissance figure, transcending the centuries of Germany's historical emasculation, linking up a true 'Germanic' heritage with the promise of a new German destiny.

The qualities that Hitler admired in Goering were those that he, to some extent, lacked, but which he recognised as characteristics of the new breed of German. 'The Reichsmarschall has been through many crises with me,' he told his staff in 1944. 'He is ice-cold in time of crisis. At such a time one can't have a better adviser than the Reichsmarschall. . . . He is brutal and ice-cold . . . you can't have a better one, a better one cannot be found.'[7] Goering's hardness, his heroism (he had not fled under fire in the November Putsch in 1923), his ruthless energy and brutality made up the political personality that Hitler admired until well into the war. Not for nothing did he appoint Goering as his successor in 1939.

Perhaps for this reason Hitler turned a blind eye to Goering's corruption. Like any Renaissance prince Goering collected great works of art, patron-ised architects and artists, ordered the designs of great civic buildings and monuments. Speer argued that 'corruption corresponded to Hitler's notion of the right of those wielding power to take possession of material goods. Authority, he thought, always needed outward show. . . .'[8] By such argu-ments Goering's piratical acquisition of art treasures, like Hitler's own, was defined as a means to protect Europe's cultural heritage, and to augment the authority of those who now controlled it. So, too, did Goering justify his extravagant and courtly life-style funded by 'gifts' from industrialists and other wealthy supporters.[9] The system of routine present-giving that developed was not defined as bribery or extortion, which is what it often was, but as a tribute to Goering's statesmanship. Those who knew the Goering household better than Hitler did were more critical. To Goebbels he had become by 1944 'more a bourgeois than a revolutionary' as a result of his restless pursuit of wealth and objects.[10] To the public at large he became what Himmler called him, 'the king of the black markets'.[11]

There is no doubt that Goering was motivated in much of this display by an uncontrollable vanity. He was vain in his own person, taking great pains with his appearance.[12] Berlin society became accustomed to discussing what he would wear or had worn on state occasions.[13] His vulgarity and ostentation were common knowledge. While this strengthened his popular appeal, it alienated those who were closer to him. Ciano thought his famous sable coat 'what a high-grade prostitute wears to the opera'.[14] General Dornberger, in charge of the V2 rocket programme, later wrote of his disgust at Goering's appearance when he came to watch the first demonstration of its launch: 'Soft Morocco leather riding-boots of glaring red with silver spurs . . . a very voluminous greatcoat of Australian opossum fur with the hide turned outwards. Platinum rings with big rubies. . . .'[15] Goering took a boyish and irresistible delight in dressing up. On one occasion when he was scheduled to meet managers of the Heinkel company in Austria to discuss vital production planning late in the war, he spent the time in Vienna's leading jewellery shops, missing the meeting altogether.[16]

His vanity had a much more serious side as well, because it sprang from the same source as his political ambition. One example may serve to illustrate this connection. During 1939 the close political links between Italy and Germany were sealed in the so-called 'Pact of Steel'. To mark the occasion the Italian King conferred on Ribbentrop, as Foreign Minister, the highest Italian civilian decoration, the Order of the Annunziata. Goering believed that he should have received the honour as the chief architect of the Axis partnership.[17] While the claim was debatable, the consequences of ignoring it were substantial. Goering refused to attend meetings with Italian leaders. He became highly critical of Italian policy, and even more so after the outbreak of war when Italy remained neutral. For months pressure was brought to bear on the Italian King to agree to give Goering a similar decoration. Since Mussolini was anxious to get economic aid from Germany, and as he became increasingly concerned that Italy might be excluded altogether from the spoils of German victory, Victor Emmanuel III was persuaded, much against his will, to concede. Goering was content only with complete capitulation, insisting on a personal letter from the King to accompany the award, as was customary.[18] Thereafter, Goering re-established cordial relations with the Italian leadership. Such personal factors inevitably bore upon public events because of the nature of leadership in the Nazi system; and they did so more with Goering than with most Nazi leaders. Even Hitler recognised the problems this raised. During the war he persistently refused to sanction the name 'Hermann-Goering Stadt' on the grounds that he was reluctant to give one particular leader a greater claim to permanence than the others. Until the end of the war the new town was known administratively as the 'area around Salzgitter'.[19]

If Hitler was by no means oblivious to the criticisms that Goering's behaviour invited, his general detachment from the squabbles of the lieutenants gave Goering, for much of the time, the benefit of the doubt. When Hitler could no longer ignore the crisis surrounding Goering's leadership in the late part of 1944 he confined himself to nothing more than severe reprimands. He argued that he had nothing to gain politically by humiliating Goering. When General Guderian begged Hitler to retire Goering from office, he replied: 'For political reasons I cannot do as you suggest. The party would never understand my motives.'[20] On grounds of sentiment he could not bring himself to break formally with one of his oldest and most loyal comrades. Goering was bound by the same ties. He told Speer late in the war that 'many years of common experiences and struggles had bound them together – and he could no longer break loose.'[21] If Goering's survival made little sense politically and strategically, it could be understood in the Nazi language of comradeship and fealty.

It should not be forgotten that Hitler and Goering, though comrades in the movement, were not intimate. Hitler used *Sie* rather than the more informal *Du* when addressing Goering. He did not include him at any time in his immediate entourage, and after the seizure of power was no longer a regular visitor at Goering's household.[22] No doubt both men recognised that it was difficult to have two kings at one court, and preferred not to encroach on each other's territory. But this did mean that Hitler's view of Goering was formed not through close and informal contact, but through regular formal meetings. This no doubt served to strengthen Hitler's idea of him as a man of action since they were in each other's company most at times of crisis, when Hitler became nervous and uncertain, and Goering became energetically decisive. Hitler's adjutant later wrote that when Hitler had to reach a decision he would punctuate his discussions with the remarks: 'I must speak to Goering first about it' or 'What does Goering say on this?'[23] The two men co-operated most closely during the period of the seizure of power, at the time of the crisis in the economy in 1936 and 1937, during the *Anschluss* and again in the period of the Polish crisis and the early stages of the war. During the latter period, Goering judged that he had been the leading influence on Hitler.[24] Although it is difficult to say with any certainty that this was the case, there is a clear correlation between these periods of increased political tension and Goering's acquisition of political power. Goering depended much more than other leading Nazis on his special political relationship with Hitler, and in this lies the explanation of his rise to power after 1933.

This is not to deny that Goering achieved much on his own initiative. He recognised the reality of the political structure of the Third Reich and used Hitler as a means to extend his own influence. But once he had gained sufficient political momentum his role became more independent so that by the Second World War he enjoyed sufficient power and prestige to make it politically inadvisable for Hitler to eliminate him from public life as his critics demanded. There was never any question of Goering suffering the fate of Röhm, for he was always ostentatiously loyal. This was all that Hitler required. Much of what Goering did in the wider world of German politics was free from Hitler's direct intervention, giving him ample room for an independent political existence. There was nothing passive or negative about Goering's political life.

Indeed Goering was extraordinarily ambitious. If we cannot altogether take seriously the claim he made at Nuremberg that he had dreamed in the 1920s of one day becoming ruler of Germany, his political history shows a man determined to make his mark.[25] Whatever setbacks his personal career experienced he was never far from the centre of affairs. He was capable of giving the impression of great activity and energy simply through his presence on so many committees and at so many vital meetings. His ability to dominate others around him gave him the advantage over those who were better administrators but who shunned the limelight. This was still true at the post-war trials of the major war criminals. Goering from the outset imposed his authority over his fellow prisoners. Even those who resented this in private subscribed to it when brought face to face with Goering. His ambition to be a figure of political influence made him a major part of the political landscape of the Third Reich despite his mistakes and his lack of any clear area of technical competency.

Goering enjoyed several advantages over other leading Nazis in his exercise of power. Perhaps the most important was his interest in collecting and disseminating secret intelligence. He was often in a position to know his rivals' plans in advance and to be able to keep one step ahead of them. His co-operative relations with Himmler throughout the period helped him to get access to information from the Gestapo and the security services.[26] In a world of conspiracy and rumour Goering found his métier. To the end of the war he never stopped intriguing in the hope that he might extract more influence or power through what amounted to a political 'black market'.

Goering was never still in the underworld of German political life, for it was here that the real politics of the Third Reich was conducted. His access to secret information, and his place in the network for gathering and communicating intelligence, also allowed him to present a distorted and more favourable impression of his political achievement than would otherwise have been possible. Information that was passed on to Hitler, for example, was carefully selected to present an optimistic assessment of events. The heavy penalties for personal failure and the strongly ideological character of political life combined to produce a situation in which Hitler was only told the intelligence it was thought he wanted to hear. Goering went to extraordinary lengths to prevent the economic intelligence services from sending to Hitler details of United States economic potential in late 1941 and early 1942, and when one such memorandum slipped through the net, he went personally to Hitler to persuade him that the figures were vastly exaggerated, and had been sent in by an officer bent only on furthering his own career.[27] Later in the war Goering's effort to persuade Hitler that Allied long-range fighters were simply conventional aircraft swept eastwards by the prevailing wind showed the same bizarre attempt to shield Hitler from the truth. Only in the last months of war did Hitler realise the extent of this misrepresentation, complaining that he had been 'lied to permanently about production figures and also about aircraft performance'.[28]

A second great advantage for Goering was his public popularity. This was partly due to his own efforts to project a political personality of great sociability and colour, for he was seldom out of the public's eye. He possessed a bluffness and humour that made him a more attractive figure on superficial acquaintance than most Nazi politicians, and allowed the public to forgive, or even identify with, his foibles. For those bourgeois who had lost out in the crisis of the war and Weimar, and whose culture was being emasculated by industrialism and 'modernity', Goering was a romantic and anachronistic expression of their own ambitions and appetites. There was a little of Goering in each of them.[29] This perhaps explains the wide currency given to stories and rumours about Goering. Many of the political jokes that circulated in the Third Reich were directed at Goering. He collected them in a large leather notebook and delighted in re-telling most of them to his friends.[30] His personal social life became part of German high society during the 1930s. He entertained lavishly and had a wide circle of acquaintances and contacts. Hitler could not tolerate too much formal social contact and left this side of state affairs as far as he could to Goering among others. This regular exposure never created anything like the 'Hitler-Myth' but it created a subsidiary myth, that Goering was a more approachable and sympathetic Nazi than his colleagues.

It was this myth that was widely accepted not just by the public at large, but by Germany's non-Nazi political circles, and by foreign opinion as well. In both Britain and the United States there were those who were prepared to distinguish between Goering and other Nazi leaders. Even the caustic Phipps believed that: 'Lunching with the Warden of New College, General Goering might pass as almost civilised.'[31] It was no mere chance that Goering was the figure chosen by British negotiators in the summer of 1939 to try to bring influence on Hitler for peace, or that Goering was favoured in Washington as a possible German delegate to an international congress on the Polish crisis after September 1939 to try to end the war. Goering still believed in the possibility in 1945 that he might be chosen by the Americans to negotiate the post-war settlement of Germany.

This reaction to Goering was partly a by-product of his popularity, partly a result of his own artful efforts to win confidence and approval while leaving his real motives obscured. The fact that he did so in a far more personable way than Hitler does not alter the character of the political tactic. He was projected as the acceptable face of Nazism, as he had been projected in 1932 and 1933 in the party's efforts to win support from industry, Catholics and nationalists. This explains why foreign statesmen misunderstood him. Ciano – who knew Goering close at hand – had no such illusions about him; nor indeed, after a brief affair in 1939, did western leaders.[32]

Within Germany Goering featured, albeit unwittingly, in the long series of conservative plans for their reconquest of German politics and the overthrow of Hitler. The reason for this was largely to do with Goering's popularity, for there was little else to attract the conservatives to him. They feared that any abrupt change in politics of the Third Reich might mean not simply the collapse of fascism but of the conservative position as well, swept away in a popular revolution. Goering was to be used instrumentally, as a way of easing the transition from one form of government to another. Some, but by no means all, of the conservatives based this optimistic view of Goering on the way in which he had behaved during 1934 in saving Germany from Röhm's 'revolution', and his apparent willingness to work with Schacht and big business during 1935 and 1936.[33] By the time of the Polish crisis much of this sympathy had evaporated, but Goering featured nevertheless in the plans drawn up in 1939 for the first serious attempt to rid Germany of Hitler. Admiral Canaris, head of the counter-espionage service, favoured using Goering for tactical purposes. Goerdeler and the Prussian Finance Minister von Popitz were both favourable disposed to using Goering as well, partly because they took Goering's peace efforts in September and October 1939 at face value. It was hoped that the 'peace party' within the Nazi leadership could be used to drive a wedge between Hitler and the rank and file of the movement.[34] There was, of course, no hope of such a tactic succeeding, not least because the conservative conspirators were implacably opposed to Goering. One of their number, Hans Dohnanyi, condemned the idea of using Goering as 'a Kerensky solution'. General Ludwig Beck, army chief-of-staff at the time Hitler took over the Supreme Command and a leading conservative opponent, told the diplomat Ulrich von Hassell that he regarded Goering as 'one of the worst of the lot'. Even the mild army commander-in-chief von Brauchitsch was reported to mistrust 'Goering's character in the highest degree'.[35] Under such circumstances the possibility of using Goering was ruled out. Although this ploy was revived again during the war, the mutual hostility between Goering and the generals only hardened.

The conservatives' flirtation with Goering was doomed to failure because of their profound misapprehension about the nature of Nazi politics in general and the character of Goering in particular. The system depended crucially upon the survival of Hitler and the 'Hitler-Myth'. There was no guarantee of political influence for any Nazi once the Führer was gone. The only occasions on which Hitler's authority was genuinely threatened – by Strasser in 1932 and Röhm in 1934 – had brought about a closing of the ranks in the party for fear of its political eclipse. The conservatives had really very little to offer except a return to the coalition politics of early 1933 when they had hoped to tame the Nazi movement. Goering, like any other Nazi leader, was not to be wooed by promises of a share of power with other groups when the Nazis already held absolute power themselves.

Goering was not, as many believed, a man of moderate views and conservative inclinations. In the context of German politics in the 1930s he was as radical as Himmler or Goebbels, for, like them, he believed in the transformation of German society along the lines of a racial community. If his ideological views were not entirely those of the party's artisan socialists – and nor for that matter were Hitler's – he was thoroughly soaked in the values and ambitions of the movement. He was entirely committed to the extension of party power and the establishment of new institutions, even if he was at times highly critical of those who ran them. He championed the ideal of community interest before private interest, whether in the economy, the research institutes or the labour movement. He was fiercely anti-Marxist, opposed to the organised working class and its political institutions, while maintaining the romantic illusion that the working classes would accept Nazism once they recognised its respect for labour. Most important of all, he accepted the crude geopolitics of Hitler's world view. He was more influential than any other Nazi in turning the economy and armed forces towards a policy of active imperialism, and enjoyed more powers than any other Nazi in constructing the New Order. The victims in all this were the Jews, against whom Goering actively struggled through the aryanisation of the economy, and the Slavs whom he regarded as fit only for German colonisation.

He was moderate in only the very limited sense that he came to prefer more stealthy and piecemeal tactics in achieving these ambitions in place of the revolutionary exuberance of the early months of Nazi rule. For one thing it was necessary to guard against what he described to Mussolini as 'the constant surprises and precipitate developments' in foreign policy.[36] For another it was necessary to utilise what other groups, such as the bureaucracy and army, had to offer while the party consolidated its power. But in every other respect he carried with him the restless activism of the movement, and its impatience with those social and political forces within Germany that threatened to compromise its historic mission. He was driven on in this by an ideological as much as a personal imperative. Without grasping the highly ideological character of Nazi politics, and the strong relationship between ideology and practice, it is difficult to make sense of political figures like Goering. Although the ideology was intellectually barren and socially specific, it played an important part in mobilising disaffected and declassé activists and in justifying what they did once in power. No other interpretation can satisfactorily encompass the Nazi rejection of German conservatism, the pursuit of empire and the elimination of the Jews.

Goering's most important contribution to the building of the new state was in replacing conservative dominance over economic and military affairs with an apparatus under his own control working for the waging of war. This became necessary at the point where big business and the armed forces were no longer willing to follow the Nazis along the path to massive war preparation and state economic control. The armed forces were concerned that Hitler's plans for conquest would again threaten Germany's security and the chances of the old military establishment surviving. Businessmen resented the loss of entrepreneurial independence and the pursuit of economic policies that threatened the direct interests of German business. Under Goering the armed forces were compelled to accept Nazi plans for want of a viable political alternative, while business fell back upon the defence of its financial and market position in the face of increasing state intervention and industrial management. How this dominance was established, and with what results has formed the largest part of this discussion, and does not need to be repeated here.

This is not to deny that there were those in the army and business world who welcomed the Third Reich, and who actively co-operated with its leaders throughout its life. Some notion of treaty revision and economic hegemony in eastern Europe was common to all conservatives. The important point was the political terms under which these goals were to be achieved. Prior to 1933 foreign policy and economic growth had been controlled in formal and informal ways by the German upper classes. It has been argued that through this control they created a political integration imposed from above, designed to avoid the radical threat that had reared up in 1848, 1861 and again in 1918, and which German conservatives assumed was always present beneath the surface of German politics. During the 1920s this political model, which was essentially Bismarck's solution to the German question, broke down, as it had been threatening to do well before 1914. Under the impact of economic crisis and international isolation mass social forces emerged of a radical right-wing character, which were mobilised by the Nazis as the most successful of the populist parties to appear under the Weimar Republic. The effect of this was to turn the Bismarckian system on its head, to impose a new integration on German society from below rather than from above. Although it took time for the conservatives to realise it, Nazism was a symptom of the frustration felt among broad sectors of the peasantry, petty bourgeoisie and nationalist working-class at the bankruptcy of the traditional elites and the interest-group politics that they practised.

The success of German fascism in 1933 also demonstrated the peculiar character of bourgeois politics in Germany. Unable to form a broad alliance of middle-class and socially conservative groups in Germany, the leading bourgeois groups abandoned mass politics and tried to shelter once again under the old conservative wing as they had done before 1914. The Nazis took advantage of this situation by attracting the support of groups in German society that were increasingly unrepresented in national politics, and increasingly revolutionary in temper. The political revolution after 1933 drew its strength from this traditional tension in German politics between the elites and the masses on the German right. Its heritage stretched back to 1848 when craftsmen, peasants, junior civil servants and teachers had once before demanded radical change. As in 1848 the conservative elites chose to follow the radicals in the hope of containing their radicalism, and with the prospect of using the army if things went wrong. But unlike 1848, the radicals could not be contained. The conservatives, whether soldiers or capitalists, followed for as long as they could but by 1936 were compelled to accept the reality of Nazi power and either capitulated and became its tools or abandoned the struggle altogether in the hope that something might be salvaged later from its overthrow.

This contest for state power, from which the new working class was forcibly excluded by both sides, derived from the very different traditions in German politics about what constituted the German nation. For the conservatives it had always been the means to an end: the survival of conservative values and traditional social power. It was not an end in itself. For all their talk of nation, the German upper classes were particularist. For all their talk of integration, their political strategies were transparently selfish. But to the social conservative masses the nation had become their chief source of historical identity and social value. Not surprisingly, under the circumstances these masses voted for a party led by people like themselves, that seemed authentically nationalistic and promised them real power.

These different views of nationhood and political practice are crucial in explaining the success of the Nazi movement. But it was a success that Nazi voters bought at a high price; for contained within this historical vision of German nationhood were the seeds of racial conflict and war. With a fearful logic the intolerant and irrational world view of the party and its supporters was imposed upon German life as if it had a universal validity. This attempt to steer a course between the conservative elites and the working-class mass was fraught with tensions and contradictions. As the efforts to create this 'Third Way' became more frantic, the party became more committed to war and to its racial policy as the best means of fulfilling the special role cast for the German nation in history. And this distorted yet further the contrast between the predominantly industrial, class society that Germany had become by the 1920s and the fantastic visions of German empire and racial community contained within the Nazi world view. The particularism of the frightened German *Mittelständ* was both more volatile and more dangerous than that of German conservatism, or German capitalism or the German working class because it was based upon a crude historicist ideology, and not upon social reality.

Goering's unhappy history reflected entirely the tension between the Nazi claim to be changing the direction of history and the necessity of adjusting to the predominant class forces in German society. Goering more than any other Nazi went a long way towards trying to resolve this tension through his extensive controls over industry and labour and his efforts to get them to serve the ambitions of the movement. But his ultimate achievement was destructive rather than creative, hastening the disappearance of what was left of Bismarck's Reich and the social groups who had run it. The subsequent attempt to mould German society to fit the Nazi image was beyond the party's means. Germany had become a modern industrial state and could not be diverted from that path by assertions of petty-bourgeois idealism.

In truth this was the core of the contradiction represented by Nazism. It was from its very nature a movement of the historical losers, an ephemeral populism thrown up by economic crisis and the distorted political and intellectual response that the crisis provoked. Had it not been for the peculiar circumstances of Germany's recent political past and the severity of the shock inflicted on the German economic structure between 1929 and 1932, it is inconceivable that Goering or even Hitler would ever have become a political figure of any significance. This was what made it difficult to reconcile Goering's illusion of being a latterday Renaissance prince with the reality of being a soap-box orator hoisted to power on the backs of disgruntled peasants and shopkeepers by courtesy of intensely insecure and nationalistic elites. Goering clutched at historical significance once he was in power, but it was hard to disguise the underlying weaknesses of his claim, or the fact that for Goering, as for the other supporters of the movement, the only way to hold on to power was ultimately through violence. By means of internal repression and war the movement postponed recognition of the historical fraud that Nazism perpetrated on Germany, but the violence was in the end self-defeating. If there is a moral in Goering's history, it is not that people get the governments they deserve, but how dangerous it is to mistake historical chance for historical necessity.

NOTES

Abbreviations in the notes are as follows:

BA	Bundesarchiv, Koblenz
BA-MA	Bundesarchiv-Militärarchiv, Freiburg i.B.
BIOS	British Intelligence Objectives Sub-Committee
CIOS	Combined Intelligence Objectives Sub-Committee
DBFP	Documents on British Foreign Policy
DDP	Dokumente der deutschen Politik
DGFP	Documents on German Foreign Policy
FD	Foreign Document
FIAT	Field Intelligence Agencies Technical
GL	Generalluftzeugmeister
HMSO	Her/His Majesty's Stationery Office
IMT	International Military Tribunal
IWM	Imperial War Museum, London
NA	National Archives, Washington D.C.
NCA	Nazi Conspiracy and Aggression
OKW	Oberkommando der Wehrmacht
RLM	Reichsluftfahrtministerium (German Air Ministry)
SA	Salzgitter Archiv, Salzgitter
TWC	Trials of the War Criminals
USSBS	United States Strategic Bombing Survey
VJP	Vierjahresplan (Four Year Plan)

The title and description of German documents has wherever possible been given in English to make them more accessible to an English readership.

CHAPTER 1   THE 'IRON MAN'

1   N. Henderson, *Failure of a Mission*, London, 1940, p. 80.
2   Goering had other nicknames – 'Scharnhorst of the Luftwaffe' and (less flatteringly) 'der Dicke', the fat one, or 'Hermann der Schreckliche', Hermann the Terrible.
3   K. Singer, *Göring – Germany's Most Dangerous Man*, London, 1940; R. Vansittart, *Black Record: Germans Past and Present*, London, 1941, p. 52.
4   Fuehrer Conference, 25.7.1943 in F. Gilbert (ed.), *Hitler Directs his War*, New York, 1950, p. 44.
5   E. Kordt, *Wahn und Wirklichkeit*, Stuttgart, 1948, p. 44.

6   There is an excellent account in R. Manvell, H. Fraenkel, *Göring*, London, 1962; see also L. Mosley, *The Reich Marshal*, London, 1974; C. Bewley, *Hermann Goering*, Göttingen, 1956; E. Butler, G. Young, *Marshal without Glory: the Life and Death of Hermann Goering*, London, 1951; W. Frischauer, *The Rise and Fall of Hermann Göring*, London, 1950.

7   H. Trevor-Roper, *The Last Days of Hitler*, 2nd ed., London, 1962, p. 54.

8   Manvell and Fraenkel, op. cit., pp. 14–16; Mosley, op. cit., p. 48.

9   Singer, op. cit., p. 51.

10   H. Goering, *Germany Reborn*, London, 1934, pp. 19–20, 23–6, 48–9.

11   F. von Wilamowitz-Moellendorff, *Carin Göring*, Berlin, 1935, pp. 24–30.

12   IMT, *Trials of the Major War Criminals*, Nuremberg, 1947, vol. 9, pp. 439–40 (hereafter IMT); K. Ludecke, *I Knew Hitler*, London, 1938, p. 129, who records Hitler's remark that his appointment of Goering would be 'excellent propaganda'.

13   On this period of Goering's life see Mosley, op. cit., pp. 87–107: Singer, op. cit., pp. 74–110; O. Dutch, *Hitler's Twelve Apostles*, London, 1939, pp. 54–5; M. Sommerfeldt, *Hermann Göring: ein Lebensbild*, Berlin, 1933, pp. 50–2.

14   Singer, op. cit., pp. 112–13.

15   For example O. Strasser, *Hitler and I*, London, 1940; W. Allen, (ed.) *The Infancy of Nazism: the Memoirs of Ex-Gauleiter Albert Krebs 1923–1933*, London, 1976; J. Goebbels, *Tagebuch 1925–6*, (ed. H. Heiber), Stuttgart, 1961.

16   H. Schacht, *76 Jahre meines Lebens*, Bad Wörishofen, 1953, pp. 350–2; F. Thyssen, *I Paid Hitler*, London, 1941, p. 131; J. and S. Pool, *Who Financed Hitler?*, London, 1979, pp. 261–4, 272–3.

17   Ludecke, op. cit., p. 429. Hitler told him that Goering was 'very useful at times, even if he is guilty of awful asininities now and then'. On the more general background see D. Orlow, *The History of the Nazi Party*, Newton Abbot, 1973, vol. 1, pp. 246–7.

18   F. von Papen, *Memoirs*, London, 1952, pp. 232–42; A. Dorpalen, *Hindenburg and the Weimar Republic*, Princeton, 1964, pp. 429–38; O. Meissner, *Staatssekretär unter Ebert-Hindenburg-Hitler*, Hamburg, 1950, pp. 216, 230, 263–4.

19   J. A. Leopold, *Alfred Hugenberg*, London, 1977, pp. 131–4.

20   Strasser, op. cit., p. 150; U. Kissenkoetter, *Gregor Strasser und die NSDAP*, Stuttgart, 1978, pp. 168–70: O. Braun, *Von Weimar zu Hitler*, New York, 1940, pp. 430–3: G. R. Treviranus, *Das Ende von Weimar*, Düsseldorf, 1968, pp. 341–5.

21   Goering, op. cit., p. 27.

22   D. M. Kelley, *22 Cells in Nuremberg*, London, 1947, p. 53. See too Goering, op. cit., pp. 23–7.

23   Singer, op. cit., pp. 51–2, 82, 121–2; Kelley, op. cit., p. 46. Goering told Kelley: 'I hated the Republic, I knew it could not last. . . . I wanted to help destroy the Republic.' On anti-semitism see Goering, op. cit., pp. 27, 73–4, 129–32.

24   J. M. Rhodes, *The Hitler Movement*, Stanford, 1980, pp. 45–8, 149.

25   IMT vol. 9, p. 439, Goering cross-examination; E. Gritzbach (ed.)., *Hermann Göring: Reden und Aufsätze*, Munich, 1938, pp. 100–20, speech of 18.6.1934 (hereafter, Goering, *Reden*); Goering, 1934, op. cit., pp. 37–8.

26   Goering, *Reden*, pp. 37–49, speech of 9.4.1933 on 'Nationalism and Socialism'; pp. 202–18, speech of 26.10.1935 on 'Party and State'.

27   T. R. Emessen (ed.), *Aus Görings Schreibtisch: ein Dokumentenfund*, Berlin, 1947, p. 78; Goering, *Reden*, pp. 22–3, speech of 3.3.1933.

28   Bewley, op. cit., p. 306.

29   Goering, 1934, op. cit., p. 77.

30 F. von Schlabrenendorff, *The Secret War Against Hitler*, London, 1966, p. 55: Goering, *Reden*, p. 27.
31 IWM Milch Documents, vol. 63, p. 6314 (hereafter MD).
32 G. M. Gilbert, *Nuremberg Diary*, London, 1948, p. 114.
33 J. Fest, *The Face of the Third Reich*, London, 1972, p. 82.
34 J. Goebbels, *Vom Kaiserhof zur Reichskanzlei*, Munich, 1937, p. 251.
35 H. Schacht, *Account Settled*, London, 1953, p. 97.
36 Christie Papers, Churchill College, Cambridge, 180/1 5 'Notes on a conversation with Göring, 28.7.1937'.
37 E. Gritzbach, *Hermann Göring*, Berlin, 1938, p. 109.
38 W. Baumbach, *Broken Swastika*, London, 1960, p. 25.
39 NA, Göring-Stabsamt papers, microcopy T84 Roll 6 frames 5269–5303, for details of Goering's appointment lists (hereafter Goering-Stabsamt).
40 Gritzbach, 1938 (2), op. cit., p. 203. Goering argued that 'when an official requires more than two or three pages of typescript to state his case, then he is as good as useless'. On his dislike of graphs and statistics see MD vol. 63, p. 6020, 'give me everything in very large clear numbers!'.
41 B. Fromm, *Blood and Banquets: a Berlin Social Diary*, London, 1943, p. 173. The cars were Mercedes-Benz.
42 U. von Hassell, *The von Hassell Diaries 1938–1944*, London, 1948, pp. 82–3.
43 von Wilamowitz-Moellendorff, op. cit., pp. 154–60. On the building of the mausoleum and the pageantry surrounding its completion see Phipps Papers, Churchill College, Cambridge, 1/12 Sir Eric Phipps to Sir John Simon, 11.6.1934, pp. 2–5.
44 E. Goering, *An der Seite meines Mannes*, Göttingen, 1967; Fromm, op. cit., pp. 172–3.
45 Gilbert, op. cit., p. 128.
46 Goering speech, May Day 1934, *Das Archiv*, 1934/5, p. 178.
47 Kelley, op. cit., p. 59.
48 Goering, 1934, op. cit., p. 51.
49 Gritzbach, 1938 (2), op. cit., pp. 116–17.
50 Kelley, op. cit., pp. 47–8. Kelley was an American doctor responsible for the health of the senior Nazi prisoners.
51 The reference to the 'last Renaissance man' was made by Goering's state secretary, Paul Koerner, at the Nuremberg trials. Goering was so pleased with the description that he adopted it forthwith. See Gilbert, op. cit., p. 248.
52 There are numerous references in Göring-Stabsamt papers, T 84 Rolls 6–9.
53 A. Speer, *Inside the Third Reich*, London, 1970, p. 266; A. Nielsen, *The German Air Force General Staff*, New York, 1959, p. 140.

CHAPTER 2 BUILDING THE GOERING EMPIRE

1 E. Gritzbach (ed.), *Hermann Göring: Reden* und Aufsätze, Munich, 1938 (hereafter Goering, *Reden*), pp. 15–16, speech of 30.1.1933.
2 K. Singer, *Göring – Germany's most Dangerous Man*, London, 1940, p. 187.
3 J. Becker, 'Zentrum und Ermächtigungsgesetz', *Vierteljahreshefte für Zeitgeschichte*, vol. 9, 1961, pp. 195–210, particularly Document 2, 'Notes of a former Centre Party deputy on the Enabling Act'; E. Matthias, R. Morsey. *Das Ende der Parteien 1933*, Düsseldorf, 1960, pp. 388–9; O. Meissner. *Staatssekretär unter Ebert-Hindenburg-Hitler*, Hamburg, 1950, pp. 289–93: G. R. Treviranus, *Das Ende von Weimar*, Düsseldorf, 1968, p. 386 ff.
4 DGFP Ser. C, vol. 1, Minutes of a Conference of Ministers, 8 February

1933, pp. 36–8; Conference of 28 February 1933, pp. 88–90; Conference of 12 July 1933, pp. 648–50.

5   F. von Papen, *Memoirs*, London, 1952, p. 241, 243; Christie Papers, 180/1 4 Notes on Gregor Strasser, 10.12.1932; H. Goering, *Germany Reborn*, London, 1934, pp. 105–7.

6   K. D. Bracher, W. Sauer, G. Schultz, *Die nationalsozialistische Machtergreifung*, Cologne, 1960, pp. 54–7.

7   J. Delarue, *The History of the Gestapo*, London, 1964, pp. 32–3; E. Crankshaw, *Gestapo: Instrument of Tyranny*, London, 1956, pp. 43–9; Beacher, op. cit., pp. 864–6.

8   H. Mommsen, 'Der Reichstagsbrand und sein politischen Folgen', *Viertel- jahreshefte für Zeitgeschichte*, vol. 12. 1964, pp. 350–413; F. Tobias, *Der Reich- stagsbrand: Legende und Wirklichkeit*, Rastatt, 1962.

9   Goering, op. cit., pp. 132–3. 1 WM FO 645 Box 156, Goering interrogations 13.10.1945 and 8.9.1945. 'They would have been arrested', he claimed, 'had there been a fire or had there not been a fire . . . a few days or possibly a week later.'

10 DGFP, Ser. C, vol. 1, pp. 88–90, Minutes of Conference of Ministers 28 February 1933; *Dokumente der deutschen Politik*, vol. 1, Berlin, 1935, pp. 44–6, 'Prussian Interior Ministry decree forbidding the activity of the German Social Democrat Party', 23.6.1933 (hereafter DDP).

11 R. Morsey, 'Der Beginn der Gleichschaltung in Preussen', *Vierteljahreshefte für Zeitgeschichte*, vol. 11, 1963, pp. 85–97; von Papen, op. cit., pp. 188–94.

12 DDP, vol. 1, p. 181, Letter from Hitler to Goering, 7.4.1933; Letter from von Papen to Hitler, 7.4.1933; P. Hüttenberger, *Die Gauleiter*, Stuttgart, 1969, p. 75; von Papen, op. cit., pp. 293–4; A. François-Poncet, *The Fateful Years*, London, 1949, pp. 76–7; Bracher, op. cit., pp. 205–6.

13 R. Diels, *Lucifer ante Portas*, Stuttgart, 1950, pp. 227–9; S. Aronson, *Reinhard Heydrich und die Frühgeschichte von Gestapo und SD*, Stuttgart, 1971, pp. 67–9, 85–93.

14 H. Pünder, *Von Preussen nach Europa*, Stuttgart, 1968, pp. 140–1; F. von Schlabrenendorff, *The Secret War against Hitler*, London,1966, pp. 40–45; Bracher, op. cit., pp. 430–46.

15 Diels, op. cit., pp. 285–7; Bracher, op. cit., pp. 430–2, 472–5. On Goering's constitutional ideas see Goering, *Reden*, pp. 50–79, speech to the Prussian Landtag on 'Prussia's Mission', 18.5.1933. On the state council see DDP, vol. 1, p. 177, 'Law over the Prussian State Council, 8.7.1933'.

16 H. Mommsen, *Beamtentum im Dritten Reich*, Stuttgart, 1966, p. 33; Bracher, op. cit., p. 148, 468–9.

17 Ibid., p. 174.

18 Delarue, op. cit., p. 44; Aronson, op. cit., pp. 172–3, 185–90.

19 G. S. Graber, *The Life and Times of Reinhard Heydrich*, London, 1981, pp. 82–9; DDP, vol. 2, Berlin, 1936, pp. 111–12, Letter from Goering to Hitler, 17.3.1934; pp. 112–13, Letter from Hitler to Goering, 1.5.1934; Speech of Goering to officials of the Interior Ministry, 7.5.1934, *Das Archiv*, 1934/5, p. 181; A. Brissaud, *The Nazi Secret Service*, London, 1974, pp. 39–41.

20 H. Höhne, *The Order of the Death's Head*, London, 1969, pp. 106–10: Fran- çois-Poncet, op. cit., pp. 134–6. There are interesting observations in Phipps Papers I, 1/12, Phipps to Simon, 5.7.1934.

21 H. Mau, 'The "Second Revolution", June 30th 1934' in H. Holborn (ed.), *Republic to Reich: the Making of the Nazi Revolution*, New York, 1972, pp. 226–31; D. Orlow, *The History of the Nazi Party*, vol. 2, Newton Abbot, 1973, pp. 106–10.

22 B. Fromm, *Blood and Banquets: a Berlin Social Diary*, London, 1943, p. 150.
23 Goering speech at Hamburg, 25.6.1934 in *Das Archiv*, 1934/5, pp. 321–2. See, too, his later remarks on demands for Habsburg restoration after the incorporation of Austria with Germany, a demand that Goering labelled 'treachery', DDP, vol. 6, Berlin, 1940, p. 198.
24 J. Leopold, *Alfred Hugenberg*, London, 1977, pp. 151–63: J. L. Heinemann, 'Constantin von Neurath and German Policy at the London Economic Conference 1933', *Journal of Modern History*, vol. 31, 1969; von Papen, op. cit., pp. 295–302.
25 Schlabrenendorff, op. cit., pp. 54–5.
26 U. von Hassell, *The von Hassell Diaries 1938–44*, London, 1948, p. 29. Von Fritsch told von Hassell that Goering had plotted against him since 1934 after bullying him into promising that the army would not interfere in the crisis over the SA. See too W. Görlitz, *The History of the German General Staff*, New York, 1953, pp. 286–7, who argues that Goering wanted control over the armed forces for himself as early as 1934.
27 A. Schweitzer, *Big Business in the Third Reich*, Bloomington, 1964, pp. 250–2; A. E. Simpson, *Hjalmar Schacht in Perspective*, The Hague, 1969, pp. 89–90.
28 U. Kissenkoetter, *Gregor Strasser und die NSDAP*, Stuttgart, 1978, pp. 127, 168–70, 193–4; Phipps Papers I, 1/12 Phipps to Simon, 25.6.1934; Phipps to Simon, 11.7.1934; A. Sohn-Rethel, *Economy and Class Structure of German Fascism*, London, 1978, p. 149.
29 Hüttenberger, op. cit., p. 86.
30 Orlow, op. cit., pp. 111–16; Höhne, op. cit., pp. 119–49; M. Gallo, *The Night of the Long Knives*, London, 1973; Mau, op. cit. pp. 236–42.
31 Phipps Papers I, 1/12 letter from Phipps to Simon, 4.7.1934. Phipps was told by von Neurath that the SA had drawn up plans for an emergency cabinet with Roehm as War Minister and head of the armed forces, and von Detten as Foreign Minister. For the discussion of the emergency decrees see DGFP Ser. C, vol. 3, p. 119, minutes of the Conference of Ministers, 3 July 1934. The telegram is reproduced in DDP, vol. 2, p. 22.
32 These included von Schleicher, A. von Hohberg und Duchwald, von Falkenhausen, von Detten, von Krausser, von Kahr, von Heydebreck, von Spreti-Weilbach, and so on.
33 DGFP, Ser. C, vol. 1, p. 648, minutes of conference of Heads of Department, 12 July 1933; vol. 3, p. 119, minutes of Conference of Ministers, 3 July 1934. At the second of these meetings Goering was twelfth in order of seniority.
34 Letter from Frick to Goering, 7.2.1934 and letter from Goering to Prussian Interior Ministry, 9.7.1934. Both are reproduced in G. Plum, 'Staatspolizei und innere Verwaltung 1934–36', *Vierteljahreshefte für Zeitgeschichte*, vol. 13, 1965, pp. 210–12.
35 NCA, Washington, 1946, vol. 3, pp. 547–50, Doc. 775-PS, Frick memorandum; IMT, vol. 9, pp. 412–15, Goering cross-examination.
36 J. L. Heinemann, *Hitler's First Foreign Minister*, Berkeley, 1979, p. 102, 117–19; E. M. Robertson, *Mussolini as Empire-Builder*, London, 1977, pp. 37, 62–3, 80; DGFP, Ser. C, vol. 1, pp. 478–9, memorandum by the Foreign Minister, 22 May 1933; p. 90, memorandum by the Ambassador to Italy, 8 November 1933: (on Poland) Ser. C, vol. 3, p. 898, Ambassador in Poland to Foreign Ministry, 1 February 1935.
37 Heinemann, op. cit., p. 118.
38 J. P. Fox, *Germany and the Far Eastern Crisis 1931–1938*. Oxford, 1982, pp. 28–30, 135–8; H. Hermann, *The Rise and Fall of the Luftwaffe*, London, 1944, pp. 107–10.

39 Heinemann, op. cit., p. 119; L. E. Hill (ed.), *Die Weizsäcker-Papiere 1933–1950*, Frankfurt a M, 1974, p. 69.

40 DGFP, Ser. C, vol. 3, pp. 559–60, memorandum of Foreign Minister, 2 November 1934; p. 560, memorandum of deputy director, Department II, 2 November 1934; pp. 548–9, memorandum by the State Secretary, 30 October 1934; pp. 733–4, memorandum of Foreign Minister, 10 December 1934.

41 DGFP, Ser. C, vol. 3, p. 596, Ambassador in Italy to Foreign Ministry, 8 November 1934.

42 Robertson, op. cit., p. 57.

43 Ibid., pp. 37, 63.

44 E. W. Bennett, *German Rearmament and the West 1932–33*. Princeton, 1979, pp. 431–2; Singer, op. cit., p. 42.

45 H. M. Mason, *The Rise of the Luftwaffe 1918–1940*, London, 1975, pp. 165, 176–7; Bracher, op. cit., pp. 727–8, 822–3.

46 F. Hossbach, *Zwischen Wehrmacht und Hitler 1934–1938*, Göttingen, 1965, pp. 71–3: Singer, op. cit., p. 179.

47 O. Dietrich, *The Hitler I knew*, London, 1955, pp. 104–5, 107–8; Christie Papers, 180/1 4, Notes of a conversation with Goering, n.d.; Görlitz, op. cit., pp. 281, 311; Hermann, op. cit., pp. 85–7.

48 Phipps Papers, I 1/15, letter from Phipps to Sir Samuel Hoare, 13.11.1935 on von Blomberg's complaints over the air force.

49 A. Nielsen, *The German Air Force General Staff*, New York. 1959, pp. 23, 27, 41–3; A. Price, *Luftwaffe Handbook 1939–1945*, London, 1977, pp. 91–100.

50 D. Irving, *The Rise and Fall of the Luftwaffe: the Life of Erhard Milch*, London, 1973, pp. 26–30; Hermann, op. cit., pp. 66–7, 84–94; E. Homze, *Arming the Luftwaffe*, Nebraska, 1976, pp. 100–1.

51 A. van Ishoven, *The Fall of an Eagle*, London, 1977, p. 161; K. Macksey, *Kesselring: the Making of the Luftwaffe*, London, 1978, pp. 47–8, 51–3; Hermann, op. cit., pp. 88–93; Mason, op. cit., pp. 245–8.

52 Phipps Papers I, 1/13, letter from Phipps to Simon, 16.3.1935.

53 Fromm, op. cit., p. 171.

54 Phipps Papers I, 1/13, letter from Phipps to Simon, 17.4.1935, p. 3.

55 For a good example see J. Bendersky, 'The Expendable Kronjurist: Carl Schmitt and National Socialism 1933–1936', *Journal of Contemporary History*, vol. 14, 1979, pp. 314–23.

56 For details see Hermann, op. cit., pp. 91–3.

57 Von Hassell, op. cit., p. 349; DGFP, Ser. C, vol. 5. p. 1068, letter from Herbert Goering to Ambassador Schulenberg, 20 May 1936; letter from Tippelskirch to Schliep, 12 October 1936; R. Vogelsang, *Der Freundeskreis Himmler*, Göttingen, 1972, p. 104.

58 DGFP, Ser. C, vol. 5, p. 511, memorandum by deputy director Department II, 6 May 1936.

59 Von Hassell, op. cit., pp. 37, 42, 97, 105; O. John, *Twice Through the Lines*, London, 1972, p. 19. John was offered a post on Goering's staff by Fritz Goering (Hermann's nephew), who had got himself a job through his family contact.

60 D. Kahn, *Hitler's Spies*, London, 1978, pp. 55–6, 178–84; Diels, op. cit., pp. 230–2; IMT, vol. 9, pp. 441–2, Goering cross-examination on telephone-tapping.

61 John, op. cit., p. 28 who was told by von Runstedt that Hitler considered Goering 'too idle'.

62 Vogelsang, op. cit., pp. 39, 60, 64.

63 Christie Papers, 180/1 4, Talk with Goering 1932.

64 Schweitzer, op. cit., pp. 113–16; A. Barkai, *Das Wirtschaftssystem des National-sozialismus*, Cologne, 1977, pp. 31–4, 88–9.
65 Christie Papers, 180/1 4, Notes on German situation, 1932. Goering wanted 'greatest possible efforts for autarky'. See too his defence of autarkic thinking in Goering, *Reden*, pp. 265–6, speech on the Four Year Plan, 28.10.1936.
66 Phipps Papers, I 1/12, Phipps to Simon, 11.6.1934, pp. 1–3.
67 F. Baerwald, 'How Germany Reduced Unemployment', *American Economic Review*, vol. 24, 1934, p. 626.
68 Bracher, op. cit., pp. 468–9, 639–41; Barkai, op. cit., p. 88.
69 Schweitzer, op. cit., pp. 100–2; M. Riedel, *Eisen und Kohle für das Dritte Reich*, Göttingen, 1973, p. 36.
70 Schweitzer, p. 498.
71 Christie Papers, 180/1 4, Notes on German situation 1932, p. 4. Goering wanted 'rearmament in full swing'.
72 Bennett, op. cit., p. 432.
73 Phipps Papers, I 1/14, letter from Phipps to Simon, 17.4.1935 on Goering's influence over Hitler during the disarmament crisis; letter from Phipps to Simon, 2.5.1935; 1/15 letter from Phipps to Hoare, 12.6.1935. Goering's arguments about doubling air force size were passed to Phipps by von Neurath.
74 L. Schwerin von Krosigk, *Memoiren*, Stuttgart, 1977, pp. 158–9.
75 H. Pentzlin, *Hjalmar Schacht*, Berlin, 1980, pp. 232–5.
76 DGFP, Ser. C, vol. 4, letter from Goering to von Neurath, 21 May 1935, pp. 179–84; letter from von Bülow to von Neurath, 26 August 1935, pp. 577–8; p. 742, memorandum by the Foreign Minister, 17 October 1935; Ser. C vol. 5, p. 197, letter from Roediger to Moltke, 18 March 1936; pp. 429–30, letter from Schacht to von Neurath, 9 April 1936; G. Weinberg, *The Foreign Policy of Hitler's Germany 1933–1936*, London, 1970, pp. 192–3.
77 D. Petzina, *Autarkiepolitik im Dritten Reich*, Stuttgart, 1968, pp. 31–2.
78 A. Schweitzer, 'Foreign Exchange Crisis of 1936', *Zeitschrift für die gesamte Staatswissenschaft*, vol. 118, 1962, pp. 244–6.
79 IMT, vol. 36, pp. 292–4, EC-293, letter from Schacht to von Blomberg, 24.12.1935; H. Schacht, *76 Jahre meines Lebens*, Bad Wörishofen, 1953, p. 457.
80 Ibid., p. 292.
81 Meissner, op. cit., p. 419. According to Sohn-Rethel, op. cit., 76–7, it was generally expected at the time that Goering would find for Schacht because Darré presented such a poor case at the hearing.
82 W. Dodd, *Ambassador Dodd's Diary*, London, 1941, pp. 320–1 on the rumours circulating in 1936 that Goering might replace Hitler as head of state.
83 Phipps Papers, I 1/15, letter from Phipps to Hoare, 7.11.1935. Schacht was reported as saying: 'Butter is short because devisen is scarce. Devisen is scarce because of the Army. I am not apprehensive because the Army, being the culprit, is bound to support the Government if the populace gets restive.' See too letter from Phipps to Hoare, 3.12.1935.
84 Riedel, op. cit., p. 77. Schacht only wanted Goering to undertake a 'funda-mental investigation' of the raw material situation, nothing more. On the exchange scandals see Dodd, op. cit., p. 287. See too Schweitzer, 1962, op. cit., pp. 243–4: IMT, vol. 9, p. 447.
85 Phipps Papers, I 1/17 letter from Phipps to Anthony Eden, 4.11.1936, who reported Schacht's earlier comments that his policy was to make Goering and the party take the blame for economic mismanagement. Goering argued at Nuremberg that he had seen through this tactic from the start. See IMT, vol. 9, p. 282, 448.

86   DGFP, Ser. C, vol. 5, pp. 393–4, circular from Reich Chancellery, 6 April 1936 for the text of the decree of 4 April.

87   W. Birkenfeld, *Der synthetische Treibstoff, 1933–1943*, Göttingen, 1963, pp. 29–31; T. Hughes, 'Technological Momentum in History: Hydrogenation in Germany, 1898–1933', *Past & Present*, vol. 15, 1969, pp. 126–30.

88   G. Meinck, *Hitler und die deutsche Aufrüstung, 1933–7*, Wiesbaden, 1959, p. 160.

89   Riedel, op. cit., pp. 67, 73–4.

90   Birkenfeld, op. cit., pp. 79–80; NCA vol. 3, pp. 868–77, doc. 1301-PS, Financing of Armament, 9 March 1936.

91   Birkenfeld, op. cit., pp. 54, 81–2. The army initially wanted the job to go to Fischer of I.G. Farben.

92   Meinck, op. cit., pp. 161–2; DGFP, Ser. C, vol. 5, p. 197, Roediger to Moltke, 18 March 1936; pp. 429–30, Schacht to von Neurath, 9 April 1936; Weinberg, op. cit., p. 248.

93   Meinck, op. cit., pp. 153–7, 162–3; Birkenfeld, op. cit., pp. 80–1; Riedel, op. cit., pp. 76–8.

94   H. Schacht, *Account Settled*, London, 1953, p. 92.

95   Foreign and Commonwealth Office London, Nuremberg Trials, Case XI documents (hereafter Case XI), Keppler Doc. Book VII, pp. 8–10, Flick Affidavit; Riedel, op. cit., pp. 17–20; Meinck, op. cit., pp. 159–61; TWC, Nuremberg, 1949, vol. 12, pp. 568–9, Koerner Affidavit; 623–30, Keppler cross-examination.

96   Schacht, 1953, op. cit., p. 105; Riedel, op. cit., pp. 77–9.

97   E. Gritzbach, *Hermann Göring*, Berlin, 1938, p. 104.

98   BA-MA, Göring-Akten, Wi I F 5.203, report of a conference with General Goering, 12.5.1936: Schweitzer, 1962, op. cit., p. 247.

99   NCA, vol. 3, p. 878, doc. 1301-PS, conference of Council of Ministers, 12 May 1936.

100 BA-MA, Göring-Akten, Wi I F 5.203, report of the meeting of the Estimates Committee over the export question, 15.5.1936.

101 Schweitzer, 1962, op. cit., pp. 253–5.

102 Phipps Papers II, 2/1 letter from Sir F. Leith-Ross to Phipps, 4.2.1937.

103 Ibid., I, 1/15 letter from Phipps to Hoare, 8.10.1935 on von Blomberg's attitude to colonies; Phipps to Hoare, 5.12.1935; 1/17 Phipps to Eden, 30.10.1936 on Schacht. The same plea was made to the French ambassador in August. See François-Poncet, op. cit., pp. 222–3. See too Dodd, op. cit., pp. 309–10, 378, 381.

104 Phipps Papers I, 1/17 letter from Phipps to Eden, 22.10.1936.

105 Christie Papers, 180/1 5 Notes of a conversation with Goering, September 1937, p. 1; report of meeting with Goering, 28.7.1937, p. 63.

106 Schweitzer, 1962, op. cit., pp. 251–8.

107 NCA, vol. 7, pp. 462–4, doc. EC-407, Minutes of 12th Meeting of Reich Defence Council, 14 May 1936.

108 W. Deist, *The Wehrmacht and German Rearmament*, London, 1982, pp. 143–8; R. O'Neill, *The German Army and the Nazi Party*, London, 1966, pp. 135–6.

109 M. Geyer, *Aufrüstung oder Sicherheit. Die Reichswehr und der Krise der Machtpolitik 1924–1936*, Wiesbaden, 1980, pp. 449–50, 458; B. A. Carroll, *Design for Total War*, The Hague, 1968, pp. 123–6.

110 G. T. Harper, *German Economic Policy in Spain during the Spanish Civil War 1936–1939*, The Hague, 1967, pp. 18–19, 24–5. *Hisma-Rowak* stood for *Compania Hispano-Marroqui de Transportes* and *Rohstoffe-und Waren-Einkaufsgesellschaft*. BA-MA, Wi I F 5.203, report from Goering currency office to von

Blomberg, 19.6.1936, p. 5 ff; von Blomberg to Goering, 31.8.1936 enclosing 'Economic Balance'; Riedel, op. cit., p. 88.
111 Ibid., pp. 82–6, 90–3.
112 Petzina, op. cit., p. 30.
113 Ibid., pp. 45–6: on Pleiger and Kehrl's recruitment see Case XI, Pleiger Doc. Book II, pp. 116–17, Koerner affidavit.
114 BA-MA Göring-Akten, Wi I F 5.203, report of a conference between Reichsbank president Schacht and senior civil servants, 20.8.1936.
115 Ibid., Voegler memorandum, July-August 1936.
116 Petzina, op. cit., p. 47; G. Ritter, *The German Resistance: Carl Goerdeler's Struggle against Tyranny*, London, 1958, pp. 34–5; IMT vol. 36, pp. 490–1, 416-EC, meeting of the Council of Ministers, 4.9.1936.
117 BA-MA Göring-Akten, Wi I F 5.203, letter von Blomberg to Goering, 7.8.1936; letter von Blomberg to Goering, 31.8.1936; letter from Colonel Thomas to Wehrmachtamt, 23.5.1936.
118 Ibid., Goering to von Blomberg, 19.6.1936, enclosing minutes of the meeting of 9.6.1936 'Financing Armaments'.
119 On VJP see W. Treue, 'Denkschrift Hitlers über die Aufgaben eines Vierjahresplans', *Vierteljahreshefte für Zeitgeschichte*, vol. 3, 1954, pp. 184–91; Riedel, op. cit., p. 88.
120 TWC, vol. 12, p. 568, NG-2918, Koerner cross-examination: 'the questions regarding the Four Year Plan that interested Hitler he asked Goering directly.'
121 Treue, op. cit., p. 184. There seems little doubt that Hitler composed the VJP memorandum himself. He later said that 'I write drafts ... only concerning matters of vital importance. It's what I did, for example, for the Four Year Plan....' See H. Trevor-Roper (ed.), *Hitler's Table Talk 1941–1944*, London, 1953, p. 57, entry for 13/14 October 1941; Pentzlin, op. cit., p. 232 on Todt. IWM FO 645 Box 156, Goering interrogation 17.10.1945, p. 8.
122 Riedel, op. cit., p. 92.
123 Simpson, op. cit., pp. 128–33; Schweitzer, 1962, op. cit., p. 271; Phipps Papers II, 2/1, letter from Leith-Ross to Phipps, 4.2.1937.
124 NCA, vol. 3, pp. 892–3, doc. 1301-PS, draft of a letter to Goering from the War Ministry, 31.8.1936; 894–5, note from Thomas to von Blomberg, 2.9.1936.
125 Case XI, doc. NI-4955, Speer memorandum, 22.8.1945.
126 IMT, vol. 36, pp. 489–91, EC 416, meeting of the Council of Ministers, 4.9.1936.
127 For text of the VJP see Treue, op. cit., p. 200ff.
128 DDP, vol. 4, Berlin, 1937, p. 268, decree of the Führer and Reich Chancellor on carrying out the Four Year Plan. 18.10.1936.
129 Goering, *Reden*, pp. 273–4, speech in the Berlin Sportpalast on 28 October 1936, concerning the tasks of the Four Year Plan.
130 Riedel, op. cit., pp. 87–9, 96–100; Case XI, Keppler doc. book VIa, pp. 12–14; book VII, pp. 1–4; TWC vol. 12, Testimony of defendant Keppler, p. 630.

CHAPTER 3   GOERING AND THE GERMAN ECONOMY

1   T. W. Mason, 'Innere Krise und Angriffskrieg', in F. Forstmeier and H.-E. Volkmann (eds). *Wirtschaft und Rüstung am Vorabend des Zweiten Weltkrieges*, Düsseldorf, 1975, pp. 158–88; idem, 'Some Origins of the Second World War', *Past & Present*, 23, 1964, pp. 81–7; A. S. Milward, 'Hitlers Konzept

des Blitzkrieges' in A. Hillgruber (ed.), *Probleme des Zweiten Weltkrieges*, Cologne, 1967, pp. 19–40.

2 See the discussion in J. Thies, *Architekt der Weltherrschaft: die Endziele Hitlers*, Düsseldorf, 1976; K. Hildebrand, *The Foreign Policy of the Third Reich*, London, 1973; A. Kuhn, *Hitlers aussenpolitisches Programm*, Stuttgart, 1970; A. Hillgruber, *Die gescheiterte Grossmacht: eine Skizze des Deutschen Reiches 1871–1945*, Düsseldorf, 1980, pp. 77–97.

3 TWC, vol. 12, p. 462, NI-051, report of Goering's speech before leading industrialists at the Preussenhaus, 17.12.1936.

4 IMT, vol. 9, p. 450, Goering cross-examination.

5 E. Gritzbach, *Hermann Göring*, Berlin, 1938, pp. 116–17.

6 Christie Papers, notes of a conversation with Goering, 3.2.1937; Goering 'had no optimism at all about the effects of the Four Year Plan on German living standards.'

7 Case XI, Prosecution Doc. Book 112, p. 293, NID-13844, lecture by State Secretary Neumann. See too DDP, vol. 5, pp. 324–5, speech of Minister-President Goering at the fifth conference of the External Organisation of the NSDAP, 2 September 1937.

8 W. Treue, 'Denkschrift Hitlers über die Aufgaben eines Vierjahresplans', *Vierteljahreshefte für Zeitgeschichte*, vol. 3, 1954, p. 206.

9 N. Baynes (ed.), *Hitler's Speeches*, Oxford, 1942, vol. 1, p. 938, speech at a meeting of the Reich Chamber of Labour, 30.4.1937.

10 Ibid., vol. 1, p. 943, proclamation at party rally, Nuremberg, 7.9.1937.

11 DDP, vol. 5, Berlin, 1938, p. 324, speech of Minister-President Goering, 2.9.1937. See too E. Gritzbach, *Hermann Göring: Reden und Aufsätze*, Munich, 1938, pp. 364–6, speech to the German Labour Front, Nuremberg, 10.9.1938; 'Labour and economy exist exclusively for the whole people' (hereafter Goering, *Reden*).

12 TWC, vol. 12, pp. 489–92, NI-12215, P. Koerner, 'Leadership and Economy', February 1938.

13 Case XI, Prosecution doc. book 112, p. 281, NID-13844, lecture by State Secretary Neumann, 29.4.1941.

14 Ibid., pp. 289–93. See too Goering, *Reden*, pp. 269–73, speech on the tasks of the Four Year Plan, 28.10.1936.

15 TWC, vol. 12, p. 462, NI-051, report of a speech by Goering before leading industrialists, 17.12.1936; Goering, *Reden*, p. 273; 'I appeal to all businesses and businessmen: do not think about your profits.'

16 Ibid., p. 277.

17 See, for example, a collection of newspaper cuttings made by Goering's staff during 1936 and 1937 in NA, Göring-Stabsamt, T84 Roll 7.

18 W. Deist, *The Wehrmacht and German Rearmament*, London, 1981, pp. 51–3, 94–5; M. Geyer, *Aufrüstung oder Sicherheit. Die Reichswehr und die Krise der Machtpolitik 1924–1936*, Wiesbaden, 1980, pp. 491–6; B. A. Carroll, *Design for Total War: Arms and Economics in the Third Reich*, The Hague, 1968, pp. 120–1, 138–9.

19 Case XI, Prosecution doc. book 118A, EC-420, memorandum from the Wehrwirtschaftsstab, December 1936; EC-408, memorandum of the War Minister 'on the Four Year Plan and preparations of the war economy', 30.12.1936; BA-MA Göring-Akten, Wi I F 5.203, letter from von Blomberg to Goering, 23.6.1936; IMT, vol. 36, p. 243, 244-EC, letter from von Blomberg to Hitler, 22.2.1937.

20 R. J. Overy, *The Nazi Economic Recovery 1932–1938*, London, 1982, pp. 28–38.

21 H. Schacht, 'Germany's Colonial Demands', *Foreign Affairs*, vol. 15, 1936–7, p. 229.

22 These differences are clear from the documents. See IMT, vol. 36, pp. 550–62, 493-EC, letter from Goering to Schacht, 22.8.1937; 569–77, 497-EC, letter from Schacht to Goering, 5.8.1937; 282–7, 286-EC, letter from Schacht to Goering, 2.4.1937; vol. 12, p. 602ff. Schacht cross-examination; DDP, vol. 5, pp. 319–21, speech by Goering at the opening of the 9th congress of the International Chamber of Commerce, 28.6.1937.

23 C. W. Guillebaud, *The Economic Recovery of Germany 1932–38*, London, 1939, pp. 275–80.

24 NCA, vol. 3, p. 883, 1301-PS, meeting of the council of ministers, 12.5.1936.

25 R. Erbe, *Die nationalsozialistische Wirtschaftspolitik im Lichte der modernen Theorie*, Zürich, 1958, p. 67.

26 Foreign Office Library, London, Box FO/646/460, Office of the Military Government of Germany, 'Report on Dresdner Bank Investigation', esp. pp. 8, 84–6, 209.

27 Ibid., pp. 54–73.

28 Ibid., pp. 72–3; TWC, vol. 13, pp. 666–7, NID-13927, letter from Kehrl to Rasche, 18.4.1940.

29 J. Borkin, *The Crime and Punishment of I.G. Farben*, London, 1979, pp. 55–63, 66–75.

30 Ibid., pp. 72–3.

31 TWC, vol. 12, p. 447, NG-1221, Goering decree on the execution of the Four Year Plan, 22.10.1936.

32 D. Petzina, *Autarkiepolitik im Dritten Reich*, Stuttgart, 1968, pp. 58–63, Case XI, Prosecution doc. book 118A, NG-1221, structure of the Four Year Plan offices; Carroll, op. cit., pp. 130–6.

33 K.-H. Ludwig, *Technik und Ingenieure im Dritten Reich*, Düsseldorf, 1974, pp. 223–5; Petzina, op. cit., pp. 119–21.

34 Speer Collection, IWM, FD 5454c/45, report of Major Drews, 19.10.1936, p. 1.

35 IMT, vol. 36, p. 379, 376-EC, Schacht to all Control Boards, 11.12.1936. This circular was inspired by a letter from Goering to Schacht in ibid., pp. 233–7, 243-EC.

36 NCA, vol. 3, p. 892, doc. 1301-PS.

37 Case XI, Prosecution doc. book 112, NI-8590, 'results of work done during the first year of the Four Year Plan, 30.10.1937'; TWC, vol. 12, p. 461, NI-051, Goering speech before leading German industrialists. On this occasion he claimed: 'I am master of German money.'

38 NCA, vol. 3, p. 902, doc. 1301-PS, conference at Field Marshal Goering's, 14.10.1938.

39 Baynes, op. cit., vol. 1, p. 121, proclamation at the opening of the Party Congress, 6.9.1938.

40 Petzina, op. cit., p. 183; on investment in aircraft industry see BA-MA, RL3 46, Chart 1, 'Investment Fuselage Industry', Chart C 'Investment Engine Industry'.

41 O. Nathan, M. Fried, *The Nazi Economic System*, London, 1944, p. 352; S. Lurie, *Private Investment in a Controlled Economy: Germany 1933–1939*, London, 1947, pp. 21–6.

42 Petzina, op. cit., pp. 91-5; J. Farquharson, *The Plough and the Swastika*, London, 1976, pp. 169–78.

43 T. Balogh, 'The National Economy of Germany', *Economic Journal*, vol. 48, 1938; S. Merlin, 'Trends in Economic Control since 1933', *Quarterly Journal of Economics*, vol. 57, 1943; A. Schweitzer, 'Profits under Nazi Planning', ibid., vol. 60, 1946; M. Palyi, 'Economic Foundations of the German Totalitarian State', *American Journal of Sociology*, vol. 46, 1941.

44 T. Mason (ed.), *Arbeiterklasse und Volksgemeinschaft*, Opladen, 1975, p. 182, Wortprotokoll der 5 Tagung der Reichsarbeitskammer 24 Nov. 1936; p. 223, Erste Anordnung zur Durchführung des VJP über die Sicherstellung des Facharbeiternachwuchses von 7 Nov. 1936; p. 226, Dritte Anordnung über die Rückführung von Metallarbeitern und Baufacharbeitern in ihren Beruf von 7 Nov. 1936. For details of other measures see K. Mandelbaum, 'An Experiment in Full Employment: Controls in the German Economy 1933–38' in Oxford University Institute of Statistics, *The Economics of Full Employment*, London, 1944, pp. 196–200. Measures included better standards of labour placement through the local Labour Offices and regular careers advice for all school-leavers.

45 TWC, vol. 12, p. 500, EC278, Goering decree. 16.7.1938.

46 NA Göring-Stabsamt, T 84 Roll 7, Frame 6369, draft of a decree on furthering the goals of the Four Year Plan, n.d.; 6371-5, letters from Schramm (head of the Handwerkskammer) to Goering, 4.11.1938 and 10.11.1938; 6592-5, memorandum of Association of German Engineers, 'Ideas concerning rationalisation', 6.12.1938, and Notes of a speech by Goering to a conference of German engineers, November 1938.

47 DDP, vol. 6, Berlin, 1941, pp. 586–7, letter from Goering to Funk, 14.12.1938.

48 See, for example, U. von Hassell, *The von Hassell Diaries 1938–1944*, London, 1948, pp. 25–8, 202.

49 DDP, vol. 3, pp. 24–8, Speech of Reichstag President Goering at the Nuremberg Reichstag, 15.9.1935.

50 DDP, vol. 6, Part II, pp. 482–4, decree over the registration of Jewish property, 26.4.1938; p. 481, decree against the efforts to disguise Jewish businesses, 22.4.1938; 484–6, third decree on the Reichsbürgergesetz, 14.6.1938; 486, law on changing the trading regulations of the German Reich, 16.7.1938.

51 IMT, vol. 27, 1208-PS, Goering to all Reich authorities, 10.12.1938.

52 Ibid., vol. 28, p. 499, 1816-PS, minutes of the conference on the Jewish question in the Reich Air Ministry, 12.11.1938.

53 Ibid., pp. 500–6, 529–38; DDP, vol. 6, part II, pp. 502–3, Goering decree on the exclusion of Jews from the German economy, 12.11.1938: pp. 503–4, decree on the restoration of the street front by Jewish businesses, 12.11.1938.

54 IMT, vol. 28, pp. 524–6.

55 For example, B. Weisbrod, 'Economic Power and Political Stability Reconsidered: Heavy Industry in Weimar Germany', *Social History*, vol. 4, 1979; D. Abraham, *The Collapse of the Weimar Republic*, Princeton, 1981, esp. pp. 119–74; G. D. Feldman, 'The Social and Economic Policies of German Big Business, 1918–1929', *American Historical Review*, vol. 75, 1969; E. Nolte, 'Big Business and German Politics: a Comment', ibid., loc. cit.

56 Case XI, Pleiger defence doc. book 3, pp. 38–9, Röchling affidavit on the reasons for the exploitation of German lowgrade iron ores.

57 Ibid., Prosecution doc. book 112, p. 28, NI-084, minutes of a meeting on 'iron scarcity and iron rationing', 16.6.1937; see too SA Pleiger-Handakten, 12/150/2 'The recent situation of Sweden's iron ore policy', 12.10.1937. For the wider question of how vital Swedish supplies of ore actually were see A. S. Milward, 'Could Sweden have stopped the Second World War?', *Scandinavian Economic History Review*, vol. 15, 1967; J. J. Jäger, 'Sweden's Iron-Ore Exports to Germany 1933–1944', ibid.

58 BA-MA, Wi I F 5.203, letter from von Blomberg to Goering, 17.8.1936; Wehrwirtschaftsstab 'Review of the raw materials position, 2 May 1936'; Wi I F 5.114, discussion of iron and steel supply under Goering, 18.6.1937;

Colonel Thomas to Hitler 'concerning the economic position of armaments', 18.9.1937.

59   Case XI, Prosecution doc. book 112, NI-090, minutes of meeting of the work committee on the iron industry and Four Year Plan Office, 17.3.1937; SA 12/150/1, report on the question of ore supply, 26.5.1937. See too M. Riedel, *Eisen und Kohle für das Dritte Reich*, Göttingen, 1973, pp. 76–83, 135–9.

60   SA 12/150 3a, statement on the memorandum of the Vereinigte Stahlwerke, 18.8.1937; letter Vereinigte Stahlwerke to Pleiger, 19.8.1937: T. Emessen (ed.), *Aus Görings Schreibtisch: ein Dokumentenfund*, Berlin, 1947, pp. 73–9, doc. 51, letter from Roechling to Goering, 27.3.1937.

61   Case XI, Prosecution doc. book 112, p. 5. NI-090, minutes of the meeting of the iron industry and Four Year Plan, 17.3.1937.

62   SA 12/150/9, Voss to Pleiger, 6.8.1937, p. 3.

63   TWC, vol. 12, p. 463, NI-051, Goering speech to leading industrialists, 17.12.1936.

64   Case XI, Prosecution doc. book 112, p. 6 NI-090.

65   Emessen, op. cit., p. 78; TWC vol. 12, p. 499, R-140, conference with leaders of the aircraft industry, 8.7.1938.

66   SA 12/150/1, conference with General Goering, 16.6.1937. For the immediate background to this decision see 12/150/1, report on the question of ore supply, 26.5.1937.

67   SA 12/150/9, letter from Voss to Pleiger, 6.8.1937 on his discussions with Schlatmann from the Economics Ministry: Case XI, Prosecution doc. book 112, NI-353, excerpts from notes taken at the meeting of 23.7.1937; TWC, vol. 12, pp. 644–5, Pleiger cross-examination.

68   SA 12/150/3a, draft of the Düsseldorf Memorandum, 24.8.1937; statement on the memorandum of the Vereinigte Stahlwerke, 18.8.1937; letter from Poensgen to Pleiger, 19.8.1937; minutes of the conference on 24.8.1937 in the Stahlhof; letter from Otto Make to Pleiger (alerting Goering to the Düsseldorf Memorandum) 26.8.1937; Emessen, op. cit., p. 81, telegram from Goering to Finance Minister, 24.8.1937; p. 82, telegram from Goering to nine industrialists, 24.8.1937; p. 83, telegram from Goering to Krupp von Bohlen, 24.8.1937; Case X, Bülow defence doc. book 1, E. Poensgen, 'Hitler und die Ruhrindustriellen', 20.1.1948, pp. 102–7.

69   DDP, vol. 5, pp. 325–6, decree of Minister President Goering over the consolidation of mining rights, 23.7.1937; SA 12/150/1, conference under Goering, 8.7.1937; 12/150/2, 'Ore-supply for the German iron industry', 22.7.1937, p. 6.

70   TWC, vol. 12, p. 645: on the wider crisis in relations between the Nazis and the Ruhr industrialists see W. Treue, 'Die Einstellung einiger deutscher Grossindustrieller zu Hitlers Aussenpolitik', *Geschichte in Wissenschaft und Unterricht*, vol. 17, 1966, pp. 497–502.

71   SA 12/150/9, letter from Pleiger to Schwerin von Krosigk, 2.12.1937, p. 5: NA Reichswerke files, T83 Roll 75, frames 3445988–90, Pleiger to all heads of Reichswerke factories, 29.4.1942; Roll 76, frames 3447630–42, Pleiger to Schacht, 3.2.1938; Case XI, prosecution doc. book 112, NI-1495, memorandum of the Reich Economics Ministry, 16.2.1938.

72   NA Reichswerke files, T83 Roll 75, frames 3445864–6, minutes of the meeting of the committee for corporate organisation of Reichswerke, 12.12.1940; 'Die Reichswerke "Hermann Göring"', *Der Vierjahrsplan*, vol. 4, 1940, pp. 1026–7; K. Lachmann, 'The Hermann Göring Works', *Social Research*, vol. 8, 1941 and vol. 9, 1942; P. Rheinländer, *Die deutsche Eisen- und Stahlwirtschaft in Vierjahresplan*, Berlin, 1939, pp. 16–17.

73 NA Reichswerke files, T83 Roll 74, frames 3445209–10, 'Founding and Growth of the Hermann Goering Works 1937–1942'.

74 Riedel, op. cit., p. 74.

75 Goering, *Reden*, p. 381, speech to the German Labour Front, 10.9.1938; A. Speer, *Spandau: the Secret Diaries*, London, 1976, pp. 126, 190–1; Rheinländer, op. cit., pp. 36–8. Goering shared Hitler's fascination for great buildings and construction projects as a permanent memorial to the early days of the movement. At the meeting on iron rationing in June 1937 he reminded his audience that 'enormous, gigantic constructions are planned for decades to come'. Cf. J. Thies, 'Hitler's European Building Programme', *Journal of Contemporary History*, vol. 13, 1978. On Salzgitter see M. Walz, *Wohnungsbau und Industrieansiedlungspolitik in Deutschland 1933–1939*, Frankfurt a M, 1979, pp. 174–87.

76 K. Lachmann, 'The Hermann Göring Works', *Social Research*, vol. 8, 1941: Goering, *Reden*, p. 881, speech to the DAF at Nuremberg, 10.9.1938.

77 SA 12/150/14, letter from Pleiger to Funk, 12.12.1939; Agreement between Pleiger and Flick, 9.10.1939; NA Reichswerke files, T83 Roll 74, frames 3445159–77, I.G. Farben volkswirtschaftliche Abteilung, 'Build-up and Development of the Reichswerke "Hermann Goering"', 19.10.1939; frames 3445356–62, List of German and Austrian firms belonging to the Reichswerke, n.d.

78 IMT, vol. 36, p. 379, 384-EC, Agreement between Schacht and Goering, 7.7.1937: Case XI, prosecution doc. book 118A, EC-248, letter from Keitel to Koerner, 14.6.1937.

79 H. Schacht, *Account Settled*, London, 1953, pp. 99–101; A. E. Simpson, 'The Struggle for Control of the German Economy, 1936–7', *Journal of Modern History*, vol. 21, 1959.

80 Schacht, op. cit., p. 103: H. Pentzlin, *Hjalmar Schacht*, Berlin, 1980, pp. 243–5. See too Speer documents, IWM, FD 5454c/45, letter from Goering to Schacht, 7.5.1937.

81 Schacht, 1953, op. cit., p. 104; IMT, vol. 36, pp. 566–7, 495-EC, Schacht to Hitler, 16.11.1937; p. 567, 494-EC, letter from Lammers (Reich Chancellery) to Schacht, 8.12.1937.

82 BA-MA, Göring-Akten, Wi I F 5.203, letter from von Blomberg to Goering, 23.6.1936 enclosing a paper on 'The organisation of fuel oil supply for the armed forces and armaments industry'; IMT, vol. 36, p. 243, 244-EC, letter from von Blomberg to Hitler, 22.2.1937.

83 Carroll, op. cit., pp. 138–9, 141–3.

84 F. Hossbach, *Zwischen Wehrmacht und Hitler 1934–1938*, Göttingen, 1965, pp. 71–3; Riedel, op. cit. p. 89.

85 N. von Below, *Als Hitlers Adjutant, 1937–1945*, Mainz, 1980, pp. 105–6.

86 T. Taylor, *Sword and Swastika*, London, 1953, pp. 123–4, 130–1, 134–5; O. John, *Twice Through the Lines*, London, 1972, pp. 27–8; von Blomberg later admitted that he had 'always been afraid of Goering's vengeance'; R. O'Neill, *The German Army and the Nazi Party*, London, 1966, pp. 35–6; H. Höhne, *The Order of the Death's Head*, London, 1969, pp. 270–2.

87 H. Deutsch, *Hitler and his Generals: the Hidden Crisis, January–June 1938*, Minnesota, 1974, pp. 80–7; A. Brissaud, *The Nazi Secret Service*, London, 1974, pp. 186–7.

88 W. Görlitz, *History of the German General Staff*, New York, 1953, pp. 311–13; Deutsch, op. cit., pp. 98–104; von Below, op. cit., p. 60.

89 Deutsch, op. cit., p. 111; Hossbach. op. cit., pp. 123–4.

90 A. von Kielmansegg, *Der Fritschprozess 1938*, Hamburg, 1949, pp. 34–5.

91 O'Neill, op. cit., pp. 199–204; Brissaud, op. cit., pp. 188–91; H. Foertsch,

Schuld und Verhängnis. Die Fritsch-Krise im Frühjahr 1938, Stuttgart, 1951, pp. 106–29.

92 Görlitz, op. cit., p. 314; Deutsch, op. cit., pp. 117–18; Höhne, op. cit., pp. 276–7; von Below, op. cit., p. 76, who recalls that during the Blomberg/Fritsch crisis many officers had the impression that it was Goering who was ruling, not Hitler.

93 Deutsch, op. cit., pp. 258–66; J. L. Heinemann, *Hitler's First Foreign Minister*, Berkeley, 1979, pp. 162–3.

94 DDP, vol. 5, p. 60, Restructuring of the Reich cabinet, 2.2.1937; pp. 92–3, Restructuring of the Reich cabinet, 26.11.1937; IMT, vol. 9, pp. 397–8, Goering cross-examination.

95 Hossbach, op. cit., pp. 121–6; Höhne, op. cit., pp. 277–8.

96 K. Abshagen, *Canaris*, London, 1956, pp. 123–4: H. Gisevius, *To the Bitter End*, London, 1948, pp. 250–1, 256–7.

97 TWC, vol. 12, pp. 482–5, NI-13629, report from Decke on the reorganisation of the Reich Ministry of Economics and the continuation of the Four Year Plan, 5.2.1938; Pentzlin, op. cit., pp. 243–7.

98 Carroll, op. cit., pp. 147–52.

99 IMT, vol. 36, pp. 275–8, 270-EC, letter from Thomas to OKW, 27.4.1938; pp. 280–1, 271-EC, letter from Funk to Lammers, 31.3.1938; letter from Lammers to Funk, 6.4.1938.

100 BA-MA, Wi I F 5.412, results of a conference with Goering, 16.7.1938.

101 NA Göring-Stabsamt, T84 Roll 7, frames 6163–4, letter from Goering to Gauleiter Mutschmann, 14.4.1938; see too TWC, vol. 12, pp. 484–5, NI-13629; pp. 543–4, NID-13894, 'Organisational questions of the Four Year Plan, 27.8.1941' in which it was claimed that Goering enjoyed 'centralised control of economics' by 1938; H. Goering, 'Einheitliche Führung und Organisation der Wirtschaft', *Der Vierjahresplan*, vol. 1, 1937, pp. 578–9.

102 B. Fromm, *Blood and Banquets: a Berlin Social Diary*, London, 1943, p. 127.

103 Ibid., p. 122; F. Winterbotham, *The Nazi Connection*, London, 1978, pp. 63–4.

104 Fromm, op. cit., pp. 233–4; D. Kelley, *22 Cells in Nuremberg*, London, 1947, p. 51.

105 Fromm, op. cit., p. 224.

106 M. Muggeridge (ed.), *Ciano's Diary 1939–1943*, London, 1947, p. 342.

107 Milch Documents, vol. 64, 6519, minutes of GL conference, 8.2.1944.

108 NA T83, Roll 5, frame 3746189, letter from General von Hanneken to Kurt Tank (Focke-Wulf) 7.1.1938; frame 3746188, letter from Tank to Ernst Udet, 11.1.1938.

109 P. Hüttenberger, *Die Gauleiter*, Stuttgart, 1969, pp. 135–6: T. Mason, *Sozialpolitik im Dritten Reich*, Opladen, 1977, pp. 247–64 for the background to the conflict. For conflicts with Darré and the Food Estate see H. Gies, 'Die Rolle der Reichsnährstandes in nationalsozialistischen Herrschaftssystem', in G. Hirschfeld, L. Kettenacker (ed), *The Führer State: Myth and Reality*, Stuttgart, 1981, pp. 276–7, 286–7.

110 BA-MA RL3 20, letter from Goering to Ley on the Volkswagen works, 15.9.1939; Milch Documents, vol. 51, p. 451, letter from Milch to Goering, 21.9.1938.

111 P. Kirchberg, 'Typisierung in der deutschen Kraftfahrzeugindustrie und der Generalbevollmächtigte für das Kraftfahrwesen', *Jahrbuch für Wirtschaftsgeschichte*, vol. 8, 1969; A. von Schell, 'Neue Wege der deutschen Motorisierung', *Der Vierjahresplan*, vol. 3, 1939.

112 For the attitude of big business circles see Christie Papers, 180/1 25, 'Memorandum by members of Big Business in Germany 1937'; 'Rough Notes of a recent conversation with a German industrialist. 1 June 1939'. On resistance

to controls see A. Schröter, J. Bach, 'Zur Planung der wehrwirtschaftlichen Mobilmachung durch den deutschen faschistischen Imperialismus vor dem Beginn des Zweiten Weltkrieges', *Jahrbuch für Wirtschaftsgeschichte*, vol. 17, 1978, pp. 42–5. On opposition from industry see Treue, 1966, op. cit., pp. 503–4.

CHAPTER 4   GOERING AND HITLER'S WAR

1   B. H. Klein, *Germany's Economic Preparations for War*, Harvard, 1959; A. S. Milward, 'Der Einfluss ökonomischer und nicht-ökonomischer Faktoren auf die Strategie des Blitzkrieges' in F. Forstmeier, H.-E. Volkmann (eds), *Wirtschaft und Rüstung am Vorabend des Zweiten Weltkriegs*, Düsseldorf, 1975, pp. 189–201: idem., 'The End of the Blitzkrieg', *Economic History Review*, 2nd Ser., vol. 16, 1963/4, pp. 499–518; A. J. P. Taylor, *1939 Revisited*, German Historical Institute Annual Lecture, 1981.

2   E. Gritzbach (ed.), *Hermann Göring: Reden und Aufsätze*, Munich, 1938, pp. 92–6, Goering speech at Kiel, 28.10.1933.

3   Christie Papers, 180/1 5, Report of a meeting with Goering 28 July 1937; also Notes of a conversation with Goering, 19 September 1937.

4   DGFP, Ser. D, vol. 1, pp. 29–39, minutes of the conference in the Reich Chancellery, 5.11.1937.

5   Christie Papers, 180/1 5, Report of a meeting with Goering, 28 July 1937, pp. 5–7; Notes from a conversation with Goering, 3 February 1937, pp. 51–4; see too G. Weinberg, *Hitler's Foreign Policy 1937–1939*, London, 1980, p. 27 who records that Goering told the French Ambassador that Czechoslovakia would be 'operated upon'.

6   Christie Papers, 180/1 5, Report of a meeting with Goering 28 July 1937, pp. 96–8. See too 100/1 4, Notes on German Situation 1932, p. 7.

7   Ibid., Notes from a conversation on 3 February, 1937, pp. 51, 54–6; Notes of a conversation with Goering n.d. (September 1937?), pp. 1–2.

8   Ibid., Report of a meeting with Goering, 28 July 1937, pp. 1, 63; Notes from a conversation with Goering, 3 February 1937, pp. 55–6. On Goering's attitude to the British upper classes see the comments in Phipps Papers I, 1/12, Phipps to Simon, 28.2.1934, pp. 2–3. Goering told Phipps that England was the place he would most like to live with 'English lawns and country houses and Oxford'.

9   Christie Papers 180/1 5, Notes from a conversation with Goering 3 February 1937, p. 52. Britain would become the 'Hauptfeind'.

10 There is a vast literature now on Hitler's foreign policy aims. See in particular J. Thies, *Architekt der Weltherrschaft: die Endziele Hitlers*, Düsseldorf, 1976; K. Hildebrand, 'La programme de Hitler et sa réalisation', *Revue d'histoire de la deuxième Guerre Mondiale*, vol. 21, 1971, pp. 7–36; A. Hillgruber, *Die gescheiterte Grossmacht*, Düsseldorf, 1980, pp. 77–96.

11 Case XI, Koerner Defence doc. book 1b, p. 8, statement of Gauleiter Uberreither.

12 TWC, vol. 12, p. 462, NI-051, report on Goering's speech to leading German industrialists, 17.12.1936.

13 Ibid., vol. 12, pp. 497–8, Goering conference with leaders of the aircraft industry, 8.7.1938.

14 Milch Documents, vol. 65, 7302–3, letter from von Brauchitsch (army c-inc) to Milch, 6.11.1939.

15 Ibid., vol. 65, 7299, letter from Goering to all Reich authorities, 7.12.1939.

16 J. L. Heinemann, *Hitler's First Foreign Minister*, Berkeley, 1979, pp. 162–3;

H. Gisevius, *To the Bitter End*, London, 1948, pp. 259–60. Cf. the discussion in
F. Fischer, *Bündnis der Eliten: zur Kontinuität der Machtstrukturen in Deutschland
1871–1945*, Düsseldorf, 1979, pp. 81–3, who argues that there was substantial continuity of social power and foreign policy attitudes over the period.

17 J. Lipski, *Diplomat in Berlin 1933–1939*, New York, 1968, p. 189, doc. 41,
    letter from Lipski to Beck (Polish Foreign Minister), 25.4.1935.
18 G. Gilbert, *Nuremberg Diary*, London, 1948, p. 138.
19 Lipski, op. cit., p. 189, doc. 41; Heinemann, op. cit., pp. 118–19; G. T.
    Harper, *German Economic Policy in Spain during the Spanish Civil War
    1936–1939*, The Hague, 1967, pp. 14–16, 24–5.
20 Heinemann, p. 152; G. Weinberg, *Hitler's Foreign Policy 1937–1939*, London,
    1980, pp. 270–1; D. Mack Smith, *Mussolini's Roman Empire*, London, 1976,
    pp. 125–7.
21 R. Luža, *Austro-German Relations in the Anschluss Era*, Princeton, 1975, p. 15.
22 DGFP, Ser. D, vol. 1, p. 385, memorandum by the German ambassador in
    Italy, 30.1.1937; Weinberg, op. cit., p. 271; P. Schmidt, *Hitler's Interpreter*,
    London, 1951, p. 64.
23 DGFP, Ser. D, vol. 1, pp. 306–8, memorandum concerning the meeting
    between Goering and Chancellor Schuschnigg, 13.10.1936; pp. 376–8,
    memorandum by the German ambassador in Italy, 16.1.1937; pp. 539–41,
    Keppler memorandum of reception by the Führer, 21.2.1938.
24 Ibid., Ser. D. vol. 1, p. 469, memorandum of visit to Goering, 8.10.1937;
    p. 450, meeting between Goering and Schmitt, 19.7.1937; p. 467, Goering
    meeting with Austrian Nazis, October 1937; p. 503, letter from von Papen
    to the Foreign Ministry, 8.2.1938; Weinberg, op. cit., pp. 267–8; B. F. Pauley,
    Hitler and the Forgotten Nazis, London, 1981, p. 188.
25 NCA, vol. 5, pp. 630–41, 2949-PS, Goering telephone conversations; J. Gehl,
    Austria, Germany and the Anschluss, Oxford, 1963, pp. 160–1, 188–93; F.
    Hesse, *Das Vorspiel zum Kriege*, Druffel Verlag, 1979, pp. 84–5.
26 DDP, vol. 6, Part I, pp. 177–8, decree on the economic revival of Austria,
    23.3.1938: N. Schausberger, 'Der Anschluss und sein ökonomische Relevanz'
    in R. Neck (ed.), *Anschluss 1938*, Vienna, 1981, pp. 245–6, 261–4.
27 DDP, vol. 6, Part I, p. 180, speech of General Field-Marshal Goering on
    building up the German Ostmark, 26.3.1938.
28 DGFP, Ser. D, vol. 1, pp. 34–6.
29 Lipski, op. cit., p. 376, doc. 87, Lipski to Beck, 19.6.1938.
30 Ibid., p. 373; pp. 382–3, doc. 91, conversation of Lipski with General
    Goering, 24.8.1938; p. 390, doc. 93, Lipski to Beck, 5.9.1938; pp. 461–2,
    Lipski diary, 15 September 1938; DGFP Ser. D, vol. 2, pp. 478–80, minute
    by Weizsäcker for the Foreign Minister, 7.7.1938; pp. 816–17, minute by
    Undersecretary of State for the Foreign Minister, 16.9.1938.
31 Lipski, op. cit., p. 394, doc. 95, Ambassador Lipski's conversations at Nurem-
    berg, 7–12 September 1938.
32 Ibid., p. 37, doc. 87, Lipski to Beck, 19.6.1938.
33 Ibid., pp. 374–5, doc. 88, Lipski to Beck, 21.6.1938; pp. 377–9, doc. 89,
    Lipski to Beck, 11.8.1938; p. 395, doc. 95.
34 Lipski, op. cit., pp. 370–2, doc. 87, Lipski to Beck, 19.6.1938; pp. 382–5,
    doc. 91, conversation of Lipski with Goering, 24.8.1938; p. 403, doc. 96,
    Lipski to Beck, 16.9.1938.
35 Heinemann, op. cit., pp. 181–3; E. von Weizsäcker, *Memoirs*, London, 1951,
    p. 154; Gilbert, op. cit., pp. 57–8, who records Goering's comments to him
    that the Munich Pact 'was a cut-and-dried affair. Neither Chamberlain nor
    Daladier were in the least bit interested in sacrificing or risking anything to
    save Czechoslovakia . . . I thought there would be an explosion. But no. We

got everything we wanted; just like that.' On the economic context see A.
Teichova, *An Economic Background to Munich*, Cambridge, 1974; B.-J. Wendt,
Appeasement 1938: wirtschaftliche Rezession und Mitteleuropa, Frankfurt, 1966;
C. A. MacDonald, 'Economic Appeasement and the German Moderates'
Past & Present, no. 56, 1972, pp. 105–35.
36 Lipski, op. cit., p. 403, doc. 96.
37 DGFP, Ser. D, vol. 4, pp. 82–3, conversation between Field Marshal Goering
and Dr. Durčansky, Slovak Minister, n.d. (c.16/17.10.1938).
38 Ibid., Ser. D, vol. 4, pp. 81–2, conversation between Field Marshal Goering
and Minister Mastny, n.d. (c.16/17.10.1938); see too, p. 148, the German
chargé d'affaires in Czechoslovakia to the Foreign Minister, 14 November
1938, who reported on an agreement reached to build an autobahn through
Czechoslovakia and a canal linking the Oder and the Danube.
39 Gisevius, op. cit., pp. 338–9: on the background and Goering's role in
Slovakia see J. K. Hoensch, *Die Slowakei und Hitler's Ostpolitik*, Cologne,
1965, pp. 240–68.
40 NCA, vol. 8, p. 202, R-133, note of a conference on 25 July 1939 with Field
Marshal Goering.
41 D. Kaiser, *Economic Diplomacy and the Origins of the Second World War*,
Princeton, 1980, pp. 263–83; P. Marguerat, *Le IIIème Reich et le pétrole
roumain*, Leiden, 1977, chs. 3–4; F. Gilbert, 'Mitteleuropa – The Final Stage',
Journal of Central European Affairs, vol. 7, 1947, pp. 58–67.
42 BA–MA, Wi I F 5.412, Results of a conference with General Goering,
16.7.1938, p. 1.
43 O. Nathan, M. Fried, *The Nazi Economic System*, London, 1944, pp. 352–8;
see Colonel Thomas's comments on living standards in BA-MA, Wi I F
5.114, lecture by Thomas, 'Rearmament and Exports', 10.6.1937, pp. 20–1.
44 R. Erbé, *Die nationalsozialistische Wirtschaftspolitik im Lichte der modernen
Theorie*, Zürich, 1958, p. 100.
45 NCA, vol. 3, p. 903, 1301-PS, conference at Field Marshal Goering's
14.10.1938; BA-MA, Wi I F 5.412, conference with Goering, 16.7.1938,
pp. 2–3. For the general background see H. Vollweiler, 'The Mobilization of
Labour Reserves in Germany', parts I and II, *International Labour Review*, vol.
38, 1938.
46 IMT, vol. 32, p. 413, 3575-PS, note on the meeting of the Reich Defence
Council, 18.11.1938; pp. 150–3, 3787-PS, Second meeting of the Reich
Defence Council, 23.6.1939.
47 DDP, vol. 7, Part I, Berlin, 1941, pp. 425–6, speech of General Goering in
the Rheinmetall-Borsig works, 9.9.1939; vol. 6, Part II, pp. 521–4, decree
over the strengthened mobilisation of female labour, 15.2.1938.
48 NCA, vol. 3, pp. 902–3, 1301-PS, conference at Field Marshal Goering's,
14.10.1938; vol. 6, pp. 722–3, 2nd meeting of the Reich Defence Council,
23.6.1939.
49 BA-MA, Wi I F 5.412, results of a conference with General Goering,
16.7.1938, pp. 1–2.
50 Ibid., p. 3.
51 Carroll, op. cit., pp. 184–8.
52 IMT, vol. 36, p. 116, 028-EC, meeting with General Thomas, 24 May 1939.
53 Ibid., vol. 27, pp. 161–2, 1301-PS, conference with Field Marshal Goering,
14.10.1938.
54 NCA, vol. 3, p. 901.
55 IMT, vol. 32, p. 413, Note on the meeting of the Reich Defence Council,
18.11.1938.
56 Ibid., vol. 27, p. 160, conference with Field Marshal Goering, 14.10.1938.

57 On the army see NCA, vol. 7, p. 851, L-79; on the navy M. Salewski, *Die deutsche Seekriegsleitung 1939–1945*, 2 vols., Frankfurt a M, 1970, vol. 1, pp. 58–65; W. Deist, *The Wehrmacht and German Rearmament*, London, 1981, pp. 83–5.
58 Salewski, op. cit., vol. 1, p. 59; see too NCA, vol. 7, p. 854.
59 O. Dietrich, *The Hitler I Knew*, London, 1955, pp. 104–7; E. M. Emme, 'Emergence of Nazi Luftpolitik as a Weapon in International Affairs', *Aerospace Historian*, vol. 7, 1960.
60 R. J. Overy, 'The Luftwaffe and Strategic Bombing', *Journal of Strategic Studies*, vol. 1, 1978, pp. 155–6.
61 BA-MA, Wi I F 5.412, conversation between Thomas and Speer, 4.10.1939.
62 Ibid., RL3 234, 'Industrial planning up to 1.4.1945', 15.10.1940; IMT, vol. 37, 043-L, 'Organisational Study 1950', 2.5.1938; vol. 9, p. 60, Milch cross-examination.
63 R. J. Overy, 'Transportation and Rearmament in the Third Reich', *Historical Journal*, vol. 16, pp. 406–7.
64 Plans on this scale were not formalised until 1940; see Speer Documents, FD 5447/45, notice of a discussion with the head of the Army Armament Office, 19.7.1940. But it is fair to assume that an army of this size is what Hitler had in mind in 1936 when he hinted at his plans for a 'powerful army'. See Deist op. cit., p. 51.
65 NCA, vol. 6, p. 729, 3787-PS, 2nd meeting of the Reich Defence Council, 23.6.1939.
66 Case XI, Prosecution doc. book 118A, NI-7835, 'Development of the production plans for gunpowder, explosives, and chemical warfare agents, 15.7.1940'.
67 Ibid., EC-282, 'Work report of Carl Krauch for the General Council of the Four Year Plan', 28.4.1939, pp. 4, 9.
68 DGFP, Ser. D, vol. 1, p. 34.
69 See, for example, DGFP, Ser. D, vol. 6, p. 2, 'Unsigned Memorandum, discussion with Goering, 16 April 1939'.
70 Case XI, Koerner Defence doc. book 1b, p. 140.
71 IMT, vol. 36, pp. 116–31, 028-EC, Meeting with General Thomas, 20.5.1939.
72 NCA, vol. 7, p. 851; see too 'Conversation with the Reich Foreign Minister, 6–7 May 1939' in M. Muggeridge (ed.), *Ciano's Diplomatic Papers*, London, 1948, p. 284.
73 Case XI, Prosecution doc. book 118a, NI-125, decree on the further tasks of the Commissioner for the Four Year Plan, 18.10.1940.
74 TWC, vol. 12, p. 498, R-140, conference with leaders of the aircraft industry, 8.7.1938.
75 Hesse, op. cit., pp. 142–3: M. Toscano, *The Origins of the Pact of Steel*, Baltimore, 1967, pp. 252–3: Warlimont, op. cit., p. 24: H. B. Gisevius, *To the Bitter End*, London, 1948, pp. 355–7: L. Schwerin von Krosigk, *Memoiren*, Stuttgart, 1977, p. 192.
76 For details see Deist, op. cit., pp. 21–35; Carroll, op. cit., pp. 179–90.
77 IMT, vol. 32, pp. 412–17, 3575-PS, note on the meeting of the Reich Defence Council, 18.11.1938.
78 NA Reichsfinanzmin., T178 Roll 15, frames 3672058–9, Schwerin-Krosigk to Goering, May 1939.
79 NCA, vol. 3, pp. 906–8, 1301-PS, Keitel to heads of armed forces, 7.12.1938; M. Geyer, 'Rüstungsbeschleunigung und Inflation: zur Inflationsdenkschrift des OKW von November 1938', *Militärgeschichtliche Mitteilungen*, vol. 23, 1981, pp. 121–69; on the money supply see J. J. Klein, 'German Money and Prices' in M. Friedman (ed.), *Studies in the Quantity Theory of Money*, Chicago,

1956, pp. 135–6; on the new finance plan of April 1939 to cope with the money problem see S. Lurie, *Private Investment in a Controlled Economy*, Columbia, 1947, pp. 33–4.

80 W. Nelson, *Small Wonder: the Amazing Story of the Volkswagen*, London, 1967, pp. 73–6.

81 Overy, 1973, op. cit., pp. 993–6.

82 A. Schröter, J. Bach, 'Zur Planung der wehrwirtschaftliche Mobilmachung durch den deutschen faschistischen Imperialismus vor dem Beginn des Zweiten Weltkriegs', *Jahrbuch für Wirtschaftsgeschichte*, vol. 17, 1978, pp. 42–5; see also A. Speer, *Spandau: the Secret Diaries*, London, 1976, pp. 88–9 for a discussion of the relations between Goering and industry at this time.

83 T. W. Mason, 'Labour in the Third Reich', *Past & Present*, vol. 12, 1966, pp. 126–39; S. Salter, 'Class Harmony or Class Conflict? The Industrial Working Class and the National Socialist Regime 1933–1945', in J. Noakes (ed.), *Government, Party and People in Nazi Germany*, Exeter, 1980, pp. 84–9.

84 Lipski, op. cit., pp. 498–99, doc. 135, Lipski to Beck, 2.3.1939.

85 M. Muggeridge (ed.), *Ciano's Diary 1939–1943*, London, 1947, p. 71, entry for 16.4.1939.

86 NCA, vol. 3, p. 847, L-79, minutes of Fuehrer conference, 23.5.1939. IWM FO 645 Box 156, Goering interrogation 11.10.1945, pp. 2–3.

87 Kelley, op. cit., p. 53; Christie Papers, 180/1 5, Notes of a Conversation with Goering, n.d.

88 Muggeridge, 1947, op. cit., p. 90, entry for 21.5.1939; Toscano, op. cit., pp. 255–7.

89 E. Homze, *Arming the Luftwaffe*, Nebraska, 1976, pp. 244–5 on underestimating foreign air strength; Muggeridge, 1948, op. cit., p. 298, 'conversation with the Reich Foreign Minister, 11.8.1939'; Toscano, op. cit., pp. 252–3.

90 See the discussions in T. W. Mason, 'Innere Krise und Angriffskrieg' in F. Forstmeier, H.-E. Volkmann, *Wirtschaft und Rüstung am Vorabend des Zweiten Weltkriegs*, Düsseldorf, 1975, pp. 158–88; E. Hennig, 'Industrie, Aufrüstung und Kriegsvorbereitung im deutschen Faschismus' in *Gesellschaft: Beiträge zur Marxschen Theorie*, vol. 5, Frankfurt a M, 1975, pp. 68–148; L. Herbst, 'Die Krise des nationalsozialistischen Regimes am Vorabend des Zweiten Weltkrieges und die forcierte Rüstung', *Vierteljahreshefte für Zeitgeschichte*, vol. 26, 1978, pp. 347–92.

91 E. Kordt, *Wahn und Wirklichkeit*, Stuttgart, 1948, p. 192; von Weizsäcker, op. cit., p. 203; NCA, vol. 8, pp. 534–5, TC-90.

92 NCA, vol. 7, p. 547, L-79, minutes of Fuehrer conference, 23.5.1939.

93 'Kriegstagebuch des Generaladmirals a.D. Albrecht, 22.8.1929' in W. Baumgart, 'Zur Anspruche Hitlers vor den Führern der Wehrmacht am 22 August 1939', *Vierteljahreshefte für Zeitgeschichte*, vol. 16, 1968, p. 149.

94 Case XI, Koerner Defence doc. book 1b, pp. 154–5; D. Irving, *The Rise and Fall of the Luftwaffe*, London, 1973, pp. 71–3.

95 Lipski, op. cit., p. 591, doc. 163, Lipski to Minister of Foreign Affairs, 31.8.1939.

96 On Goering's earlier efforts see DGFP, Ser. C, vol. 5, pp. 571, 581, 1068. On Nazi policy towards Russia see G. Weinberg, *Germany and the Soviet Union, 1939–41*, Leiden, 1972, pp. 33–45; W. Birkenfeld, 'Stalin als Wirtschaftsplaner Hitlers 1939–1941', *Vierteljahrschrift für Sozial- und Wirtschaftsgeschichte*, vol. 51, 1966.

97 A. Speer, *Inside the Third Reich*, London, 1970, pp. 101–2; L. E. Hill (ed.), *Die Weizsäcker-Papiere 1933–1950*, Frankfurt a M, 1974, pp. 159–60: J. Toland, *Adolf Hitler*, New York, 1976, pp. 544–49.

98 Hillgruber, op. cit., pp. 88–9: Hesse, op. cit., pp. 101–2; J. Hencke, *England*

in Hitlers politischen Kalkul, Boppard a R, 1973, pp. 308–9 who argues that Goering genuinely sought peace with England and a political alliance with Schacht and the moderates. This argument fails to take into account the poor relations between Goering and the liberals or the fact that Hitler and Goering were clearly co-ordinating their efforts. For the background of Goering's contacts with the British see C. A. MacDonald, *The United States, Britain and Appeasement 1936–1939*, London, 1981, pp. 81, 89; B.-J. Wendt, *Economic Appeasement: Handel und Finanz in der britischen Deutschland-Politik 1933–1939*, Düsseldorf, 1971, pp. 549–554: Schmidt, op. cit., pp. 54–5.

99 Lipski, op. cit., p. 556, doc. 148, letter from Goering to Lipski, 11.8.1939; p. 585, doc. 163, Lipski to Minister of Foreign Affairs, 31.8.1939.

100 Macdonald, 1981, op. cit., p. 165; Wendt, 1971, op. cit., pp. 606–10 for a discussion of the Wohlthat/Wilson talks in June 1939; Hesse, op. cit., pp. 142–3; see too R. F. Holland, 'The Federation of British Industries and the International Economy 1929–1939', *Economic History Review*, 2nd ser., vol. 34, 1981, pp. 297–8.

101 D. Kahn, *Hitler's Spies*, London, 1978, p. 183; Lipski, op. cit., pp. 591–9, doc. 163, Lipski to Minister of Foreign Affairs, 31.8.1939; F. Hesse, *Hitler and the English*, London, 1954, pp. 91–3; U. von Hassell, *The von Hassell Diaries 1938–1944*, London, 1948, pp. 68–9.

102 H. Groscurth, *Tagebücher eines Abwehroffiziers*, Stuttgart, 1970, p. 202, entry for 9.9.1939.

103 Lipski, op. cit., pp. 581–2, doc. 163; B. Dahlerus, *The Last Attempt*, London, 1948, pp. 31–2; A. von Ribbentrop, *Deutsch-englische Geheimverbindungen*, Wuppertal, 1967, pp. 341–54.

104 Muggeridge, 1947, op. cit., p. 91, entry for 21 May 1939.

105 Kordt, op. cit., pp. 192–4; N. von Below, *Als Hitlers Adjutant 1937–1945*, Mainz, 1980, pp. 92, 185: on Goering's failure to notify Ribbentrop see DGFP, Ser. D, vol. 6, p. 743 and vol. 7, p. 124.

106 H. Höhne, *Codeword Direktor*, London, 1971, p. 217: Kahn, op. cit., p. 183.

107 NCA, vol. 8, pp. 534–5, TC–90.

108 Ibid., p. 594; N. Henderson, *Failure of a Mission*, London, 1940, pp. 274–80: D. Kelley, *22 Cells in Nuremberg*, London, 1947, p. 53.

109 Groscurth, op. cit., p. 193, entry for 29.8.1939; von Weizsäcker, op. cit., p. 209.

110 Henderson, op. cit., pp. 258–9; A. Cienciala, *Poland and the Western Powers 1938–1939*, London, 1968, pp. 241–3, 248–9; von Ribbentrop, op. cit., pp. 460–3, 564–6.

111 F. Hesse, *Hitler and the English*, London, 1954, p. 92; Gisevius, op. cit., pp. 361–2, 365–6, 374–5; Weizsäcker, op. cit., pp. 191–2, 203.

112 R. Manvell, H. Fraenkel, *Göring*, London, 1968, pp. 164–5 for an account of the last hours before the British declaration of war. They record that Goering telephoned Ribbentrop but not what was said. The alleged remark can be found in A. Kesselring, *Memoirs*, London, 1955, p. 42.

113 Hesse, 1954, op. cit., p. 91. The remark was reported by Hewel of the Foreign Ministry. See too N. Bethell, *The War Hitler Won*, London, 1972, pp. 361–3.

114 Ibid., pp. 286–8, 359; P. W. Ludlow, 'Scandinavia Between the Great Powers', *Särtryck ur Historisk Tidskrift*, 1974, pp. 9–13; B. Martin, 'Das "Dritte Reich" und die Friedens-Frage im Zweiten Weltkrieg', in W. Michalka (ed.), *Nationalsozialistische Aussenpolitik*, Darmstadt, 1978, pp. 527–9.

115 Muggeridge, 1947, op. cit., p. 152, 163. Count Magistrati reported to Ciano on 14 September that Goering finally 'seems to have been persuaded of the advisability of Italy's remaining neutral'.

116 Bethell, op. cit., pp. 288–9; Ludlow, op. cit., p. 15.
117 Hesse, 1954, op. cit., p. 93; Bethell, op. cit., pp. 363–4, 370–1; DGFP, Ser. D, vol. 8, p. 141, memorandum of the conversation between the Fuehrer and M. Dahlerus in the presence of Field Marshal Goering, 26.9.1939.
118 Bethell, op. cit., p. 118. On British attitudes see the interesting comments in Groscurth, op. cit., pp. 352–4, 'Notes of Legationsrat von Etzdorf on the foreign political situation, 21.10.1939'.
119 Ibid., pp. 387–9, 'Vortragsnotiz über Auftrag an Birger Dahlerus zur Fühlungnahme mit England 26.10.1939'; Ludlow, op. cit., pp. 29–34; C. Burkhardt, *Meine Danziger Mission 1937–1939*, Munich, 1960, p. 346, records that Hitler told him in the summer of 1939 that he would like to meet with 'Marshal Ironside' to resolve Anglo-German differences.
120 DGFP, Ser. D, vol. 8, p. 141; F. Taylor (ed.), *The Goebbels Diaries 1939–1941*, London, 1982, p. 51, entry for 17.11.1939. Goering told Goebbels that peace initiatives were 'all over'. See too Groscurth, op. cit., pp. 385–6, 'Notes of a secret speech by Hitler before the Reichsleiter and Gauleiter, 24.10.1939'.
121 Bethell, op. cit., pp. 288–9; S. Friedländer, *Prelude to Downfall: Hitler and the United States 1939–1941*, London, 1967, pp. 37–9.
122 DGFP, Ser. D, vol. 8, pp. 856–7, discussion between Goering and Sumner Welles, 5.3.1940.
123 Groscurth, op. cit., p. 403, 'File note, 4.11.1939'; Gilbert, op. cit., pp. 135–40 for details of Goering's attitude to Ribbentrop: A. Zoller, *Hitler privat: Erlebnisbericht seiner Geheimsekretärin*, Düsseldorf, 1949, p. 166.
124 S. Hedin, *German Diary*, Dublin, 1951, p. 39.
125 DGFP, Ser. D, vol. 8, pp. 397–8, Ribbentrop to German legation in Sweden, 11.11.1939.
126 Case XI, Prosecution doc. book 118a, 3324-PS, speech by Funk on the war economy, 14.10.1939. See too DDP, vol. 7, part I, pp. 403–9, War-Economy Decree, 4.9.1939, which called for necessary cuts in civilian living standards.
127 BA-MA, Wi I F 5.412, Note on the speech by General Thomas, 13.11.1939, p. 8.
128 DGFP, Ser. D, vol. 8, p. 193, memorandum of a conversation between the Fuehrer and Count Ciano, 1.10.1939; p. 141, memorandum of the conversation between the Fuehrer and M. Dahlerus, 26.9.1939; BA-MA Wi I F 5.412, conference on carrying out the Krauch Plan, 17.11.1939.
129 Ibid., note of the conference on 11.12.1939, p. 1.
130 Case XI, Prosecution doc. book 118a, NI-7835, 'Development of the production-plans for gunpowder and explosives, 15.7.1940'.
131 Speer Documents, FD 1434/46 169, 'Comparative review of the munitions programmes 1938–1942'.
132 NA Reichsfinanzmin., T178 Roll 15, frames 3671912–17, Statistical review of the Reich budget, 1938–1943, November 1944; frames 3671758–63, report on war finance, 15.10.1943.
133 Ibid., frames 3672058–60, letter from Schwerin von Krosigk to Goering, May 1939; see too 3671791–3, memorandum over spending power and war finance, 1940, 13.2.1940; on cutting consumption see DDP, vol. 7, part I, pp. 403–9, War-Economy Decree, 4.9.1939.
134 NA Reichsfinanzmin., T178 Roll 15, frames 3671805–7, letter from Ley to Funk, 13.12.1939; frames 3671803–4, letter from Ley to von Krosigk, 1.12.1939 and 13.12.1939.
135 Ibid., frames 3671816–8, letter from von Krosigk to Funk, 21.11.1939; 3671841–3, letter from von Krosigk to Goering, 13.12.1939; frames 3671869–80, letter from the Economics Ministry to von Krosigk. 19.1.1940.
136 Ibid., frames 3678852–56, Price Commissioner Wagner to von Krosigk,

21.12.1939; L. Graf Schwerin von Krosigk, *Staatsbankrott*, Stuttgart, 1974, pp. 295, 298–300.

137 Ibid., frames 3671912–7, 'Statistical Review of the Reich Budget 1938 to 1943', November 1944.

138 Case XI, Prosecution doc. book 112, pp. 293–4, NID-13844, lecture by State Secretary Neumann, 29.4.1941.

139 NCA, vol. 6, p. 723, 3787-PS, 2nd meeting of the Reich Defence Council, 10.7.1939; on 'idle' factories see Speer Documents, FD 5445/45, letter from Goering to Funk, 6.12.1939, p. 2; Goering decree, 29.11.1939; BA-MA, Wi I F 5.412. Conference with General Thomas, 13.11.1939, pp. 1–2.

140 Case XI, Prosecution doc. book 112, p. 304, Neumann lecture.

141 USSBS, Report 77, *German Motor Vehicles Industry Report*, p. 8.

142 R. Wagenführ, *Die deutsche Industrie im Kriege*, Berlin, 1963, pp. 37, 56; B. Klein, *Germany's Economic Preparations for War*, Harvard, 1959, p. 105. By 1942 80 per cent of all construction was for military or military industrial purposes.

143 M. Steinert, *Hitler's War and the Germans*, Ohio, 1977, pp. 53, 64–5, 92–3; DDP, vol. 7, part I, pp. 403–9, War Economy Decree, 4.9.1939; pp. 388–9. Decree of the Plenipotentiary for the Economy, 27.8.1939; p. 429, speech by Field Marshal Goering, 9.9.1939; L. Lochner, *What About Germany?*, London, 1943, pp. 142–5.

144 Wagenführ, op. cit., p. 174. The Wehrmacht took 44 per cent of all textiles, 43 per cent of all leather, 40 per cent of all paper, etc.

145 Speer Documents, FD 5454 b/45, Deutsche Institut für Wirtschaftforschung, 'The Measurement of German Industrial Production during the War', June 1942, p. 9.

146 Ibid., FD 4809/45 VJP, 'Report on the general economic situation', 28.2.1940 and 20.8.1941.

147 Ibid., report of 22.2.1941, p. 4.

148 BA-MA, Wi I F 5.118, part 2, letter from Goering to the Economics Ministry, 22.7.1940.

149 IMT, vol. 31, pp. 235–6, 2852-PS, minutes of the meeting of the ministerial committee for Reich defence, 16.10.1939.

150 Schröter and Bach, op. cit., pp. 42–5; BA-MA, Wi I F 5.412, conference with General Thomas 13.11.1939, pp. 2–9.

151 Ibid., note of a conference in the Economics Ministry, 3.10.1939, pp. 1–2; conference with General Thomas, 13.11.1939, pp. 7–8; speech by General Thomas to heads of industry, 18.12.1939, pp. 8–9: Speer Documents, FD 5454 d/45, speech of General Thomas, 29.11.1939, pp. 3–5; FD 5445/45, Labour supply situation, 15.2.1940, pp. 1–4.

152 BA-MA, Wi I F 5.412, note of a conference with General Thomas, 1.11.1939, pp. 2–3.

153 SA 12/150/35, letter from Todt to Pleiger, 23.12.1939; letter from Goering to Pleiger, 7.9.1939.

154 Ibid., Circular from Todt to all leading authorities on conserving iron, 19.12.1939.

155 BA-MA, Wi I F 5.412, note of a conference in the Economics Ministry, 3.19.1939, p. 1.

156 Ibid., War programme for the vehicle industry, 1.1.1940; USSBS, Report 77, pp. 5, 8–9.

157 BA-MA, Wi I F 5.412, note of a discussion between General Thomas and Dr. Blank, 20.9.1939.

158 NA T177, Roll 31, frames 3719731–5, note of a conference in the War Ministry concerning the Opel works, 17.4.1936; Overy, 1973, op. cit.,

pp. 407–8; BA-MA RL3/84, Air Ministry report on the Opel works and the armed forces, 24.8.1936.

159 Ibid., Wi I F 5.412, conference with General Thomas, 5.10.1939; note of a discussion between Colonel Hünermann and Prof. Lüer, 29.9.1939.

160 Milch Documents, vol. 65, 7107–8, Luftwaffe General Staff, discussion points on Opel, 10.10.1941, pp. 1–2: USSBS Report 77, pp. 7–11.

161 BA-MA, Wi I F 5.412, discussion between General Thomas and Porsche (Volkswagen), 21.9.1939 and 4.10.1939; BIOS Final Report 768, *The German Automobile Industry*, HMSO, 1946, p. 11; K. Hopfinger, *Beyond Expectation: the Volkswagen Story*, London, 1954, pp. 131–2; USSBS Report 88, *Volks-wagen-Werke, Fallersleben*, pp. 3–4.

162 BA-MA, Wi I F 5.412, Extracts from the notes of a conference with General Thomas, 23.10.1939, p. 4. On the scale and layout of the Volkswagen plant see USSBS Report 88, pp. 6–7.

163 IMT, vol. 27, pp. 201–2, 1375–PS, letter from Hans Frank to the VJP Office, 25.1.1940.

164 BA-MA, Wi I F 5.3352, Goering decree on the skilled worker shortage, 28.9.1939; Review by the Plenipotentiary for the Economy, 17.10.1939; Speer Documents, FD 4809/45, VJP reports 19.2.1940 and 3.5.1940.

165 Ibid., FD 5454 d/45, speech by General Thomas to the Reich Group Indu-stry, 29.11.1939; FD 5445/45, Goering decree, 29.11.1939, 'Transition from peace to war economy'.

166 TWC, vol. 12, p. 528, 3324–PS, speech by Funk, 14.10.1939.

167 O. Dietrich, *The Hitler I Knew*, London, 1955, p. 189.

168 NA Göring-Stabsamt, T84 Roll 8, passim.

169 von Below, op. cit., pp. 60, 76.

170 IMT, vol. 33, p. 149, 3787–PS, 2nd meeting of the Reich Defence Council, 23.6.1939.

171 Ibid., vol. 32, pp. 412–13, 3575–PS, note of the meeting of the Reich Defence Council, 18.11.1938.

172 Ibid., vol. 31, p. 225, 2852–PS, minutes of the meeting of the Ministerial Council for Defence of the Reich, 1.9.1939; pp. 227–39, meetings of the Ministerial Council, 4.9., 8.9., 19.9., 16.10., 15.11., 1939; DDP, vol. 7, part I, p. 393, Decree of the Fuehrer over the formation of a Ministerial Council for Defence of the Reich, 30.8.1939.

173 Case XI, Prosecution doc. book 119, NI-1162, minutes of the meeting of the VJP General Council, 20.12.1939.

174 TWC, vol. 12, pp. 529–30, NG-1177(1), letter from Goering to Funk and to all VJP commissioners, 7.12.1939; IMT, vol. 9, pp. 382–3, Goering cross-examination; Case XI, Prosecution doc. book 119, memorandum of the Reich Chancellery, 11.12.1939; H. Schacht, *76 Jahre meines Lebens*, Bad Wörishofen, 1953, pp. 494–8.

175 TWC, vol. 12, pp. 531–2, NG-1177(2), memorandum of Willkuhn to Lammers, 8.12.1939; p. 533, NG-1177(4), letter from Koerner to Lammers, 18.1.1940; pp. 543–4, NID-13894, 'Organisational questions of the Four Year Plan', 27.8.1941. On the announcement in January 1940 see F. Taylor, op. cit., Goebbels diary, 6.1.1940.

176 IMT, vol. 9, p. 784, Goering cross-examination; Speer Documents, FD 5445/45, Fuehrer decree over the appointment of a Reich Minister for Weapons and Munitions, 17.3.1940; Goering decree 20.3.1940; FD 5454 d/45, draft of a Goering decree, 23.2.1940.

177 TWC, vol. 12, p. 575, NI-125.

178 BA-MA, Rl3 159, 'Supply programme no. 15, 1.9.1939; Milch Documents, vol. 65, 7410-11, notes for the discussion with General Goering, 13.12.1938;

NA T177 Roll 31, frame 3719681, 'Supply figures for air equipment, 1.4.1938'.
179 BA-MA, RL3 46, 'Average prices for different weapons and their armament', n.d.
180 Salewski, op. cit., vol. 1, pp. 463–70.
181 Case XI, Prosecution doc. book 118a, NI-7835, 'Development of the production plans for gunpowder, explosives and chemical warfare agents', 15.7.1940, pp. 2–3.
182 BA-MA, Wi I F 5.412, 'War programme for the vehicle industry', 1.1.1940; USSBS Report 77, pp. 7–11.
183 W. Baumbach. *Broken Swastika*, London, 1960, p. 8; F. Taylor, op. cit., p. 70, Goebbels diary, 20.12.1939, 'Our air victory is the Führer's great joy'; p. 109, entry for 1.2.1940 'With the Führer ... Overall, our Luftwaffe is magnificent. It is the best weapon for attack, and the most reliable defence.'
184 R. J. Overy, *The Air War 1939–1945*, London, 1980, p. 23.
185 Ludlow, op. cit., pp. 48–50.
186 Friedländer, op. cit., p. 100.
187 Groscurth, op. cit., p. 414, 'Minutes of the talk by Hitler to the heads of the Armed Forces', 23.11.1939; on the decision to attack Russia see A. Hillgruber, *Hitlers Strategie: Politik und Kriegführung 1940–41*, Frankfurt a M, 1965, pp. 157–91, 218–19; Warlimont, op. cit., pp. 110–12.
188 Hesse, 1954, op. cit., pp. 107–8.
189 Ibid., pp. 105–6.
190 BA-MA, Wi I F 5.412, results of a conference with Goering, 16.7.1938.
191 Irving, op. cit., pp. 64–6, 75–6, 107–8.
192 Klein, op. cit., p. 160.
193 Homze, op. cit., pp. 244–5: Baumbach, op. cit., pp. 30–1.
194 Overy, 1980, op. cit., p. 197.
195 D. Dempster, D. Wood, *The Narrow Margin: the Battle of Britain and the Rise of Airpower*, London, 1961, pp. 248–9, 461, 463, 478–80.
196 Irving, op. cit., pp. 72–3.

CHAPTER 5   BUILDING THE NAZI EMPIRE

1 G. Eley, *Reshaping the German Right: Radical Nationalism and Political Change after Bismarck*, New Haven, 1978, esp. pp. 336–48; F. Fischer, *Germany's Aims in the First World War*, London, 1967; D. Calleo, *The German Problem Reconsidered*, Cambridge, 1978, pp. 36–49.
2 Christie Papers 180/1 5, notes of a conversation, 28.7.1937.
3 IMT, vol. 32, 3575-PS, meeting of Reich Defence Council, 18.11.1938.
4 DDP, vol. 6, part 1, pp. 177–8, Decree on the economic recovery of Austria, 23.3.1938; p. 377, decree on carrying out the VJP in the Sudeten German regions, 10.10.1938. See too N. Schausberger, 'Der Anschluss und seine ökonomische Relevanz' in R. Neck (ed.), *Anschluss 1938*, Vienna, 1981, pp. 245–6, 261–4.
5 NA T177, Roll 3, frame 3684568, Economic Inspectorate Prague to Air Ministry, 30.3.1939; frames 3684480–2, OKW report over mobilisation preparations in Bohemia and Moravia, 15.7.1939; BA-MA, RL3 24, report of an official visit to Prague from 26.2 to 2.3.1940; RL3 18, Folder 1, report from Udet to Goering, December 1939; Case XI, Prosecution doc. book 168, NID-15635, Reich Finance Ministry file note, 17.2.1939. It was pointed out in the note that Hans Kehrl had been instructed to purchase shares in

major Czech concerns (including the Skoda works) before the occupation of Bohemia in March.

6   The large hydrogenation plant at Brüx in the Sudetenland was set up under the Reichswerke in 1939, as a state-owned concern.

7   Case XI, Prosecution doc. book 112, p. 281, NID-13844, Neumann lecture; see also NA Reichswerke files, T83 Roll 75 frames 3446018–25, letter from Voss to Goering, 7.11.1941. On the construction projects see C. Schneider, *Stadtgründung im Dritten Reich: Wolfsburg und Salzgitter*, Munich, 1979, pp. 66, 77–8, 83–6.

8   NA Göring Stabsamt, T84 Roll 7, frames 6704–5, note on trustee administration, 21.4.1942.

9   Case XI, Prosecution doc. book 112, p. 290, NID-13844, Neumann lecture.

10 Ibid., p. 149, NID-13797, letter from Koerner to von Krosigk, 7.10.1940.

11 M. Riedel, *Kohle und Eisen für das Dritte Reich*, Göttingen, 1973, pp. 234–43; SA 12/150/1, note of a conference with Goering on 29.4.1938; K. Rothschild, *Austria's Economic Development between the Two Wars*, London, 1947, pp. 79–83.

12 F. Thyssen, *I Paid Hitler*, London, 1941, pp. 48–9. They were officially distrained on 13 October 1939 and confiscated on 14 December.

13 NA Reichswerke files, T83 Roll 74, frames 3445159–77, I.G. Farben volkswirtschaftliche Abteilung, 'Build-up and development of the Reichswerke A.G.', 19.10.1939; frame 3445754, Index of businesses belonging to the Reichswerke A.G. concern as of 31.12.1943; Roll 75, frames 3446029–64, Dresdner Bank, Volkswirtschaftliche Abteilung, 'The Reichswerke "Hermann Goering" concern, 21.12.1940'.

14 F. Morton, *The Rothschilds*, London, 1962, pp. 224–6; A. Teichova, *An Economic Background to Munich*, Cambridge, 1974, pp. 82–3, 91–2.

15 SA 12/150/12, letter from Nathow to Pleiger, 22.2.1939, letter from Steinbrinck to Pleiger, 30.1.1939; *Conditions in Occupied Territories (5): the Penetration of German Capital into Europe*, HMSO, 1942, pp. 10–11. The Petschek holdings were brought together to form the basis of the Sudetenländische Bergbau A.G., a major Reichswerke subsidiary providing lignite for hydrogenation.

16 Case XI, Prosecution doc. book 168, Finance Ministry memorandum on 'Transfer of investments to AG Reichswerke (Holding)', 9.1.1940; TWC, vol. 13, pp. 666–7, NID-13927, letter from Hans Kehrl to Karl Rasche, 18.4.1940; p. 710, Rasche cross-examination.

17 NA Reichswerke files, T83 Roll 77, frames 3449313–28, 'Distribution of the shareholding in Skoda works and Brünner Waffenwerke', 6.11.1940; Case XI, Pleiger doc. book 7b, pp. 30–9, 'The economic development of the Sudetenländische Bergbau A.G. during the years 1939–1945', 28.5.1945; pp. 50–9, Holst affidavit, 3.6.1948 on Poldihütte and Ferdinands Nordbahn; pp. 85–9, minutes of a meeting of the Reichswerke board, 20.5.1941; TWC, vol. 13, pp. 662–5, NID-15640, Reich Finance Ministry on 'The purchase of shares in the iron and machine industry of the Protectorate', 28.10.1939.

18 Teichova, op. cit., pp. 91–2; Morton, op. cit., pp. 225–6.

19 Case XI, Pleiger doc. book 7a, pp. 17–19, 'The legal position of the Witkowitz Gewerkschaft', 21.10.1939.

20 NA Reichswerke files, T83 Roll 75, frame 3446239, Reich Statistical Office, 'The Witkowitzer Bergbau-und Eisenhüttengewerkschaft, 31.3.1944'; Case XI, Pleiger doc. book 7a, pp. 82–7, 'Resolution of the board of the Witkowitzer Gewerkschaft', 14.12.1942.

21 Ibid., pp. 38–45, 'Business report of the financial year 1940 by the Vorstand of the Gewerkschaft, 10.6.1941'; p. 62, Fiscal Report, 1942.

22 Ibid., p. 57, 'Fiscal Report of the Gewerkschaftvorstand of Witkowitzer

Gewerkschaft 1941', September 1942; pp. 134–6, Minutes of the first meeting of the council for the administration of enemy property, Supplement 9, 9.7.1943.

23 Speer Documents, FD 264/46, Index of firms, HGW Iron, steel and coal bloc, pp. 1–4.

24 D. Kaiser, *Economic Diplomacy and the Origins of the Second World War*, Princeton, 1980, pp. 264–6, 277–9; D. Eichholtz, 'Die IG-Farben-Friedens-planung', *Jahrbuch für Wirtschaftsgeschichte*, vol. 5, 1966.

25 Christie Papers 180/1 5, Report of meeting with Goering, 28.7.1937; Notes from conversation with Goering, 3.2.1937.

26 DGFP, Ser. D, vol. 5, p. 387, memorandum on arms deal with Jugoslavia, 9.2.1939; p. 409, memorandum by director of economic policy dept on arms sales to Jugoslavia, 27.2.1939; BA-MA, Wi I F 5.412, note of a discussion with General Thomas, 20.9.1939, concerning Jugoslavia; R. Schönfeld, 'Deutsche Rohstoffsicherungspolitik in Jugoslawien 1934–1944', *Vierteljahreshefte für Zeitgeschichte*, vol. 24, 1976, pp. 220–33.

27 Kaiser, op. cit., pp. 264–5.

28 DGFP, Ser. D, vol. 6, pp. 91–6, German-Roumanian Economic Treaty, 23.3.1939; pp. 161–6, Wohlthat report on negotiations in Bucharest, 27.3.1940; pp. 1021–2, Foreign Ministry to legation in Romania, 30.7.1939.

29 M. Pearton, *Oil and the Roumanian State*, Oxford, 1971, p. 231; A. Hillgruber, *Hitler, König Carol und Marschall Antonescu*, Wiesbaden, 1954, pp. 156–7.

30 P. Marguerat, *Le IIIᵉ Reich et le pétrole roumain 1938–1940*, Leiden, 1977, pp. 201–2; *Conditions in Occupied Territories*, op. cit., p. 23; BIOS Final Report 513, *Notes on the Organisation of the German Petroleum Industry during the War*, p. 7.

31 Marguerat, op. cit., p. 180; *Conditions in Occupied Territories*, op. cit., p. 29; K. Lachmann, 'The Hermann Göring Works', *Social Research*, vol. 8, 1941, p. 34.

32 Hillgruber, op. cit., p. 156; K. Lachmann, 'More on the Hermann Göring Works', *Social Research*, vol. 9, 1942, pp. 316–17; DDP, vol. 8, Berlin, 1942, p. 704, 'Protocol on German-Roumanian co-operation in carrying out a Ten Year Plan for building up the Roumanian economy, 4.12.1940'.

33 NA Göring-Stabsamt, T84 Roll 6, frames 5512–3, file note, 1.9.1942; DGFP, Ser. D, vol. 12, pp. 223–4, Memorandum of the Foreign Ministry on the Goering-Antonescu conversations, 8.3.1941. For the general background to the disputes see E. Campus, 'Die Hitlerfaschistische Infiltration Rumäniens 1939–1940', *Zeitschrift für Geschichtswissenschaft*, vol. 5, 1957; N. N. Constantinescu, 'L'exploitation et le pillage de l'économie roumaine par l'Allemagne hitlérienne dans la période 1939–44', *Revue roumaine d'histoire*, vol. 3, 1964, pp. 110–12.

34 L. Neal, 'The Economics and Finance of Bilateral Clearing Agreements: Germany 1934–38', *Economic History Review*, 2nd Ser., vol. 32, 1979, pp. 398–403.

35 Kaiser, op. cit., pp. 130–66.

36 DGFP, Ser. D, vol. 6, p. 885, secret protocol between Germany and Roumania, July 1939; p. 886, Roumanian Economics Minister to Minister Clodius, 8.7.1939; pp. 432, 485, Minister in Roumania to Foreign Ministry, 18.3.1939, 13.5.1939; vol. 7, pp. 105, 368, Minister in Roumania to Foreign Ministry, 17.8 and 28.8.1939; IWM, Milch Documents, vol. 65, 7335–8, letter from Udet to Goering, 4.7.1939 on 'the Position of Exports to the Balkans'; 7384, notice of a conference with Goering, 2.5.1939; 7390, letter from Udet to Milch; NCA, vol. 8, pp. 203–4, Note of a conference with General Goering, 25.7.1939; Kaiser, op. cit., pp. 269–71.

37   DGFP, Ser. D, vol. 8, pp. 49–50, memorandum from Economic Policy Dept, 11.9.1939; vol. 6, p. 157, minister in Jugoslavia to Foreign Ministry, 30.3.1939.
38   Case XI, Prosecution doc. book 125, PS-1707, memorandum of a meeting, 13.10.1939.
39   Ibid., letter from Goering to Funk, 9.10.1939.
40   DDP, vol. 7, part II, p. 604, Decree on the introduction of the VJP in the eastern areas, 30.10.1939; DGFP, Ser. D, vol. 9, p. 527, 'Competence for foreign economic relations of the occupied territories', 7.6.1940. The powers were assigned in Fuehrer decrees on 12 October 1939, 19 May and 5 June 1940.
41   TWC, vol. 13, p. 847, EC-207, Fuehrer decree concerning the economy of the newly occupied eastern territories, 29.6.1941.
42   BA-MA, RL3 18 File 4, GL report on aluminium production in Norway. See too A. S. Milward, *The Fascist Economy in Norway*, Oxford, 1972, pp. 207–8.
43   NA Reichswerke files, T83 Roll 76, frames 3447665–90, report on the coal industry from Pleiger to Goering, 15.8.1941; Riedel op. cit., pp. 276–7.
44   Case XI, Prosecution doc. book 124, NI-10797, Memorandum of a meeting of 21.1.1941 over the founding of Kontinentale Öl.
45   R. J. Overy, 'The Luftwaffe and the European Economy 1939–1945', *Militärgeschichtliche Mitteilungen*, vol. 21, 1979, pp. 57–62.
46   DGFP, Ser. D, vol. 9, pp. 526–7; p. 683, letter from Goering to Weizsäcker, 22.6.1940.
47   NCA, vol. 7, p. 467, EC-410, Goering to all Reich ministers, 19.10.1939; BA-MA, RL3 45, GL Liaison office in Bohemia, Moravia and Poland, report for 20.1.1940.
48   A. S. Milward, *The New Order and the French Economy*, Oxford, 1970, p. 77.
49   IMT, vol. 27, pp. 200–2, 1375-PS, Frank to VJP office in Poland, 25.1.1940; vol. 36, pp. 299–306, 305-EC, Conference on eastern questions with Goering, 12.2.1940; Case XI, Pleiger doc. book 9, pp. 34–41, 'Foundries in the Government General', 7.12.1942.
50   NCA, vol. 7, p. 608, EC-620, letter from Goering on the exploitation of the economy of the occupied western territories, 26.8.1940.
51   DGFP, Ser. D, vol. 8, pp. 66–8, 'The Greater Economic Sphere', 1.6.1940; DDP, vol. 8, pp. 692–701, decree of W. Funk over the organic building up of the European economy, 1.9.1940; R. E. Herzstein, *When Nazi Dreams Come True*, London, 1982, pp. 103–25; Milward, 1970, op. cit., pp. 38–44 on France; N. Rich, *Hitler's War Aims: The Establishment of the New Order*, London, 1974; K. Wittmann, *Schwedens Wirtschaftsbeziehungen zum Dritten Reich, 1933–1945*, Munich, 1978, pp. 204–40; D. Eichholtz, 'Die IG-Farben Friedensplanung', *Jahrbuch für Wirtschaftsgeschichte*, vol. 5, 1966.
52   NCA, vol. 7, pp. 210–11, EC-137, Goering to the Economy and Armaments Office, 'German influence with foreign enterprises', 9.8.1940. See too pp. 79–86, EC-43, Reich Economics Ministry, 'Acquisition of shares of important foreign enterprises in south-east Europe', 16.8.1940; pp. 543–7, EC-485, Goering conference, 1.10.1940.
53   Case XI, Prosecution doc. book 167, NID-16958, Kehrl to Reich Textile Commissioners, 12.8.1940.
54   SA 12/155/4, P. Rheinländer, 'Vorschlag zur Ausgestaltung der Eisenindustrie im Grossdeutschen Wirtschaftsraum nach dem Kriege', autumn 1940.
55   A. Speer, *The Slave State*, London, 1981, pp. 76–7.
56   D. Eichholtz, *Geschichte der deutschen Kriegswirtschaft 1939–1945*, Berlin, 1969, vol. 1, pp. 294–338, document collection 'Ruhrmontankonzerne'; R. Jeske, 'Zur Annexion der polnischen Wojewodschaft Schlesien durch Hitlerdeutsch-

land im zweiten Weltkrieg', *Zeitschrift für Geschichtswissenschaft*, vol. 5, 1957, pp. 1073–5, 1087.

57 Case XI, Prosecution doc. book 125, 2207-PS, Goering decree, 1.11.1939; SA 12/150/1, Goering to Terboven, 30.10.1939; 12/150/14, 150/14, letter from Koerner to Pleiger, 21.11.1939; note of a conference, 31.10.1939; NA Reichswerke files, T83 Roll 76, frames 346860–1, letter from Pleiger to Koerner, 13.3.1940; Case XI, Prosecution doc. book 115, NI-1250, letter from Reichswerke to Preussag, 23.7.1940; DDP, vol. 7, part II, pp. 680–1, Announcement of the development of Chief Trustee Office East, 7.11.1939.

58 Case XI, Prosecution doc. book 125, 2207-PS, Himmler decree, 10.11.1939; Pleiger doc. book 8, pp. 1–4, Winkler affidavit.

59 Ibid., Pleiger doc. book 10, pp. 34–41, File note 'Foundries in the General Government'.

60 NA Reichswerke files, T83 Roll 76, frames 3446876–7, letter from Pleiger to Koerner, enclosing letters from Krupp, 10.4.1940; frames 344684–6, Pleiger to Krupp, 8.4.1940; Roll 80, frame 3452589, letter from Koerner to Pleiger, 30.8.1940; Case XI, Prosecution doc. book 113, NID-14954, note of a discussion between Flick and Koerner, 2.8.1940.

61 Case XI Transcript, vol. 231, p. 14842.

62 Ibid., Pleiger defence doc. book 10, p. 1, Gritzbach affidavit.

63 NA Reichswerke files, T83 Roll 81, frames 3452359–66, 'Supply company for the iron ore mines in Lorraine and Meurthe-et-Moselle', 1944.

64 Case XI, Pleiger doc. book 10, pp. 3–9, Beckenbauer affidavit.

65 Ibid., Gritzbach affidavit, 21.4.1948.

66 NA Göring-Stabsamt, T84 Roll 7, frames 6322–6, 'The economic reunion of Luxembourg with the German economy', 1938.

67 D. Eichholtz, W. Schumann (eds), *Anatomie des Krieges*, Berlin, 1969, p. 274, doc.127, letter from Hoesch A.G. to Koerner, 2.8.1940.

68 Case XI, Prosecution doc. book 113, NI-3153, letter from Flick to Burkühl, 23.6.1940; NI-3528, letter from Flick to Goering, 2.11.1940; NI-3530, letter from Flick to Goering, 1.11.1940: NA Reichswerke files, T83 Roll 74, frames 3445217–25, 'Foundation and growth of the HGW 1937–42', 17.6.1948.

69 Ibid., Roll 81, frames 3452364–6, 'Supply Company' 1944; Case XI, Prosecution doc. book 165, NID-15558, letter from Koerner to Pleiger, 29.10.1940.

70 NA Reichswerke files, T83 Roll 81, frame 3452366.

71 Case XI, Prosecution doc. book 165, NID-15558, letter from Koerner to Pleiger, 29.10.1940.

72 Ibid., Prosecution doc. book 113, NI-049, Economic Group Iron Producing Industry to Pleiger, 5.2.1941; Pleiger doc. book 10, pp. 30–6, 'Works Transfer Agreement between HGW and the Chief of Civil Administration, Lorraine'.

73 DGFP, Ser. D, vol. 10, p. 93, Commissioner of the Four Year Plan to the Foreign Ministry, 2.7.1940; vol. 9, p. 683, Goering to Weizsäcker, 22.6.1940.

74 Milward, 1970, op. cit., pp. 48–9.

75 Ibid., pp. 49–50, 52–9: DGFP, vol. 10, pp. 128–9, circular of the Four Year Plan Office, 5.7.1940; pp. 170–3, Ribbentrop to Goering, 9.7.1940.

76 NA Reichswerke files, T83 Roll 76, frame 3447887, Minutes of a conference in the Economics Ministry, 27.6.1941.

77 Riedel, op. cit., pp. 276–80.

78 SA 12/155/4, Rheinländer memorandum, Autumn 1940.

79 Ibid., pp. 19–22, 38–40.

80 Ibid., pp. 21–2, 34–5.

81 Ibid., pp. 10–19, 23–31. On the role of Vienna see D. Orlow, *The Nazis in the Balkans*, Pittsburgh, 1968, pp. 137–8. See also DDP, vol. 8, p. 698, Decree on the organic building-up of the European economy, 1.9.1940.

82 Case XI, Pleiger doc. book 5a, pp. 79–81, von Krosigk to Funk, 11.12.1940. See too NA Göring Stabsamt, T84 Roll 7, frames 6707–10, letter from Winkler to Goering, 16.4.1942; Reichswerke files, T83 Roll 76, frames 3447886–9, Minutes of meeting in the Economics Ministry, 27.6.1941; IMT, vol. 13, 150 ff. Funk cross-examination.

83 Milch Documents, vol. 65, 5316–8, report of a conference with Reichmarschall Goering and the representatives of the aircraft industry, 13.9.1942.

84 NA Reichswerke files, T84 Roll 74, frames 3445227–56, list of firms and directors, Reichswerke A.G. 'Hermann Goering'.

85 See, for example, TWC, vol. 12, p. 670, NID-13436, 'Aryanisation report from the Boehmische Escompte Bank', 6.8.1941. There were many similar reports, primarily from Poland and Czechoslovakia.

86 H. Höhne, *The Order of the Death's Head*, London, 1969, pp. 387–99; H. Krausnick et al., *The Anatomy of the SS State*, London, 1968, pp. 68–9.

87 IMT, vol. 28, pp. 533–9, 1816-PS.

88 G. S. Graber, *The Life and Times of Reinhard Heydrich*, London, 1981, pp. 188–91; Krausnick, op. cit., pp. 68–88.

89 See, for example, H. Goering, *Germany Reborn*, London, 1934, pp. 131–2, 'Only he who has observed the activities of Jews in Germany ... can fully understand the necessity of what has now been done. The Jewish question has not yet been completely solved.'

90 NCA vol. 3, pp. 525–6, 710-PS, letter from Goering to Heydrich, 31.7.1941; A. Speer, *The Slave State*, London, 1981, pp. 256–7.

91 Case XI, Prosecution doc. book 126, NI-4769, letter from Pleiger to Speer, 12.12.1943; NI-4784, Reichswerke memorandum on labour allocation, 22.6.1942: USSBS Special Report 3, *The Effects of Strategic Bombing upon the Operations of the Hermann Goering Works*, Washington, 1947, p. 68.

92 IMT, vol. 27, pp. 356–7, 1584 (3)-PS, Himmler to Goering, 9.3.1944, 'Use of prisoners in the aircraft industry'; Case XI, Prosecution doc. book 112, p. 316, NID-13613, letter from Himmler to Pohl, 31.1.1942; Prosecution doc. book 126, NID-12324, memorandum on Mauthausen woodworking plant, 12.12.1941; NO-1913, telegram from SS Construction Main Office to Pohl, 22.7.1942. On poor productivity see NO-19143, letter from Hohberg to Pohl, 6.8.1942.

93 Ibid., NID-14599, list of workers who died or were killed at Salzgitter/Watenstedt.

94 NA Reichswerke files, T83 Roll 76, frames 3446957-82, report of the board of the Sudetenlaendische Treibstoffwerke, 24.7.1941; frame 3447040, report of the board, September 1942.

95 Ibid., frames 3447692–3, letter from Goering to Pleiger, 24.10.1941.

96 G. Gilbert, *Nuremberg Diary*, London, 1948, p. 82.

97 IMT, vol. 9, pp. 344–6.

98 H. Trevor-Roper (ed.), *Hitler's Table Talk 1941–1944*, London, 1973, pp. 70, 479; D. Mack Smith, *Mussolini's Roman Empire*, London, 1976, pp. 226–8, 234.

99 A. Speer, *Spandau: the Secret Diaries*, London, 1976, pp. 58–61.

100 H. Groscurth, *Tagebücher eines Abwehroffiziers*, Stuttgart, 1970, p. 414, Minutes of a talk by Hitler to the heads of the armed forces, 23.11.1939; M. Muggeridge (ed.), *Ciano's Diary 1939–1943*, London, 1947, p. 351. Ciano reported von Bismarck's view that Goering's influence with Hitler was waning because he 'admonishes him too much'; E. Goering, *An der Seite meines Mannes*, Göttingen, 1967, pp. 204–7.

101 Eichholtz and Schumann, op. cit., p. 163, 'Grüne Mappe, June 1941'; Speer

Documents, FD 5454 d/54, conference with Goering, 19.3.1941. On iron ore see BA-MA, RL3 18, RLM report no. 31, 27.9.1941, pp. 1–2.

102 IMT, vol. 28, p. 8, 1743-PS, 'Guidelines for the leadership of the economy', June 1941; Eichholtz and Schumann, p. 316, doc. 150, file note of a discussion with Goering, 26.2.1941; Speer Documents FD 1434/46 no. 176, statement concerning the occupation of the Caucasian mineral oil region, 16.7.1941.

103 TWC, vol. 13, p. 847, EC-207, Fuehrer decree, 29.6.1941.

104 IMT, vol. 36, pp. 135–57, 126-EC, 'Economic guidelines for the economic organisation of the East', 23.5.1941; TWC vol. 13, pp. 350–1, NI-3777, Goering decree, 27.7.1941, 'concerning German economic policy in the occupied eastern territories'.

105 Case XI, Prosecution doc. book 124, NI-2021, 'Memorandum on Russian mineral oil economy, 22.7.1941', pp. 1–3; NA Reichswerke files, T83 Roll 81, frames 3452275–6, Goering decree on the eastern economy, 27.7.1941.

106 NA T177, Roll 14, frame 3698645, GL report, 13.8.1941; BA-MA, RL3 18, RLM short report no. 31, 27.9.1941.

107 A. Dallin, *German Rule in Russia*, London, 1981, pp. 305–6, 310–17.

108 NA Reichswerke files, T83 Roll 80, frames 3453057–60, file note on the organisation of the Russian economy, 4.8.1941; TWC, vol. 12, pp. 857–72, NI-440, directive from Koerner to all Reich authorities, 20.11.1941.

109 Case XI, Prosecution doc. book 124, NI-2021, von Hanneken memorandum on Russian mineral oil industry, 22.7.1941; NI-10797, Memorandum of a meeting of 21.1.1941, p. 2; NI-10162, minutes of the second meeting of the managerial board of Kontinentale Öl, 13.6.1942; NA Reichswerke files, T83 Roll 80, frames 3452597–9, meeting of Economic Staff East, 24.9.1941.

110 Case XI, Prosecution doc. book 124, NI-5581, Economic Group Iron and Steel Industry to all heads of firms, 21.8.1941; NA Reichswerke files, T83 Roll 79, frames 3451471, Goering decree on establishment of BHO; Dallin, op. cit., pp. 384–5.

111 Ibid., frames 3451490-3, 'Second work report of BHO, Dec. 1942'; Roll 80, frames 3452609-10, letter from Pleiger to the Economics Ministry, 10.4.1942.

112 Ibid., frame 3452641, 'Report on the activity of the BHO, 31.5.1942'; Speer Documents, FD 5444/45, Goering decree 'over trusteeship for armaments works in the occupied east', 28.10.1941; OKW memorandum, 'Claims on industrial firms for arms production in the occupied eastern areas', n.d.

113 See the long correspondence between Goering, Rosenberg and Koch in NA Göring-Stabsamt, T84 Roll 7, frames 6712–48; see too Reichswerke files, T83 Roll 80, frames 3452442–7, Rosenberg to Goering, 20.11.1943; 3452473–4, Rosenberg to Goering, 6.1.1943.

114 Ibid., Roll 79, frames 3451474–1540, 'Second work report of the BHO, December 1942'; TWC, vol. 13, p. 895, NI-5261, meeting of the administrative council of the BHO, 31.3.1943.

115 Eichholtz and Schumann, op. cit., pp. 410–11, doc. 216, letter from Goering to Economic Staff East, 2.11.1942; pp. 411–12, doc. 217, 'Principles for the leadership of the "godfather" firms of the BHO', 3.11.1942; Dallin, op. cit., pp. 385–8.

116 USSBS, Special Report 3, pp. 54a, 65–8; Speer Documents, FD 264/46, Index of firms in HGW Montanblock.

117 NA Reichswerke files, T83 Roll 74, frames 3445183–98, Reich Economics Ministry, 'Composition and Structure of the Reichswerke concern. Position as of 31.3.1941'; Roll 75, frames 3446065–74, 'The growth of state enterprises in private legal form', 1944.

118 USSBS Special Report 3, pp. 38, 60: USSBS Report 106, *Hermann Goering Werke Braunschweig-Hallendorf*, Washington, 1947, pp. 1–3.

CHAPTER 6   THE ERA OF EGOTISM AND INCOMPETENCE

1   A. Speer, *Spandau: the Secret Diaries*, London, 1976, p. 63.
2   Speer Documents, FD 5447/45, Thomas to armaments inspectorates 'Reorientation of Armaments', p. 2; Notice of a discussion with the head of the Army Armament Office, 19.7.1940; letter from Goering to Funk, 22.7.1940; FD 5078/45, Conference on the Plassenburg with Todt, 5/6.6.1940, p. 1.
3   Ibid., FD 5447/45, Thomas to Goering, 15.7.1940.
4   Ibid., FD 5447/45 'Development of the armament position with regard to 8.8 cm. Flak munitions, August 1940'; FD 5450/45 file note on the conference in the Reich Transport Ministry, 17.9.1941.
5   BA-MA, RL3 234, report from Tschersich to Udet, 13.10.1940.
6   Speer Documents, FD 5447/45 'Reorientation of Armaments'.
7   Ibid., FD 5450/45, 'Increase in Luftwaffe production', 27.6.1941; 'Expanded air armament programme, 6.7.1941', pp. 4–5; BA-MA, RL3 157, 'Provisional supply plan "Elch-Programm" ', 13.8.1941.
8   M. Salewski, *Die deutsche Seekriegsleitung 1939–1945*, Frankfurt a M, 1970, vol. 1, pp. 261, 437–9; Speer Documents, FD 5450/45, Admiral Raeder to Keitel, 'Completion of the building programme for new U-boats'; USSBS, Report 92, *German Submarine Industry*, Exhibit P.
9   Ibid., FD 5444/45, Conference of Armaments Inspectors, 22.1.1941, pp. 64–5; FD 5445/45, letter from Goering to Funk, 6.12.1939; FD 5446/45, letter from Thomas to Syrup (Reich Labour Ministry), 22.2.1940; FD 4809/45, conference with Goering, 9.2.1940.
10 Ibid., FD 5445/45, Goering decree, 29.11.1939.
11 Ibid., FD 5447/45, letter from Goering to Funk, 22.7.1940; FD 4809/45, Reich Economics Ministry decree, 21.2.1940; FD 5078/45, contribution for the conference of German military attachés, 26.8.1940.
12 Ibid., FD 5450/45, Goering decree, 18.2.1941.
13 Ibid., FD 5450/45, notice for the Chief of OKW, 6.7.1941; FD 5450/45, letter from Todt to all armed forces, 11.7.1941.
14 Ibid., FD 5450/45, file note on the conference in the Reich Transport Ministry, 17.9.1941; WiRüAmt minute, 19.7.1941, 'on the Fuehrer's guidelines on the future conduct of the war, 14.7.1941'.
15 NA Göring-Stabsamt, T84 Roll 6, frames 5312–3, report from Gauleiter Bürckel to Goering, 11.9.1942.
16 Speer Documents, FD 5450/45, 'Current situation in the area of raw materials, July 1941', pp. 1–2.
17 Ibid., p. 3 'Aluminium plan 1941'; NA Göring-Stabsamt, T84 Roll 6, frame 5254, report from Milch to Goering 'on the French aluminium and bauxite capacity', 4.1.1943; USSBS Report 20, *Light Metals Industry of Germany*, part 1, pp. 16–21.
18 Milch Documents, vol. 50, p. 57, letter from Goering's adjutant to Milch, 25.5.1942.
19 R. J. Overy, 'The Luftwaffe and the European Economy 1939–1945', *Militärgeschichtliche Mitteilungen*, vol. 21, 1979, pp. 58–9, 64–5; P. Façon, 'Aperçus sur la collaboration aéronautique franco-allemande 1940–1943', *Revue d'histoire de la deuxième Guerre Mondiale*, vol. 27, 1977, pp. 97–100.
20 USSBS Special Paper no. 4, *Food and Agriculture*, pp. 105–6, and Exhibit D, E, F.
21 E. Homze, *Foreign Labour in Nazi Germany*, Princeton, 1967, pp. 28–38, 64–6.
22 USSBS Special Report no. 3, pp. 66–7; SA 12/141/1–2, Labour report 2nd qtr 1941, Salzgitter/Watenstedt.

23 Homze, op. cit., pp. 57, 65, 232; H. Pfahlmann, *Fremdarbeiter und Kriegsgefangene in der deutschen Kriegswirtschaft*, Darmstadt, 1968, pp. 133–7.
24 See for example CIOS report XVII-I, *German Activities in the French Aircraft Industry*, HMSO, 1946, p. 59; Speer Documents, FD 362/45 monthly report of the Arado-Bureau, Paris, April 1943; NA T177, Roll 14, frame 3698947, Armaments Inspectorate XI, report for May 1941.
25 Case XI, Pleiger doc. book 5a, 79–81, letter from von Krosigk to Funk, 11.12.1940; NA Reichswerke files, T83, Roll 77, frames 3448198–201, visit of the Reich Finance Minister to the Sudetenland, 16.7.1943.
26 Case XI, Pleiger doc. book 7a, pp. 48–51, 5th meeting of the management board of the Witkowitzer Gewerkschaft, 30.6.1942; Resolution of the management board, 14.12.1942; doc. book 8, pp. 34–45, BHO report on financial year 1943, 6.6.1944; pp. 58–65, Mining Administration Upper-Silesia report for the Reichswerke on investment plans, 24.6.1941.
27 BA-MA, RL3 18, file 4, report over proposed aluminium works in Norway, 25.8.1941; RL3 52, Defence Economic Staff, Norway, situation report, 14.6.1941; RL3 54, situation report, April 1942; A. S. Milward, *The Fascist Economy in Norway*, Oxford, 1972, pp. 207–8.
28 Speer Documents, FD 778/46, meeting of the Advisory Board of the Flugmotorenwerke Ostmark, 16.12.1941, 16.10.1942, 14.8.1943; Milch Documents, vol. 51, pp. 564–70, GL minute on the 'visit and conference at the Flugmotorenwerke Ostmark', 30.4.1943.
29 CIOS Report, XXX-6.
30 Overy, op. cit., pp. 56–7, 63–4.
31 Case XI, Prosecution doc. book 112, p. 140, NI-932.
32 L. Graf Schwerin von Krosigk, *Staatsbankrott*, Stuttgart, 1974, pp. 233–4; NA Reichswerke files, T83, Roll 76, frames 3446932–3, letter from Todt to Koerner, 9.5.1940; 3446950–2, letter from Todt to Pleiger, 23.4.1940.
33 Case XI, Pleiger doc, book 5a, pp. 1–23, Pleiger to Goering, 'Reorganisation of the "Hermann Goering" Concern', 20.4.1940.
34 Ibid., p. 25, letter from Goering to Pleiger, 15.8.1940.
35 NA Reichswerke files, T83, Roll 75, frame 3445769, letter from Koerner to Pleiger, 15.11.1940; frames 3445813–41, 'Report of the Work Group of the committee for the organisation of the Reichswerke concern'; USSBS Special Paper 3, pp. 43–4; Control Office for Germany and Austria, GED 43/0/34, *The Hermann Göring Complex*, June 1946, pp. 24–6.
36 Case XI, Pleiger doc. book 5a, p. 39, letter from Pleiger to Goering, 22.8.1940.
37 Ibid., pp. 24–6, Goering to all Reichswerke leaders, 15.8.1940.
38 Ibid., pp. 32–4, letter from Goering to Pleiger, 15.8.1940; see also pp. 54–5, letter from Goering to Pleiger, 31.8.1940.
39 NA Reichswerke files, T83 Roll 75, frame 3445868, minutes of the meeting of the committee for the organisation of the concern, 12.12.1940; frames 3445799–803, discussion with director Delius, 28–29.11.1940.
40 A. S. Milward, *The New Order and the French Economy*, Oxford, 1970, p. 84.
41 Milch Documents vol. 63, 6024, conference with the Reich Marshal, 28.10.1943. In the Luftwaffe factories over 50 per cent of the workforce was of conscriptable age.
42 Speer Documents FD 5444/45, WiRüAmt, 'Die Ersatzlage der Wehrmacht', 22.2.1941; FD 5447/45, file note on the conference with Field Marshal Keitel, 17.8.1940. The armed forces also promised to release 400,000 men for winter work in arms factories.
43 Ibid., FD 5444/45, Labour Situation, 15.2.1940; WiRüAmt, 'Ersatzlage', p. 38; 'Rationalisation of manpower in the civilian sector', 27.1.1942, p. 1.

276   *Notes to pages 147–56*

44   IMT, vol. 27, pp. 65–6, 1206-PS, note of instructions from the Reich Marshal on 7.11.1941. On female labour see BA-MA, Wi I F 5.2602, F. Sauckel report, 'The programme for labour supply', 20.4.1942, pp. 3–12.
45   Milch Documents, vol. 63, 6017–44, minutes of the conference with the Reich Marshal on the allocation of labour, 28.10.1943.
46   R. J. Overy, 'German Aircraft Production 1939–1942', unpublished Ph.D. thesis, Cambridge University, 1977, p. 274.
47   A. Speer, *Inside the Third Reich*, London, 1970, pp. 208–13.
48   Speer, 1976, op. cit, p. 62; see too the discussion in Speer Documents, FD 5444/45, WiRüAmt, conference of inspectors, 22.2.1941, pp. 64–7. To Thomas the key to a better economic performance was the 'exploitation of more rational methods'.
49   See, for example, Speer Documents, FD 5450/45, Reich Transport Ministry to Goering, 27.8.1941; letter from Todt to Keitel, 30.7.1941; letter from Todt to Raeder, 30.7.1941; WiRüAmt, report 'on the management of material resources for the armed forces in the period 1.9.1940 to 1.4.1941', 10.7.1941.
50   Ibid., memorandum of the Fuehrer, 11.9.1941.
51   Ibid., FD 1434/46 no.170, 'Umstellung der Rüstung', March 1942, pp. 7–13. Decrees on rationalisation were issued on 11.9., 19.9., 10.10, and 23.10.1941.
52   D. Eichholtz, W. Schumann (eds), *Anatomie des Krieges*, Berlin, 1969, p. 331, doc. 161, 'Circular from Udet on calling together an Industrial Council for the aircraft industry', 22.5.1941;BA-MA, RL3 252, 'Preconditions for carrying through the "Goering-Programme" ', 18.10.1941; Milch Documents, vol. 53, pp. 1150–1: Speer Documents, FD 4355/45, 'Increased efficiency in the manufacture of aircraft equipment', 15.8.1941.
53   C. Webster, N. Frankland, *The Strategic Air Offensive against Germany*, London, 1961, vol. 4, p. 496.
54   R. Wagenführ, *Die deutsche Industrie im Kriege*, Berlin, 1963, pp. 178–9.
55   Overy, thesis, op. cit., pp. 260–73 for details.
56   Case XI. Pleiger doc. book 2, passim; TWC, vol. 12, p. 640, Pleiger cross-examination.
57   For example NA Göring-Stabsamt, T84 Roll 6, frames 5269–5303, Appointments for the Reich Marshal, 25.9.1942 – 7.12.1942; frame 5443, Goernnert to Gritzbach, 11.11.1942, office diary.
58   Ibid., frame 5274, 'Journey plan for the journey of 10/11 Dec. 1942'; Roll 8, frame 7577, orders for the journey of the Reich Marshal to the Fuehrer headquarters, 16.4.1942, are both typical examples.
59   IMT, vol. 31, pp. 225–39, 2852-PS, minutes of the meetings of the Reich Defence Council 1.9., 4.9., 8.9., 19.9., 16.10., 15.11.1939; P. Hüttenberger, *Die Gauleiter*, Stuttgart, 1969, p. 153.
60   U. von Hassell, *The von Hassell Diaries*, London, 1948, p. 104.
61   D. Irving, *The Rise and Fall of the Luftwaffe*, London, 1971, p. 136.
62   See, for example, the clash over contracts for small businesses in NA Göring-Stabsamt, T84, Roll 7, frame 6375, Schramm to Goering, 4.11.1938; frames 6371–3, Schramm to Goering, 10.11.1938; frame 6369, Draft of an order on furthering the aims of the VJP, n.d. See too the crisis surrounding the Brenninkmeyer department store in Leipzig: ibid., frames 6163–5, Goering to Gauleiter Mutschmann, 14.4.1938; frames 6176–7, letter from NSDAP Kreisleitung Leipzig to Reich Economics Ministry, 2.2.1938; or the crisis surrounding the appointment of the mayor of Düsseldorf in J. Noakes, 'Oberbürgermeister and Gauleiter. City Government between Party and State' in G. Hirschfeld, L. Kettenacker (eds), *The Führer-State, Myth and Reality*, Stuttgart, 1981, pp. 194–224.

63 Speer Documents, FD 5447/45, Oskar Henschel to General Thomas, 28.8.1940; E. Heinkel, *He 1000*, London, 1956, pp. 161–2, 233.

64 For example Speer Documents, FD 5444/45, WiRüAmt report, 27.1.1942, pp. 1–2; Protocol of the conference of inspectors, 22.2.1941, pp. 64–6; Case XI, Prosecution doc. book 81, NI-966, letter from Bormann to Lammers on Gauleiter Simon. For a wider discussion of this question see Hüttenberger, op. cit., p. 158, 166–7, 183–5; I. Kershaw, *Popular Opinion and Political Dissent in the Third Reich*, Oxford, 1983, pp. 297–312, 314–17.

65 BA-MA, RL 1 speech of the Reich Marshal before the Gauleiter in Munich, 18.11.1943; H. Trevor-Roper (ed.), *The Bormann Letters*, London, 1954, p. 147.

66 Speer Documents, FD 5454c/45, chart of Amt für deutsche Roh – und Werkstoffe, 1.2.1937.

67 Quoted in Irving, op. cit., p. 120.

68 Speer Documents, FD 3742/45, File 1, Reich Economics Ministry to Goering, 15.5.1944.

69 Ibid., FD 5444/45, 'The rationalisation of manpower in the civilian sector', 27.1.1942; report of General Thomas on the military and economic situation, 23.1.1942, pp. 11–13; BA-MA, RL2 9, 'Problems of the German arms industry: report prepared by General Unruh, October 1943–June 1944', pp. 3–4, 10; Speer, 1970, op. cit., pp. 217–20; J. P. Cullity, 'The Growth of Government Employment in Germany, 1882–1950', *Zeitschrift für die gesamte Staatswissenschaft*, vol. 123, 1967, pp. 202–4.

70 E. N. Peterson, 'The Bureaucracy and the Nazi Party', *Review of Politics*, vol. 23, 1966, pp. 176–80; J. Caplan, 'Bureaucracy, Politics and the National Socialist State' in P. Stachura (ed.), *The Shaping of the Nazi State*, London, 1978, pp. 234–5, 250–1; P. Hüttenberger, 'Nationalsozialistische Polykratie', *Geschichte und Gesellschaft*, vol. 2, 1976, pp. 439–42.

71 Milch Documents, vol. 63, 6026, Conference with the Reich Marshal, 28.10.1943.

72 Ibid., 6027–8.

73 A. Bagel-Bohlan, *Hitlers industrielle Kriegsvorbereitung 1936 bis 1939*, Koblenz, 1975, pp. 137–8.

74 Speer Documents, FD 5078/45 Folder 1, file note of discussion between Milch and General Fromm. Fromm argued that technical personnel and skilled labour were now in much greater demand in the army because of motorisation and mechanisation. See too FD 5078/45 Folder 2, letter from Todt to Keitel, 26.4.1940; Speer, 1970, op. cit., pp. 212–13.

75 Wagenführ, op. cit., p. 34.

76 Milch Documents, vol. 63, 6164, minutes of a meeting with the Reich Marshal and GL, 14.10.1943.

77 Ibid., vol. 65, 7409, data for the report to the Reich Marshal, 13.12.1938; vol. 57, 3137–8, notes of a meeting with Goering, 15.2.1937.

78 H. Trevor-Roper (ed.), *Hitler's Table Talk 1941–1944*, London, 1973, p. 633; see too BA-MA, RL2 9, Unruh report, pp. 4, 17–18.

79 Speer Documents, FD 5450/45, OKW memorandum 'on the technical equipment of the armed forces', 19.9.1941, p. 2. See too Milch's report to the Luftwaffe Chief-of-Staff, arguing the same thing; BA-MA, RL3 6, report from Milch to Jeschonnek, 23.1.1942, pp. 2–4.

80 Speer Documents, FD 5450/45, OKW memorandum, pp. 2–4; Milch Documents, vol. 63, 6165–6.

81 Speer Documents, FD 1434/46 no. 167, letter from Todt to Keitel, 24.1.1941. See too Speer, 1976, op. cit., pp. 88–9, 'Industrialists were given

the floor only to speak on special technological problems. No military, let alone political questions were ever discussed in their presence.'

82 BIOS Final Report 537, *Investigation of Production Control and Organisation in German Factories*, p. 7; BA-MA RL3 244, leader of Special Committee F 1 to Air Ministry, 20.9.1943.
83 Speer Documents, FD 3210/45, letter from Admiral Lahs to heads of all air firms, 1.1.1945.
84 Ibid., FD 5450/45, WiRüAmt report, 10.7.1941; Milward, 1965, op. cit., pp. 106–9: Wagenführ, op. cit., pp. 36–7, 49–51.
85 NA T177, Roll 12, frames 3695691–704, General Bauer, 'Basic principles of aeronautical technology', 1939; Roll 14, frames 3698887–916, 'Rationalisation of the production of aircraft equipment', 1.6.1941.
86 Speer Documents, FD 1434/46, no. 167, speech of Minister Speer to the Gau economic advisers, 17.4.1942, pp. 10–12.

CHAPTER 7   THE FAILURE OF THE LUFTWAFFE

1 K. Singer, *Göring: Germany's Most Dangerous Man*, London, 1940, p. 15.
2 R. Suchenwirth, *Command and Leadership in the German Air Force*, New York, 1969, pp. 131–65.
3 P. Deichmann, *German Air Force Operations in Support of the Army*, New York, 1962, pp. 12–42; G. Förster, *Totaler Krieg oder Blitzkrieg*, Berlin, 1967, pp. 155–9; H. Boog, *Die deutsche Luftwaffenführung 1935–1945*, Stuttgart, 1982, pp. 194–204.
4 R. J. Overy, 'From "Uralbomber" to "Amerikabomber": the Luftwaffe and Strategic Bombing', *Journal of Strategic Studies*, vol. 1, 1978, pp. 155–6; Boog, op. cit., pp. 153–7; Christie Papers, 180/1, Notes of a conversation with Goering, n.d. and 28.7.1937.
5 IMT, vol. 9, p. 452, Goering cross-examination.
6 E. Heinkel, *He 1000*, London, 1954, pp. 216–17; BA-MA, RL3 158, Aircraft programme Plan 10, January 1939; Supply programme 11, 1.4.1939; RL3 159, Aircraft-production programme 16, 28.10.1939; RL3 146, Supply plan 20, 'Goering-Plan', 15.9.1941; Milch Documents, vol. 65, 7409–11, notes for a meeting with Goering, 13.12.1938.
7 NA T177, Roll 14, frames 3698585–7, report from Luftwaffe General Staff for the GL, 9.8.1939.
8 IMT, vol. 9, p. 452; Heinkel, op. cit., p. 214.
9 D. Irving, *The Rise and Fall of the Luftwaffe*, London, 1971, pp. 65–7, 75–6.
10 IMT, vol. 9, pp. 45–6, 57, Bodenschatz cross-examination; 57–60, Milch cross-examination; K. H. Völker, *Dokumente und Dokumentarfotos zur Geschichte der deutschen Luftwaffe*, Stuttgart, 1968, pp. 460–66.
11 H. S. Dinerstein, 'The Impact of Air Power on the International Scene, 1930–1939', *Military Affairs*, vol. 19, 1955, pp. 67–8. See too W. Wark, 'British Intelligence on the German Air Force and Aircraft Industry, 1933–1939', *Historical Journal*, vol. 25, 1982.
12 BA-MA, RL3 131, Aircraft production programme no. 5, 1.4.1937.
13 K. Gundelach, 'The German Air Force', *Aerospace Historian*, vol. 18, 1971, p. 88.
14 A. Nielsen, *The German Air Force General Staff*, New York, 1959, pp. 23, 27, 41–3; Boog, op. cit., pp. 38–41; R. Suchenwirth, *Historical Turning Points in the German Air Force War Effort*, New York, 1959, pp. 14–15.
15 Völker, op. cit., p. 156, doc. 59, 'Dienstanweisungen für den Generalluftzeugmeister, 6.2.1939'; p. 164, doc. 62, 'Dienstanweisungen für den Chef des

Generalstabes der Luftwaffe, 1.3.1939'; Milch Documents, vol. 65, 7406, reorganisation of the RLM, 23.1.1939; vol. 62, 5189, conference with the Reich Marshal, 21.3.1942; IMT, vol. 9, pp. 59–60, Milch cross-examination; Boog, op. cit., pp. 41–6.

16 BA-MA, RL1 1, speech of the Reich Marshal before the Gauleiter, 8.11.1943, pp. 1–3.

17 O. Dietrich, *The Hitler I Knew*, London, 1955, pp. 104–5, 245; H. Groscurth, *Tägebücher eines Abwehroffiziers, 1938–1940*, Stuttgart, 1970, p. 416, 'Minutes of the talk by Hitler to the heads of the armed forces, 23.11.1939'. On the July speech see DDP, vol. 8, p. 235, Reichstag speech of the Fuehrer, 19.7.1940.

18 R. J. Overy, *The Air War 1939–1945*, London, 1980, pp. 22–3, 197–8; W. Schellenberg, *The Schellenberg Memoirs*, London, 1956, pp. 125, 216; Boog. op. cit., pp. 91–9, 118–23.

19 H. Trevor-Roper, *Hitler's War Directives*, London, 1964, pp. 74–9, Directive no. 16, 16.7.1940; p. 79, Directive no. 17; K. Klee, *Dokumente zum Unternehmen Seelöwe*, Göttingen, 1959, pp. 305–9, doc. 11 'Memorandum of General Jodl on a landing in England, 12.7.1940'; p. 324, 'Preparation of a Luftwaffe campaign against England, 30.7.1940'; K. A. Maier et al., *Das Deutsche Reich und der Zweite Weltkrieg*, Stuttgart, 1979, vol. 2, pp. 375–83.

20 Luftwaffe Operations Staff Ic, 'Comparative Survey of RAF and Luftwaffe Striking Power, 16.7.1940' in D. Dempster, D. Wood, *The Narrow Margin*, London, 1961, pp. 106–10.

21 BA-MA, Wi I F 5.376 part 1, 'Losses of front-line aircraft 1.8.1940–31.3.1941', 15.4.1941; part 2, 'Losses of front-line aircraft 10.5–30.9.1940', 10.10.1940; OKW review of front-line aircraft numbers, 1939–41.

22 Dempster, Wood, op. cit., p. 115.

23 O. Bechtle, 'German Air Force Operations against Great Britain; address in Berlin, 2.2.1944' reproduced in *RAF Quarterly*, vol. 19, 1947–8, pp. 48–56; see Goering's discussion of the problems of the Blitz in Milch Documents, vol. 63, 5866–9, Goering speech to the Gauleiter, November 1943.

24 Milch Documents, vol. 63, 6085.

25 M. Salewski, *Die deutsche Seekriegsleitung 1939–1945*, Frankfurt a M, 1970, vol. 1., pp. 261–7; E. Raeder, *Struggle for the Sea*, London, 1959, pp. 83–92.

26 A. Lee, *The German Air Force*, London, 1946, pp. 206–8; Boog, op. cit., pp. 204–14; A. Lee, *Goering: Air Leader*, London, 1972, pp. 141–2.

27 R. J. Overy, 'Hitler and Air Strategy', *Journal of Contemporary History*, vol. 15, 1980, pp. 405, 412–13; Deichmann, op. cit., pp. 12–14, 126; Boog, op. cit., pp. 499–504.

28 Speer Documents, FD 5454 d/45, report of discussion with Goering, 19.3.1941; W. Warlimont, *Inside Hitler's Headquarters*, London, 1964, pp. 75, 280; A. Lee, *Goering: Air Leader*, London, 1972, p. 172.

29 H. Plocher, *The German Air Force versus Russia 1941*, New York, 1965, pp. 38–45: Overy, 1980(1), op. cit., pp. 49–55.

30 Ibid., p. 150.

31 Milch Documents, vol. 63, 5900–1, Goering speech before the Gauleiter, 8.11.1943.

32 R. Wagenführ, *Die deutsche Industrie im Kriege*, Berlin, 1963, p. 29.

33 These figures disguise wide differences in the structure weight of aircraft. In 1944 British aircraft had an aggregate weight of 208 m. lbs, German aircraft 199 m. lbs.

34 NA T177, Roll 31, frame 3719681, 'Supply figures for aircraft equipment,

1.4.1938'; frame 3719526, RLM 'Supply from 1.4.1937'; Milch Documents, vol. 65, 7410–11, report for the Field Marshal, 13.12.1938.

35 Völker, 1968, op. cit., p. 211, 'Instruction for planning the expansion of the Luftwaffe, 7.11.1938'; Milch Documents, vol. 56, 2928–9, letter from Siebel to Udet, 7.10.1940.

36 BA-MA, RL3 237, Studie 1036.

37 C. Bewley, *Hermann Göring in the Third Reich*, New York, 1962, p. 306: see too DDP, vol. 6, part 2, pp. 621–2, Speech by Goering on rebuilding the German Luftwaffe, 1.3.1938.

38 Milch Documents, vol. 63, 5901–2, Goering spech before the Gauleiter, 8.11.1943.

39 Ibid., 6316–7, discussion with the Reich Marshal, 9.10.1943.

40 Ibid., vol. 13, 32–3, GL conference, 7.4.1942; 224–5, GL conference, 27.4.1942; vol. 62, 5258, conference with Goering, 8.8.1942.

41 Nielsen, op. cit., pp. 138–45; H. Hermann, *The Rise and Fall of the Luftwaffe*, London, 1944, pp. 66–7, 84–8; E. Homze, *Arming the Luftwaffe*, Nebraska 1976, pp. 100–1.

42 NA T177, Roll 37, frames 3727564–5, letter from Kurt Tank to Kesselring, 13.6.1942; BA-MA, RL3 6, report of a discussion between Goering and Messerschmitt, 9.3.1942; Milch Documents, vol. 13, 16 ff., GL conference, 10.3.1942; H. Conradis, *Design for Flight*, London, 1960, 'The causes of the defeat of the German Luftwaffe 1939–1945, Memorandum of Kurt Tank', pp. 207–8.

43 Nielsen, op. cit., pp. 46–9, 143–7; Boog, op. cit., pp. 41–6, 49–51.

44 USSBS, *The Defeat of the German Air Force*, January 1947, pp. 7–8 on rates of attrition. Fighter losses averaged 20 per cent a month in 1940 and 1941.

45 Gundelach, op. cit., pp. 88–91; A. Galland, *The First and the Last*, London, 1955, pp. 205–6, 217–20. On the crisis over aero-engine reserves see Milch Documents, vol. 44, 6923, 7107, 7047; BA-MA, RL3 7, letter from Jeschonnek to Milch, 23.6.1942; RL3 282, report from the air force supply office, aero-engines for 1943, 14.12.1942.

46 Milch Documents, vol. 44, 6894, protocol of Gl conference, 23.11.1942.

47 CIOS report XXV-45, *German Aircraft Maintenance*, HMSO, 1946; CIOS report XXVII-64, *German Aircraft Maintenance and Overhaul Methods*, HMSO, 1946. On comparative levels of serviceability see Overy, 1980(1), pp. 150–1.

48 B. H. Klein, *Germany's Economic Preparations for War*, Harvard, 1959, pp. 198–9; H. Schliephake, *The Birth of the Luftwaffe*, London, 1971, pp. 57–8; USSBS, *Defeat of the German Air Force*, pp. 3–4, on the decline in training standards; Suchenwirth, 1959, op. cit., pp. 20–8.

49 Hermann, op. cit., pp. 84–94.

50 Overy, 1980(1), op. cit., pp. 155–62.

51 Milch Documents, vol. 56, 5224–5, Organisation of the Technical Office; Völker, 1968, op. cit., p. 142, 'Order of the Reich Air Minister on the organisation of the RLM', 2.6.1937.

52 Ibid., p. 156, 'Regulations for the Generalluftzeugmeister', 6.2.1939; Irving, op. cit., pp. 50–5; K. Macksey, *Kesselring: the Making of the Luftwaffe*, London, 1978, pp. 47–53.

53 Heinkel, op. cit., p. 180.

54 Ibid., p. 185.

55 H. Herlin, *Udet: a Man's Life*, London, 1960, p. 196.

56 NA T177 Roll 19, frames 3704714–5, RLM Vollmacht Messerschmitt, 15.11.1939; BA-MA, RL3 246, Koppenberg to Goering, 19.8.1939; Milch Documents, vol. 57, 3234, letter from Goering to Koppenberg, September 1938.

57 R. J. Overy, 'German Aircraft Production 1939–1942', unpublished Ph.D thesis, Cambridge University, 1977, pp. 117–89 on the German aircraft industry.

58 Heinkel, op. cit., pp. 237–71; Speer Documents, FD 4355/45, vol. 5, letter from Messerschmitt to Udet, 20.3.1941; BA-MA, RL3 6, report of a discussion between Goering and Messerschmitt, 9.3.1942.

59 A. van Ishoven, *Messerschmitt*, London, 1975, pp. 158–9.

60 C. G. Grey, *Luftwaffe*, London, 1944, pp. 101–8, 120–6; Hermann, op. cit., pp. 30–2, 57–8; W. Green, *Warplanes of the Third Reich*, London, 1970, p. 374.

61 NA T177 Roll 12, frames 3695932–5, Report of the conference of the specialist group for construction questions, Dessau, 19.10.1934.

62 Ibid., Roll 14, frames 369888–9, Bauer report 'Rationalisation of aircraft equipment'; BIOS Final Report 537, *Investigation of Production Control and Organisation in German Factories*, HMSO, 1947, pp. 7–8; O. Mooyer, 'Neuzeitliche Berufserziehung in der Luftfahrtindustrie', *Der Vierjahresplan*, vol. 3, 1939, pp. 518–22.

63 CIOS report XXX-94, *Administration, Plastics, Production Tooling, Spare Parts and Servicing in the German Aircraft Industry*, HMSO, 1946. On the Ju 88 see NA T177 Roll 14, frame 3698915.

64 See, for example, Milch Documents, vol. 56, Siebel aircraft company to Udet, 7.10.1940: see too CIOS report XXX-94, pp. 18–19.

65 NA T177 Roll 12, frame 3695911, report from General Bauer, 1935, p. 2.

66 See CIOS report XXX-94; BIOS Final Report, 537, passim.

67 USSBS Report 20, *The Light Metal Industry of Germany*, p. 13.

68 Milch Documents, vol. 62, 5237, conference with the Reich Marshal, 29.6.1942; BA-MA, RL1 18, Industrial Council, 'The adaptation of aircraft construction to the raw material and components position', March 1944; Irving, op. cit., p. 126; Wagenführ, op. cit., p. 76.

69 BIOS Final Report 537, pp. 7–8.

70 NA T177 Roll 32, frames 3720914–941, Statistical Office. 'The Aircraft Industry 1933–1936', February 1938, p. 9.; Mooyer, op. cit., p. 522, 'that [the Meister] must be convinced National Socialists is an obvious requirement'.

71 CIOS Report XXV-42, *Survey of Production Techniques in the German Aircraft Industry* HMSO, 1946, p. 6.

72 BA-MA, RL3 84, RLM report 6.10.1936; NA T177, Roll 3, frame 3684346, letter from RLM to WiRüAmt, 6.9.1939.

73 Irving, op. cit., p. 58; see too M. Biehl, 'Um die Prinzipien des Serienbaus von Kampfflugzeuge in England', *Der Vierjahresplan*, vol. 2, 1938, pp. 471–9.

74 Milch Documents, vol. 63, 6202–3, conference with the Reich Marshal, 14.10.1943.

75 BA-MA, RL3 46 chart 1, 'Investment in fuselage construction', chart 2, 'Investment in aero-engine construction'; RL3 36, 'Construction in the Aircraft Industry 1939–1943', shows the following decline in building work: (1939/40=100)
     1940/1 52   1941/2 54   1942/3 24

76 N. Kaldor, 'The German War Economy', *Manchester School*, vol. 14, 1946, p. 35; Klein, op. cit. pp. 107–8.

77 Milch Documents, vol. 53, 1163, speech by Milch to the Industrial Council, 18.9.1941; see too BA-MA, RL3 33, 'Position of capacity use in the aircraft industry', pp. 2–3.

78 BA-MA, RL3 6, letter from the plenipotentiary for machine-tools to Milch, 16.8.1941: Milch Documents, vol. 53, 1163–4: Speer Documents, FD

5450/45, 'Position in the machine tools sector', 30.6.1941: BA-MA, RL3 33, 'Situation of machine-tools in the aircraft industry', p. 3.

79 Klein, op. cit., p. 109; A. Milward, *The German Economy at War*, London, 1965, pp. 92–3.

80 Speer Documents, FD 4921/45 folder 1, Special committee F2, report of 10.11.1942.

81 Milch Documents, vol. 62, 5288–9, 5315–7, report of the conference between Goering and representatives of the aircraft industry, 13.9.1942; vol. 53, 764–86, Lahs to Milch, 2.11.1942; Speer Documents, FD 3210/45, letter from Lahs to all heads of aircraft firms, 1.1.1945.

82 Ibid., p. 5.

83 Ibid., vol. 5, letter from Messerschmitt to Tschersich (RLM), 13.3.1940, p. 2.

84 BA-MA, RL2 9, report from General Unruh, 'Problems of the German Armaments Industry', pp. 42–3.

85 Van Ishoven, op. cit., pp. 73–86.

86 Overy, thesis, op. cit., pp. 177–88 for a discussion of the attitudes of the aircraft industrialists.

87 Milch Documents, vol. 53, 791–4, minutes of a conference at the RLM on the reorganisation of the Messerschmitt company, 23.4.1942; NA Göring-Stabsamt, T84 Roll 6, frame 5257, Bormann to Goering, 29.10.1942.

88 Heinkel, op. cit., pp. 161–2.

89 Grey, op. cit., p. 142.

90 Ibid., pp. 144–6.

91 Milch Documents, vol. 57, 3212, letter from Goering to Milch, June 1941. Milch's powers were strengthened again in January 1942: vol. 53, 1073, letter from Goering to Milch, 8.1.1942. See too Irving, op. cit., pp. 124–5, 132–2; Herlin, op. cit., pp. 226–44.

92 Milch Documents, vol. 53, 1020, 'New organisation of the offices of the GL'; vol. 56, 2433–4, letter from Bäumker to Milch, 10.1.1942; Irving, op. cit., pp. 143–4; Suchenwirth, op. cit., pp. 103–4.

93 Milch Documents, vol. 63, 6204.

94 Ibid., vol. 57, 3213, letter from Goering to Milch, 20.6.1941; G. Thomas, *Geschichte der deutschen Wehr – und Rüstungswirtschaft 1918–1943/5* (ed. W. Birkenfeld), Boppard am Rhein, 1966, p. 488, RLM conference report 'on the armament programme of the Luftwaffe, 26.6.1941'.

95 BA-MA, RL3 6, letter from Milch to Jeschonnek, 23.1.1942, pp. 3, 6.

96 Speer Documents, FD 4355/54, 'Increased productivity in the manufacture of aircraft equipment', 15.8.1941; Milch Documents, vol. 53, 1150–68, Milch speech to the leaders of production rings, 18.9.1941; BA-MA, RL3 252, 'Preconditions for carrying out the "Goering-Programme" ', 18.10.1941.

97 Milch Documents, vol. 54, 1555, order from Goering founding the Industrial Council, 14.5.1941.

98 CIOS Report XXX-94, p. 21: A. Speer, 'Selbstverantwortung in der Rüstungsindustrie', *Der Vierjahresplan*, vol. 7, 1943, p. 242.

99 Speer Documents, FD 4921/45 folder 1, p. 6. Floorspace was reduced by 18 per cent per unit, material used by 25 per cent.

100 CIOS Evaluation Report 149, *Junkers Aircraft Targets*, p. 7.

101 Speer Documents, FD 4969/45 BMW report 2, 'The despatch of supplies since the beginning of the war', p. 25; FD 3224/45 I, Henschel aero-engine works, 'Increased productivity since the outbreak of war', 28.12.1943.

102 BA-MA, RL3 252, 'Preconditions for carrying out the "Goering-Programme" ', 18.10.1941, p. 204: Milch Documents, vol. 53, 772–3, report

from Lahs to Milch, 2.11.1942. The amount of labour increased by only 120,000 in 1942 from 1,739,000 to 1,859,000.

103   Speer Documents, FD 5665/45, Junkers interrogation reports, (v) General Statistical Data, section 3; FD 5504/45, charts C, D, E; FD 4904/45, 'Development of the Messerschmitt labour force'.

104   Ibid., FD 3224/45 I, Henschel report, 28.12.1943.

105   Milch Documents, vol. 53, 754–63, General of Bombers to Milch, 27.11.1942.

106   L. E. Simon, *German Research in World War Two*, New York, 1947, pp. 93–8; Milch Documents, vol. 56, 2430–40, letter and report from Bäumker to Milch, 10.1.1942, 'Organisation of Research on Air Equipment'.

107   Speer Documents, FD 783/46, Rothe Handakten, 'Development costs of prototypes, 19.10.1943'.

108   Ibid., FD 4335/45, vol. 5, 48–52, letter from Messerschmitt to Udet enclosing report 'Applied research and pure research in wartime', 2.1.1940; Milch Documents, vol. 53, 802–18, report from Lusser (Heinkel) to Milch, 'Memorandum on development and development planning in German air armament', 15.1.1942; letter from Tank to Goering, 7.7.1941, printed in Conradis, op. cit., pp. 141–2; Boog, op. cit., pp. 47–8, 51–9.

109   BA-MA, RL3 6, minutes of a meeting over the Me 210, 12.3.1942; report of a discussion between Goering and Messerschmitt, 9.3.1942; RL3 16, report from Luftwaffe testing command to Goering on He 177, 13.8.1942; report on He 177 from Heinkel to the RLM, 12.9.1942, pp. 1–11.

110   Ibid., RL3 7, letter from Jeschonnek to Milch, 23.6.1942 and 14.7.1942; RL3 6, letter from Milch to Jeschonnek, 23.1.1942.

111   Milch Documents, vol. 63, 6164, minutes of the conference with the Reich Marshal, 23.10.1943. On the problem of excessive modification see BA-MA, RL2 9, Unruh report, pp. 4, 17–18, 42–3; Milch Documents, vol. 13, 16, Hertel report at GL conference, 10.3.1942.

112   Overy, 1980(1), op. cit., p. 150.

113   Milch Documents, vol. 53, 756, General of Bombers to Milch, 27.11.1942; vol. 51, 353–5, Petersen to Milch, 10.9.1942. On Milch's arguments for air defence see vol. 51, 426, letter from Milch to Goering, 23.6.1943.

114   Ibid., vol. 56, 2621–2, General Peltz to Milch, 10.9.1942; vol. 53, 706–10, Head of the Luftwaffeführungsstab, report on air force requirements, 19.5.1944; 1160–1, Milch speech to the Industrial Council, 18.9.1941 for a statement of the strategy.

115   Lee, 1976, p. 172.

116   Milch Documents, vol. 63, 5877: 'In my opinion', said Goering, 'air defence of the Reich is most decisive'; vol. 51, 425, Goering to Milch, 28.7.1943.

117   Ibid., vol. 63, 5963–6, conference with the Reich Marshal, 2.11.1943 in the Messerschmitt works; 6290-308, conference with the Reich Marshal, 9.10.1943.

118   NA T321, Roll 10, frames 4746751–2, letter from the Führungsstab to the Luftwaffe Chief of Staff, 5.5.1944; frames 4745754–64, Führungsstab report 'on the aircraft situation in bomber units': Heinkel, op. cit., pp. 233–5.

119   Suchenwirth, op. cit., pp. 289–90.

120   Heinkel, op. cit., p. 233.

121   Milch Documents, vol. 63, 5862–3; vol. 64, 6594–6627, minutes of the conference with the Reich Marshal, 28.11.1943, for the discussion of Goering's ideas on the bombing campaign.

122   Nielsen, op. cit., p. 174; Milch Documents, vol. 51, 479.

123   Ibid., vol. 63, 6310, conference with the Reich Marshal, 9.10.1943; vol. 53, 732, telegram from Goering to Milch 'on industrial measures for the battle

with England', 12.10.1943; NA T321, Roll 10, frames 4747765–7, Führungs-stab 'Study of the aircraft situation', Appendix 3.

124 Milch Documents, vol. 62, 5208.

125 Ibid., vol. 64, 6595–27, discussion with the Reich Marshal, 28.11.1943; NA T321, Roll 10, frames 4746460–3, Führungsstab, war diary 21.11.1943, 'Brief study: campaign against the Russian armaments industry, 9.11.1943'; on Britain ibid., frames 4746464–6.

126 L. Lochner (ed.), *The Goebbels Diaries*, London, 1948, p. 347, entry for 10.9.1943.

127 NA T321, Roll 10 frames 4746764–5, 'Study of the aircraft situation', Appendix 1.

128 Irving, op. cit., p. 172: W. Green, *Warplanes of the Third Reich*, London, 1970, pp. 345–6.

129 Lochner, op. cit., p. 436.

130 H. Picker, *Hitlers Tischgespräche im Führerhauptquartier*, Stuttgart, 1976, p. 474, entry for 28.7.1942.

131 Milch Documents, vol. 62, 5277–315, report of the conference between Goering and representatives of the air industry, 13.9.1942.

132 Speer, 1971, op. cit., pp. 225–7; D. Irving, *The Virus House*, London, 1967, pp. 266–70.

133 Baumbach, op. cit., p. 84; see too H. Heiber (ed.), *Hitlers Lagebesprechungen*, Stuttgart, 1962, fragment 27, Fuehrer address to divisional commanders, 28.12.1943.

134 Simon, op. cit., pp. 69–81.

135 K.-H. Ludwig, *Technik und Ingenieure im Dritten Reich*, Düsseldorf, 1974, pp. 217–18; Simon, op. cit., pp. 79–80.

136 A. Beyerchen, *Scientists under Hitler*, New Haven, 1977, pp. 123–67; S. Goudsmit, *ALSOS; the Failure in German Science*, London, 1947, pp. 14–56.

137 BA-MA, RL1 20, Bäumker to Richter (RLM), 26.5.1942; Heisenberg to Bäumker, 26.5.1942; Bäumker to Heisenberg, 26.5.1942.

138 C. Ramsauer, 'Zur Geschichte der deutschen Physikalischen Gesellschaft in der Hitlerzeit', *Physikalische Blättter*, vol. 1. 1947; K.-H. Ludwig, *Technik und Ingenieure im Dritten Reich*, Düsseldorf, 1974, pp. 241–5, 157–9; Simon, op. cit., pp. 94–104.

139 BA-MA, RL1 20, Goering decree on the leadership of research, 29.5.1942; Conference of State Secretaries, 5.6.1942.

140 Ibid., letter from Prof. Prandtl to Milch, 26.1.1942 and 18.4.1942; letter from Dr Seewald to Milch, 24.3.1942; letter from Tank to Milch, 1.4.1942; Milch Documents, vol. 56, 2430–45, report from Bäumker to Milch 'Organisation of air force research', 10.1.1942.

141 BA-MA, RL1 20, Seewald to Milch, 24.3.1942; Milch to Seewald, 13.3.1942.

142 Milch Documents, vol. 56, 2561-4, 'Remarks on the organisation of air force technology', 20.5.1944; Simon, op. cit., pp. 106–7.

143 BA-MA, RL1 20, letter from Seewald to Milch, 14.9.1943; BIOS Final Report, 170, pp. 9–10, Seewald interview.

144 A. Price, *Instruments of Darkness*, London, 1967, p. 48.

145 M. Ziegler, *Rocket Fighter*, London, 1961, p. 157.

146 BA-MA, RL1 20, letter from Goering to Milch, 24.7.1942; Speer, 1971, op. cit., p. 225; NA Stabsamt, T84, Roll 8, frames 7976–80, conference on the Reichsforschungsrat, 4.7.1942; Beyerchen, op. cit., pp. 155–6, 189–90.

147 BA-MA, RL1 20, letter from Goering to Milch, 24.7.1942: Simon, op. cit., pp. 79–80.

148 BA-MA, RL1 20, letter from Admiral Witzell to Goering, 9.10.1942, pp. 2–8; Ludwig, op. cit., pp. 241–5; Simon, op. cit., pp. 106–7.

149 Goudsmit, op. cit., pp. 191–3.
150 A. Speer, *The Slave State*, London, 1981, pp. 140–52, 185–200; Goudsmit, op. cit., p. 188.
151 Irving, 1973, op. cit., pp. 265–6.
152 NA T321 Roll 10, frame 4766477, Goering orders, 6.12.1943; frame 46746530, Chefsache, 6.1.1944.
153 Ibid., frame 4746527, 'Imminent danger in the north, 6.1.1944'; frame 4746560, Instructions for combat in the event of an enemy landing in Portugal, 4.2.1944; frame 4746650, Goering orders, 15.3.1944.
154 J. Killen, *The Luftwaffe: a History*, London, 1967, pp. 230–40. By 8 June Luftflotte 3 defending northern France had only 80 operational fighters left.
155 Boelcke, op. cit., p. 396, conference of 6–8.7.1944.
156 A. Verrier, *The Bomber Offensive*, London, 1968, pp. 267–76.
157 On the 'Fighter Staff' see D. Eichholtz, W. Schumann (eds), *Anatomie des Krieges*, Berlin, 1969, pp. 443–4, Order from Speer on 1.3.1944 on the development of a Fighter Staff; Milch Documents, vol. 56, 2701–13, Milch memorandum 'The Fighter Staff', n.d.
158 Ibid., vol. 63, 6113, 6118, conference with the Reich Marshal, 3.10.1943.
159 Ibid., 6113.
160 J. Steinhoff, *The Last Chance. The Pilots' Plot against Göring 1944–1945*, London, 1977, p. 9; H. Guderian, *Panzer Leader*, London, 1952, p. 445.
161 Steinhoff, op. cit., pp. 125–7.
162 Case XI, Prosecution doc. book 120, NOKW-244, Luftwaffe Chief-of-Staff to Milch, 17.11.1943, pp. 1–2.
163 Ibid., p. 5.
164 Boog, op. cit., pp. 527–32.
165 Galland, op. cit., pp. 251–3; Steinhoff, op. cit., pp. 120–32.
166 IWM Library, AD 1 (K) report 348/1945, 'The Collapse viewed from within: the Memoirs of General Koller, the German Chief of Air Staff', pp. 8, 42.
167 H. Trevor-Roper (ed.), *The Goebbels Diaries: the Last Days*, London, 1978, p. 126, entry of 13.3.1945.
168 Koller, memoirs, p. 4.
169 Ibid., p. 8.
170 D. Irving, *Hitler's War*, London, 1977, p. 708.
171 Ibid., pp. 707–8, 727–8; Trevor-Roper, 1978, op. cit., pp. 197–9, 249–51; Galland, op. cit., pp. 235–6.
172 Trevor-Roper, 1978, op. cit., p. 196.
173 Koller to Goering, 'morale in the Luftwaffe', 17.1.1945, reprinted in Steinhoff, op. cit., pp. 115–16.
174 Ibid., pp. 120–32.
175 Speer, 1981, op. cit., pp. 242–4.
176 Trevor-Roper, 1978, op. cit., p. 107.
177 Koller, memoirs, p. 41.

CHAPTER 8   THE DECLINE OF THE GOERING EMPIRE

1 E. Goering, *An der Seite meines Mannes*, Göttingen, 1967, p. 204, who alleges that Hitler refused to see her husband for two weeks before the launch of the attack on Russia, telling him that 'this is my war alone'.
2 BA-MA, Wi I D 82, WiRüAmt, 'File note of meeting with Goering, 7.3.1942'.
3 W. Schellenberg, *The Schellenberg Memoirs*, London, 1956, pp. 125, 216–17.
4 Milch Documents, vol. 63, 6085–6, conference with the Reich Marshal, 28.10.1943.

5 NA Göring-Stabsamt, T84 Roll 8, frames 8013–35, Goering to all Reich authorities, 'adjustment of the war economy to the armaments programme', 17.11.1941; frame 8005, notice on a speech by the Reich Marshal, 20.5.1942.

6 Speer Documents, FD 5450/45, WiRüAmt report, 10.7.1941; B. A. Carroll, *Design for Total War*, The Hague, 1968, pp. 229–30.

7 NA Göring-Stabsamt, T84 Roll 8, frame 8035, Goering to Bouhler, October 1941.

8 A. Speer, *Inside the Third Reich*, London, 1971, p. 183; Carroll, op. cit., p. 229.

9 BA-MA, Wi I F 5.412, discussion between Speer, Keitel and Thomas, 14.3.1942.

10 A. S. Milward, *The German Economy at War*, London, 1965, pp. 64–70.

11 Speer Documents, FD 1434/46 no. 170, 'Reorientation of Armaments', March 1942, pp. 13–16.

12 Ibid., FD 5450/45, WiRüAmt minute, 19.7.1941, on 'Directives of the Fuehrer on 14.7.1941 on the future conduct of the war'; FD 1434/46 no. 170, pp. 4–7.

13 G. Thomas, *Geschichte der deutschen Wehr-und Rüstungswirtschaft, 1918–1943/5* (ed. W. Birkenfeld), Boppard am Rhein, 1966, pp. 478–82, Fuehrer Memorandum 10.1.1942, on 'Armament 1942'; pp. 483–7, Fuehrer decree, 10.1.1942; NA Reichswerke files, T83 Roll 76, 3447503–4, Fuehrer decree, 21.3.1942; Speer Documents, FD 5454a/45, Fuehrer decree, 2.4.1942 'for unity in the war economy to maximise output'; FD 1434/46 no. 170, pp. 15–16; H. Trevor-Roper (ed.), *Hitler's Table Talk 1941–44*, London, 1973, pp. 157–8, talk with Todt and Pleiger, 29.12.1941.

14 Speer, op. cit., p. 196.

15 Speer Documents, FD 5444/45, WiRüAmt report, 27.1.1942; Thomas, op. cit., pp. 470–7, WiRüAmt 'the furthering of armaments', 23.12.1941.

16 Speer Documents, FD 5450/45, Fuehrer order, 11.9.1941; FD 1434/46 no. 170, p. 28. The armed forces published a number of decrees to fit in with Hitler's directives: 'Directives in the area of personnel, 23.10.1941' and 'Technical equipment of the Wehrmacht, 19.9.1941'. See too Thomas, op. cit., p. 288, who records the OKW decree of 10.10.1941 'on the adaptation of the production needs of the Wehrmacht to the productive capabilities of the economy'. IMT, vol. 27, pp. 65–6, 1206-PS, note of the statements of the Reich Marshal in the discussion of 7.11.1941.

17 Speer, op. cit., pp. 191–3.

18 Ibid., pp. 193–5; NA Göring-Stabsamt, T84 Roll 8, frame 8259, Journey plan for 8.2.1942.

19 Speer, op. cit., pp. 195–6.

20 BA-MA, Wi I F 5.412, 'Draft of a Fuehrer order for the establishment of an armaments minister of the Reich', n.d.

21 NA Göring-Stabsamt, T84 Roll 8, Appointments of the Reich Marshal, January 1942; D. Irving, *The Rise and Fall of the Luftwaffe*, London, 1973, p. 145.

22 D. Orlow, *The History of the Nazi Party, 1933–1945*, Newton Abbot, 1973, pp. 379–80; NA Reichswerke files, T83 Roll 74, frames 3445212–3, 'Foundation and Growth of the Hermann Goering Works, 1937–1942', 17.6.1947.

23 Trevor-Roper, op. cit., p. 237, entry for 24.1.1942; Speer, op. cit., p. 202.

24 W. Boelcke (ed.), *Deutschlands Rüstung im Zweiten Weltkrieg, Hitlers Konferenzen mit Albert Speer*, Frankfurt a M, 1969.

25 Speer Documents, FD 5454a/45, Fuehrer decree, 2.4.1942.

26 Speer, op. cit., pp. 132–60: on the significance of architecture in the Third

Reich see J. Dülffer, J. Henke, J. Thies, *Hitlers Städte: Baupolitik im Dritten Reich*, Cologne, 1978, pp. 3–25.
27 Trevor-Roper, op. cit., pp. 227–302. Himmler was a special guest of Hitler's seven times between 20 January and 8 February 1942, though much of their discusion must have centred around the impending conference on the Jewish question at Wannsee.
28 Ibid., pp. 304–5; Speer, op. cit., pp. 196–8.
29 Speer Documents, FD 1434/46 no. 167, speech of Speer to the *Gauleiter*, 20.2.1942, pp. 1–2.
30 P. Hüttenberger, *Die Gauleiter*, Stuttgart, 1969, pp. 166–7; IMT vol. 9, p. 356, Goering cross-examination: 'But at that time [1942] the Fuehrer had already begun to intervene much more strongly and directly in [economic] problems'; Orlow, op. cit., pp. 375–9.
31 A. Speer, 'Selbstverantwortung in der Rüstungsindustrie', *Der Vierjahresplan*, vol. 7, 1943; NA Göring-Stabsamt, T84 Roll 8, frame 8007, 'Decree over the area of responsibility for the self-responsible agencies in the armament economy', 20.4.1942.
32 Speer Documents, FD 1434/46 no. 167, speech to *Gau* economic advisers, 17.4.1942, pp. 22–4.
33 Carroll, op. cit., pp. 235–41.
34 Speer, 1971, op. cit., p. 215; Irving, op. cit., p. 145.
35 Speer, 1971, op. cit., pp. 201–2, 205.
36 Ibid., p. 206.
37 Ibid., pp. 206–7.
38 Ibid., pp. 218–19; Speer Documents, FD 1434/46 no. 167, Speer speech, 17.4.1942, p. 8; IMT, vol. 9, p. 356.
39 NA Göring-Stabsamt, T84 Roll 8, frame 8040, notice for the Reich Marshal for the meeting with the Fuehrer, 3.4.1942.
40 Irving, op. cit., p. 155.
41 NA Göring-Stabsamt, T84 Roll 8, frame 8096, 'Decree on "Central Planning" in the VJP, April 1942'.
42 Ibid., Roll 6, frame 5620.
43 NA Reichswerke files, T83 Roll 75, frames 3446008–17, Pleiger proposal on the structure of the Hermann Goering Works, 9.11.1941; frames 3446018–25, Voss to Goering, 7.11.1941.
44 Control Office for Germany and Austria, *The Hermann Goering Complex*, GED 43/0/34, June 1946, pp. 28–9, 46–7.
45 NA Reichswerke files, T83 Roll 74, frames 3445213–4, 'Foundation and Growth of the Hermann Goering Works, 1937–1942', 17.6.1947.
46 Ibid., Roll 75, frames 3445997–8, letter from Goering to Pleiger, 23.3.1942; frames 3446014–5, Pleiger proposal, 9.11.1941.
47 On reprivatisation see ibid., Roll 77, frames 3449408–11, letter from Roehnert to Waffen-Union, 6.1.1943; Göring-Stabsamt, T84 Roll 8, frame 7699, letter from Goernnert to Gritzbach, 11.7.1942; TWC Transcripts of Case XI, vol. 201, pp. 14843, 14859–62, 14875; Speer Documents, FD 787/46, letter from Roehnert to Goering, 26.2.1943.
48 NA Reichswerke files, T83, Roll 77, frame 3449223, letter from Meindl to Roehnert, 28.10.1942; Speer Documents, FD 787/46, Protocol of the meeting of the managerial board of Steyr-Daimler-Puch, 13.8.1943, pp. 3–4. A major share in Rheinmetall Borsig A.G. was retained by the state-funded Bank der deutschen Luftfahrt: see Control Office for Germany, op. cit., p. 28.
49 NA Reichswerke files, T83 Roll 77, frame 3449216, letter from Roehnert to Simmering-Graz-Pauker A.G., 5.3.1944; frames 3449240–1, letter from

Meindl to Roehnert, 26.9.1942; Speer Documents, FD 787/46, Steyr-Daimler-Puch general meeting, 13.8.1943.

50 NA Reichswerke files, T83 Roll 77, frame 3449231, Simmering-Graz-Pauker A.G. to Roehnert, 28.11.1942; 3449233–4, file note on reprivatisation, 9.10.1942.

51 Milward, op. cit., p. 87.

52 Carroll, op. cit., pp. 237–40.

53 Irving, op. cit., pp. 157–9.

54 NA Göring-Stabsamt, T84 Roll 8, frame 7350, letter from Goering to Sauckel, 26.10.1942; frames 7352–3, letter from Goering to Sauckel and Speer, 27.10.1942: Milch Documents, vol. 63, 6031–3, conference with the Reich Marshal, 28.10.1943, on the allocation of manpower.

55 Carroll, op. cit., p. 237.

56 NA Reichsfinanzmin. T178, Roll 16, frames 3672591–2, letter from von Krosigk to Goering, 1.1.1942; frames 3672677–8, letter from von Krosigk to Goering, 3.2.1942.

57 NA Göring-Stabsamt, T84, Roll 9, frames 8842–4, letter from Lammers to Goering, 14.3.1942, 'on securing the price level 14.3.1942'; Roll 8, frames 8109–10, circular from Goering to all Reich authorities, 22.4.1942.

58 NA Reichsfinanzmin, T178 Roll 16, frame 3672708, letter from von Krosigk to Goering, 4.3.1942.

59 H. Pfahlmann, *Fremdarbeiter und Kriegsgefangene in der deutschen Kriegswirtschaft*, Darmstadt, 1968, pp. 93–5.

60 NA Göring-Stabsamt, T84 Roll 9, frames 8651–2, letter from Goering to Keitel, 31.7.1942; K. Brandt, *Management of Agriculture and Food in the German Occupied and other areas of Fortress Europe*, Stanford, 1953, pp. 195–7, 202–8, 227–32.

61 NA Göring-Stabsamt, T84 Roll 8, frame 7337, Bohle (Auslands-Organisation) to Goering, 12.9.1942; frames 7888–91, notice on the meeting of the *Gauleiter*, 5.8.1942; frame 7893, Evaluation of the discussions with the *Gauleiter* and the Military commanders of the occupied areas, 14.8.1942.

62 Ibid., Roll 8, frames 7912–7, Results of a meeting with the leaders of German offices in the occupied countries, 6.8.1942.

63 Ibid., Roll 6, frames 6035–6, results of a conference with General Keitel, Minister Backe and Marshal Goering, 26.8.1942.

64 Trevor-Roper, op. cit., pp. 528–32, conversation of 23.6.1942; for the general background see USSBS Special Paper 4, *Food and Agriculture*, pp. 105–6, Exhibits D, E; Brandt, op. cit., pp. 145–8, 610–14.

65 IMT, vol. 9, 397–8, Goering cross-examination.

66 Speer, 1971, op. cit., pp. 222–5; Speer Documents, FD 5450/45, file note of a discussion in the Reich Transport Ministry, 17.9.1941, pp. 2–3; letter from Transport Minister to Goering, 27.8.1941.

67 D. Petzina, *Autarkiepolitik im Dritten Reich*, Stuttgart, 1968, p. 182: W. Meier-Dörnberg, *Ölversorgung der Kriegsmarine 1935 bis 1945*, Freiburg i B, 1973, pp. 68–81: M. Pearton, *Oil and the Roumanian State*, Oxford, 1971, pp. 256–9.

68 NA Göring-Stabsamt, T84 Roll 6, frames 5607–11, report of the Oil conference, 10.7.1942; frame 5433–6, letter from Goernnert to Gritzbach, 9.11.1942.

69 Ibid., frame 5617, report of the oil conference. The Russians were reported to have 3–4,000 oil engineers, Germany only 850.

70 Ibid., frame 5615.

71 Ibid., frames 5661–97, report over the oil conference at Goering's Headquarters, 21.11.1942.

72 Ibid., frames 5670–7.

73 Ibid., frame 5472, letter from Goernnert to Bodenschatz on synthetic oil, 27.9.1942. On the general background see W. Birkenfeld, *Der synthetische Treibstoff*, Göttingen, 1963, pp. 165–76.

74 NA Göring-Stabsamt, T84 Roll 6, frame 5967, notices for the Fuehrer, n.d; Irving, op. cit., p. 153.

75 Milch Documents, vol. 65, 5315–8, report of the conference between Goering and representatives of the aircraft industry, 13.9.1942; 5258, conference notes, 18.8.1942.

76 NA Göring-Stabsamt, T84 Roll 6, frame 5686, report of the oil conference, 21.11.1942.

77 Ibid., Roll 8, frame 8320–1, letter from Goering to Bormann, 24.5.1942: 'I have spoken briefly to the Fuehrer that no Fuehrer-decision can be taken which involves my jurisdiction without my agreement and knowledge'; frame 8100, letter from Goering to Ribbentrop, 28.3.1942.

78 C. Bekker, *The Luftwaffe War Diaries*, London, 1966, pp. 355–69; J. Fischer, 'Über den Entschluss zur Luftversorgung Stalingrads. Ein Beitrag zur militärischen Führung im Dritten Reich', *Militärgeschichtliche Mitteilungen*, vol. 6, 1969.

79 NA Göring-Stabsamt, T84, Roll 6, frame 5635, oil conference, 10.7.1942.

80 Irving, op. cit., pp. 183–96.

81 W. Görlitz, 'The Battle for Stalingrad', in H.-A. Jacobsen, J. Rohwer, *Decisive Battles of World War Two*, London, 1965, pp. 242–51.

82 Irving, op. cit., p. 197.

83 See the opinion of the prison doctor at Nuremberg. D. Kelley, *22 Cells in Nuremberg*, London, 1947, pp. 47–8.

84 A. Nielsen, *The German Air Force General Staff*, New York, 1959, pp. 146–7.

85 L. Lochner (ed.), *The Goebbels Diaries*, London, 1948, p. 309, entry for 22.5.1943, p. 377, entry for 27.7.1943. See too W. Boelcke (ed.), *The Secret Conferences of Dr. Goebbels October 1939–March 1943*, London, 1971, p. 262, entry for 20.7.1942.

86 NA Göring-Stabsamt, T84 Roll 6, frame 5480, Gritzbach to Goernnert, 31.8.1942.

87 Trevor-Roper, op. cit., pp. 596–598: 'those of the Party who still have any connection with business must now make their final decision: either they must abandon all such connections, or they must resign from their official positions.'

88 TWC vol. 12, 893, NI-5261, letter from Koerner to Pleiger, 31.3.1943.

89 H. Höhne, *Codeword: Direktor*, London, 1971, pp. 98–100.

90 Ibid., pp. 188–215; G. Perrault, *The Red Orchestra*, London, 1967, pp. 199–218.

91 Höhne, op. cit., pp. 160–86.

92 Lochner, op. cit., pp. 197–203, entry for 2.3.1943, pp. 235–7, entry for 18.3.1943; Speer, 1971, op. cit., pp. 259–61; Orlow, op. cit., pp. 418–19.

93 Speer, 1971, op. cit., pp. 263–5; Lochner, op. cit., pp. 214–15, 221–2.

94 Speer, 1971, op. cit., pp. 264–5. Although Speer thought Goebbels's absence deliberate, he had in fact fallen ill with a kidney infection: Lochner, op. cit., pp. 252–3. Himmler said to Speer a few months later that 'it would be very unwise to try to motivate the Reich Marshal again': Orlow, op. cit., pp. 419–20.

95 Speer, 1971, op. cit., p. 265; U. von Hassell, *The von Hassell Diaries 1938–1944*, London, 1948, pp. 213–14, 235–6; Lochner, op. cit., pp. 198–9; J. van Lang, *The Secretary: Martin Bormann*, New York, 1979, pp. 162, 203–4.

96 Speer, 1971, op. cit., p. 265.

97 Lochner, op. cit., p. 262, entry for 20.4.1943.

98 Irving, op. cit., pp. 202–3, 213–14.

99 E. Georg, *Die wirtschaftliche Unternehmungen der SS*, Stuttgart, 1963, pp. 9–11, 119–41: A. Speer, *The Slave State*, London, 1981, pp. 14–25, 60–74.

100 Ibid., pp. 74–5; Speer, 1971, op. cit., pp. 372–3.

101 M. Riedel, *Eisen und Kohle für das Dritte Reich*, Göttingen, 1973, pp. 276–80; BA-MA, Wi I F 5.412, correspondence between Goering, Bormann and Minister Schmitt, March 1941.

102 A. van Ishoven, *Messerschmitt*, London, 1975, pp. 158–64.

103 Speer, 1971, op. cit., p. 266.

104 Including, among others, Jeschonnek, Milch, von Greim, Himmler, Goebbels, Bormann, Guderian.

105 Milch Documents, vol. 63, 6119–20, minutes of a conference with the Reich Marshal, 23.10.1943.

106 Milch Documents, vol. 56, 2648–55, minutes of a meeting on production in occupied Europe and Italy, 12.11.1942; 2658–61, letter from GL dept C to Milch, 22.10.1942; 2667, Planning Office to Milch, 17.11.1942.

107 Case XI, Prosecution doc. book 120, NOKW-260, Goering decree, 4.9.1943; 1510-PS, Speer decree, 29.10.1943.

108 Ibid., NID-14601, Goering decree, 2.10.1943.

109 Milch Documents, vol. 63, 6087, conference with the Reich Marshal, 28.10.1943; 6216–7, conference notice, 14.10.1943.

110 Ibid., 6118–9.

111 D. Irving, *Hitler's War*, London, 1977, p. 574: 'the devastation actually works in our favour, because it is creating a body of people with nothing to lose – people who will therefore fight on with utter fanaticism.'

112 Milch Documents, vol. 63, 6084–5, conference with the Reich Marshal, 28.10.1943.

113 Speer, 1981, op. cit., p. 217; Hüttenberger, op. cit., pp. 184–5.

114 Speer, 1981, op. cit., p. 218.

115 Milch Documents, vol. 63, 5934–5, report of a meeting at Junkers Aircraft Works, 4.11.1943; 6195–202, conference of the Reich Marshal with the Industrial Council, 14.10.1943; vol. 64, 6402, conference with the Reich Marshal, 1.5.1944. On the telephone conversation see 6520, minutes of the GL conference with Goering, 8.1.1944.

116 Ibid., 6510–11, points from the discussion with Goering, 4.3.1944; vol. 63, 6200–3, 6213; vol. 51, 416–7, letter from Goering to Milch, 21.11.1943; Speer, 1981, op. cit., pp. 231–4.

117 Ibid., pp. 233–4, 236–7; Speer, 1971, op. cit., pp. 334–42.

118 Speer, 1981, op. cit., pp. 224–8; Milch Documents, vol. 64, 6403–5, conference with the Reich Marshal, 1.5.1944; 6453–62, conference with the Reich Marshal, 19.4.1944; 6505, points from the discussion with the Fuehrer, 5.3.1944.

119 Irving, 1973, op. cit., pp. 285–6; Speer, 1981, op. cit., chs 5, 6, 8.

120 H. Trevor-Roper (ed.), *The Bormann Letters*, London, 1954, pp. 145–6, letter from Martin to Gerda Bormann, 31.10.1944; pp. 146–7, letter from Martin to Gerda Bormann, 4.11.1944; van Lang, op. cit., p. 316.

121 Orlow, op. cit., pp. 467–8; Speer, 1981, op. cit., pp. 127–8, 133–4, 202–16; E. Georg, *Die wirtschaftliche Unternehmungen der SS*, Stuttgart, 1963, pp. 101–6, 124–44.

122 Speer, 1981, op. cit., pp. 240–4.

123 Milch Documents, vol. 64, 6325–47, conference with the Reich Marshal, 29.5.1944 over the Me 262; Boelcke, 1969, op. cit., pp. 388–9, 396–7, conferences of 19–22.6.1944, 6–8.7.1944.

124 H. Heiber (ed.), *Hitlers Lagebesprechungen*, Stuttgart, 1962, pp. 781–8, 793–883, 896–906, 915–21.

125 A. Lee, *Goering: Air Leader*, London, 1976, p. 196.
126 G. Gilbert, *Nuremberg Diary*, London, 1947, p. 118.
127 Ibid., p. 62, 94, 97–8, 212–19; Kelley, op. cit., pp. 61–2; A. Speer, *Spandau: the Secret Diaries*, London, 1976, pp. 73–4.
128 Gilbert, op. cit., pp. 240, 264.
129 Ibid., p. 42; see too IMT, vol. 9, 450–2; Kelley, op. cit., pp. 53, 58–9.
130 Ibid., p. 130; Speer, 1976, op. cit., p. 73; 'Goering wanted to use the Nuremberg trial as the first step in creating a legendary image of the Hitler era': M. Biddiss, 'The Nuremberg Trial: Two Exercises in Judgement', *Journal of Contemporary History*, vol. 16, 1981, pp. 602–3.
131 Gilbert, op. cit., pp. 48–9, 110, 124, 127. Goering said he would 'strangle [Bormann] with his bare hands'. Speer, 1976, op. cit., p. 9, who wrote 'Goering took all the responsibility, only to employ all his cunning and his energy to deny that he bore specific guilt.'
132 Gilbert, op. cit., pp. 65, 95–6, 207.
133 Ibid., p. 128.
134 Ibid., p. 112; Speer, 1976, op. cit., p. 74.
135 Gilbert, op. cit., p. 270.
136 Ibid., p. 275.

CHAPTER 9   GOERING AND THE POLITICS OF THE THIRD REICH

1 BA-MA, RL1 5, letter from Goering to Hitler, n.d.; letter from Goering to Jodl, 23.4.1945; telegram from Hitler to Goering, 23.4.1945.
2 E. Goering, *My Life with Goering*, London, 1967, pp. 120–9.
3 K. D. Bracher, *The German Dictatorship*, London, 1973, p. 350.
4 R. Diels, *Lucifer ante Portas*, Stuttgart, 1950.
5 H. Trevor-Roper, *Hitler's Table Talk 1941–1944*, London, 1973, p. 206.
6 A. Zoller, *Hitler privat*, Düsseldorf, 1949, p. 208.
7 F. Gilbert, *Hitler Directs his War*, New York, 1950, p. 44, conference of 25.7.1943.
8 A. Speer, *Spandau: the Secret Diaries*, London, 1976, p. 129. He recalls Hitler's remarks to him that in the new Nazi empire 'The German agencies and authorities are to have wonderful buildings, the governors palaces'; A. Speer, *The Slave State*, London, 1981, p. 297.
9 E. Butler, G. Young, *Marshal without Glory*, London, 1951, pp. 168–9.
10 L. Lochner, *The Goebbels Diaries*, London, 1947, p. 247.
11 W. Schellenberg, *The Schellenberg Memoirs*, London, 1956, p. 300.
12 D. Kelley, *22 Cells in Nuremberg*, London, 1947, pp. 49–50.
13 B. Fromm, *Blood and Banquets: a Berlin Social Diary*, London, 1943, pp. 82, 207.
14 M. Muggeridge (ed.), *Ciano's Diary 1939–1943*, London, 1947, p. 430.
15 W. Dornberger, *V2*, London, 1954, p. 239.
16 E. Heinkel, *He 1000*, London, 1956, p. 235.
17 Muggeridge, op. cit., pp. 91, 205.
18 Ibid., pp. 238, 253–4.
19 C. Schneider, *Stadtgründung im Dritten Reich: Wolfsburg und Salzgitter*, Munich, 1979, pp. 86–8.
20 H. Guderian, *Panzer Leader*, London, 1952, p. 445.
21 A. Speer, *Inside the Third Reich*, London, 1971, p. 427.
22 O. Dietrich, *The Hitler I Knew*, London, 1955, pp. 145, 203; N. von Below, *Als Hitlers Adjutant 1937–1945*, Mainz, 1980, pp. 238–9.
23 Ibid., pp. 60, 76.

24 IMT, vol. 9, p. 441, Goering cross-examination: 'The chief influence on the Fuehrer, at least up till the end of 1941 or the beginning of 1942, if one can speak of influence at all, was exerted by me ... all in all, I do not believe any one had more influence on the Fuehrer than I had.'

25 Kelley, op. cit., p. 46, 'I wanted to help destroy the Republic and to be, perhaps, the ruler of the new Reich'. According to W. Dodd, *Ambassador Dodd's Diary 1933–1938*, London, 1941, p. 317, Goering told the French ambassador in 1936 that in the event of Hitler's death or retirement he was to succeed the Fuehrer as ruler of Germany.

26 H. Höhne, *Canaris*, London, 1979, p. 372; Schellenberg. op. cit., p. 300.

27 Ibid., pp. 216–17. Goering handed back the report with the remark, 'Everything you have written is utter nonsense. You should have a psychiatrist examine your mental condition.'

28 A. Galland, *The First and the Last*, London, 1955, pp. 158, 189; D. Irving, *Hitler's War*, London, 1977, p. 703.

29 There is an interesting discussion of Goering's popularity in H. B. Gisevius, *To the Bitter End*, London, 1948, pp. 307–10.

30 D. Kahn, *Hitler's Spies*, London, 1978, pp. 181–2; U. von Hassell, *The von Hassell Diaries 1938–1944*, London, 1948, records a large number of the political jokes of the period, the bulk of them about Goering; Dietrich, op. cit., p. 240.

31 Phipps Papers, I 1/12, telegram from Phipps to Simon, 21.3.1934.

32 N. Bethell, *The War Hitler Won*, London, 1972, pp. 287–9; S. Friedländer, *Prelude to Downfall: Hitler and the United States 1939–1941, London, 1967, pp. 37–41.*

33 L. Graf Schwerin von Krosigk, *Memoiren*, Stuttgart, 1977, pp. 158–9, 168–9.

34 K. Abshagen, *Canaris*, London, 1956, p. 113; von Hassell, op. cit., pp. 74–5, 81–2, 97; O. John, *Twice through the Lines*, London, 1972, pp. 57–8.

35 Von Hassell, op. cit., pp. 83, 88; on 'Kerensky solution' see H. Deutsch, *The Conspiracy against Hitler in the Twilight War*, London, 1968, p. 295. Though he worked closely with the military conspirators, Dohnanyi was a judge not a soldier.

36 DGFP, vol. 6, p. 251, unsigned memorandum of conversation between Goering and the Duce, 15.4.1939.

BIBLIOGRAPHY AND SOURCES

A UNPUBLISHED SOURCES

1 *Bundesarchiv-Militärarchiv, Freiburg im Breisgau*
   RL 1 Reichsminister der Luftfahrt
   RL 2 Generalstab der Luftwaffe
   RL3 1 – 16 Generalluftzeugmeister Handakten
   RL 3 – RL 37 Reichsluftfahrtministerium
   Wehrwirtschaft-und Rüstungsamt Wi I F 5.114–5.3352
   Göring-Akten, Wi I F 5.203

2 *Churchill College Archives, Cambridge*
   Christie Papers
   Phipps Papers

3 *Foreign and Commonwealth Office Library, London*
   Nuremberg Trials, Case XI, 'The Ministries Case', background documents

4 *Imperial War Museum, London*
   Milch Documents, volumes 1–65
      (The originals of these documents are now to be found in the Bundesarchiv.
      I was able to consult them before they were restituted to Germany in the
      early 1970s and have kept the original references used by the Museum.)
   Speer Documents
      Wehrwirtschafts-und Rüstungsamt documents
      Zentrale Planung
      Rothe Handakten, Roehnert Handakten (Junkers)
      Vierjahresplan
   Nuremberg Trials, Case X, background Documents
   United States Strategic Bombing Survey Reports
   Private Firms
      AGO Flugzeugwerke
      ATG Maschinenfabrik
      Arado Flugzeugwerke
      Bayerische Flugzeugwerke
      Bayerische Motorenwerke
      Brandenburgische Motorenwerke
      Daimler-Benz
      Deutsche Lufthansa
      Gerhard Fieseler Werke

Flugmotorenwerke Ostmark
Focke-Wulf Flugzeugbau
Gothaer Waggonfabrik
Ernst Heinkel A.G.
Henschel Flugmotorenbau
I. G. Farben
Junkers Flugzeug-und Motorenwerke
Luftfahrtbedarf A.G.
Luther Werke
Messerschmitt A.G.
Mitteldeutsche Metallwerke
Mitteldeutsche Motorenwerke
Reichswerke 'Hermann Goering' A.G.
Rheinmetall Borsig A.G.
Schaefer Propellor
Steyr-Daimler-Puch
Vereinigte Aluminiumwerke
Wiener-Neustadt Flugzeugwerke

5 *National Archives, Washington D.C., microfilmed documents*
Göring-Stabsamt, T84 Rolls 6–9
Reichsluftfahrtministerium T177 Rolls, 3,12,14,17,19,23,31–2,42,48
OKL Luftwaffenführungsstab T321, Roll 10
Kurt Tank correspondence T83, Roll 5
Focke Wulf papers, T177 Roll 37
Reichswerke files, T83 Rolls 74–81
Reichsfinanzministerium, von Krosigk – Goering correspondence, T178, Rolls
    15–16
Reichswirtschaftsministerium T71, Roll 2

6 *Salzgitter A.G., Konzernarchiv, Salzgitter*
Reichswerke files
Pleiger Akten

7 *University Library, Cambridge*
Combined Intelligence Objectives Sub-Committee Reports
British Intelligence Objectives Sub-Committee Reports

B PUBLISHED SOURCES

W. Baumgart, 'Zur Ansprache Hitlers vor den Führern der Wehrmacht am 22
    August 1939', *Vierteljahreshefte für Zeitgeschichte*, vol. 16, 1968.
N. Baynes (ed.), *Hitler's Speeches*, 2 vols, Oxford, 1942.
W. Boelcke (ed.), *Deutschlands Rüstung im Zweiten Weltkrieg: Hitlers Konferenzen mit
    Albert Speer*, Frankfurt a M, 1969.
W. Boelcke (ed.), *The Secret Conferences of Dr Goebbels*, London, 1970.
Documents on British Foreign Policy, HMSO: 2nd series, vols 1–19, 1946–82; 3rd
    series, vols 1–9, 1949–55.
Documents on German Foreign Policy, 1918–1945, HMSO: Series C, vols 1–6,
    1957–83; Series D, vols 1–13, 1949–64.
Dokumente der deutschen Politik, 8 vols, Berlin, 1935–42.
D. Eichholtz, W. Schumann (eds), *Anatomie des Krieges*, Berlin, 1969.

T. R. Emessen (ed.), *Aus Görings Schreibtisch: ein Dokumentenfund*, Berlin, 1947.
F. Gilbert (ed.), *Hitler Directs his War*, New York, 1950.
E. Gritzbach (ed.), *Herman Goering: Reden und Aufsätze*, Munich, 1938.
F. Halder, *Kriegestagebuch*, 3 vols, Stuttgart, 1962–4.
H. Heiber (ed.), *Hitlers Lagebesprechungen*, Stuttgart, 1962.
L. E. Hill (ed.), *Die Weizsäcker-Papiere, 1933–1950*, Frankfurt a M, 1974.
K. Klee (ed.), *Dokumente zum Unternehmen Seelöwe*, Göttingen, 1959.
T. Mason (ed.), *Arbeiterklasse und Volksgemeinschaft*, Opladen, 1976.
M. Muggeridge (ed.), *Ciano's Diplomatic Papers*, London, 1948.
Nuremberg Trials, International Military Tribunal, *Nazi Conspiracy and Aggression*, 8 vols, Washington, 1947.
Nuremberg Trials, International Military Tribunal *The Trial of the Major War Criminals*, Nuremberg, 1947, 23 volumes of transcripts, 17 volumes of documents.
Nuremberg Trials, International Military Tribunal, *Trials of the War Criminals*, 12 vols, Nuremberg, 1949.
H. Picker (ed.), *Hitlers Tischgespräche im Führerhauptquartier*, Stuttgart, 1976.
A. von Ribbentrop (ed.), *Deutsch-englische Geheimverbindungen*, Wuppertal, 1967.
W. Treue, 'Der Denkschrift Hitlers über die Aufgaben eines Vierjahresplans', *Vierteljahreshefte für Zeitgeschichte*, vol. 3, 1954.
H. Trevor-Roper (ed.), *Hitler's Table Talk 1941–1944*, London, 1953.
H. Trevor-Roper (ed.), *The Bormann Letters*, London, 1954.
H. Trevor-Roper (ed.), *Hitler's War Directives*, London, 1964.
K. H. Völker (ed.), *Dokumente und Dokumentarfotos zur Geschichte der deutschen Luftwaffe*, Stuttgart, 1968.
Das Archiv
Der deutsche Volkswirt
Der Vierjahresplan
Nationalsozialistische Monatshefte
Wirtschaft und Statistik

C DIARIES AND MEMOIRS

W. Allen (ed.), *The Infancy of Nazism: the Memoirs of Ex-Gauleiter Albert Krebs 1923–1933*, London, 1976.
W. Baumbach, *Broken Swastika*, London, 1960.
N. von Below, *Als Hitlers Adjutant, 1937–1945*, Mainz, 1980.
O. Braun, *Von Weimar zu Hitler*, New York, 1940.
C. Burkhardt, *Meine Danziger Mission 1937–1939*, Munich, 1960.
B. Dahlerus, *The Last Attempt*, London, 1948.
R. Diels, *Lucifer ante Portas*, Stuttgart, 1950.
O. Dietrich, *The Hitler I Knew*, London, 1955.
W. Dodd, *Ambassador Dodd's Diary, 1933–1938*, London, 1941.
W. Dornberger, *V2*, London, 1954.
A. François-Poncet, *The Fateful Years*, London, 1949.
A. Fredborg, *Behind the Steel Wall: Berlin 1941–43*, London, 1944.
B. Fromm, *Blood and Banquets: a Berlin Social Diary*, London, 1943.
A. Galland *The First and the Last*, London, 1955.
G. M. Gilbert, *Nuremberg Diary*, London, 1948.
E. Goering, *An der Seite meines Mannes*, Göttingen, 1967.
E. Goering, *My Life with Goering*, London, 1967.
H. Groscurth, *Tagebücher eines Abwehroffiziers, 1938–1940* (eds H. Krausnick, H. Deutsch), Stuttgart, 1970.
H. Guderian, *Panzer Leader*, London, 1952.

U. von Hassell, *The von Hassell Diaries, 1938–1944*, London, 1948.
S. Hedin, *German Diary*, Dublin, 1951.
E. Heinkel, *He 1000*, London, 1956.
N. Henderson, *Failure of a Mission*, London, 1940.
F. Hesse, *Das Vorspiel zum Kriege*, Druffel Verlag, 1979.
F. Hosssbach, *Zwischen Wehrmacht und Hitler 1934–1938*, Göttingen, 1965.
O. John, *Twice Through the Lines*, London, 1972.
H. Kehrl, *Krisenmanager im Dritten Reich*, Düsseldorf, 1973.
W. Keitel, *The Memoirs of Field Marshal Keitel*, London, 1965.
D. M. Kelley, *22 Cells in Nuremberg*, London, 1947.
A. Kesselring, *Memoirs*, London, 1955.
E. Kordt, *Wahn und Wirklichkeit*, Stuttgart, 1948.
J. Lipski, *Diplomat in Berlin, 1933–1939*, New York, 1968.
L. Lochner (ed.), *The Goebbels Diaries*, London, 1948.
K. Ludecke, *I Knew Hitler*, London, 1938.
E. von Manstein, *Lost Victories*, London, 1958.
O. Meissner, *Staatssekretär unter Ebert-Hindenburg-Hitler*, Hamburg, 1950.
M. Muggeridge (ed.), *Ciano's Diary 1938–1943*, London, 1947.
F. von Papen, *Memoirs*, London, 1952.
E. Raeder, *Mein Leben*, 2 vols, Tübingen, 1956–7.
E. Raeder, *Struggle for the Sea*, London, 1959.
J. von Ribbentrop, *The Ribbentrop Memoirs*, London, 1954.
H. Schacht, *Account Settled*, London, 1953.
H. Schacht, *76 Jahre meines Lebens*, Bad Wörishofen, 1953.
W. Schellenberg, *The Schellenberg Memoirs*, London, 1956.
P. Schmidt, *Hitler's Interpreter*, London, 1951.
L. Schwerin von Krosigk, *Memoiren*, Stuttgart, 1977.
A. Speer, *Inside the Third Reich*, London, 1970.
A. Speer, *Spandau; the Secret Diaries*, London, 1976.
O. Strasser, *Hitler and I*, London, 1940.
F. Taylor (ed.), *The Goebbels Diaries, 1939–1941*, London, 1982.
F. Thyssen, *I Paid Hitler*, London, 1941.
G. R. Treviranus, *Das Ende von Weimer*, Düsseldorf, 1968.
H. Trevor-Roper (ed.), *The Goebbels Diaries: the Last Days*, London, 1978.
W. Warlimont, *Inside Hitler's Headquarters*, London, 1964.
E. von Weizsäcker, *Memoirs*, London, 1951.
F. Winterbotham, *The Nazi Connection*, London, 1978.
A. Zoller, *Hitler privat. Erlebnisbericht seiner Geheimsekretärin*, Düsseldorf, 1949.

D   SECONDARY SOURCES: BOOKS

D. Abraham, *The Collapse of the Weimar Republic*, Princeton, 1981.
K. Abshagen, *Canaris*, London, 1956.
L. Addington, *The Blitzkrieg Era and the German General Staff, 1865–1941*, Rutgers, 1971.
S. Aronson, *Reinhard Heydrich und die Frühgeschichte von Gestapo und SD*, Stuttgart, 1971.
A. Bagel-Bohlan, *Hitlers industrielle Kriegsvorbereitung 1936 bis 1939*, Koblenz, 1975.
A. Barkai, *Das Wirtschaftssystem des Nationalsozialismus*, Cologne, 1977.
H. Bauer, *Hitler's Pilot*, London, 1958.
C. Bekker, *The Luftwaffe War Diaries*, London, 1966.
E. W. Bennett, *German Rearmament and the West 1932–33*, Princeton, 1979.
V. Berghahn (ed.), *Germany in the Age of Total War*, London, 1981.

W. Bernhardt, *Die deutsche Aufrüstung 1934–1939*, Frankfurt a M, 1969.
N. Bethell, *The War Hitler Won*, London, 1972.
C. Bewley, *Hermann Göring*, Göttingen, 1956.
A. Beyerchen, *Scientists under Hitler*, New Haven, 1977.
W. Birkenfeld, *Der synthetische Treibstoff 1933–1945*, Göttingen, 1963.
H. Blood-Ryan, *Göring: the Iron Man of Germany*, London, 1938.
H. Boog, *Die deutsche Luftwaffenführung 1935–1945*, Stuttgart, 1982.
J. Borkin, *The Crime and Punishment of I. G.`Farben*, London, 1979.
R. Bowen, *German Theories of the Corporate State*, New York, 1947.
K. D. Bracher, *The German Dictatorship*, London, 1973.
K. D. Bracher, W. Sauer, G. Schultz, *Die nationalsozialistische Machtergreifung*, Cologne, 1960.
R. Brady, *Business as a System of Power*, New York, 1943.
K. Brandt, *Management of Agriculture and Food in the German Occupied and Other Areas of Fortress Europe*, Stanford, 1953.
A. Brissaud, *The Nazi Secret Service*, London, 1974.
M. Broszat, *Der Staat Hitlers*, Munich, 1969.
G. Bry, *Wages in Germany*, Princeton, 1960.
A. Bullock, *Hitler: a Study in Tyranny*, London, 1962.
E. Butler, G. Young, *Marshal without Glory: the Life and Death of Hermann Goering*, London, 1951.
W. Carr, *Arms, Autarky and Aggression*, London, 1972.
W. Carr, *Hitler: a Study in Personality and Politics*, London, 1978.
B. A. Carrol, *Design for Total War: Arms and Economics in the Third Reich*, The Hague, 1968.
A. Cienciala, *Poland and the Western Powers*, London, 1968.
H. Conradis, *Design for Flight: the Kurt Tank Story*, London, 1960.
G. A. Craig, *The Politics of the Prussian Army*, Oxford, 1955.
E. Crankshaw, *Gestapo, Instrument of Tyranny*, London, 1956.
A. Dallin, *German Rule in Russia*, London, 2nd edn, 1981.
P. Deichmann, *German Air Force Operations in Support of the Army*, New York, 1962.
W. Deist, *The Wehrmacht and German Rearmament*, London, 1982.
W. Deist, M. Messerschmidt, H.-E. Volkman, W. Wette, *Ursachen und Voraussetzungen der deutschen Kriegspolitik*, Stuttgart, 1979.
J. Delarue, *The History of the Gestapo*, London, 1964.
D. Dempster, D. Wood, *The Narrow Margin: The Battle of Britain and the Rise of Air Power*, London, 1961.
H. Deutsch, *The Conspiracy against Hitler in the Twilight War*, London, 1968.
H. Deutsch, *Hitler and his Generals: the Hidden Crisis January – June 1938*, Minnesota, 1974.
A. Dorpalen, *Hindenburg and the Weimar Republic*, Princeton, 1964.
J. Dülffer, *Weimar, Hitler und die Marine*, Düsseldorf, 1973.
J. Dülffer, J. Henke, J. Thies, *Hitlers Städte: Baupolitik im Dritten Reich*, Cologne, 1978.
O. Dutch, *Hitler's Twelve Apostles*, London, 1939.
D. Eichholtz, *Geschichte der deutschen Kriegswirtschaft 1939–1945*, vol. 1, Berlin, 1969.
R. Eicke, *Warum Aussenhandel? Eine Lebensfrage für das deutsche Volk*, Berlin, 1938.
G. Eley, *Reshaping the German Right: Radical Nationalism and Political Change after Bismarck*, New Haven, 1978.
R. Erbe, *Die nationalsozialistische Wirtschaftspolitik im Lichte der modernen Theorie*, Zürich, 1958.
J. Farquharson. *The Plough and the Swastika*, London, 1976.
J. Fest, *The Face of the Third Reich*, London, 1972.

J. Fest, *Hitler*, London, 1974.

G. Feuchter, *Geschichte des Luftkrieges*, Frankfurt a M, 1964.

F. Fischer, *Germany's Aims in the First World War*, London, 1967.

F. Fischer, *Bundnis der Eliten: zur Kontinuität der Machtstruktur in Deutschland 1871–1945*, Düsseldorf, 1979.

W. Fischer, *Deutsche Wirtschaftspolitik 1918–1945*, Opladen, 1968.

H. Foertsch, *Schuld und Verhängnis. Die Fritsch-Krise im Früjahr 1938*, Stuttgart, 1951.

G. Förster, *Totaler Krieg oder Blitzkrieg*, Berlin, 1967.

F. Forstmeier, H.-E. Volkmann (eds), *Kriegswirtschaft und Rüstung während des Zweiten Weltkrieges 1939–1945*, Düsseldorf, 1975.

F. Forstmeier, H.-E. Volkmann (eds), *Wirtschaft und Rüstung am Vorabend des Zweiten Weltkrieges*, Düsseldorf, 1975.

J. P. Fox, *Germany and the Far Eastern Crisis, 1931–38*, Oxford, 1982.

F. Friedenburg, *Die Rohstoffe und Energiequellen im neuen Europa*, Oldenburg, 1943.

S. Friedländer, *Prelude to Downfall: Hitler and the United States, 1939–1941*, London, 1967.

W. Frischauer, *The Rise and Fall of Hermann Goering*, London, 1950.

M. Gallo, *The Night of the Long Knives*, London, 1973.

J. Gehl, *Austria, Germany and the Anschluss*, Oxford, 1963.

E. Georg, *Die wirtschaftliche Unternehmungen der SS*, Stuttgart, 1963.

M. Geyer, *Aufrüstung oder Sicherheit: die Reichswehr und der Krise der Machtpolitik 1924–1936*, Wiesbaden, 1980.

H. Goering, *Germany Reborn*, London, 1934.

W. Görlitz, *The History of the German General Staff*, New York, 1953.

S. Goudsmit, *Alsos: the Failure of German Science*, London, 1947.

G. S. Graber, *The Life and Times of Reinhard Heydrich*, London, 1981.

W. Green, *Warplanes of the Third Reich*, London, 1970.

C. G. Grey, *Luftwaffe*, London, 1944.

E. Gritzbach, *Hermann Göring*, Berlin, 1938.

C. W. Guillebaud, *The Economic Recovery of Germany 1932–1938*, London, 1939.

J. L. Heinemann, *Hitler's First Foreign Minister*, Berkeley, 1979.

J. Henke, *England in Hitler's politischen Kalkul*, Boppard a R, 1973.

H. Herlin, *Udet: a Man's Life*, London, 1960.

H. Hermann, *The Rise and Fall of the Luftwaffe*, London, 1944.

R. E. Herzstein, *When Nazi Dreams Come True*, London, 1982.

F. Hesse, *Hitler and the English*, London, 1954.

K. Hildebrand, *The Foreign Policy of the Third Reich*, London, 1973.

A. Hillgruber, *Hitler, König Carol und Marschall Antonescu*, Wiesbaden, 1954.

A. Hillgruber, *Hitlers Strategie: Politik und Kriegführung 1940–1941*, Frankfurt a M, 1965.

A. Hillgruber (ed.), *Probleme des Zweiten Weltkrieges*, Cologne, 1967.

A. Hillgruber, *Die gescheiterte Grossmacht: eine Skizze des Deutschen Reiches 1871–1945*, Düsseldorf, 1980.

F. H. Hinsley, *Hitler's Strategy*, Cambridge, 1951.

G. Hirschfeld, L. Kettenacker (eds), *The Führer State: Myth and Reality*, Stuttgart, 1981.

A. Hitler, *Mein Kampf* (ed. D.C. Watt), London, 1969.

J. K. Hoensch, *Die Slowakei und Hitlers Ostpolitik*, Cologne, 1965.

H. Höhne, *The Order of the Death's Head*, London, 1969.

H. Höhne, *Codeword: Direktor*, London, 1971.

H. Höhne, *Canaris*, London, 1979.

H. Holborn (ed.), *Republic to Reich: the Making of the Nazi Revolution*, New York, 1972.

E. Homze, *Foreign Labour in Nazi Germany*, Princeton, 1967.

E. Homze, *Arming the Luftwaffe*, Nebraska, 1976.

K. Hopfinger, *Beyond Expectation: the Volkswagen Story*, London, 1954.

P. Hüttenberger, *Die Gauleiter*, Stuttgart, 1969.

D. Irving, *The Virus House*, London, 1967.

D. Irving, *The Rise and Fall of the Luftwaffe: the Life of Erhard Milch*, London, 1973.

D. Irving, *Hitler's War*, London, 1977.

A. van Ishoven, *Messerschmitt*, London, 1975.

A. van Ishoven, *The Fall of an Eagle*, London, 1977.

E. Jäckel, *Hitler's Weltanschauung*, Wesleyan, 1972.

H. Jacobsen, J. Rohwer, *Decisive Battles of World War Two*, London, 1965.

G. Janssen, *Das Ministerium Speers: Deutschlands Rüstung im Krieg*, Frankfurt a M, 1968.

D. Kaiser, *Economic Diplomacy and the Origins of the Second World War*, Princeton, 1980.

D. Kahn, *Hitler's Spies*, London, 1978.

I. Kershaw, *Popular Opinion and Political Dissent in the Third Reich*, Oxford, 1983.

A. von Kielmansegg, *Der Fritschprozess 1938*, Hamburg, 1949.

J. Killen, *The Luftwaffe: a History*, London, 1967.

U. Kissenkoetter, *Gregor Strasser und die NSDAP*, Stuttgart, 1978.

B. H. Klein, *Germany's Economic Preparations for War*, Harvard, 1959.

H. Krausnick et al., *The Anatomy of the SS State*, London, 1968.

A. Kuhn, *Hitlers aussenpolitisches Programm*, Stuttgart, 1970.

J. von Lang, *The Secretary: Martin Bormann*, New York, 1979.

B. Leach, *German Strategy against Russia, 1939–1941*, Oxford, 1973.

A. Lee, *The German Air Force*, London, 1946.

A. Lee, *Goering: Air Leader*, London, 1972.

J. A. Leopold, *Alfred Hugenberg*, London, 1977.

L. Lochner, *What about Germany?*, London, 1943.

L. Lochner, *Tycoons and Tyrants. German Industry from Hitler to Adenauer*, Chicago, 1954.

C. D. Long, *The Labour Force under Changing Income and Employment*, Princeton, 1958.

K. H. Ludwig, *Technik und Ingenieure im Dritten Reich*, Düsseldorf, 1974.

S. Lurie, *Private Investment in a Controlled Economy: Germany 1933–1939*, London, 1947.

R. Luža, *Austro-German Relations in the Anschluss Era*, Princeton, 1975.

C. A. Macdonald, *The United States, Britain and Appeasement 1936–1939*, London, 1981.

K. Macksey, *Kesselring: the Making of the Luftwaffe*, London, 1978.

D. Mack Smith, *Mussolini's Roman Empire*, London, 1976.

K. Maier, H. Rohde, B. Stegemann, H. Umbreit, *Die Errichtung der Hegemonie auf dem europäischen Kontinent*, Stuttgart, 1979.

R. Manvell, H. Fraenkel, *Göring*, London, 1962.

P. Marguerat, *Le IIIème Reich et le pétrole roumain*, Leiden, 1977.

W. Maser, *Nuremberg: a Nation on Trial*, London, 1979.

H. M. Mason, *The Rise of the Luftwaffe, 1918–1940*, London 1975.

T. W. Mason, *Sozialpolitik im Dritten Reich*, Opladen, 1977.

W. Meier-Dörnberg, *Ölversorgung der Kriegsmarine 1935 bis 1945*, Freiburg i B, 1973.

G. Meinck, *Hitler und die deutsche Aufrüstung 1933–1937*, Wiesbaden, 1959.

W. Michalka (ed.), *Nationalsozialistische Aussenpolitik*, Darmstadt, 1978.

W. Michalka, *Ribbentrop und die deutsche Weltpolitik 1933–1940*, Munich, 1980.

A. S. Milward, *The German Economy at War*, London, 1965.

A. S. Milward, *The Fascist Economy in Norway*, Oxford, 1972.

A. S. Milward, *The New Order and the French Economy*, Oxford, 1970.

H. Mommsen, *Beamtentum im Dritten Reich*, Stuttgart, 1966.

F. Morton, *The Rothschilds*, London, 1962.

L. Mosley, *The Reich Marshal*, London, 1974.

K.-J. Müller, *Armee, Politik und Gesellschaft in Deutschland, 1933–1945*, Paderborn, 1979.

V. Muthesius, *Der Krieg der Fabriken*, Berlin, 1941.

O. Nathan, M. Fried, *The Nazi Economic System*, London, 1944.

R. Neck (ed.). *Anschluss 1938*, Vienna, 1981.

W. Nelson, *Small Wonder: the Amazing Story of the Volkswagen*, London, 1967.

F. Neumann, *Behemoth*, London, 1942.

A. Nielsen, *The German Air Force General Staff*, New York, 1959.

J. Noakes (ed.). *Government, Party and People in Nazi Germany*, Exeter, 1980.

R. O'Neill, *The German Army and the Nazi Party*, London, 1966.

D. Orlow, *The Nazis in the Balkans*, Pittsburgh, 1968.

D. Orlow, *The History of the Nazi Party, 1919–1945*, 2 vols, Newton Abbot, 1973.

R. J. Overy, *The Air War 1939–1945*, London, 1980.

R. J. Overy, *The Nazi Economic Recovery, 1932–1938*, London, 1982.

B. F. Pauley, *Hitler and the Forgotten Nazis*, London, 1981.

M. Pearton, *Oil and the Roumanian State*, Oxford, 1971.

H. Pentzlin, *Hjalmar Schacht*, Berlin, 1980.

G. Perrault, *The Red Orchestra*, London, 1967.

D. Petzina, *Autarkiepolitik im Dritten Reich*, Stuttgart, 1968.

H. Pfahlmann, *Fremdarbeiter und Kriegsgefangene in der deutschen Kriegswirtschaft*, Darmstadt, 1968.

J. Piekalkiewicz, *Secret Agents, Spies and Saboteurs*, Newton Abbot, 1974.

H. Plocher, *The German Air Force versus Russia, 1941*, New York, 1965.

J. and S. Pool, *Who Financed Hitler?*, London, 1979.

A. Price, *Instruments of Darkness*, London, 1967.

A. Price, *The Luftwaffe Handbook 1939–1945*, London, 1977.

H. Pünder, *Von Preussen nach Europa*, Stuttgart, 1968.

P. Rheinländer, *Die deutsche Eisen-und Stahlwirtschaft im Vierjahresplan*, Berlin, 1939.

J. M. Rhodes, *The Hitler Movement*, Stanford, 1980.

M. Riedel, *Eisen und Kohle für das Deutsche Reich*, Göttingen, 1973.

G. Ritter, *The German Resistance: Carl Goerdeler's Struggle against Tyranny*, London, 1958.

E. M. Robertson, *Hitler's Pre-War Policy and Military Plans*, London, 1963.

E. M. Robertson, *Mussolini as Empire-Builder*, London, 1977.

G. von Roon, *German Resistance to Hitler. Count von Moltke and the Kreisau Circle*, London, 1971.

K. Rothschild, *Austria's Economic Development between the Wars*, London, 1947.

M. Salewski, *Die deutsche Seekriegsleitung 1939–1945*, 2 vols, Frankfurt a M, 1970.

F. von Schlabrenendorf, *The Secret War against Hitler*, London, 1966.

H. Schliephake, *The Birth of the Luftwaffe*, London, 1971.

C. Schneider, *Stadtgründung im Dritten Reich: Wolfsburg und Salzgitter*, Munich, 1979.

A. Schweitzer, *Big Business in the Third Reich*, Bloomington, 1964.

L. Schwerin von Krosigk, *Staatsbankrott: Finanzpolitik des Deutschen Reiches 1920–1945*, Stuttgart, 1974.

W. Shirer, *Berlin Diary*, London, 1941.

L. E. Simon, *German Research in World War II*, New York, 1947.

A. E. Simpson, *Hjalmar Schacht in Perspective*, The Hague, 1969.

K. Singer, *Göring – Germany's Most Dangerous Man*, London, 1940.

A. Sohn-Rethel, *Economy and Class-Structure of German Fascism*, London, 1978.

M. Sommerfeldt, *Hermann Göring: ein Lebensbild*, Berlin, 1933.
A. Speer, *The Slave State*, London, 1981.
P. Stachura (ed.), *The Shaping of the Nazi State*, London, 1978.
J. Steiner, *Power, Politics and Social Change in National Socialist Germany*, The Hague, 1976.
M. Steinert, *Hitler's War and the Germans*, Ohio, 1977.
J. Steinhoff, *The Last Chance. The Pilots' Plot against Göring 1944–1945*, London, 1977.
F. Sternberg, *Germany and a Lightning War*, London, 1938.
N. Stone, *Hitler*, London, 1980.
R. Suchenwirth, *Historical Turning Points in the German Air Force War Effort*, New York, 1959.
R. Suchenwirth, *The Development of the German Air Force 1919–1939*, New York, 1968.
R. Suchenwirth, *Command and Leadership in the German Air Force*, New York, 1969.
A. J. P. Taylor, *The Origins of the Second World War*, London, 1961.
A. J. P. Taylor, *1939 Revisited*, German Historical Institute Lecture, London, 1980.
T. Taylor, *Sword and Swastika*, London, 1953.
A. Teichova, *An Economic Background to Munich*, Cambridge, 1974.
J. Thies, *Architekt der Weltherrschaft: die Endziele Hitlers*, Düsseldorf, 1976.
G. Thomas, *Geschichte der deutschen Wehr-und Rüstungswirtschaft 1918–1943/45* (ed. W. Birkenfeld), Boppard a R, 1966.
F. Tobias, *Der Reichstagsbrand: Legende und Wirklichkeit*, Rastatt, 1962.
J. Toland, *Adolf Hitler*, New York, 1976.
M. Toscano, *The Origins of the Pact of Steel*, Baltimore, 1967.
H. Trevor-Roper, *The Last Days of Hitler*, London, 1947.
O. Ulshöfer, *Einflussnahme auf Wirtschaftsunternehmungen in den besetzten nord, west und südost-europäischen Ländern während des Zweiten Weltkrieges*, Tübingen, 1958.
R. Vansittart, *Black Record: Germans Past and Present*, London, 1941.
A. Verrier, *The Bomber Offensive*, London, 1968.
R. Vogelsang, *Der Freundeskreis Himmler*, Göttingen, 1972.
K.-H. Völker, *Die deutsche Luftwaffe 1933–1939*, Stuttgart, 1968.
R. Wagenführ, *Die deutsche Industrie im Kriege*, Berlin, 1963.
M. Walz, *Wohnungsbau und Industrieansiedlungspolitik in Deutschland 1933–1939*, Frankfurt a M, 1979.
C. Webster, N. Frankland, *The Strategic Air Offensive against Germany*, 4 vols, HMSO, 1961.
G. Weinberg, *The Foreign Policy of Hitler's Germany 1933–1936*, London, 1970.
G. Weinberg, *Germany and the Soviet Union 1939–1941*, Leiden, 1972.
G. Weinberg, *Hitler's Foreign Policy 1937–1939*, London, 1980.
B.-J. Wendt, *Appeasement 1938: wirtschaftliche Rezession und Mitteleuropa*, Frankfurt a M, 1966.
B.-J. Wendt, *Economic Appeasement: Handel und Finanz in der britischen Deutschlandpolitik 1933–1939*, Düsseldorf, 1971.
F. von Wilamowitz-Moellendorff, *Carin Göring*, Berlin, 1935.
K. Wittmann, *Schwedens Wirtschaftsbeziehungen zum Dritten Reich, 1933–1945*, Munich, 1978.
M. Ziegler, *Rocket Fighter*, London, 1961.

E SECONDARY SOURCES: ARTICLES

The following abbreviations have been used:
AEcR   American Economic Review

DVP   *Der Vierjahresplan*
EcHR   *Economic History Review*
JCH   *Journal of Contemporary History*
JMH   *Journal of Modern History*
JWG   *Jahrbuch für Wirtschaftsgeschichte*
MGM   *Militärgeschichtliche Mitteilungen*
P&P   *Past and Present*
RDGM   *Revue d'histoire de la Deuxième Guerre Mondiale*
VfZ   *Vierteljahreshefte für Zeitgeschichte*

F. Baerwald, 'How Germany Reduced Unemployment', *AEcR*, vol. 24, 1934.
T. Balogh, 'The National Economy of Germany', *Economic Journal*, vol. 48, 1938.
L. Baudin, 'An Outline of Economic Conditions in France under the German Occupation', *Economic Journal*, vol. 55, 1945.
O. Bechtle, 'German Air Force Operations against Great Britain: address in Berlin, 2.2.1944', *RAF Quarterly*, vol. 19, 1947/8.
J. Becker, 'Zentrum und Ermächtigungsgesetz', *VfZ*, vol. 9, 1961.
J. Bendersky, 'The Expendable Kronjurist: Carl Schmitt and National Socialism 1933–1936', *JCH*, vol. 14, 1979.
M. Biddiss, 'The Nuremberg Trial: Two Exercises in Judgement', *JCH*, vol. 16, 1981.
M. Biehl, 'Um die Prinzipien des Serienbaus von Kampfflugzeuge in England', *DVP*, vol. 2, 1938.
W. Birkenfeld, 'Stalin als Wirtschaftsplaner Hitlers', *Vierteljahreshefte für Sozial-und Wirtschaftsgeschichte*, vol. 51, 1966.
A. Bullock, 'Hitler and the Origins of the Second World War', *Proceedings of the British Academy*, vol. 53, 1967.
E. Campus, 'Die Hitlerfaschistische Infiltration Rumäniens 1939–1940', *Zeitschrift für Geschichtswissenschaft*, vol. 5, 1957.
J. Caplan, 'Bureaucracy, Politics and the National Socialist State', in P. Stachura (ed.), *The Shaping of the Nazi State*, London, 1978.
N. N. Constantinescu, 'L'exploitation et le pillage de l'économie roumaine par l'Allemagne hitlérienne dans la période 1939–1944', *Revue roumaine d'histoire*, vol. 3, 1964.
J. P. Cullity, 'The Growth of Governmental Employment in Germany 1882–1950', *Zeitschrift für die gesamte Staatswissenschaft*, vol, 123, 1967.
H. Dinerstein, 'The Impact of Air Power on the International Scene 1930–1939', *Military Affairs*, vol. 19, 1955.
J. Dülffer, 'Der Beginn des Krieges 1939: Hitler, die innere Krise und das Mächte-system', *Geschichte und Gesellschaft*, vol. 2, 1976.
D. Eichholtz, 'Probleme einer Wirtschaftsgeschichte des Faschismus in Deutsch-land', *JWG*, vol. 2, 1963.
D. Eichholtz, 'Die IG-Farben-Friedensplanung. Schlüsseldokumente der faschist-ischen "Neuordnung des europäischen Grossraums"', *JWG*, vol. 5, 1966.
D. Eichholtz, 'Zum Anteil des IG-Farben-Konzerns an der Vorbereitung des Zweiten Weltkrieges', *JWG*, vol. 8, 1969.
P. Einzig, 'Hitler's New Order in Theory and Practice', *Economic Journal*, vol. 51, 1941.
T. Elmshirst, 'The German Air Force and its Failure', *Journal of the Royal United Services Institute*, vol. 91, 1946.
E. M. Emme, 'Emergence of Nazi Luftpolitik as a Weapon in International Affairs', *Aerospace Historian*, vol. 7, 1960.
W. Eucken, 'On the Theory of the Centrally Administered Economy. An Analysis of the German Experiment', *Economica*, vol. 15, 1948.

P. Façon, 'Aperçus sur la collaboration aéronautique franco-allemande 1940–1943', *RDGM*, vol. 27, 1977.

G. D. Feldman, 'The Social and Economic Policies of German Big Business 1918–1929', *American Historical Review*, vol. 75, 1969.

J. Fischer, 'Über den Entschluss zur Luftversorgung Stalingrads. Ein Beitrag zur militärischen Führung im Dritten Reich', *MGM*, vol. 6, 1969.

J. Foster, 'Rumäniens Weg in die deutsche Abhängigkeit. Zur Rolle der deutsche Militärmission 1940/1', *MGM*, vol. 21, 1979.

M. Geyer, 'Rüstungsbeschleunigung und Inflation: zur Inflationsdenkschrift des OKW von November 1938', *MGM*, vol. 23, 1981.

H. Gies, 'Die Rolle des Reichnährstandes im nationalsozialistischen Herrschaftssystem' in G. Hirschfeld, L. Kettenacker (eds), *The Führer State: Myth and Reality*, Stuttgart, 1981.

F. Gilbert, 'Mitteleuropa – the Final Stage', *Journal of Central European Affairs*, vol. 7. 1947.

H. Goering, 'Einheitliche Führung und Organisation der Wirtschaft', *DVP*, vol. 1, 1937.

H. Goering, 'Wiederaufbau der Ostmark', *DVP*, vol. 2, 1938.

K. Gundelach, 'The German Air Force', *Aerospace Historian*, vol. 18, 1971.

H. Handke, 'Zur Rolle der Volkswagenpläne bei der faschistischen Kriegsvorbereitung', *JWG*, vol. 1, 1962.

M. Hauner, 'Did Hitler want a World Dominion?', *JCH*, vol. 13, 1978.

J. L. Heinemann, 'Constantin von Neurath and German Policy at the London Economic Conference 1933', *JMH*, vol. 31, 1969.

E. Hennig, 'Industrie, Aufrüstung und Kriegsvorbereitung im deutschen Faschismus', *Gesellschaft: Beiträge zur Marxschen Theorie*, vol. 5, 1975.

L. Herbst, 'Die Krise des nationalsozialistischen Regimes am Vorabend des Zweiten Weltkrieges und die forcierte Rüstung', *VfZ*, vol. 26, 1978.

K. Hildebrand, 'La programme de Hitler et sa réalisation', *RDGM*, vol. 21, 1971.

R. F. Holland, 'The Federation of British Industry and the International Economy 1929–1939', *EcHR*, 2nd ser., vol. 34, 1981.

T. Hughes, 'Technological Momentum in History: Hydrogenation in Germany 1898–1933', *P&P*, vol. 15, 1969.

P. Hüttenberger, 'Nationalsozialistische Polykratie', *Geschichte und Gesellschaft*, vol. 2, 1976.

J. J. Jäger, 'Sweden's Iron-ore Exports to Germany 1933–1944', *Scandinavian Economic History Review*, vol. 15, 1967.

G. Janssen, 'Todt et Speer', *RDGM*, vol. 21, 1971.

W. Jensen, 'The Importance of Energy in the First and Second World Wars', *Historical Journal*, vol. 11, 1968.

R. Jeske, 'Zur Annexion der polnischen Wojewodschaft Schlesien durch Hitlerdeutschland im Zweiten Weltkrieg', *Zeitschrift für Geschichtswissenschaft*, vol. 5, 1957.

N. Kaldor, 'The German War Economy', *Manchester School*, vol. 14, 1936.

P. Kirchberg, 'Typisierung in der deutschen Kraftfahrzeugindustrie und der General bevollmächtigte für das Kraftfahrwesen', *JWG*, vol. 8, 1969.

B. H. Klein, 'Germany's Preparations for War: a Re-examination', *AEcR*, vol. 38, 1948.

J. J. Klein, 'German Money and Prices' in M. Friedman (ed.), *Studies in the Quantity Theory of Money*, Chicago, 1956.

H. Koppenberg, 'Deutschlands Luftfahrtindustrie ist Grossindustrie', *DVP*, vol. 3, 1939.

K. Lachmann 'The Hermann Göring Works', *Social Research*, vol. 8, 1941.

K. Lachmann, 'More on the Hermann Göring Works', *Social Research*, vol. 9, 1942.

R. Lindholm, 'German Finance in World War II', *AEcR*, vol. 37, 1947.

P. W. Ludlow, 'Scandinavia between the Great Powers', *Särtryck ur Historisk Tidskrift*, 1974.

C. A. Macdonald, 'Economic Appeasement and the German Moderates', *P&P*, no. 56, 1972.

K. Mandelbaum, 'An Experiment in Full Employment: Controls in the German Economy 1933–1938', in Oxford University Institute of Statistics, *The Economics of Full Employment*, London, 1944.

B. Martin, 'Das "Dritte Reich" und die Friedens-Frage im Zweiten Weltkrieg' in W. Michalka (ed.), *Nationalsozialistische Aussenpolitik*, Darmstadt, 1978.

T. W. Mason, 'Some Origins of the Second World War', *P&P*, no. 29, 1964.

T. W. Mason, 'Labour in the Third Reich', *P&P*, no. 33, 1966.

T. W. Mason, 'Innere Krise und Angriffskrieg' in F. Forstmeier, H.-E. Volkmann (eds), *Wirtschaft und Rüstung am Vorabend des Zweiten Weltkrieges*, Düsseldorf, 1975.

T. W. Mason, 'Intention and Explanation: a Current Controversy about the Interpretation of National Socialism' in G. Hirschfeld, L. Kettenacker (eds), *The Führer State: Myth and Reality*, Stuttgart, 1981.

H. Mau, 'The "Second Revolution", June 30th 1934', in H. Holborn (ed.), *Republic to Reich: the Making of the Nazi Revolution*, New York, 1972.

S. Merlin, 'Trends in Economic Control since 1933', *Quarterly Journal of Economics*, vol. 57, 1943.

A. S. Milward, 'The End of the Blitzkrieg', *EcHR*, 2nd ser., vol. 16, 1963/4.

A. S. Milward, 'Could Sweden have Stopped the Second World War?', *Scandinavian Economic History Review*, vol. 15, 1967.

A. S. Milward, 'Hitlers Konzept des Blitzkrieges' in A. Hillgruber (ed.), *Probleme des Zweiten Weltkrieges*, Cologne, 1967.

A. S. Milward, 'Der Einfluss ökonomischer und nicht-ökonomischer Faktoren auf die Strategie des Blitzkriegs' in F. Forstmeier, H.-E. Volkmann (eds), *Wirtschaft und Rüstung am Vorabend des Zweiten Weltkrieges*, Düsseldorf, 1975.

H. Mommsen, 'Der Reichstagbrand und seine politischen Folgen', *VfZ*, vol. 12, 1964.

O. Mooyer, 'Neuzeitlicher Berufserziehung in der Luftfahrtindustrie', *DVP*, vol. 3, 1939.

R. Morsey, 'Der Beginn der Gleichschaltung in Preussen', *VfZ*, vol. 11, 1963.

W. Murray, 'German Air Power and the Munich Crisis' in B. Bond, I. Roy (eds), *War and Society*, vol. 1, 1976.

L. Neal, 'The Economics and Finance of Bilateral Clearing Agreements: Germany 1934–38', *EcHR*, 2nd ser., vol. 32, 1979.

J. Noakes, 'Oberbürgermeister and Gauleiter: City Government between Party and State' in G. Hirschfeld, L. Kettenacker (eds), *The Führer State: Myth and Reality*, Stuttgart, 1981.

E. Nolte, 'Big Business and German Politics: a Comment', *American Historical Review*, vol. 75, 1969.

R. J. Overy, 'Transportation and Rearmament in the Third Reich', *The Historical Journal*, vol. 16, 1973.

R. J. Overy, 'The German pre-war aircraft production plans', *English Historical Review*, vol. 90, 1975.

R. J. Overy, 'The Luftwaffe and the European Economy', *MGM*, vol. 21, 1979.

R. J. Overy, 'From "Uralbomber" to "Amerikabomber": the Luftwaffe and Strategic Bombing', *Journal of Strategic Studies*, vol. 1, 1978.

R. J. Overy, 'Hitler and Air Strategy', *JCH*, vol. 15, 1980.

R. J. Overy, 'Hitler's War and the German Economy: a Reinterpretation', *EcHR*, 2nd ser., vol. 35, 1982.

M. Palyi, 'Economic Foundations of the German Totalitarian State', *American Journal of Sociology*, vol. 46, 1941.

E. N. Peterson, 'The Bureaucracy and the Nazi Party', *Review of Politics*, vol. 23, 1966.

D. Petzina, 'Die Mobilisierung deutscher Arbeitskräfte vor und während des Zweiten Weltkrieges', *VfZ*, vol. 18, 1970.

G. Plum, 'Staatspolizei und innere Verwaltung 1934–1936', *VfZ*, vol. 13, 1965.

J. Radkau, 'Entscheidungsprozesse und Entscheidungsdefizite in der deutschen Aussenwirtschaftspolitik 1933–1940', *Geschichte und Gesellschaft*, vol. 2, 1976.

C. Ramsauer, 'Zur Geschichte der deutschen Physikalischen Gesellschaft in der Hitlerzeit', *Physikalische Blätter*, vol. 1, 1947.

H. Schacht, 'Germany's Colonial Demands', *Foreign Affairs*, vol. 15, 1936–7.

N. Schausberger, 'Der Anschluss und seine ökonomische Relevanz' in R. Neck (ed.), *Anschluss 1938*, Vienna, 1981.

A. von Schell, 'Neue Wege der deutschen Motorisierung', *DVP*, vol. 3, 1939.

R. Schönfeld, 'Deutsche Rohstoffsicherungspolitik in Jugoslawien 1934–1944', *VfZ*, vol. 24, 1976.

A. Schröter, J. Bach, 'Zur Planung der wehrwirtschaftlichen Mobilmachung durch den deutschen faschistischen Imperialismus vor dem Beginn des Zweiten Weltkrieges', *JWG*, vol. 17, 1978.

A. Schweitzer, 'Profits under Nazi Planning', *Quarterly Journal of Economics*, vol. 60, 1946.

A. Schweitzer, 'Foreign Exchange Crisis of 1936', *Zeitschrift für die gesamte Staatswissenschaft*, vol. 118, 1962.

G. Siebel, 'Luftfahrt Unternehmer', *DVP*, vol. 1, 1937.

A. E. Simpson, 'The Struggle for Control of the German Economy 1936/37', *JMH*, vol. 21, 1959.

W. Solveen, 'Die Neuordnung der deutschen Eisenwirtschaft', *DVP*, vol. 1, 1937.

A. Speer, 'Selbstverantwortung in der Rüstungsindustrie', *DVP*, vol. 7, 1943.

B. Stegemann, 'Hitlers Ziele im ersten Kriegsjahr 1939/40', *MGM*, vol. 22, 1980.

H. Stuebel, 'Die Finanzierung der Aufrüstung im Dritten Reich', *Europa-Archiv*, vol. 6, 1951.

A. Teichova, 'Aspects of Capital Accumulation in Interwar Central-east European Industry', *History of European Ideas*, vol. 3, 1982.

J. Thies, 'Hitler's European Building Programme', *JCH*, vol. 13, 1978.

W. Treue, 'Die Einstellung einiger deutscher Grossindustriellen zu Hitlers Aussenpolitik', *Geschichte in Wissenschaft und Unterricht*, vol. 17, 1966.

H. Vollweiler, 'The Mobilisation of Labour Reserves in Germany', parts I and II, *International Labour Review*, vol. 38, 1938.

W. Wark, 'British Intelligence on the German Air Force and Aircraft Industry, 1933–1939', *Historical Journal*, vol. 25, 1982.

F. Zipfel, 'Hitlers Konzept einer Neuordnung Europas' in D. Kurse, *Aus Theorie und Praxis der Geschichtwissenschaft*, Berlin, 1972.

L. Zumpe, 'Kohle-Eisen-Stahl 1936/7: Unterdrückung oder Interessenprofilierung', *JWG*, vol. 19, 1980.

INDEX

Abysinnia, 45
Adam Opel motor company, 99, 161
aircraft: Ar 234, 196; He 177, 85, 160, 167, 193, 196, 217; Ju 88, 85, 105, 167, 184, 190; Ju 288, 193; Me 110, 217; Me 210, 183, 193, 217; Me 262, 200, 228
aircraft production, 75, 102, 106, 143–4, 148, 149–50, 176–7, 180–7, 195–6, 214, 217–18, 228
air defence, 173–4, 194–5, 201–2, 225–6
Air Office, 32
air rearmament, 37–8, 85
Alpine-Montangesellschaft, 113, 140
Alsace-Lorraine, 111, 122, 123–4, 125, 134, 143
aluminium production, 119, 141, 143, 184–5
American Mineworkers' Union, 104
Anschluss, 79–80, 110, 234
Antonescu, Marshal Ion, 117
Arbed trust, 123, 124
'Armament 1942' decree, 207
'Asia' (Goering's train), 100
Astra oil company, 117
Augsburg, 187
Auschnitt, Max, 117
Auskämm-Aktionen, 140
Austria, 32, 66, 77, 79–80, 81–2, 89, 111, 112, 113, 114, 122, 123, 129, 140, 143, 216, 233
autarky, 36, 40–1, 44–5, 54–5, 56–7
Autobahnen, 46
Aviation Bank, 56, 183

Backe, Herbert, 57, 215
Balbo, General Italo, 32
Balkans, 32, 79, 93, 107, 110, 116–18, 125, 200
Baltic, 200
Bank der deutschen Luftfahrt, *see* Aviation Bank
Baptism of Fire (film), 93
'Barbarossa', 205
Battle of Britain, 106, 170–2
Battle of France, 170
Bauer, General, 162, 184
Bavaria, 6, 7, 31

Bayerische Motorenwerke (BMW), 7, 187, 190
Beamish-Fock, Baroness Huldine, 6
Beck, Jozef, 81
Beck, General Ludwig, 237
Belgium, 121
Berchtesgaden, 46
Berg-und Hüttenwerksgesellschaft Ost (BHO), 133
Berlin, 8, 25, 36, 121, 132, 157, 208, 226, 233
Bessarabia, 90
'Big Week', 201, 226
Bismarck, Herbert von, 29
Bismarck, Prince Otto von, 3, 4, 72, 240
'Blitz', 173, 196, 225
Blitzkrieg, 76, 78, 85, 103, 207–8
Blomberg, Field Marshal Werner von, 31, 33, 37, 40–1, 42; and rearmament, 43–4, 46, 49, 53, 58; and Blomberg/Fritsch crisis, 68–70, 71, 72, 208
Blomberg-Fritsch crisis, 68–72, 80, 237
Bodenschatz, General Carl, 35, 213
Bohemia, 77, 82, 111, 116, 120, 126, 129, 213
Bolshevik Party, 22
bombing, 173–4, 175, 184, 191, 195–7, 225, 228
'booty commands', 132
Bormann, Martin, 155, 188, 208, 209–10, 218, 221, 223, 227–8, 229
Bosch, Carl, 56
Bouhler, Philip, 206
Brassert, Henry, 63
Brauchitsch, Field Marshal Walter von, 237
Britain, 77, 82, 85, 90, 91, 93, 103, 104–5, 106, 109, 116, 117, 130, 150, 167, 179, 186, 195, 196, 205, 206, 236
British Empire, 77, 90
Brüning, Heinrich, 10
Brünner Waffenwerke, *see* Czech Armaments Works
Buna rubber, 57
bureaucracy, 157–9

Cameroon, 43

Canaris, Admiral Wilhelm, 237
Carinhall, 20, 36, 154, 219
Carol, King of Roumania, 116, 117
Caucasus, 216, 217, 219
Celle, 216
Central Planning Board, *see Zentrale Planung*
Charlemagne, 13, 164
China, 32
Christie, Group Captain M. G., 77, 109
Churchill, Sir Winston, 154
Ciano, Count Galeazzo, 89, 233, 236
coal nationalisation, 126, 223
colonies, 29, 43
'Columbia' oil company, 133
Commission of Reorganisation, 27
concentration camps, 26, 129
Concordia oil company, 133
Continental System, 146
Copsa Mica si Cugir mining company, 117
Council of Ministers, 59
Coventry, 172
Crimea, 131
Croatia, 120
Croneiss, Theo, 223
Czech Armaments Works, 113–14, 117, 143
Czechoslovakia, 66, 80, 81–2, 87, 89, 100, 111, 113, 116, 122, 123, 138, 140, 143

Dahlerus, Birger, 91, 93–4
Daluege, Kurt, 26, 84
Danzig, 32, 38, 41, 88–9, 91–2
Darré, Walther, 39, 41–2, 47
Davis, William, 94
Denmark, 6
de Wendel iron and steel company, 124
Diels, Rudolf, 24, 28, 231
Differdange foundry, 124
Dniepropetrovsk, 133
DNVP, 11
Dohnanyi, Hans von, 237
Donetz Basin, 132, 133
Dornberger, General Walther, 233
Dornier, Claus, 183
Dorpmüller, Julius, 216
Dorsch, Xavier, 227
Dresdner Bank, 56, 113
Durčansky, Ferdinand, 81
Düsseldorf Memorandum, 65

Economic Council, 154
economic recovery, 36–7, 53–5
Edelweiss Chapel, 6
Eisenhower, General Dwight D., 228
'Elch' air programme, 149
Eltz-Rubenach, Paul Freiherr von, 70
Enabling Law, 23
England, *see* Britain

Fascist Party, 7, 32
Feder, Gottfried, 36–7
Fighter Staff, 201, 228
final solution, 128, 229
First World War, 4, 5, 32, 35, 45, 63, 71,
84, 85, 103, 109, 130, 158, 177, 181, 188, 215
Flick, Friedrich, 124
Focke-Wulf aircraft company, 156, 183
forced labour, 128–30, 141–2, 226–7
foreign exchange crisis, 38–9, 45
Forschungsamt, 35, 92
Four Year Plan (Second), 15, 34, 37, 46–7, 48–9, 50–3, 56–62, 65–6, 69, 74, 79, 82, 85–6, 89, 91, 95, 96, 98, 99, 100–1, 110ff, 122ff, 130, 132, 133, 134, 146, 147, 151, 153, 157, 199, 206, 208, 209, 210, 212, 214, 215, 216, 222, 223, 224
Four Year Plan (Third), 86, 101
France, 32, 63, 77, 82, 85, 90, 103, 106, 107, 116, 117, 118, 121, 122, 123, 125, 139, 143–4, 146
Frank, Hans, 120, 121, 122
Frederick the Great, 47, 154, 164
Freikorps, 6
Freundeskreis, 35
Frick, Wilhelm, 25, 26–7, 28, 31, 101
Fritsch, General Werner Freiherr von, 30, 70–1
Funk, Walther, 42, 62, 71, 87, 98, 101, 119, 127, 140, 155, 206, 211, 221, 222

Galland, General Adolf, 194
Geheime Staatspolizei (Gestapo), 26–7, 28, 31, 70, 127, 129, 221, 223
General Council (FYP), 57, 101
Generalluftzeugmeister (GL), 181
German Air Force, 17; and early build up, 33–4; in Spain, 79, 85; and Poland, 93, 102–3, 106, 119, 131, 143, 152, 153, 156; growth in 1930s, 165–6; and strategic bombing, 166–8; and early campaigns, 169–70; and Battle of Britain, 170–3; and air strength, 175; and reserves, 179; and production crisis, 181–93; and air defence, 194–5; and research, 197–200; and final collapse, 201–3; and Stalingrad airlift, 219, 220, 224–5, 227–8
German air intelligence, 171
German army, 29–30, 33, 53; and Blomberg-Fritsch crisis, 68–71; and rearmament, 85–6, 119, 121, 139, 151–2, 158–60, 174
German Communist Party (KPD), 24, 25
German National Front, 29
German Navy, 33, 85
German Social Democratic Party (SPD), 24, 25
German Sixth Army, 219
Goebbels, Josef, 7, 8, 14, 28, 30, 34, 36, 73, 155, 196, 202, 203, 208, 221–2, 228, 232, 238
Goerdeler, Carl, 45, 46, 58, 237
Goering air programme, 149
Goering, Albert, 114
Goering, Carin, 6, 7, 18
Goering, Edda, 73
Goering, Emmy, 18, 34

Goering, Heinrich, 4

Goering, Herbert, 35

Goering, Hermann Wilhelm: and role in the Third Reich, 1–4; early life, 4–6; contact with Hitler, 7; as Reichstag deputy, 8–9; as party 'ambassador', 9–10; and seizure of power, 10–11; personality, 11–15; administrative style, 16–18; influences upon, 18–19; and alleged drug addiction, 20; as Prussian Interior Minister, 23–7; and Reichstag Fire, 25–6; and conflict with SA, 26–8; and Gestapo, 26–7; and Roehm crisis, 28–31; and foreign office, 31–2; and military aviation, 32–4; wedding, 34; and economic affairs, 36–7; and rearmament, 37–9; and foreign exchange crisis, 39–42; and colonies, 43; and Spanish Civil War, 44; and Four Year Plan, 46–7; economic ideology of, 51–3; contest with Schacht, 53–5; and economic policy, 53–6; and FYP organisation, 57–60; and Jewish question, 61–2; and conflict with Ruhr, 62–5; and founding of Reichswerke, 65–8; and Blomberg/Fritsch crisis, 68–71; promoted Field Marshal, 71; personal popularity of, 73; relations with other Nazis, 73–4; and foreign expansion, 76–7; and total war, 78; and foreign affairs, 78–9; and *Anschluss*, 79–80; and Czech crisis, 80–2; and war preparations, 82–6; and problems of rearmament, 86–8; and Polish crisis, 88–92; peace initiatives of, 90–5; and economic mobilisation, 95–6; and war finance, 96–7; and organisation of war economy, 99–102; and peace feelers in 1940, 104; and German strategy, 107–8; imperialist ideas of, 109–10; and central Europe, 111–16; and the Balkans, 116–18; organisation of New Order, 118–22; conflicts with Ruhr, 123–6; and reconstruction plans, 126–7; and final solution, 127–8; and forced labour, 128–30; in invasion of Russia, 130–3; and Russian economy, 132–4; and production crisis, 138–40; and exploitation of Europe, 140–2; and labour problems, 142–3; and Reichswerke reorganisation, 144–6; compared with Napoleon, 146; and labour mobilisation, 147–8; and inefficiency, 148–50; in conflict with army and industry, 151–2; qualities of leadership, 153–5; and links with Nazi Party, 155–7; and problems of bureaucracy, 157–8; and role of military, 158–62; military attitudes of, 164–5; and air strategy, 165–7; and air force organisation, 169; and early campaigns, 169–70; and Battle of Britain, 170–2; and poor preparation of air force, 172–4; loss of strategic direction, 174–5; military values of, 177–9; and aircraft production crisis, 180–8; and reform of production, 189–91; and quality of aircraft, 192–3; ideas on defence of, 193–5; and new Luftwaffe, 195–7; and German research, 197–200; and 1944 invasion, 200–1; and collapse of air force, 201–3; turning point in career, 206–8; efforts to replace Todt, 207–8; and control of war economy, 209–12; and Reichswerke reprivatisation, 212–14; and prices and wages, 215; and food crisis, 215–16; and transport, 216; and failure of oil strategy, 216–17; and aircraft output, 217–18; and Stalingrad airlift, 219; and his critics, 220; and Red Orchestra, 220–1; political intrigues of, 221–2; and links with SS, 222–3; and loss of powers, 224; and air force failure, 225–6; and underground construction, 226–7; and final eclipse of power, 228; at Nuremberg Trials, 228–30; death, 230; loyalty to Hitler, 231–2; personal qualities of, 232; corruption and vanity, 232–3; and political relationship with Hitler, 234–5; ambitions of, 235; popularity of, 236; and German conservatives, 237–8; contribution to Third Reich, 238–9; historical assessment of, 240–1

Goering-Programme, 36

Goernnert, Ministerialrat, 16

Greater German Reich, 107–20

Gritzbach, Erich, 16

Guderian, General Heinz, 234

Hagedange foundry, 124

Haiti, 5

Harpener Bergbau company, 124

Hassell, Ulrich von, 32, 155, 237

Haupttreuhandstelle Ost, 122

Heinkel, Ernst, 181, 183, 188, 199

Heinkel aircraft company, 156, 233

Heisenberg, Werner, 197, 198

Henderson, Sir Nevile, 92

Henschel aircraft company, 156, 190

Hermann-Goering-Stadt, 112, 127, 233

Hess, Rudolf, 2, 73, 100, 101

Heydrich, Reinhard, 27, 73, 128, 208

Hilferding, Rudolf, 52

Himmler, Heinrich: and police powers, 27–8; and Roehm purge, 30–1, 35, 36, 42; and Blomberg/Fritsch crisis, 69–70, 73, 122; and Jewish question, 127, 208, 209–10, 218, 221–3, 226, 227

Hindenburg, Oskar von, 10

Hindenburg, Field Marshal Paul von, 9, 11, 28, 31

Hindenburg Programme, 85

Hitler, Adolf, 1–2; meets Goering, 7; attitude to Goering, 8–10; and seizure of power, 10–11, 14, 15; and political system, 16–17, 18; and influence over Goering, 19, 20, 22; and Nazi revolution, 22–5, 32; and attitude to Goering, 34, 36–7; and food crisis, 38–9; and autarky, 40–2; and FYP, 45–7, 48, 49, 53, 56, 59–60; and

Hitler, Adolf (cont.)
  Schacht's fall, 68; and army crisis, 69–71,
    72, 73, 76; foreign policy of, 77–9; and
    Anschluss, 80, 81; and rearmament, 85–6;
    and Danzig, 89; and Second World War,
    90–2; and Britain, 93–4, 100, 101; and
    war production, 102; and wartime
    strategy, 103–7, 110, 113, 118, 119, 125;
    and Jewish question, 128; and Barbarossa,
    130–1, 138–9, 140, 142, 152, 154, 159,
    160, 161, 164, 165; appoints Goering
    Reichsmarschall, 170; and Battle of
    Britain, 172; and air strategy, 174, 177;
    and air defence, 194–5; and bombing,
    196; and 'terror' weapons, 197–8, 200,
    201, 202, 203, 205; and total war, 206–8;
    and appointment of Speer, 208–12, 215,
    216, 217, 218, 219, 220, 221, 222, 224;
    and new Luftwaffe, 225–6; and
    underground factories, 226–7, 228,
    229–30; and relationship with Goering,
    231–2, 234–8, 241
Hoesch steel company, 124
Hohenzollern, Prince August Wilhelm, 9
Holland, 117, 118, 121
'Hossbach' conference, 77, 80, 86
Hugenberg, Alfred, 11, 23, 29, 31, 39
Hungary, 32, 116
Hüttenverwaltung Westmark, 124

IG Farben, 56–7, 62, 63, 85, 111, 122
Ilgner, Max, 56
iron and steel industry, 62–5, 122, 140–1
iron ore, 44, 63–5, 107, 131
Ironside, General Edmund, 94
Italy, 7, 32, 45, 49, 59, 77, 79, 93, 105, 224

Japan, 32, 105, 150
Jeschonnek, General Hans, 174, 180, 194,
    195
Jewish question, 61–2, 111, 127–8, 238
Jodl, General Alfred, 53, 160
Jugoslavia, 116, 118, 146
July Crisis, 90
Junkers aircraft company, 105, 183, 188,
    190, 192

Kammler, Hans, 227
Kammhuber, General Josef, 194
Karlsruhe, 5
Kehrl, Hans, 45, 113, 121, 133
Keitel, Field Marshal Wilhelm, 2, 44, 73,
    101, 160, 206, 221
Keppler, Wilhelm, 37, 41–2, 44, 45, 46, 47,
    57, 63, 73
Kesselring, Field Marshal Albert, 34, 41
'Kindergarten', 216
Koch, Erich, 120, 133, 156
Koerner, Paul, 16, 35, 57, 66, 100, 101, 124,
    144, 145, 212, 220
Koller, General Karl, 20, 202, 203
Kontinentale Öl, 117, 119, 132–3
Koppenberg, Heinrich, 119

Krauch, Carl, 56–7, 85, 116
Kristallnacht, 61–2
Krivoi-Rog, 133
Krupp AG, 65

labour controls, 84, 147–8, 214
Labour Front, 36, 74, 84
Lammers, Hans, 73, 101, 221
Landfried, Friedrich, 71, 222
League of Nations, 29
Lenin, 22–3
Ley, Robert, 28, 36, 42, 73, 74, 88, 96, 99,
    221–2
Lichterfelde military academy, 5
Linz, 112, 126, 129
Little Entente, 32
living standards, 50–1, 83, 96–8
Loerzer, Bruno, 35
London, 114, 117, 172, 195
Lorraine, *see* Alsace-Lorraine
Lufthansa, 34
Luftwaffe, see German Air Force
Luxembourg, 123, 124

Madagascar, 128
Maikop, 217
Malaxa works, 117
MAN truck company, 99
Mediterranean, 104, 105, 130, 174, 193, 206
Meinberg, Wilhelm, 66
Mein Kampf, 26, 76
Messerschmitt, Willi, 183, 185, 188, 190,
    223
Metz, 123
Mexico City, 104
Middle East, 105
Milch, Field Marshal Erhard, 16, 33, 37,
    149, 157, 161, 168, 177; and aircraft
    production, 178–81, 184–6; and reform of
    production, 189–93, 195, 197, 199; and
    collapse of Luftwaffe, 200–2, 206, 208,
    211, 214, 216, 217, 218, 219, 221–2, 224,
    225–6
Ministry: Agriculture, 43, 57; Air, 26, 157,
    158, 169, 178, 183, 185, 188, 192, 196,
    198, 203, 211, 220–1, 223, 224, 226;
    Defence (War), 35, 41, 43, 46, 70, 71,
    166; Economics, 30, 39, 42, 43, 44, 46,
    53, 57–8, 64, 71, 96, 101, 127, 134, 140,
    147, 155, 233; Education, 198; Finance,
    37, 96, 113, 143, 213; Foreign Affairs,
    44, 78, 80, 91, 120, 125; Interior, 27;
    Labour, 57; Prussia, 45, 57; Transport,
    216; Weapons and Munitions, 101, 214
Mitteleuropa, 77
Mooney, William, 93
Moravia, 82
Moscow, 147
motor industry, 88, 97, 99
Munich, 7, 8, 9
Munich crisis, 81, 84, 92, 100
Mussolini, Benito, 3, 7, 32, 45, 49, 59, 79,
    224, 223, 238

Napoleon, 13, 138, 146, 154, 164
National Socialist Party (NSDAP), 6, 7; and
1928 elections, 8; and seizure of power,
9–11, 13, 19, 22–3; and Roehm purge,
29–31, 43, 45; and FYP, 47–9; and
empire, 109–10, 127, 151; and role of
Goering in, 155–7, 162
Nazi Party, *see* National Socialist Party
Nazi-Soviet Pact, 90, 92, 104
Netherlands, *see* Holland
Neumann, Erich, 96, 113, 128
Neurath, Constantin Freiherr von, 29, 32,
70, 78, 79, 114, 120
New Order, 2, 107, 110, 117, 118, 119, 135,
146, 157, 163, 238
New Plan, 54
Night of the Long Knives, 3, 29–31, 34, 36
Nikopol, 133
North Africa, 107
Norway, 118, 120, 143, 146, 200
nuclear research, 197–8
Nuremberg, 40, 73
Nuremberg Laws, 61
Nuremberg Party Rally: (1936); 46; (1937),
51; (1938), 60
Nuremberg Trials, 20, 76, 89, 130, 166,
228–30, 235

Oberkommando der Wehrmacht (OKW),
209, 216
Obersalzburg, 46
oil, 41, 83, 107, 122, 131, 132–3, 216–17
Operation Steinbock, 225
Order of the Annunziata, 233
Organisation Todt, 227
Ostfasergesellschaft, 133

Pact of Steel, 233
Papen, Franz von, 24, 25, 26, 29
Peltz, General Dietrich, 225
Petrol-Block, 117, 133
Petschek family, 133
Phipps, Sir Eric, 34, 236
Planck, Max, 197
Pleiger, Paul, 16, 45, 65–6, 119, 123, 124,
133, 144–5, 151, 213, 228
Plenipotentiary for (War) Economy, 68, 69,
71, 101
Plenipotentiary for the Machine Industry,
187
Poensgen, Ernst, 98, 113, 125
Poland, 32, 38, 77, 79, 81, 87, 89, 90, 92,
93, 100, 102, 116, 118, 120–1, 122, 125,
141, 143, 146, 169, 214
Poldihütte, 114
Polish campaign, 169
Polish crisis, 81, 88–93, 234, 236, 237
Popitz, Johannes, 237
Portugal, 200
Prague, 82, 113
Preussische Staatsbank, 133
Price Commissioner, 45, 58
'Production Battle', 60

'Production Miracle', 201
Protectorate, *see* Bohemia
Prussia, 4, 23–4, 25–6, 28–9, 31, 35, 109,
153
Prussian Ministry of the Interior, 27
Prussian State Council, 26, 31

Raeder, Admiral Erich, 172
Rasche, Karl, 56, 113
rationalisation, 61, 148–50, 206–8
Raw Material and Foreign Exchange Office,
40, 157
rearmament, 44, 45–6, 50–1, 84–8
Red Army, 133
Red Orchestra spy ring, 220
Reich Chamber of Labour, 51
Reich Court-Martial, 220
Reich Defence Council, 44, 71, 87, 100,
154, 221
Reichsbank, 39, 56, 58, 87, 101
Reichsforschungsrat, 199
Reichskreditkasse, 133
Reichstag, 8, 10, 13, 23, 25, 28, 220
Reichstag Fire Emergency Decree, 25
Reichsvereinigung Kohle, 119, 123
Reichswerke AG 'Hermann Goering', 64–8,
98, 111ff, 117, 122ff, 134, 144–6, 154,
212–14, 220, 222, 223, 224
Resita iron and steel works, 117
Rheinländer, Paul, 122
Rheinmetall-Borsig AG, 213
Rhineland air programme, 37
Ribbentrop, Joachim von, 70, 73, 78–9, 80,
89–92, 93, 94, 104, 120, 221, 233
'Robinson' (Goering's train), 100
Röder, Manfred, 221
Roehm, Ernst, 8, 23, 28, 30–1, 234, 237
Roehm Affair, *see* Night of the Long Knives
Roehnert, Helmut, 213
Rome, 109
Roosevelt, Franklin Delano, 104, 154
Rosenberg, Alfred, 73, 120, 133, 221
Rosenheim, Bavaria, 4
Rote Kappelle, see Red Orchestra
Rothschild, Louis, 113
Roumania, 41, 116, 131, 216
Royal Air Force (RAF), 166, 170–2, 176,
225
Ruhr, 24, 113, 122, 124, 125–6, 127, 134,
151, 207, 213
Rümanische-Deutsche AG für
Eisenindustrie und Handel, 117
Russia, *see* Soviet Union
Rust, Bernhard, 199

SA (Sturm Abteilung), 7, 8, 23, 24, 25–6,
27, 28–31, 37, 40
Salzgitter, 64, 98, 112, 123, 128, 141, 233
Sauckel, Fritz, 141, 156, 210, 212, 214, 215,
221, 223, 226
Saur, Karl-Otto, 227
Scandinavia, 121, 122
Schacht, Hjalmar, 9, 15, 37; and

rearmament, 38–9; and food crisis, 39–41, 42; and rearmament, 43–5; and FYP, 48–50; and economic policy, 53–6; and 1937 crisis, 58–9, 63; resignation, 68–9, 71, 72, 78, 87, 101, 208
Schell, General Adolf von, 75
Schirach, Baldur von, 229
Schleicher, General Kurt von, 11, 30–1
Schmitt, Guido, 79
Schmitt, Kurt, 30, 31, 37, 38
Schmitz, Hermann, 56
Schneider-Creusot, 124
Schulze-Boysen, Harro, 220
Schuschnigg, Kurt von, 80
Schwerin von Krosigk, Lutz Graf, 38, 55, 87, 96, 144, 215
'Second Revolution', 29, 237
Seewald, F., 199
Seville, 44
Seyss-Inquart, Artur, 120
Sicherheits-Dienst (SD), 228
Siebel aircraft company, 190
Silesia, 93, 111, 112, 122, 125, 126
Skoda works, 113, 140, 143, 213
Slovakia, 77, 81, 120
Sonnemann, Emmy, *see* Goering, Emmy
Soviet air force, 175
Soviet Union, 41, 45, 77, 81, 85, 90, 94, 104, 106, 107, 111, 118, 121, 126, 127, 129, 130–4, 143, 146, 155, 160, 172, 174–5, 176, 186, 189, 196, 204, 206, 207, 214, 217, 229
Spain, 44, 79, 109
Spandau prison, 138
Spanish Civil War, 44, 45
Speer, Albert, 20, 46, 99, 122, 138, 148, 152, 158, 162, 179, 197, 199, 208–15, 216, 218, 221, 223, 224, 226–7, 232, 234
SS (Schutzstaffel), 4, 24, 36, 69–70, 127–8, 129, 130, 198, 200, 202, 203, 210, 220, 221, 222–3, 226–8, 229
'stab-in-the-back' legend, 6
Stahlverein, *see* Vereinigte Stahlwerke
Stalin, Josef, 104, 151
Stalingrad, 127, 194, 205, 219, 221
Standard Oil Co., 133
Strasser, Gregor, 11, 24, 30–1, 237
Streicher, Julius, 73
submarine production, 106, 139, 141
Sudetenland, 77, 80, 81, 113
Suez Canal, 130
Sweden, 6, 7, 63
Syrup, Friedrich, 57

Tank, Kurt, 183, 188
taxation, 96
Technical Office (Air), 181–2
Third International, 81

Thomas, General George, 53, 68, 84, 86, 98, 101, 119, 131, 139, 140, 149, 150, 157, 161, 208, 211, 212, 214
Thuringia, 156, 210
Thyssen, Fritz, 9, 113, 124
Todt, Fritz, 46, 61, 87, 98, 101, 140, 149, 161, 206–8, 210, 211–12
Togoland, 43
'Turnip Winter', 97

Udet, Colonel Ernst, 16, 34, 149, 155, 181, 183, 185–6, 187, 189, 191–3, 195, 197, 199, 206, 217
Ukraine, 120, 121, 132, 133, 156
United States, 85, 93, 104, 105, 106, 111, 150, 167, 179, 186, 189, 204, 206, 235, 236
United States Army Air Forces, 166
Uralbomber, 167

V1, 197, 225
V2, 197, 225, 233
Vansittart, Lord Robert, 2
Veldenstein, Nuremberg, 5
Vereinigte Stahlwerke, 45, 65, 113
Versailles Settlement, 6, 12, 36, 43, 76, 87, 122, 188
VIAG (State holding company), 113
Vichy regime, 144
Victor Emmanual III, 233
Vienna, 62, 80, 113, 127
Vitkovice works, 114, 115, 143
Voegler, Albert, 45, 65, 98, 199
Volksgemeinschaft, 4
Volkswagen, 88, 99

Waffen-Union, 213
Wagener, Otto, 36–7
Wagner, Josef, 47, 58
Wannsee Conference, 128
war finance, 96
Warsaw, 121, 122, 169
Washington DC, 93, 236
Watenstedt, 129
Weimar Republic, 6, 7, 12, 22, 49, 236, 239
Welles, Sumner, 94
Westminster Bank, 117
Wever, Colonel Walther, 167
Wilhelmine Reich, 5–6, 109
Wimmer, General Wilhelm, 34
Winkler, Hans, 112
Wirtschaftsführungsstab Ost, 131
Wirtschaftsstab Ost, 131
Witkowitzer Bergbau und Eisenhütten Gewerkschaft, *see* Vitkovice works

Zentrale Planung, 212
Z-Plan, 85, 102